A Father's Quest

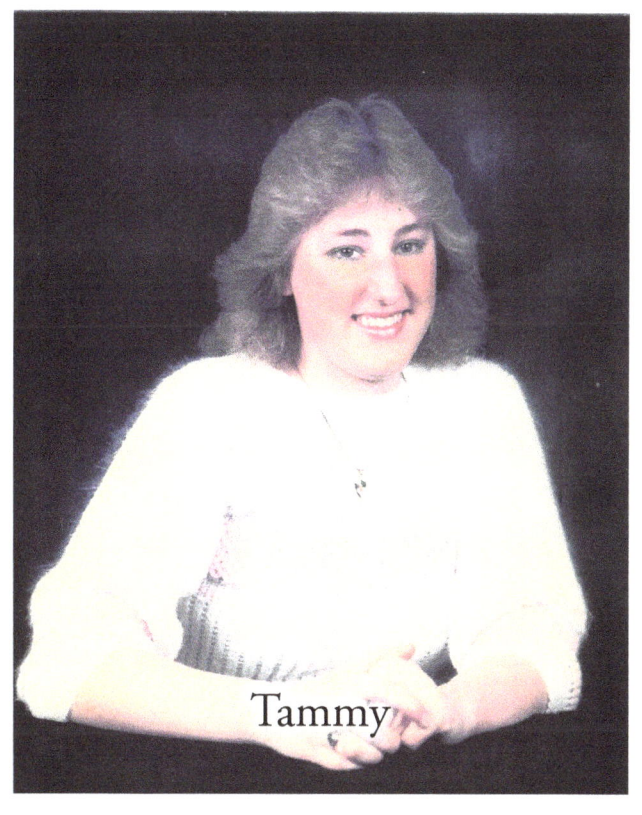

Tammy

Wayne McColley

ISBN 978-1-63844-600-2 (paperback)
ISBN 978-1-63844-602-6 (hardcover)
ISBN 978-1-63844-601-9 (digital)

Copyright © 2021 by Wayne McColley

All rights reserved. No part of this publication may be reproduced, distributed, or transmitted in any form or by any means, including photocopying, recording, or other electronic or mechanical methods without the prior written permission of the publisher. For permission requests, solicit the publisher via the address below.

Christian Faith Publishing, Inc.
832 Park Avenue
Meadville, PA 16335
www.christianfaithpublishing.com

Printed in the United States of America

Contents

Introduction 5
Chapter 1: Tammy's Death 11
Chapter 2: Early Years 19
Chapter 3: Life on the Frodl Farm 32
Chapter 4: Life on the Lukken Farm 48
Chapter 5: We Moved Three Times in One Year 56
Chapter 6: The Place Where My Parents Would Live
the Rest of Their Lives 59
Chapter 7: The Navy Years 71
Chapter 8: Marriage and Early Years 87
Chapter 9: The Birth of Our Children 100
Chapter 10: Buying the Farm and the Early Years 108
Chapter 11: Farm Depression and the Exchange Students 133
Chapter 12: The Nineties 160
Chapter 13: The First Year after Tammy's Death 194
Chapter 14: The Investigation into Tammy's Death 224
Chapter 15: The Second Year after Tammy's Death 250
Chapter 16: The Third Year after Tammy's Death 272
Chapter 17: The Turn of the Century 315
Chapter 18: The Elections 344
Chapter 19: The Fifth Year after Tammy's Death 348
Chapter 20: The Sixth Year after Tammy's Death 382
Chapter 21: The End of the Nightmare 391
Chapter 22: The Horses and the Wagon Trains 434
Chapter 23: The Medium 468
Chapter 24: Life after We Got Custody of the Girls 479
Chapter 25: The Calm before the Storm 512
Chapter 26: Leading up to the Power of Prayer 518

Chapter 27: The Power of Prayer 522
Chapter 28: Dogs throughout the Years 544
Chapter 29: The Stroke 560
Chapter 30: The Journey through Cancer 598

Introduction

Why would I want to write a book? When I was in school, a long time ago, I hated anything to do with English. Over the years, I have developed an interest in writing. I think it started in the Navy, writing letters. Twenty years later, I started writing short stories. Once in a while, some I shared and some I kept to myself. I shared all of them with my wife, Ruth. When our daughter Tammy died in 1997, I started writing a lot. I didn't want to forget anything about her. That was when I started to think about writing a book. A couple of years later, we went to a medium. I never mentioned my desire to write a book. She told me, "You are going to write a book someday." Over the years when we talked to friends about Tammy and her daughters and all the things we were going through, many of our friends said, "You should write a book." I decided to name it *A Father's Quest*. The definition of *quest* is "the act of seeking or looking for something"; to go on a quest or to search for something, an adventure or expedition, as in medieval romance. I was only planning to write about Tammy. Now over twenty years later, I am going to do it. I still think it will be about Tammy, only about much more. Over the years, Ruth and I have had a good life, but we have had a lot of struggles. Ruth had cancer and beat it. I have had a stroke and don't have full use of the right side of my body. It is impossible to write, right-or left-handed, so I type with my left hand and one finger. My brain is affected, so this is not easy. I think this big project is good therapy for my brain.

My brother Dallas has been a big inspiration for me. Dallas has written a book on the McColley history. He spends his retirement years researching all about family history. I really enjoy reading about our past relatives. I read them over and over again. It seems I can almost live their lives with them. One of my goals is that my great-great-grandchildren can live my life with me by reading about my life. Over one hundred years later, when my grandchildren are reading this book, I hope they will say, "This the best gift my grandpa could give me." At first I thought I didn't have a very interesting life. But the more I have written, I began to think that maybe some things are interesting. I am going to write about some things you may not want your children to read.

For you to understand some of the things I am going to write about, you have to look to the Bible. God talked to Moses and Jonah.

> And the Angel of the Lord appeared to Moses in a flame of fire from the midst of a bush. (Exodus 3:2)

It doesn't tell how God talked to Jonah.

In Jonah 1:1, it says, "Now the word of the Lord came to Jonah." Someone has talked to me twice. The first time, I felt it was God. The second time, I don't know; maybe it was the devil.

As I get older, I think we planned our lives with God's help before we were born.

> I knew you before I formed you in your mother's womb. Before you were born I set you apart. (Jeremiah 1:5)

God gave us free will so we might not follow everything in our plan. We have angels with us to help us. Maybe they are sending messages to us all the time. If only we could, or would, listen. As you read this book, you will realize I wasn't alone.

One of the first Sundays in January 2019, when Ruth and I went to church, Pastor Barb met us at the door. I told her that Mayo was going to look in my bladder for cancer in February. I had it before. She said, "Your life reminds me about Job's life in the Bible." Satan took almost everything from Job. But Job never lost faith in God. Satan took his children, his livestock, and his land away. Job never lost faith in God. In the end, God gave his children, livestock, and land back to Job. Job was several times richer than when Satan took these things away from him. Job lived to be 140 years old. It's a lesson from the Bible that takes thought.

Our daughter, Tammy, died. Before her death, I got a message from, I believe, the devil, or Satan that I was going to lose one of my children. How could this be? Even as I kept my faith in God, Tammy died. In the end after numerous struggles, we raised Tammy's two girls. They were the highlight of my life.

I started farming in 1974 on nothing. I was lucky in the beginning. God and angels were with me. We built a big and somewhat profitable operation. Ten years later, in 1984, I almost lost everything. I almost lost my faith in God. We went on, and I again built a much more profitable operation on the same farm with God's help.

I had high blood pressure all my life. I got diabetes when I was fifty-three years old. I had a life-threatening stroke at seventy-two years of age. I got bladder cancer at seventy-three years of age. I had surgery three times in twenty-two months for bladder cancer. Now I have been cancer-free for almost a year. Most of my life I considered to be in good health. Maybe I was just trying to fool myself.

I almost died thirteen times. I survived with God's help. He never let me down.

1. When I was twelve years old, I fell from jumping from stone to stone. I was unconscious for six hours. I had a skull fracture. I was in the hospital for six days.
2. When I was seventeen years old, I skipped school with two guys. While passing on a hill driving way too fast, we were within feet of hitting the oncoming car. An angel threw the car in the ditch. We should have died.
3. When I was thirty-one years old, I was sitting in water using a drill to drill holes to mount a new hog waterer. I got electrocuted from the drill. An angel must have told Ruth to unplug the cord. I was seconds away from death.
4. When I was thirty-five years old, we came home from my parents' late afternoon on a Sunday. It looked like a storm was coming. We had some chores to do, and Ruth said,

"As soon I get the kids in the house, I'm coming out to help you before it rains." I went to the granary to set up the mill and grind feed. I was within inches of the switch when lightning struck the mill. If my finger were on the switch, I could have been killed. Ruth was right under a big tree when the lightning stuck the tree. We both could have been killed.

5. When I was sixty-two years old, we were on a wagon train. Ruth was with me on a wagon pulled by horses. The horses ran away. When they were coming out of a ditch, the reins broke. We were going down a long hill with a curve at the bottom. I knew we would fly out of the wagon. Jim Malone (riding a mule) and our son Bob (riding a horse), one on each side, grasped the horses and stopped them. Afterward when I saw Jim Malone, I always said, "You are one of the persons that saved our lives."

6. When I was sixty-three years old, we were going on a wagon train to the state of Georgia. Bob was pulling a horse camping trailer with the four horses and the girls. I was driving another pickup with the surrey and the hay. It was just before morning. My shoulder started to bother me. I took off my seat belt. I went to sleep while driving the pickup. We went in the ditch, and the trailer jackknifed. The trailer came through the cab. My seat was behind the cab when everything stopped. When Bob came up to us, he said, "Someone had to be with you. You could have been killed." Neither Ruth nor I had a scratch or a sore spot. God and the angels were with us.

7. When I was sixty-four years old, I was in a corn bin. The sump was plugged. I was poking a long rod down, trying to unplug the sump. The auger was running. Suddenly the corn started flowing. I went down with the corn. The corn was up to my chest. I was seconds away from death. Ruth for no reason shut the auger off. An angel must have been with us.

8. When I was seventy-two years old, I suffered a stroke. I couldn't talk or swallow. The right side of my body was completely paralyzed. At first I couldn't move at all. I was never afraid. I knew that God was with me.
9. When I was seventy-two years old and walking somewhat, I fell coming out of the bathroom in the morning. I thought I broke my arm. Bob took me to the emergency room. I had a female doctor. I complained about the pain in my hip. She asked me to get off the bed and walk a little. When I sat on the bed, I passed out and quit breathing. They had a crash crew come in, but they couldn't get my heart beating. The doctor then asked Bob, "Should we keep trying or just let him go?" She figured that I was without oxygen to my brain too long.
10. When I was seventy-three years old, we celebrated Christmas on the night of the twenty-sixth. At nine o'clock, I had to use the bathroom. Ruth took me. When I was sitting on the toilet, I quit breathing. My whole body turned dark gray. Ruth called for help. When Bob saw me, he immediately called the ambulance. Doreen, Brenda, and Jodi came into the room. Jodi knew how to perform CPR. The bathroom was not that big. She was trying to come up with a plan to get me off the toilet to the floor. Brenda was shaking my hand and hollering at me. Suddenly I was breathing. A policeman came into the bathroom. The first thing that came into my mind was, "How come all these people are with me?" I think an angel was with me. God didn't want me yet.
11. When I was seventy-three years old, on the tenth of August, I was again sitting on the toilet when I quit breathing. Bob and Justin had just come into the house. Bob called the ambulance. Justin and Bob carried me to the south room and sat me on the lift chair. When the ambulance crew was there, I came to. I couldn't figure out what just happened.
12. When I was seventy-three years old, in mid-August, I was throwing up blood in the bed in the early morning. Jodi

called the ambulance. When the ambulance was going through Kasson, the person that was taking care of me yelled to the driver, "Turn on the siren and don't stop for anything." The next night my temperature went up to 105 degrees.
13. When I was seventy-four years old, on the seventh of December, when we were going to the Mayo Clinic in Rochester, I got a premonition that I was going to die that day. Just before I was called to my eye appointment, I told Ruth, "I feel terrible." When I got into the doctor's office, I passed out. My blood pressure was 40/20.

I don't think that many people experienced having so many close calls with death as I did. I would have never made it through life without God and my guardian angel or more angels with me. It would not be easy to get through life alone.

Some parts of the book, I am only going to write from memories. I have a good memory from years ago, and that's easier. For some chapters I am going to have to do some research, to be sure I get it right. I feel that God wants me to do more thing with my life. Sometimes I have thought, "Is life still worth it? I might be happier in heaven. My body doesn't do what I want it to do anymore."

I almost gave up on writing the book many times in the last two years. It was my wife, Ruth, and my children that kept me writing by giving me encouragement.

If it wouldn't be for my daughter-in-law, Jodi, helping me write the book, and her daughter, Janessa, for putting the pictures in the book, I could never have written the book without her help.

I would like to thank Diana Vang for correcting my writings. She has made me a lot better writer than when I started. THANK YOU! THANK YOU to everyone involved!

I also think my guardian angel was helping me write the book. Memories that I had forgotten came into my mind as I was writing. At certain times, I was just typing without thinking at all.

I hope you enjoy reading my book, *A Father's Quest*.

Chapter 1

Tammy's Death

The morning of Sunday, January 5, 1997, we got up early to go to church. It was snowing and windy. The weather was not good. We decided against going to church. At eight fifteen, Tammy's car went by our place going east toward her house. We figured she worked at the nursing home last night. I had just gotten pigs in the last days. I had gone several months without pigs. I went outside and did chores. After dinner I took a nap lying on our living room couch. Ruth, my wife, woke me up from my nap, saying that Tammy's house was on fire. A neighbor had just called Ruth on the phone. Bob, our son, was going in his pickup, and Ruth and I were going to take our car. We got stuck going out of our garage.

Ruth said, "Go with Bob, I'm going to shovel out the car."

I think God was looking out for Ruth. Ruth didn't see the house on fire. Tammy lived four miles east of us on the same road. I bought the farm from Adline Hrtanek less than two years ago. I sold the buildings and five acres to Tammy and Garry for the same amount as I paid per acre for the farm. As we got close to the house, we could see the flames coming out of the windows.

I told Bob, "I hope they got out of the house."

Tammy's car was on the road. Bob parked his pickup right past Tammy's car. As I got out of the pickup, I could see Tammy sitting in the front seat looking back at the house. I didn't see her face. But she was a fairly tall blond lady. Kayla and Sarah were sitting in the back seat. I immediately felt relieved that they were okay. We walked past Tammy's car toward the house.

As we got closer to the house, someone said, "Tammy is in the house."

I looked back toward the car, and Tammy wasn't there. There was no one sitting in the front seat. Bob started running toward the house. I was afraid he would go inside.

I hollered, "Stop, stop."

Bob stopped.

I asked Tammy's husband, Garry, "Why didn't you get Tammy out?"

He said that he set a ladder up to the upstairs bedroom window and had gone into the house but couldn't find her. I asked him, "Were you in the room?" He said he was, but he couldn't find her. He said he was in the barn when the fire started. I thought that the girls went to the barn with Garry. There were dressed perfectly, with coats, caps, gloves, and boots. I couldn't believe the fire was so bad that the firemen or the police weren't there. How could the fire get so bad so soon?

Bob and I then took Kayla and Sarah to our house as I couldn't watch the house burn or to have them watch. When we got home, I had to tell Ruth that Tammy was dead. At first both of us didn't show any emotions. We couldn't believe what just happened. I thought I had to call three people while I could still do it. First, I called Pastor Nelson. Next, I called my brother Dallas. Next, I called Ruth's sister Eva. There was no answer. Then I called Ruth's brother Howard. Pastor Nelson and his wife, Doris, came to our house right away. Ruth hadn't done the dishes, and Doris did them and cleaned up the kitchen. The kitchen was never too much to clean up. Ruth always kept it clean. To the west of us, there was a blizzard. All of my family lived west of us. It was impossible for any of them to make it to our place. East of us the weather was not so bad. Howard called his brother and sisters right away. Soon all of Ruth's family were at our house. Ruth's family remarked that there wasn't any smell of smoke on our granddaughters' or their clothes. We have a big house, and Ruth's family and we were sitting in the dining room. Our granddaughters were in the living room. Sometime later, I went into the living room to check on them. The TV was left on when we left to go to the fire. There was a movie on TV that had a house on fire. The girls sat in awe as they watched the movie. I didn't say anything, but I turned off the TV. I didn't want the girls to see this. It was a mistake to have the TV on. It was hard for three-and four-year-old children to separate the fire on TV from the fire at their house. Soon a policeman came to our house to talk to the girls. He talked to the girls alone in the living room. Several police cars and several other cars were in our yard. I assumed they belonged to Garry's family. None of them came to the door. If they would have come to the door, I would have invited them in. Toward nighttime, Ruth's family left, and I went outside to do the chores. Walking back up to the house, it finally hit me that Tammy had died. Early in the evening, Howard's two sons, Kevin and Kris, came to our house. They were dairy farmers. They had milked their cows early so they could come up to our house. I asked them to stay until Garry came to get the girls. Garry came about ten at night.

Sarah and Kayla

When Ruth and I went to bed, we couldn't sleep. I held Ruth in my arms while she was crying. Finally, she went to sleep, but I heard her sobbing all night. I remembered the voice in the pig barn six months ago that told me that I was going to lose a child. Was it an angel or the devil? Was I losing my mind? Maybe I was mentally ill. I recalled being at Uncle Stanley's funeral twenty years ago. He was fifty-three years old. His funeral was in January too. I was fifty-three years old now. I remembered how the thought came into my mind sitting in church at his funeral. I was going to die at fifty-three, or it was going to be something worse. It was worse. I remembered the last time I had seen Tammy. Two days ago, on the Friday night before Tammy died, she came to our house. She said that Garry told her to go see her folks. This was something that he never said before. She said he was going to come over to our place on his snowmobile. She wasn't here very long before he called and told Tammy to come home right now! The last thing Tammy said to me was, "I can't wait until the girls get old enough to tell him where to go." I started thinking about my life. It was the longest night of my life. Many long nights were soon to come.

My mother and my dad came the next morning. Several other people from my family also came. The sheriff called in the morning, saying that they found Tammy's body in the basement. They sent her body up to the cities to have an autopsy done. Late in the morning, the fire marshal and a sheriff's deputy came to our house. Ruth and I took them into our office so everyone wouldn't hear what they told us. They told us that the girls started the fire with a cigarette lighter to a blanket on the couch on the south side of the living room. According to the burn pattern of the two-by-fours, that was where the fire was started. After they started the fire, the girls went out to the barn and told Garry that the house was on fire. I believed them at first, but Ruth never did.

In the afternoon we went to the funeral home to plan Tammy's funeral. Bob, Doreen, Brenda, Ruth, and I went. Pastor Nelson also went. Garry was there with his mother and his sisters.

The first thing the funeral director said to me was, "Tammy was married, and you and your family are not next of kin. You have nothing to say."

I said, "How can you say that? Ruth and I are her parents."

He told me again, "You have nothing to say, you are not next of kin."

I started to get very mad and upset. Pastor Nelson said something that calmed everyone down. The funeral was going to be in our church. The wake was going to be Wednesday night at the Dibble Funeral Home, and the service was going to be in our church on Thursday. Garry wanted Tammy cremated, and Doreen wanted Tammy buried. I told Garry that I had a life insurance policy on Tammy and that I had paid the premium since her birth. I gave this policy to Tammy a year ago. It was big enough to pay for her funeral and her burial. Garry was very unhappy, but he finally agreed. We finally agreed that there were going to be three pallbearers from his side of the family and three from our side. We picked Keven, Kris, and Cory. Cory was the oldest son of my brother Rick.

The *Post Bulletin* interviewed Garry for the article in the newspaper. He said Tammy loved to work. Working at the nursing home was a stressful job. She told us that she couldn't take working more than four days a week. She was working all the hours to support her family. Garry wasn't working at all. He was fired from his job at MTM in Dodge Center the previous May. He had only worked part-time since then, and very little the month before the fire. In the paper they listed the cause of the fire as careless handling of smoking materials. Garry said that Tammy was a smoker, and the article implied that she died from smoking in bed. I never saw Tammy smoke since she was born. She was at our house many times, for long periods of time, and we never saw her smoke. Her autopsy showed that she had zero nicotine in her body. She didn't die in bed from smoking! He, on the other hand, was a heavy smoker, and he didn't mention that. I became very upset and mad from reading the article in the paper.

We all went to see a person who took care of the cemetery the next day. We had to pick out a plot. Doreen wanted me to buy enough plots for all of us. Bob and I did. I wanted to pay that day. The lady that took care of the cemetery talked me out of paying her that day. After Tammy's funeral, I didn't want it to end. I found it to be impossible to finish up the loose ends. In a month I went to pay. Garry had paid for her plot. Bob and I paid for the other plots. It was a big mistake I would have to carry the rest of my life. I should have paid the first day. I wanted to own the plot that Tammy was buried in.

In the time following Tammy's death but before the funeral, several things started bothering us about the fire. How could the house burn so much before the fire department got there? Bob and I were there and left with the girls before either the fire department or the sheriff's deputy was there. We questioned the sheriff's office about this. They came to our house and told us that Garry had first gone to the Tucker Farm. Tucker is sixty-five years old and retarded. Tucker looked up the number in the telephone book, and the line was busy, and he never called back! Therefore, the fire was never reported. A half hour or so later, Garry went to another neighbor and reported the fire. This was the neighbor who called Ruth.

The day of wake, a member of the snowmobile club came to our house with a check for $500. She was a thin young blond girl in her early twenties who worked with Tammy. She said she brought the check to us because she wanted to be sure the money went to Kayla and Sarah and not to Garry. She was sure that Garry would spend the money right away.

The wake was from five until eight. Tammy's casket was at the front of the room. It was unopened because Tammy's body was 60 percent burned. Ruth and I stood on the east side at the room. That was where the line started. There was always a long line. Garry stood in the front, next to Tammy's casket. But he was hardly ever there. Bob, Doreen, and Brenda stood on the west side of the room. Soon people were giving me the cards instead of putting them in the box. I soon had so many that I didn't know what do with them. Evidently, they didn't want Garry to get them. It was almost nine before everyone got through.

Tammy's funeral was on a Thursday, January 9. The weather was bad the night before and that day. Our family met in a Sunday school room. Some people were telling me, "You know that Tammy was murdered." My sister-in-law—Rick's wife—Carol had a conversation with Garry's mother. His mother said, she could foresee a problem with Kayla and Sarah. She said, "Wayne will try and take the girls away from Garry. If Wayne or anyone else tries to take the girls away from Garry, he will kill Wayne or anyone else who tried." I think she was threatening me. She knew Garry was capable of murder. Did he murder Tammy? Family members of Tammy took almost half of the church. Ruth and I sat in the front pew with Garry, Kayla, Sarah, and his mother. Bob, Doreen, and Brenda sat in the next pew. I made a mistake picking out the songs. I wanted the song "Jesus Loves Me." Tammy's daughters, Kayla and Sarah, were so young, and I thought it was a song for them. When I was in church and that song was sung, I started crying. I was again in the front pew at Tammy's funeral. It took me twenty years to get over it. Now I kind of like the song but still get an uneasy feeling. Pastor Nelson did a good job with Tammy's funeral, but my mind was thinking about the fire. Was Tammy murdered? The church had made a tape of the service that the pastor gave me later.

When we went to the cemetery, there was a six-foot snowbank between where we could park and Tammy's burial place. Thankfully, the snowbank was so hard we could walk over it. The pallbearers had to carry her casket over this snowbank. Everyone that went to the cemetery couldn't walk over the snowbank, and they had to stay in their cars. They set up a tent or a shelter for us to sit in at Tammy's burial place.

Next, we went back to church for lunch. Stella Nelson seated us and waited on us. She made a good, lasting impression on me that I would never forget. I didn't have an appetite. I ate very little. I had not eaten since Tammy's death. Garry's family didn't want to stay for lunch. Usually, the funeral director would pay for the lunch and that would be part of the bill. But he wouldn't, and the women of the church asked Garry to pay. He refused! I immediately paid the bill. Garry's family wanted to divide up the flowers in the church. Tammy was dead, and all they wanted was the flowers! I got carried up in this. It was a mistake! They were mad at me for not inviting them into our house the day of the fire. I was supposed to go outside and go up to each car and personally invite them in. I was numb from losing Tammy! I couldn't think clearly. None of Garry's family told Ruth or me sorry for our loss. I went to get Ruth, and they took most of the flowers that they liked. Before they were done fighting over the flowers, almost all our guests had left. I really felt guilty about this. I should have greeted every one of them. I should have left Garry's family to fight among themselves, and Ruth and I should have stayed in the dining room. Spending time with our guests would have meant more to us than the flowers.

Pastor Nelson set up a fund at our bank where people could donate money for Tammy's girls. I could put the money from the cards there. Eva and Nado Bernard were put in charge of this fund. They were Tammy's sponsors at her baptism.

On Tuesday, January 14, we were called by the nursing home personnel where Tammy worked, and we were asked to come down. As soon as we got there, they took us in the office and shut the door. They had taken up a collection of almost $500 and wanted to be sure the money would be set aside for the girls rather than Garry getting it. They said there were some other things they wanted us to know. The first was that there was a $100,000 life insurance policy on Tammy and that the girls were listed as beneficiaries. They also told us that Tammy was coming to work with bruises and one time with a mark on her face. They were convinced that Garry was beating her. I didn't know what to do about this information. But I must do something!

It became impossible to sleep. In the next months, I would live my whole life over. It was not so simple as to lose our daughter and be able to mourn. We didn't have time to mourn. It was turning into a nightmare.

Chapter 2

Early Years

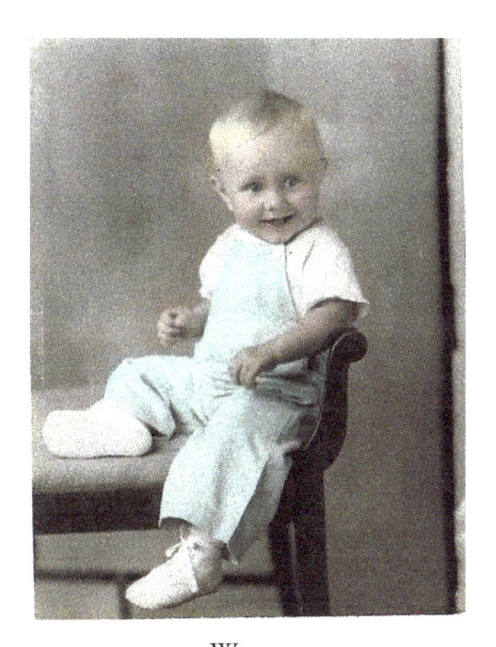

Wayne

After Tammy's death, if I thought about the fire or Tammy, it was impossible to get to sleep. I lay awake all night. During this time, I lived my whole life over, from earliest time until the time of Tammy's death.

I was born December 21, 1943, at 1:10 PM. My dad was in World War II. Nine months before my birth, he was stationed in Miami, Florida. At this time, Mom could be with him. She worked at Sears. I don't know what time, but she came back to her parents' farm in Waseca, Minnesota, before I was born. Dr. McIntire delivered me. Dr. McIntire was a friend of my Grandpa Larson. In the 1930s, he kept race horses at my grandpa's farm. I remember Grandpa and Mom telling me how they raced the horses across the pasture. I was born in the Waseca Hospital. Mom and I stayed ten days. The hospital was built on ground my mother's Grandpa Emil Krassin sold to them. My mother worked at Swifts, a poultry processing plant, in Waseca, after I was born. The first two years of my life, I lived on my grandparents' farm. I developed a close relationship with my grandpa. He died when I was thirty-three. He was always my favorite person.

I can remember many things before the age of two. I always knew my grandfather was all Norwegian and that my grandmother was all German. Neighbors got together often and talked about the war with Germany. Most of them were Germans. At night when it was dark and after I had listened to this talk, I was afraid of my grandmother because she was a German. My grandfather often said, "There are too many Germans living here." Later in life, my grandfather told me many times, "Marry a full-blood Norwegian." I did. I don't know what he meant about this. He married a German.

I couldn't remember my first haircut, but the barber told me about it every time I had a haircut. It was almost like I could remember. My mother stood beside me while the barber was cutting my hair. I was crying. Grandpa and Uncle Roger stood outside looking in the window at me. They were making faces, trying to make me laugh. I started to cry and scream more. The longer they were there, the more I screamed. Tobin was the older barber, and McCarthy was the younger. Tobin was gone by the time I was a teenager. McCarthy always told me the story every time I came in. When I graduated from high school, McCarthy wanted me to go to barber school and go into business with him. I really liked him, but I didn't want to be a barber. I wonder now how my life would have turned out if I would have been a barber. Tammy would have never met Garry in Waseca.

I remember sitting on a wagon pulled by two horses. Grandpa and Grandma and Uncle Roger were picking corn by hand and throwing the ears into the wagon. There was a little bit of snow on the ground. Grandpa's dog Brownie was with us. After supper, Grandpa went outside and shoveled the corn into the crib. I believe this time was shortly before I turned two. My sister was a baby at this time, and I think my great-grandmother was watching her. Sometime after I turned two, the war was over, and my dad come home. I was afraid of him at first, for a long time. I didn't want to leave my grandpa. At the dinner table, I was afraid to sit next to him. I sat next to my mother until the time I went to the Navy.

Around March 15, 1944, my mother took a train ride with a lady from Sherburn, Minnesota, to North Carolina. Her husband was a buddy of my dad. I was three months old at this time. The train stopped in Washington, DC. There was an older couple who let my mom and dad stay with them during this time. My mother got Christmas cards from them for several years. My sister Sandra was born December 15, 1944. Over sixty years later, Ruth and I visited the same train station in Washington, and the same clock was on the wall.

Deloris McColley, Wayne, and Sandra

I can remember shelling corn with my grandpa. It was a corn sheller where you turned a large wheel and put in an ear of corn. The corn cob came out the side and the kernels came out the bottom. I have one today. My sister was not old enough to walk. My grandpa carried her in the bushel basket on top of the corn on his shoulder while I held unto his other hand. The corn crib was at least seven hundred feet from the henhouse. This was a fun job that I looked forward to.

I can remember once when my grandpa went alone to Thor, Iowa. He was raised in Thor. He went to visit friends and relatives. I would miss him and was glad when he come back. When I was older, I went with him. As soon as I got out of the Navy, I took him to Thor. He often talked about his friends but never talked about his relatives. He often talked about farming 320 acres for two years near the town of Hartland, Minnesota. He never said who owned the farm. My brother Dallas did some research on these farms about a hundred years later. Grandpa's half brother George owned 160 acres, and his dad, Martin, owned the next 160 acres. I asked my Uncle Roger about this. He didn't know his grandfather owned part of the farm. I think my grandpa was deeply hurt when they sold the farm and he had to quit farming. On a wagon train in 2013, I drove a team of horses past this land and into the town of Hartland over a hundred years later. I could imagine that my grandpa drove a team of horses on this same road into Hartland over a hundred years ago.

There are other things I remember, but I am not sure they were before the age of two. I walked through the woods to a creek where my grandpa and Uncle Roger were working on rebuilding a bridge. It was taken out by a flood. I was supposed to stay in the house. I had snuck out. Grandpa told me there were Indians in the woods and they were going to get me. He said, "Run back to the house, and stay on the field road before they get you." I ran fast, and I was scared for a long time. I didn't do that again.

I was not afraid of dogs; the dogs were afraid of me. I would go up to dogs and bite their ears. They would run away howling. I am not sure if I remember this. My mother told this story many times.

The buildings on my grandparents' farm were more than three quarters of a mile from the road. The road came in from the west. It was almost a thousand feet through other land to reach his farm. This was called a cart way at that time. It was a road that we called the grade. Grandpa had a gate where his farm started, and we always had to open it. They drove through the pasture and woods to the buildings. At the building there was another gate which had to be opened every time. There was a hill right away. The tires wore out the grass, and when it rained, the water ran. When the ruts got so deep they picked a different place to drive. There was only one place they never drove except in the winter. That was where the snowplow went. They had to leave the car sitting by the grade when it was wet in the spring, and they walked in. Before 1936, they actually drove in from the east through the river. When the river was high, they couldn't go. On these times they drove through Johnny's Krassin farm. My grandparents didn't like doing this, and they preferred driving through the river. It was a 166-acre farm; 106 acres were woods. There were 60 acres in four fields. The biggest field was called the flat. There was a river on one side, and a creek went through the middle of the farm. The woods consisted of small hills, steep hills, and cliffs. There was a ninety-foot-tall windmill, the tallest one around. We could see it from miles away. The farmstead was in a valley, and there were a lot of tall trees. The windmill was made out of iron, so it was rusty. My Uncle Stanly and Norman Klatt took it down in the late 1950s.

My grandmother's Grandfather Martin Krassin homesteaded this land in 1855. He died at the age of fifty-seven, and at this time he owned about 920 acres. He had five sons and wanted to give each son a farm. He bought half of the land three years before his death. My Great-grandfather Emil was twelve years old at the time of his death. Emil got 207.5 acres of this land. My grandmother and grandfather, Edward and Pearl Larson, got 166 acres from Emil. My mother and father, Harry and Deloris, got twenty-three acres of this land and sold it later to my brother Dallas. There is a Krassin cemetery on a knoll, on Dallas's land. Dallas feels that Reuben Prechel, a relative of the Krassins, purchased the stone for this cemetery in the 1950s. It has twenty-three names including the names of my great-great-great-grandparents.

Wayne 9 Months Old

    I remember when Grandpa sold his 1931 Chevy. He had just bought a 1936 Chevy and did not trade in the 1931 Chevy. I was there when a couple of guys come to look at it. I don't know if it was brown or it was all rust. My grandpa loved to deal. He sold them the Chevy. The '36 was black. We would fill up milk cans with water and put them in the trunk. We would then take them to the field, pour water in one gopher hole, and stand at the other hole with a baseball bat and hit the gophers when they came out. That was fun. He tied sacks of corn and oats to the fender and took them to the elevator to have it ground. Before the 1931 Chevy, my grandpa had Model Ts. Once he traded a Model T pickup for a race horse. This horse didn't make a good race horse, but he hitched it to another horse, and that was his team until the mid-1950s. This horse lived to be older than forty. He bought a brand-new 1925 Model T. My grandmother drove the Model Ts but never learned to shift a car. I have a 1920 Model T pickup. It's harder to drive. Hardly no one knows how to drive it. During this time my grandmother called the grocery store with a list. My grandpa just picked them up and paid for them. In a few years the grocery stores didn't do this anymore. Now because of the Internet, you can order groceries online and they delivery them to your house.

I don't remember my grandpa buying the Model F20 Farmall tractor. I never remember him driving it. Uncle Roger would always drive it. In the 1950s, he traded it for a WC Allis tractor, and he drove it. I remember walking up to an oat field during threshing. Roger was loading bundles with a team of horses. When he finished, he had to go down a steep hill through the woods. I think he was going too fast because all of a sudden, the whole wagon tipped over.

I stayed with my grandparents many times. Sometimes with my sister and sometimes alone. At night my grandma would mix up bread dough. I helped her knead the dough. Then she would let it rise throughout the night. She always got up between four and five in the morning. When I got up, I could smell the bread baking. It smelled good and fresh bread tasted so good. In the summer, when I got up in the morning, she was often working in the garden, which was about nine hundred feet from the house.

I was not much older than two when my grandpa taught me how to play checkers. We played often. Both of my grandparents loved to play cards. As soon as we would come, we always played cards. Neighbors came over often to play cards. We didn't have TV; I think life was better then.

I remember once when my grandpa's two half brothers and his brother Andrew were there. They were shooting a rifle. They were throwing pennies up in the air and shooting them. They hardly ever missed. I was never that good.

My grandparents often went to visit his brother Andrew in Albert Lea. Often they stopped at our home and took my sister and me along. My grandpa and his brother were always playing jokes on someone. Andrew didn't have a bathroom. He had an outhouse. He told my grandpa, "Wait for someone to go in, and we are going to play a good one on them." He had mounted a tape recorder under the seat, and he was waiting to plug it in. Soon someone went in. All of a sudden, a voice said, "Would you move over to the other hole? I'm working down here." They were always trying to come up with something. Andrew and his wife, Lillie, and grandpa's brother Alfred and his wife often came to my grandparents' home together. Andrew and Lillie played the violin, and Alfred played the banjo. They came often, and it was fun listening to them.

My grandpa told me many stories, but I can't remember many of them. One I can really remember is when my grandpa was ten in 1897. It was May 1. It was a Norwegian custom to hang a May basket on a neighbor's house. Grandpa was going to hang a May basket on Christerfor's house. He was barefooted, and when he started to run away from the house, the hired man saw him. They had a mad bulldog, and the hired man yelled, "Sic him, sic him." My grandpa ran as fast as he could. The bulldog was gaining on him, and my grandpa was getting tired. Soon my grandpa stopped and started yelling, "Sic him, sic him." The bulldog ran right past Grandpa.

Grandpa had a definition for cigarettes. "Fire on one end and a fool on the other end."

At this time, they had several restaurants in Waseca. My grandpa knew every waitress in every one. He liked to tease them. We always sat at the counter so we were closest to the waitress when they weren't busy. Every time we went to town, we stopped at two or three restaurants. He had a cup of coffee, and I had a bottle of pop. Coffee and pop were five cents each. Once in a while, we had ice cream cones. Grandpa said he once got a cone that had a fly in the bottom. We always threw the bottom of the cone away. Ice cream cones were a dime.

When I was five, Grandpa taught me how to shoot a rifle. He sat a can on a fence post next to the house. He said he did this for his nephew Robert Kelly. He said to him, "If you can hit it, you can have the rifle." Robert shot, but Grandpa didn't put any bullets in the rifle. He set it up where he would have hit the house. He didn't deserve to get the rifle. This was a lesson I never forgot. I have the rifle today.

They picked me up often to go fishing with them. We fished from shore mainly for bullheads. We sometimes fished for Northern Pike. We were always lucky. My grandpa's sister and her husband,

Lettie and Art Anderson, had a cabin up north. My grandpa also had a bachelor brother who lived on the lake in a bus. They took me there several times, and it was a lot of fun. When I was fifteen and just got my driver's license, I went up north with my grandparents and drove Grandpa's car all the way. I really felt important.

My grandparents got a TV right before Queen Elizabeth became queen. We skipped school to watch the big celebration. That was a big deal since we had never seen a TV before. After that we often went over to their house after supper to watch TV. It was black and white. We didn't get a color set for another twenty years.

In August 1923, my grandparents got a state schoolboy from Owatonna, Minnesota. His name was Chester Schafer. He stayed with them for ten years. When I was ten years old, my grandparents took me along to visit Chester in Marshfield, Wisconsin. He worked for the railroad, as a mechanic. He took me to work with him and let me drive a train. He stopped the train on the turntable and turned it around with me sitting in the train by myself. That was the biggest thing I had ever done in my life. After I got married, we visited Chester and his wife, Evelyn, many times. I miss him and Evelyn.

Edward Larson Farm, Waseca MN 1967

My grandpa's barn was over a hundred feet long. He had fourteen wood-milking stanchions. There was no cement in the barn. The gutters behind the cows were made of wood. He carried the manure from the gutter to the horse-drawn manure spreader which sat right outside the barn. In the winter when there was snow, he used a sleigh pulled by horses. He pitched the manure on from the barn and then off while the horses were pulling it through the field. Until the late 1940s, they milked cows by hand. Then he bought a Marlow milking machine. There was a bucket that sat on the ground, and the teat cups were attached to the cows' teats. He sold cream so we had to separate the milk. We had a separator to do this, and we turned a crank by hand. We dumped the milk in the top, and the separator separated the cream from the skim milk. He took the cream to the creamery in Waseca. When I went with him, he always bought me an orange drink called Green Spot. He fed the skim milk to the hogs. He mixed it with feed in the winter in a feed cooker. The feed cooker consisted of a hung cast-iron tub. It was surrounded by a jacket to the ground. It had a door on the bottom where you built a fire and was used to heat the feed. He dumped the warm feed into the troughs. He kept some banty chickens in the barn in the winter and outside during the summer. He didn't feed them anything; they found something to eat by themselves. Grandpa had this favorite banty rooster, and he would fight with it. The rooster would try to scare everyone away. I would always be looking for the rooster and run away when I saw him.

Roger and Lorna (McColley) Larson

    My mother's brother Roger married my dad's sister Lorna. They were both my uncle and aunt before they were married. They got married at my Grandparent McColley's farm in 1951. They got married in the front room of my grandparents' house. Lorna's brother Lyle sang a song at the wedding, "Three Coins in a Fountain." We went to the first part of the wedding dance. Grandpa Larson was a really good dancer. We had to go home early in the evening. I did not like going home. It would have been a lot more fun to stay at the dance. Grandpa's brothers Alfred and Andrew and his wife, Lillie, played at the wedding dance. My Grandpa Larson's sister and her husband, Lettie and Art Anderson, bought a farm for them to rent two miles away. Grandpa was sixty-five years old at this time and quit milking the cows.

    Chickens were my grandpa's favorite. Shortly before I was born, he built a new chicken house which held two hundred chickens. They filled up thirty dozen egg cases. When they got one case full of eggs, they took it to town to sell them. They got over two hundred chicks ever spring in the mail. They started them outside in brooder house in the spring. In the fall my grandpa had everyone over at night to catch the chickens. They roosted in trees. We had a chicken-catcher. The chicken-catcher was a thin, six-foot firm rod. It had a hook on one end and a handle on the other end. We could reach up into a tree with the chicken-catcher and grab their leg with the hook and pull them out of a tree.

Grandpa could catch a fly in the air while the fly was flying past him. I would practice and practice, and I got almost as good as Grandpa was. We would hold the fly in our hands underwater until we drowned the fly. Then we put the fly on the table and covered the fly completely with salt. In about four to five minutes, when the salt became hard because of the water, we broke up the salt with a pencil. Soon the fly would walk and then fly away. It was really fun, and it always worked. I have showed this trick to my kids several times.

Grandpa would offer us a dollar if we could put our elbow in our ear. We tried and tried, but we couldn't do it. There were always rabbits outside. Grandpa would give us a saltshaker and tell us if we could get some salt on the rabbits' tail we could catch the rabbit. We spent hours but never got close enough to get salt on their tails. We were never bored. We didn't need a lot of toys to stay busy.

Family reunions were real important to both of my grandparents. Men wore suits with vests. Women always wore dresses. We had the picnic at least one year at the Clear Lake Park in Waseca. Grandpa's brother Andrew was the national champion player of horseshoes. They always played horseshoes. When they were playing, they always took off their suit coats.

I had one thing I didn't like about my grandpa. He carried garden snakes in his pocket. When I didn't expect it, he pulled the snake out of his pocket and tried to hand it to me. He told me often that he used to put a snake into his teacher's desk in school. I was really scared of snakes, and I am still scared of them today. My grandmother was terribly afraid of snakes. I don't know how she put up with him. Grandpa was a trickster, and he liked to have fun. When we went there on Halloween night to get a treat, Grandpa always said, "If you want a treat, you have to do a trick." We went outside and tried to make the windows rattle.

A FATHER'S QUEST

Grandpa Larson's Farm······Pearl and Ed Larson

Chapter 3

Life on the Frodl Farm

Shortly before my dad came home from the war, my mother and her father-in-law, my Grandpa McColley, met with Lewis Frodl and rented the farm from him. At first they rented it on shares. After three years they changed it to cash rent. Lewis Frodl come to visit about once a month. He drove a Model A Ford. In 1950 he traded the Model A for a brand-new Ford. He was a fun person to visit with. Mom had saved $3,000 during the war, and my dad saved $2,000. This was money with which they were going to start farming. My Grandpa McColley owned the farm next to it. He bought it in 1942, the year before I was born. I was the oldest grandchild of both grandparents. They all treated me special. My mother came from a family of three. Her two brothers were Stanley and Roger. My dad came from a family of ten: Dale, Marlin, Lorna, Lyle, Lenard, Duane, David, Judith, and Clifford. There were twenty-five years' difference from my dad's age and the age of his youngest brother. Both of my parents were an oldest child. Their farm was ten miles from my Grandpa Larson's farm and four miles from the town of Otisco, eight miles from Waseca. We took turns living with both grandparents until we could move on the farm.

Harry, Duane, Lyle, David, Dale (Top), Lenard, Marlin,
Judy, Cliff, Grant, Freda, Lorna (Bottom)

Grant and Freda McColley 1942

We moved on the farm March 1, 1946. I was two years old. It was a big and nice house. There was one bedroom downstairs and four bedrooms upstairs. Every bedroom had a large walk-in closet. There was a large pocket door between the dining room and the parlor or front room. We closed this door in the winter and didn't heat the front room. There were three large porches. The house was heated with a wood stove in the kitchen and a kerosene stove in the dining room. There was no bathroom or running water. We had to carry in water and kept it in a crock. We had a dipper hanging in the crock, and we didn't waste any water. If you didn't drink all the water, you put it back. We had a reservoir in the wood stove, and that was where we heated the water. There was no heat upstairs. Ice formed on the windows. In the winter we put on our pajamas downstairs and ran upstairs and got under the covers.

I think Dad started milking with eight cows. They milked by hand, and they sold cream. He started with a gray team of horses, Duke and Don. He had a Minneapolis Moline R tractor. An ember flew out the muffler and hit me in the eye; I could feel it for years. I did not like that tractor, and I was afraid of it. Dad tried to get me to ride with him on the tractor, but I was scared. We didn't have electricity, and I can remember the lamps in the house and the lanterns in the barn. We had an icebox in the kitchen to keep things cool. I can remember plainly going to town for ice. I knew where the icehouse was. We didn't always have ice. Dad planted corn with horses and used a check wire so we could cultivate it both ways. He cultivated with the R. He made hay with the horses. He mowed it, raked it and put the hay up loose with a hay loader. I think my Grandpa McColley had a corn picker. Dad bought a threshing machine the first year he farmed. He plowed with the R. I remember the 1937 Chevy we had. Grandpa McColley also had a 1937 Chevy. We got electricity in 1947. That was a big change. We started milking with a Marlow milking machine. We got two Surge milkers in 1952. We hung a strap around the cow to hold the milkers up. We started selling milk in 1947 and had a cooler to keep it cool. A person from the creamery started picking the milk up at our farm that we had put in milk cans.

Before Dad got out of the Army, he was stationed in the Galapagos Islands. He got bone cancer in his foot while there. I think he had surgery on his foot while he was there. He had surgery on his foot twice after he come home. The last time was 1949. He wore a cast on his foot and was on crutches. His brothers, mainly Lyle, did his work. Lyle would often sing to my mother. My mother had a guitar, and she played and sang in her younger years. My dad went to a touch doctor in Mankato. It was on a farmstead close to town. Sometimes there were a hundred people there. You got a number, and the doctor didn't spend more than a minute with you, and it cost a dollar. You had to pay a dollar when you got the number. People traded numbers. People who came in early bought several numbers then sold them to people that didn't want to wait. Many people made money by trading numbers. After going to the touch doctor for some time, my dad's foot started draining. One night a small bone came out. It was a lot better, but he suffered from pain all his life. When he was almost eighty, he had his foot amputated. He always drew a disability check from the Army.

Lyle with Queen and Beauty at the Frodl Farm

In January 1949, my dad bought a new 1948 WC Allis tractor and a mounted two-row corn picker. He had one of the few two-row mounted corn pickers. He did a lot of custom work opening corn fields. He had a blacksmith make an extension of the clutch so I could reach it from the seat and stop the tractor. I was five when I started to work in the field. When I drove, the tractor pulling the hay rack and the hay loader was behind. The hay windrows were a long way behind me from where I sat on the tractor. I sometimes got off the row on the corners. Dad really swore at me. He made me feel bad about leaving the hay. I soon got good at it. Dad leveled the hay on the rack laying down three slings. When we got it loaded, we took the rack to the barn to unload the hay. We were able to hook up the sling and pull it up to the hay mow. My Uncle Lenard always lay on the hay, and the hay was pulled around him. The hay was pulled up into the hay mow, and he was tripped out with the hay. The hay and Lenard fell together in the barn. Lenard always worked in the hay mow, leveling the hay. It took a big crew to put up hay. Two people were always in the field loading hay. One person hooked the slings and tripped the slings. Two people leveled off the hay, and it took one to drive the tractor pulling up the hay rope. We made hay with my grandpa. He had a lot of boys, so we had a big crew.

I started pulling the grain binder at five years old also. Dad cut off the tongue on the binder so he could use the tractor instead of the horses. I drove the tractor, and Dad sat on the grain binder. It had a tier to tie the bundles. There was a carrier on the right side, and when we got seven bundles, we dropped them. Grandpa Larson often came over at night and set the shocks with six bundles on the edges with the oats pointing up and one laid over the top to shed rain. The shocks looked like small teepees. While we worked we always visited. Grandpa always told stories, and he had a real interest in me. This was a fun time. I looked forward to this time. The shocks usually sat for two weeks to a month to dry before threshing.

Right before we started threshing, all the neighbors came over to our house to decide on the order we were going to thresh. In the early years we had a big crew, and it took almost a month. Mom always served a big lunch. One by one the neighbors got combines.

Dad sold the threshing machine in 1955 after threshing and bought a combine. That was the first year we raised soybeans. The threshing machine had to be run setting perfectly level. Dad dug a little on every wheel, backed the threshing machine in the holes, checked the level, then pulled the threshing machine ahead, and dug some more. He did this until it was perfect. The threshing machine was run with a long belt from the tractor. In the early years they loaded bundles in the field on racks pulled by horses. They brought the bundles to the threshing machine and pitched the bundles into the machine. The oats went into a wagon, and one wagon was replaced by another wagon, and a man unloaded the wagon in an elevator to the granary. The oats were stored in the granary. Boys usually leveled the oats in the wagons. Straw went out the back of the threshing machine in a long tube with a blower to a straw pile. It took a big crew. I usually went along. It was an exciting time. They often had horses run away, and in later years, horses were replaced with tractors. A small boy often drove the tractor. The wives tried to have the best meals, and it was fun to eat with the men. All the houses had a big dining room. They always served afternoon lunch with sandwiches and cake. The men always had a beer, and the boys always had pop. When they were threshing at our place, our pastor always came out for afternoon lunch and had a beer with the men. After we finished threshing, we had everyone over to our house to settle up. Some farmers had a bigger oat crop, and they paid others for their extra work. After we were finished settling up, the grown-ups played cards, and the kids played. Mom always served a big lunch with sandwiches and cake.

We had a granary with a lean-to on the side and another on the back. The lean-tos were our machine shed. We had a hammer mill in the granary. It was run by the tractor and a long belt. We shoveled corn on a wagon from the corn crib. We backed up it up to the door beside the mill and the belt. We shoveled the corn in the mill along with oats that were kept in the granary. There was a bin in the granary beside the mill where we kept the ground feed. We hauled the feed to the barn in a cart to feed the cows. I got up early in the summer and had it done before my dad got up. My dad's four brothers—Lyle, Lenard, Duane, and David—often came up to help. They usually didn't all come up at the same time. They rode their horses, Beauty and Queen, over. When they got to our place, they sent the horses home. Grandpa was waiting to put the horses in the pasture. Queen was Beauty's mother.

When I was five, my mother said I was going to cut off chickens' heads so she could butcher them. My dad got sick when he did it. I hated that job! She butchered them in the kitchen, and it smelled terrible. I soon hated anything to do with chickens, including eating chickens. My job was to feed the chickens. One evening I came in for supper, and my mom asked if I had fed the chickens. I said, "I would do it after supper." She said, "You will do it now. You know it is supposed to be done before supper." So I went out and did it. When I came in, my sister and mom were doing the dishes. I couldn't believe how fast they had eaten. She said, "You have missed supper, next time feed the chickens earlier." I never forgot it; I think it made me a lot more responsible person. I had to help my dad with the milking. One night the yard light was burned out. I said, "I am afraid of the dark." Dad said he would go down and turn on the lights, then I should come down. I played around and didn't pay any attention. So Dad came up mad. "Now you can help with the dishes and then come down." My dad sat until I got there, and then we had to do all the milking, and it got really late. I didn't do that again.

In 1949 we had a big wind storm. It blew part of the lean-to off the barn. Frodl had a smaller lean-to built on the barn. We kept pigs in the lean-to, so we got rid of them. Dad decided to buy forty heifer calves from Wisconsin. He was planning on selling half of them when they had their calves and to keep half to milk. We had the new lean-to ready early, but the calves never came. They come late in the fall when weather was bad. The calves all got pneumonia, and half of them died. We didn't have any to sell. This was a big setback for my dad.

At this time, we got a collie puppy. She was a natural cattle dog. She went out to the pasture to get the cows. She never had to be told. She always got them just before milking. Her name was Lucky. We never shut the barnyard gate since she lay on the porch and watched it. My mother always had several horses, and sometimes they were able to get out. We sometimes had cows in a pasture along a road, and we had to open gates. Lucky was afraid to ride in a car, so she met us there. My mother raised a hundred geese a year. She butchered them in the fall and sold them. This was her money. She had an incubator to hatch the eggs. She kept it in the basement. We had a high fence to pen the geese up at night. My sister Lucky and I always went to get them. Lucky pushed them with her long nose. We were always able to keep them together. Mom saved this money to buy things for the house.

In 1950, Dad bought a 1946 Ford car. In the winter, when it was below zero, it didn't start. The winter was much colder then. The climate had changed. Mom would hook a horse to the car. Mom would lead the horse to pull the car, and my dad would sit inside the car and start it. Every time we drove the car in the winter, we did this. The heater worked a little bit better on the Ford. We always had so many blankets to keep warm. It was a little bit better than the 1937 Chevy, but not much. In the winter Dad drained the oil out of the tractor and brought the oil in the house and set it next to the wood stove. In the morning he put the oil back in the tractor. Warm oil made the tractor start easily.

Dad dumped the milk out of the milker into a pail. I carried the pails to the milk room. We had a strainer set on the top of the cans, and I dumped the milk into the strainer. When I was eight I was able to lift the cans four feet high into the cooler.

My job was to throw down loose hay from the haymow. I would get the hay stuck in the haymow on purpose. I would then jump on it and fall in front of the cows and do it again. When I was ten I got to milk cows while Dad was milking a new heifer. My mom milked when my dad was working the fields. My dad enjoyed cooking, and Mom sometimes said, "If you cook supper, I will milk the cows."

My sister and I had a pony to ride named Topsy. My mother had this same pony when she was a young girl. Topsy died of old age, and we got a new pony. I think he was about twelve hands high. We got him as a colt, and we name him Tarzan. My mother had a palomino named Golden Lady. She got the horse as a gift from her Uncle Art Anderson. She raised several colts. One time when her grandmother, Grandma Krassin, was staying with us, she led the colt in the house so her grandma could see it. One of the colts always bit me on the shoulder when I went past her stall.

My uncles and aunt were not much older than I was. My Uncle Clifford was two years younger than I was. Today we call him Cliff. When we were kids, we knew him as Kip. Lyle was Buck, Lenard was Bim, and Duane was Dewey. David was always called David. When he was grown up, they called him Dave. We often walked over to each other's house and played. My grandmother was the most organized person I knew. When I stayed overnight, she gave me a list of things to do along with the rest of her kids. We had to get everything done on our list before we could play. We had big imaginations. We were in the army attacking another army. We were cowboys pretending to be the person we saw in the movies. Otisco had free outside movies on Saturday nights in the summer. They were mostly westerns. That was a big thing for Otisco. Every neighbor was there. Otisco was a really small town. It had a creamery, bank, blacksmith, bar, grocery store, and church. There were only a dozen houses. On Sundays my grandpa's family came to visit. There were a lot of kids, and we often played softball. I often thought that I wanted a lot of kids. It was fun. For Christmas when I was six, I got a toy Oliver tractor with a mounted two-row corn picker. When I was seven I got a pull-type combine. I took really good care of them. I have them sitting on a shelf today.

In 1954, my grandpa quit farming and went to work in Herters in Waseca making fiberglass boats. Farmers couldn't get Social Security back then. My grandpa was fifty-seven years old then. Most of his boys were out of school. He wanted to get Social Security. My dad rented half of Grandpa's farm, and a neighbor, Bud Priebe, rented the other half. I couldn't understand why Dad didn't rent all of it. They changed the law so that farmers could draw Social Security in 1956. My Grandpa Larson retired at the end of 1956 at the age of seventy. He only paid into Social Security one year and drew it for over twenty years.

My Uncle Lenard was in a car accident in 1954. The person driving was killed. Lenard had a broken back. I can remember how scared my grandmother was. He had to be in a cast from his neck to his legs for a long time. My grandmother didn't know if he would walk again. Lenard was a very determined person. He was going to be stronger than anyone. I think I got this determination and stubbornness from Lenard all my life and after my stroke. When we moved March 1, 1956, he could pick up two hundred pounds of potatoes with one sack in each hand and carry them up the basement steps. He suffered from this all his life with back problems. He died at seventy-one years old. Lenard was afraid to climb a ladder. My dad and Lenard were the only brothers afraid to climb. His other brothers teased him. Lenard decided he would do something that his brothers would be afraid to do. My grandpa had a forty-foot-tall silo without a roof that was empty. Lenard climbed to the top of the silo and then walked completely around the edge of the silo. His brothers were afraid to do it. My grandmother was really mad. Lenard could have fallen and been killed. He could overcome being afraid if he really set his mind to it, but he was still afraid to climb. He worked a year building barns. All his brothers said Lenard was the most stubborn person there was.

It was shortly before this time when my dad wanted my grandpa to mortgage his farm and buy two more farms that were next-door and were for sale. He wanted his brothers to farm with him. My dad was a staff sergeant in the Army, and he was used to being boss. He was always in pain from his foot and wanted someone else to do the work. Dad wanted to be a manager. My grandpa realized that this wasn't going to work. Lyle and I talked about this many times.

Picture at School

    I started first grade in school at the age of four. There was one girl, Marlys, in my class. She was my girlfriend for that year. My Aunt Judy was in fourth grade, and my Uncle David was in eighth grade. There were about twenty kids in school. We walked to school, but sometimes Grandpa McColley took us. My sister started the next year. There were three other kids in her grade. One was a boy, Charles, who become my best friend. We stayed at each other's houses many times. Another girl was Beverly. After we graduated from high school, I dated her a few times. The other girl was Janet. She was very pretty with her carrot-red hair and freckles. She was my girlfriend throughout the rest of country school. She was so smart she was advanced a grade and put in my class. She was best friends with my sister, and she stayed at our house often. When she started high school, she met another guy whom she married. My Uncle Kip started school the next year. Nadine Mittlested was my teacher the first two years. She married Ivan Sheffert at the end of the school year. She was my next-door neighbor five years later. Ruth Mittelstadt, not related to Nadine, was my next teacher. Her parents lived in our neighborhood.

Priebe School District 22

We had a real nice country school. It was called the Priebe School District 22. There were two bathrooms, one for the boys and one for the girls. The school had a drinking fountain. There was a basement with good-size windows. There was a kitchen in the basement. There was also a well on one side of the basement. There was also a furnace. We came in the school and went down a few steps to the basement. We went up a few step to the coat room. Then we went into the main rooms where our desks were. On the west wall there was a long row of blackboards. The bathrooms were in the back. There was also a large porch on the back of the school. When the weather was bad, we played games in the basement. The driveway went all the way around the school.

The teacher taught each grade sitting at a table at the front of the room. Each grade sat, in turn, around the table. The teacher taught eight grades and several subjects. The main subjects were reading, writing, spelling, arithmetic, and history. We had songbooks, and she taught music to everyone at once. We were supposed to be doing our work, but we were listening to her teaching the other grades. We often learned things early. When I was in second grade, I learned things she was teaching the fourth graders. Sometimes I didn't understand things when I was in the third grade, and when I was in the fifth grade, I learned it while listening to her teaching third grade. Everyone got along. There was no bullying. I never knew of someone who got punished. When we went to high school, we were way ahead of kids who went to town school. County school was almost a thing of the past since schools we were consolidating. When schools closed, kids went to town. Our school was the most modern, and they stayed open longer than most.

Two weeks before Christmas vacation, the school board came in to set up a stage in the front of the room. All we did was practice for the Christmas program. It was a big deal. We had to learn our parts by heart. Today everyone can read their parts. School has really gone backward over time. The school was full for the program. All my grandparents came. A big lunch was served.

Ruth Mittelstadt loved to play softball. If we worked hard in the morning, we often got to play softball all afternoon. Ruth always hit a home run. Once the ball went down the chimney. We only had one ball, so we had to quit. One school board member came and took down the stove pipes and got the ball back. I see Ms. Mittelstadt once in a while. I always thank her for the success I have in my life.

Once in a while my Grandpa Larson picked us up from school. Everyone who was going our way rode with him. Often twelve kids were in the car. We had no seat belts then and had never heard of such a thing. When everyone had gotten in, Grandpa said, "I want to talk to the teacher." One kid went in, but Grandpa said, "Hurry back." He always left before the teacher made it out. Everyone had a good laugh. He did it every time. Thinking about it today, the teacher wasn't so dumb to have that pulled on her more than twice.

I made the mistake of carrying my spelling book inside my shirt. We could walk on the road. It was two miles. When the weather was nice, we walked across the field. There was a creek between home and school, so we crossed over a bridge either way. Both ways we had a hill to go down and then back up. We walked across the field the day I lost my spelling book. The book cost my dad $2, and I really caught heck. From then on, I refused to study spelling. The rest of the time I went to school, I often had to stay after. One night she kept me after school until six o'clock. I just sat in my desk, staring at the blackboard. A farmer, Freddy Nelson, found the book that fall, but it was ruined. I have worked all my life trying to learn how to spell.

In the winter of 1951, we had a lot of snow. We were snowed in for thirty days in March. Grandpa took all the kids from our way to school every day by horses pulling a sled. He also picked us up at night. My Uncle David always came along. My other uncles stayed home from high school because the bus couldn't come. They were doing chores while Grandpa was taking us to school. The horses often got stuck. David shoveled them out. Dad hauled the milk to Otisco, four miles away, by horses and sled. He also picked up groceries. At the end of March, a snowplow came. All the neighbors shoveled in front of the snowplow. We didn't have the equipment back then that we have now.

One day in the winter, we decided to snowball the school bus. The bus stopped, and some big kids caught us. They were mainly my uncles. They took us to the bus, and the driver said he would give us a ride home if we promised never to snowball the bus. We never did that again. We had never ridden in a bus before. It was kind of a big deal for us.

One day the neighbor kids stopped at our place in the morning before school. They asked, "Where is your mom and dad?"

I said, "The old man is milking, and the old lady is in the house making my lunch."

Mom heard me, and I got my mouth washed out with soap. I never made that mistake again.

Ruth Mittelstadt stayed with her parents and rode a bicycle to school. After two years, she bought a brand-new car. Dad said he would buy her bike for my sister and one for me if we would get rid of our ducks. My sister's bike was really good, but my bike was junk. The handlebars broke off. My Uncle Stanley welded on a steering wheel. I was the only kid who had a steering wheel on a bike.

It was the summer of 1954. We had just got a television set. Grandma and Grandpa Larson wanted to go to Niagara Cave in Harmony. They wanted their whole family to go. We had to take three cars. By then I had two brothers: Dallas, born in 1950, and Richard, born in 1952. We were also going to visit my dad's Army buddy Orval Erickson afterward. He lived on a farm not far from Harmony by Pilot Mound. He really had a Norwegian accent, and it was fun listening to him talk. They had a pretty farm in the valley surrounded by hills. We left their place after supper. The roads had a lot of curves. We went through Pilot Mound, and then there were more curves. Soon we went up a long hill, and the curves were gone. Three quarters of the way up this hill was a farmstead some distant from the road on the left. I could see their lights. I was always asking my mother questions about who lived there. Mom said, "Your girlfriend lives there, should we stop?" I said "No." My future wife was living there. There were six girls. If we had stopped, I wouldn't have known which one she was.

In 1955, Frodl wanted to sell the farm. We didn't have the money to buy it. Dad spent the whole year looking for another farm to rent. He bought some new machinery that spring, planning on finding another farm to rent. I don't remember when, but the horses, Duke and Don, were gone. A few years earlier, we bought a second tractor, a 1937 WC Allis. We traded the threshing machine for a combine after threshing in 1955. I was eleven, and I thought I could do everything. Finally, it was fall, and there was no farm to rent. Dad got a job working for a farmer. We were going to live on a farm six miles from Waldorf, which was eleven miles from New Richland. We were going to go to school in New Richland. We had a sale November 15, 1955. It was the worst day of my life up to now. Before the sale, my dad bought a new 1955 Chevy car. He could never wait. Otto Fredrick was the auctioneer. He spent too much time selling the machinery. It was milking time before he started selling the cows, and a lot of people had left by then. They went really cheap. I thought we should have kept the cows until mid-February and milked them. When Dad paid off the bank, he didn't have enough money to pay for the car. I knew they started farming with $5,000, and now it was gone. I felt they had just gone broke. On December 21, I turned twelve.

Freda and Grant McColley

Chapter 4

Life on the Lukken Farm

We moved to the farm on March 1, 1956. We had kept the 1948 WC Allis tractor, the manure spreader, two cows, and two horses from the sale. We bought an extra calf when a cow had a calf. We butchered one calf and sold one calf. By having two cows, one was milking all the time. The cow wouldn't give up her milk when we milked her. So we had to let one calf suck while we milked her. We had to get one gallon a day, and that was a challenge to get a gallon faster than the calf could. We milked the cow once every day except Sunday. The calves took care of the rest. There was a real small barn where we kept the horses and cows, barely big enough for them. There was also a bigger barn but in poor shape. Dad also kept the 1946 Ford since he had to drive to work now. Dad got paid $200 a month. Roy and Marcie Lukken always treated me good, and I liked them. They paid me some for helping on the farm. Their home farm was ten miles north of the farm where we lived. They fixed up the house some for us. We had running water, a water heater, and a shower. As soon as it got warm, they put in a septic tank and a toilet. Dad did all the work, using a cistern as a septic tank. He had no experience with plumbing but was able to figure it out. It was sure nice to have a bathroom and to be able to take a shower. The house was much smaller than the one on the Frodl farm. The kitchen was fairly big. We boys shared a bedroom right above it. The living room was a smaller size. There would have been a really small bedroom downstairs, but that room was changed into a bathroom. There was a small bedroom upstairs that my parents used. My sister slept in the hall.

When I was in country school, I thought I was the most popular kid in school. We were starting at the end of the year. I had a hard time making friends in the town school. They assigned another boy to show me around the first week. I thought I had to stay with him all the time, and he soon got sick of me. When other boys asked me to do something with them, I said no. Soon no one liked me. When the boy showed me my locker, it was being used by a girl. He said, "For now, just use it." I was so bashful, and so was the girl, that we never asked to have it changed. If the girl was at the locker, I stayed away. I often got to class late, I would get lost in the halls. Part of the school building was on three floors; part of the building was on two floors. The floors didn't match. We had to go down steps to get on the other level. It was real confusing. We had to ride the school bus over one hour each way. We got on the bus before seven and got off after five. I got along better on the bus. I was sick to my stomach all the time just thinking about school. When the weather got nice, we ran to the football field. It was a mile away. I had never heard of football before. We played a little in the spring. I really liked playing football in physical ed. Next year I could go out for football. I couldn't imagine how I could get my folks to pick me up at school after practice.

My great-grandma Edith Krassin died May 12, 1956, at eighty-four years old. She was born on Valentine's Day. I was playing in the barn when my mother told me. I had never experienced anyone dying before. She was confined to a bed for the last four months of her life. She was in a coma and out of a coma several times. Right before she died, while my Aunt Lorna was watching her, she opened up her eyes and told Lorna goodbye. Back then my grandma took care of her mother in her home. Dr. Norman visited her at home. Now she would have been in a rest home. Taking care of my great-grandmother was terribly hard on Grandma's health. Great-grandma had a will leaving her three grandchildren $200 each and giving what was left to my grandmother. I remember my grandmother talking about this. Great-Grandmother didn't have $600 left. My grandparents decided to give each of the grandchildren $200 anyway. Great-grandma always gave me a silver dollar for my birthday. I still have all of them.

Roy Lukken had a big lawn mower that you walked behind. They had a big lawn, and I often had the job of mowing it. We had a power mower at home, and I always mowed the lawn. We had a big garden, and I really got into gardening. I spent a lot of time working there. I kept it perfect. It seemed that we spent all summer living off the garden. I didn't like food from the garden. In my mind, you were poor if you ate anything from the garden. I have never gotten over this. We had neighbors, Jules and Mary Schlaak, who lived a half mile from us. Jules was a first cousin of my Grandma Larson. Mom wanted me to go up to their place and mow the lawn. I didn't want to go. Finally, I went, and Jules paid me good, and I had a lot of fun with him. Mom often went up to visit with Mary, and I always went along.

Our family didn't go to church much at the time. Grandpa Larson's father was a strict religious dad. He wouldn't allow any music, any instruments, or any guns in their home. My grandpa and his brothers hid the violin and the rifles in the barn. Andrew had a violin, and Grandpa had a rifle. The strictness turned Grandpa off on religion. My Grandpa McColley went to church regularly, and their first four children were baptized. During the Depression, the church asked them too often for money that they didn't have. They quit going. In 1951, when my Uncle Lyle went in the Navy, my grandmother said that before her boys went into the service, they had to be baptized. The younger six were baptized at the same time. My parents always took us to Sunday school. My dad took us, and he sat in the car waiting for us. There was a man from church that always sat with my dad in the car visiting with him. We also went to vacation Bible school at church in the summer for one week. It was my mother's idea, and she took us. In 1956, during Bible school, they asked everyone to come up to the altar and confess our belief in God. Every day a few more kids went up. Two other boys and I refused to go up. Throughout the week, we talked among ourselves. On the last day we all agreed we wanted to be born again in spirit. We went up to the altar and confessed our belief in God and Jesus.

I have always felt different in my heart since that time. We went to church at the end of vacation Bible school. One of the teachers got up and talked about how she was so proud that the three toughest kids had been born again. I was confirmed in 1957. The pastor said we had to go to church in order to be confirmed. I was afraid to talk to my dad. I thought I had learned everything and I would not be confirmed. We had to learn the creeds, the Lord's Prayer, and parts of the Bible by heart. The pastor confirmed me anyway. Mom had the whole family over. My dad worked that Sunday and missed it. After I graduated from high school, my family started going to church regularly before my brothers were confirmed. My sister and I had been good at going to church regularly, and my brothers had not been such good churchgoers.

In August 1956, we had a McColley family reunion in Mineral Springs Park in Owatonna. I was playing with my Uncle Clifford, the Wakefield boys, and Lawrence Peterson in a creek. I was jumping from stone to stone. At two o'clock I slipped and I was knocked out. My dad decided it was best to take me to the hospital in Waseca. They took me in the car. I didn't come to until eight o'clock in the evening. All my grandparents were there. The first thing they asked me was, "Do you know me?" The doctor had warned everyone that I might have amnesia. I knew everyone. I had a terrible headache. The only time I have had that bad of a headache was when I had a stroke. I had this terrible headache for days. When I had the stroke, the headache lasted less than a minute. They said I had a skull fracture and it would affect my right eye. I could go blind in that eye. I had to stay in the hospital for one week. When I got out, they said I couldn't have any excitement or play in any sports for three months. The day I got home, a neighbor's barn, right across the road from our house, burned down. Mom couldn't keep me from watching from the window.

I had to get glasses, and I never liked them. I had perfect vision in my left eye, and I could never see any better with glasses. My mother kept telling me, "You will go blind in that eye if you don't wear your glasses." When I started driving, I took the glasses along but never wore them. My eye slowly got better. When I was in my thirties, I passed the eye exam and could drive without my glasses. I really felt bad that I couldn't play football that fall. I have never had an interest in football since.

In the fall of 1956, my brother Dallas started school. He could not talk well enough so that anyone could understand him. My brother Ricky could talk to him and tell everyone what he said. My dad's aunt was Dallas's schoolteacher. She soon had him talking. At first I had to stay in study hall while the other kids had physical education. I still had some trouble making friends, but it became easier. I soon had two really good friends. I did not get lost anymore and had a locker alone. Over the noon hour, we could walk uptown. We could buy used comic books at the drugstore. After we read them, we could sell them back. I always had a little money that I had saved from getting paid by Roy Lukken and Jules Schaak. Every boy had a squirt gun. The bus driver said if we didn't have a gun to check into a box upfront, we couldn't get on the bus. That eliminated the boys from getting into a squirt gun fight. Football games were played during the day. We often walked across the field to an old abandoned hemp plant. It was fun exploring it. I really liked shop class. We made a radio. We mounted it on a small piece of plastic with an end bent up. It had a condenser and a few transistors. We all bought a set of earphones. When I took it home, I ran a long electric fence wire from my bedroom to a tree. I hooked it to the radio and could hear it. I could get about three stations. That was the most fun project I ever made.

Mom worked at Birds Eye during the sweet corn harvest that fall. She worked nights, so my dad would be home most of the time. Sandy and I watched Dallas and Ricky most of the time. I didn't realize at that time that it cost them something for the hospital when I had my skull fracture.

That fall when Dad was harvesting on our farm, I rode on the grain tank, sitting behind Dad combining. The grain tank was a place to store the grain before unloading it into a wagon or truck. The combine didn't have a cab. It had a two-row corn head. There weren't very many farmers who picked corn with a combine. I got to chop corn stocks with an A. John Deere tractor with a two-row chopper. It was slow going, but I thought it was fun. Dad plowed with an R. John Deere tractor and a five-fourteen bottom plow. It plugged up often. After Dad turned at the end, he got off the tractor and walked, keeping the plow clean. When he got across the field, he got back on the tractor and turned around. The R. always stayed the furrow. There was no one driving the tractor. Perhaps Dad was ahead of time. Sixty years later, now a tractor can drive itself.

In January 1957, my sister got sick. I think she had colitis. She missed four months of school. A teacher came to our house a couple times a week. My sister was smart, so she kept up with her class.

In the spring of 1957, my dad was starting a Haggie self-propelled sprayer. It had one big tire on the front and two small ones on the back. It had no cab. It had a crank on the front, so if the battery was dead, you could crank it. That was what dad was doing. The sprayer was in gear, and when it started, the big wheel pushed my dad into the machine shed and broke all his ribs on the right side of his body. It took a long time to heal. Dad couldn't stand up straight, and it was terribly painful. It was planting season, and Roy wanted dad to come back to work soon. Dad went back sooner than he should have. Dad told Roy that he would stay until the first of March then he was done. When harvest was done, Roy offered a raise in pay. My dad quit March 1, and we moved.

Dad wanted to teach me how to cultivate corn that summer, but Mom always said she had things for me to do. I thought I could be real help to my dad. I didn't learn how to cultivate. Looking back years later, Mom didn't want me to get interested in farming. After Dad got hurt, I think it was her idea that Dad quit.

Grandma Larson inherited a 160-acre farm in North Dakota from her Uncle Steve Krassin in October 1933. Steve was married. His wife died in 1920. They had no children. I don't know if she had visited the farm before, but she wanted to go in 1957. My Uncle Roger and Aunt Lorna went with Grandpa and Grandma Larson. When they were in Devil's Lake, North Dakota, Grandma had a heart attack. My Uncle Stanley, his wife, Myrtle, and my parents went to North Dakota right away. Grandma Larson had to stay in the hospital six weeks. We started school before she got out. Grandpa stayed up there all the time except for one week when he came home to do some business. The rest of the kids took turns going to North Dakota every week. Marcie watched us some of the time during the day. When Grandma came home from the hospital, she stayed with us for some time. Mom had a bed set up in the living room for her. About this time, she got diabetes. She lost a lot of weight and could control diabetes with pills. Her grandfather, Gottfried Gehring, had diabetes too. He went blind. They put up ropes between the buildings so he could go outside. On the last day of his life, he could see again. He died when he was seventy-eight years old. My grandpa bought a brand-new 1957 Ford car soon after my grandma was staying with us. He bought a stick-shift transmission. He was certain he would not be able to learn how to drive with an automatic transmission.

We had electric fence around the small pasture. I had to check it every night. I always took Ricky along. He grabbed ahold of it. He told me if it was working. But Ricky didn't always tell the truth. He would sometimes say the fencer wasn't working. I would grab the wire and really get a shock. He thought it was funny. One time Mom had Ricky check the fence. Ricky said it didn't work. Mom stepped across the wire and really got a shock. Rick really caught hell, and he deserved it.

The whole family went out to the field after picking corn and picked up corn off the ground that the picker had left. We got enough to feed the livestock for a year. Roy bought a brand-new 720 John Deere tractor that fall with a four-row shock chopper. When I got off the bus after school, I was able to start it and go to the field by myself. That was really something!

Ben Krause owned the farm across the road from us. He had just built a new barn. His daughter and son-in-law lived there. Several times that summer and fall the cows didn't get milked. Ben's son-in-law was out drinking and didn't come home to milk the cows. Ben went to our church, and Dad knew him well. Dad always went and told him when the cows didn't get milked. Ben Krause lived about five miles from us. He lived on a farm my Great-great-grandfather Martin Krassin once owned.

My Uncle Marlin and his wife, Jeraine, visited us several times when we lived on the Lukken farm. They lived on the south edge of the cities on a steep hill. We visited them once. They lived on an old farmstead. There was a tunnel between the house and the barn. Marlin was a cabinetmaker. They had a cabinet shop in the barn. I was really impressed with everything. The sawdust smelled so good.

After Christmas vacation, I told everyone that I would be moving away. I became more popular. I soon had more friends, and they were sorry that I would be moving. Toward the end of January, Dad told me that Ben Krause had offered him his farm across the road from us. He was going to help him to start farming again. I was really happy for we would soon be milking cows again. I thought about that for about three weeks. Then we were going to move. My parents never told me why. I think it was Mom's decision. She didn't want to go broke again. We moved March 1, 1958.

Chapter 5

We Moved Three Times in One Year

On March 1, 1958, we moved on the Murphy farm. No one had lived in the house for some time. Dad rented the buildings for $30 a month. It was on a two-hundred-acre farm. Roy Lukken rented the land. A brother of my Great-great-grandfather Martin Krassin homesteaded this land. It was a big house. Part of the house was built much sooner than the second half. It was not in good shape. There was no running water or bathroom. We had to use an outhouse. As soon as the frost came out, we had to dig a new hole for the outhouse. My dad did not have a job, and my mother borrowed $200 from her dad. We heated the house with a woodstove. Dad stayed busy cutting wood with only a handsaw. We had a small barn, and it was good enough for the little livestock we had. There were a lot of woods, hills, and a big cliff overlooking the river. Clifford often came over, and we enjoyed exploring the woods. There was a big bridge with an overhead structure. We threw cherry bombs off the bridge, and they exploded under the water. That was fun to do. Steve Krassin's farm was a short distance away. No one lived there, and it was fun going through the buildings. The rumor was Steve Krassin hid a big jug of coins. We looked and looked and never found them. Maybe someone else had found them earlier and said nothing. I often rode my horse, Tarzan, through the woods.

    I went to Waseca High School. A kid named Jerry Cawley showed me around. He was captain of every sport. I did not have anything in common with him and did not spend much time with him. Fifty years later, we became good friends. I still had trouble making friends, but I always had some.

In April, my mother and Dad got jobs at Herters in Waseca. Dad worked making gunstocks, and Mom worked at filling orders. I didn't like coming home from school when no one was home. I decided at that time, when I got married and had children, my wife wasn't going to work.

In September, my folks rented another farmstead from Johnny Krassin. The place was right next to Grandma and Grandpa Larson. It was only a short distance through the woods. Martin Krassin owned this farm once too. Dad paid $60-a-month rent. It had a really nice house without a bathroom. We had to dig a new hole for the outhouse right away. As soon as we moved in, Johnny's son Arvin met a girl in Chicago and was going to get married. We had to move.

Uncle Stanley came over one day. He told us that a farmer was building a new house and that he wanted to sell the old house. Mom told her parents. The next day they came up and told Mom that they would sell her six acres and we should have the house moved. They had 166 acres. By selling Mom 6 acres, they would have 160 acres left. They charged Mom $600. They wanted Mom to live close to them. They needed help.

We decided to move our livestock into Grandpa's barn. Dad bought enough hay bales to block off a corner of the barn so it would stay warmer. The hay mow had twelve-inch-wide boards, with a one inch between them. The wind really blew through them. When it was really windy, it had a creepy sound. When the wind was strong, I felt like I was hearing things. I was afraid of the barn at times. I was in the barn in October of 1958. It was really windy, and a voice said, "You are going to be a farmer someday."

I answered, "Being a farmer is a hard life, I will always be poor and have no money."

The voice said, "You will always pay yourself first."

I answered, "I want to be a cabinetmaker like my Uncle Marlin. He always has a new car and a lot of money."

The voice said, "You are going to be a very successful farmer."

I answered, "I am not going to be a farmer."

In John 3:8, it says:

> The wind blows where it wishes and you hear the sound of it, but cannot tell where it comes from and where it goes. So is everyone who is born of the Spirit.

God talked to Moses through an angel. Maybe that just happened. Both Moses and Jonah didn't want to do what they were told. They fought against it. If you believe in the Bible, and God talked to them, can you believe that God talked to only two people? I think that God talked to more people than you can count. The Bible is a lesson for us.

Much later, I found out that Uncle Marlin never got a car paid for and that he didn't have the money that I had thought. Marlin was someone I always looked up too.

The next year I worked for Lorentz Frank. He did a lot of custom hay baling. I always stacked the bales behind the baler; I had no help stacking the bales. I did every year until I graduated from high school. Sometime after I graduated, Lorentz called me to come over and he wanted to talk to me about something. He said that there was an eighty-acre farm for sale a half mile away from his farm. The house had burned down long ago, but there was a good barn. He said that I could buy it cheap and that he would help me to get started farming. I told him no; that was the last thing I wanted to do. At different times, I told my dad that I didn't want to be a farmer. But at other times when I was thinking about the angel, I told my dad that I was going to be a farmer. He advised me not to rent a farm but buy one. But it would be impossible. You cannot do it without a lot of help.

In the fall, Dad bought a chain saw and cut down trees where we were going to set the house. Grandma Larson enjoyed watching the fire from the trees or brush especially at night. Dad and I watched the mover jack up the house and get it ready to move. I rode inside the house while they were moving it. We had a basement dug before we moved the house. The movers set the house on big pillars, and we had the basement built afterward. It cost my parents $4,000 total for the land, the house moving, and the basement.

Chapter 6

The Place Where My Parents Would Live the Rest of Their Lives

Harry and Deloris's Place

We moved January 1, 1959. Dad's brother Duane helped us move. It was a short distance to move. We hauled everything in a wagon pulled by our tractor. We had a wood furnace down in the basement. By the time I left home, I thought I had put up enough wood to last me a whole life time. I always had a big stack of wood to split with an axe. We had a septic tank put in, so we had a bathroom but had no well. The bathroom was really small, so we had a shower in the basement. Every night I took the wagon, pulled by our tractor, down to my grandparents' house. We had eight milk cans that I filled with water. When I got home, I carried the cans into the entryway. Every time you went to the bathroom, you had to take a pail of water to flush the toilet. My grandparents really looked forward for me to come for water and to visit. It was late in the summer before my dad had enough money to dig a well. He had Born Well dig the well. Forty years later, Born Well dug a well for my son Bob. Stanley Born came over one day. I had a lot of fun visiting with him about digging the well for my dad. He could remember both of my grandpas. He remembered digging the well for Grandpa McColley in 1942 or 1943. After the well was dug, Grandpa and his boys moved the windmill to the new well. They moved the windmill standing up from the old well to the new well. I didn't know that. That was a really enjoyable day. I think Stanley was in his eighties when they dug Bob's well.

We cut logs out in the woods to build a barn. We hauled the logs over to Lorentz Frank's place where he had a saw mill. We had a big crew to saw them into two-by-fours and boards. Dad had bought some beer for everyone to drink. When I worked for Lorentz, we always had a beer for dinner. He didn't care how old I was. Dad hauled one load of lumber home with the tractor; I sat on the top of the load. I was drunk. When we got home, I just sat on the load. My mother yelled, "What is wrong with you, Wayne? Get off and help us." My dad said, "Just leave him alone."

We built a one-story barn, twenty-four by forty feet, by ourselves. We had room for chickens. I didn't like them. I had to take care of them. One time we had a dog that had puppies in the manger. We also had a cat that had kittens at the other end of the same manger. When the dog was there, both the puppies and the kittens nursed at the same time. When the cat was there, they nursed together. The puppies and the kittens didn't care whether they nursed from a dog or a cat. The dog and the cat didn't care either. We had a stall and manger together for our horses, Lady and Tarzan. We had a stall and manger for our two cows. We also had calves' pens.

That fall I was in the tenth grade. We had a big essay to write. I didn't like writing, but I enjoyed this big project. We were to pick three things we would want to do for a career. We had to write about the education we would need, the money we would make, and the things we would do. For number 1, I picked architect. I would make the most money, and that was important. I would need to go to college for six years. For second place, I picked carpenter. They made more money than a cabinetmaker. I could learn on the job; I wouldn't have to go to college. I felt it would be easier to get a job as a carpenter than a cabinetmaker. For a third choice, I picked farmer. I didn't want to be a farmer, but God or an angel told me that I was going to be a farmer. From the research I had done on being a farmer, I knew it would take a lot of money to start. And it was the lowest-paying career. If one didn't have a family farm, it was almost impossible. I thought I wouldn't have to be a farmer, but on the other hand, I knew that I was going to be a farmer. I also had to give a speech on the career of my choice. I had so bad a stomachache from thinking of giving the speech I could hardly talk. If I would have chosen a career in the year 2000, I would have chosen an agricultural journalist. For a grade, I got an A on the essay and a failing grade on the speech. We also took several tests to show what career would be the best for us. Then we met with a counselor. Her advice to me was to be a nurse. At that time, I had never heard of a male nurse. If she told anyone, I would have been be so embarrassed. Little did I know at that time that later in life, I became a nurse for my future wife for a year.

When I was old enough to get my driver's license, Grandpa Larson took me for the driving test. I was going to drive his car. He said, "As soon as you pass the test, you can drive Grandma and me up north to go fishing." I didn't make many mistakes, but I drove too slowly, and I didn't pass. The next week when I took the test, I was not going to make this mistake again. I drove way too fast and didn't pass. Finally, the third time, I got it right, and we went up north fishing.

I was riding the school bus in 1959. The bus stopped at the railroad tracks. It was the law back then that a kid always had to run across the tracks looking both ways for a train. When we came to the north-south tracks, next to the Catholic school, a station wagon had been hit by the train. All the kids were lying dead between the tracks. I have never been able to get this sight out of my mind. James

Zimmerman lost his wife and all six children. Two years later, James Zimmerman married a widow with six children. Most of the kids had the same names as his dead children.

Shortly after this time, my Uncle Stanley, Mom, and I went to a sale. It was Johnny Robinson's sale. He was a neighbor to Stanley, and he had died. Stanley bid on the black 1946 Ford. He got it for $95, and it was my car. I got to drive it to school. Stanley had two daughters, Judy and Shirley. He treated me like a son. We did many things together. He taught me how to weld. He was a Raleigh Dealer. He called on farm customers, selling them things. He carried everything in the back of his pickup. He had built an enclosure for his pickup. He built in shelves and drawers, and he kept it very neat. He took me with him many days. He taught me how to drive a truck. Stanley had a small acreage, and he had four cows. He milked them at the same time, morning and night. He went down to the barn early, sat on a pail, waiting for the exact time to start.

Chester Schafer and his family visited Grandma and Grandpa Larson one weekend in the summer. I don't remember the year. I was at my grandparents' early watching for their car to arrive. I could remember driving the train when my grandparents took me to visit Chester. I really liked Chester. I couldn't wait to see him. When they got there, Chester started to wrestle with his two sons. It was fun watching them. Chester always encouraged everyone to compete. My Aunt Myrtle challenged me to race with her. I could run fast and thought it would be easy to beat Myrtle. We would run from the house to the henhouse and then back to the house. Myrtle started out fast, and I never caught up with her. I have never seen anyone run as fast as Myrtle. I was so embarrassed!

That year we celebrated Thanksgiving Day at Grandparents Larson's home. After we got done eating, Stanley said, "I will wash the dishes, and Wayne will dry them." I thought I was too old to do dishes. I did not want to help. It was women's work. Stanley taught me a lesson that day. I helped him, and I had fun doing it. We laughed the whole time. My mother took pictures of us doing the dishes. Stanley always had a way of making it fun to help him. Doing dishes was not women's work.

Wayne and Stanley

My dad told me to go to college, but he had no idea how I or we could pay for it. He never offered to help me. I gave up the idea of being an architect. In the senior year, a student could get a job and work in the afternoon. I got a job working as a carpenter for Lyle Neuman. We built two houses right away. Next he decided to build a hamburger shop and named it Lyle's Drive. He sold small hamburgers, three for a quarter. He decided to run it himself. So now I was out of a job. In the meantime, I had trouble with the 1946 Ford. The transmission locked up in two gears at once. My dad decided I should trade it for a 1953 Ford.

My Grandpa Larson's brother Alfred had died, and his funeral was on Saturday, March 7, 1960. My parents went to the funeral, and I was driving the car on Main Street at noon. I knew some kids on the sidewalk. I wanted to show off in my new car. A car was stopped at a red light. I wasn't paying attention and ran into the back of the car. It didn't do any damage, but the female wanted the police to come. We exchanged driver's licenses. She said, "You are a damn McColley." She walked around her car swearing, "Them damn McColleys, them damn McColleys." I was so embarrassed that I stood on the sidewalk, acting like I wasn't involved. I think she had something to do with Lenard or Duane. The motor mounts were broken, and the fan went through the radiator. Uncle David worked part-time at Springler's gas station. It was two blocks away. I could drive the car that far. They were not working on anything, so I could put my car in the garage. We went to a junkyard and bought the motor mounts for $40 and the radiator for $10. David helped me fix the car, and there were no other charges. I had it fixed before my parents got home.

There was a girl, Joan, who walked to school. I picked her up a couple times a week and gave her a ride to school. I wanted to take her to the prom but never got up enough nerve to ask her. Soon someone else asked her, and she eventually married him. Jerry Torbert, a friend of mine, wanted me to ask Sue. She was a good friend of Jerry's date. I called her one night. When I asked her, she said, "Yes," and hung up right away. The next day when I went to school, everyone knew that I was taking her to the prom. She was so excited that she told everyone at school. After the prom, the four of us went to the Stables Supper Club in Albert Lea. I had never been at a fancy place like that before. As a family, we had never eaten at a restaurant before. Once in a while, we went to a root beer stand and had hamburgers and fries. I didn't know how to order off the menu. I didn't even know what a salad was. I was so embarrassed that I never asked her out again.

I was a senior, and I had a new car, new to me anyway. I liked to show it off. Two other kids and I skipped school one day. We were going to go to our home since no one was home. I was driving way too fast. I passed on a hill, and all of a sudden a car was right in front of me. We were so close we couldn't miss. I froze and closed my eyes. All of a sudden, I opened my eyes. We were in the ditch facing the other way. There had to have been an angel with me. It wasn't time for me and the other two kids to die. I was going eighty miles an hour. I was at the crest of the hill, and the other car was right in front of me. The car I was passing was directly beside my car. We should have been killed. By the time we had got out of the car, my Uncle Roger and Aunt Lorna were there. Roger said they would take me to their farm and get a tractor and pull me out. The other two kids would have to walk back to town. I asked Roger not to tell my dad. Lorna said she was going to tell him, but it would be better that I told my dad first. I didn't think Roger would have told my dad. I asked

Roger when I was writing the book if he would have told my dad. He told me, "No, I wouldn't have told your dad."

When I graduated from high school, they held the exercises in a large auditorium. It had a large stage. There were a hundred kids in our class. When our name was called, we went up on the stage and received our diploma. We were to stay on the stage until everyone had their diploma. Then members of our family or friends could come up on stage and congratulate us. All the other students standing close to me had long lines of people waiting to congratulate them. I was standing alone. No one came up to me. I was so embarrassed! The only thing I could think was, all the men in my family were in the military. They were sick of standing in lines. I decided right there that I was going to come up and congratulate all my future children regardless how long I had to stand in line. I was soon in the military, and I got sick of standing in lines. But I would never use this as an excuse to stop me from congratulating my children.

I was only seventeen and five months when I graduated. Everyone had to be eighteen to get a job. At that time, even if you were eighteen, it was not easy to get a job. My Uncle Stanley had a small Case tractor with a cultivator. Robert Mishek, a former schoolteacher, had a small farm by Clear Lake. He decided to plant evergreen trees and sell them in a few years as Christmas trees. Mishek had a tile plant, a ready-mix company, and a mail order business for churches and schools. Stanley worked for Mishek years ago in the tile plant. He called Stanley and wanted him to cultivate the Christmas trees. Stanley hired me to do it. Now at least I had a job! I had to also hoe around the trees. Mishek was out often checking on me. I was doing a good job for him, and he offered me a job in the mail order business. I had worked for him a month when he asked me to get a license to drive a truck. I had to be eighteen years old to get a license to drive a truck. I told him that I was seventeen years old. I got laid off. I wasn't old enough to work there. In a week, he called me back to work. I would only wrap packages in the mail order business. I liked the job. He also had a trailer park. I mowed the grass there on Saturdays, and I plowed the snow in the winter with an International Scout. Plowing snow with the Scout was fun! Mishek was conducting the mail order business in a small two-story building next to his house and also in the basement of his house. That fall he decided to build a new building on the land where the Christmas trees were.

In the fall of 1961, I bought a 1960 Ford Galaxy. It was bright yellow, and it was pretty, at least to me. My dad had made a few payments on the 1953 Ford. So he made me give the 1953 Ford to my sister Sandy. The next summer I had an appointment with Kietzer Oil, where I bought gas, to come to where I worked every Friday to pick my car up and wash it and bring it back to work. It cost me $.75.

Jerry Frederick worked there. We became friends, and he asked me to go to the Kato Ballroom in Mankato. We went every Friday night. I didn't know how to dance, but when the band played the Circle Two Step, I always went out to the dance floor and pretended to dance. You had a new partner every two minutes. The girls were glad when they could dance with a new partner instead of me. One night I got a new partner who was older and overweight. I was hoping that the two minutes would go fast. Right away she knew that I didn't know how to dance. She said, "I'm going to keep you until you know how to dance." At the end of the dance, I sort of knew how. She was the best dance partner I could have had. Now I could ask a girl to dance.

Mishek had horses on his farm for his kids. There was an old barn. I sometimes had to take care of the horses, and that was fun. He also had an old John Deere self-propelled sprayer without a cab. A couple times a year, I drove the sprayer, spraying weed along the farm. It was fun driving the sprayer. I knew I would never be a farmer, but if I were ever a farmer, I wanted to have a John Deere self-propelled sprayer. One day when I was doing chores, I found an old pool table. I asked Mishek if I could have the pool table. It was worthless! Mishek sold me the pool table for $5. I took the bumpers off the side of the table. I covered the sides with a green material and the bottom of the table. Grandma Larson crotcheted new pockets for the table. She told me that if we ever bet on a pool game, she was going to cut the pockets off. I had it in the basement of our house. We had a lot of company that came to play pool. One Sunday, my Grandma

Larson played a game of pool against my Grandma McColley. I don't remember who won, but it was sure fun watching them. They both sometimes cheated so much it was hard to see who won. It was hilarious! We were having so much fun with the pool table that I bought a new one. I sold the old pool table to someone in Janesville. Than all of a sudden, the fun was gone. The new pool table just sat in the basement.

Mishek had the new building built. It had to be painted and shelves had to be set up. Mishek hired additional people to help. One was Eddie Babcock, a painter, and the other was Jim Duckworth, a person that worked construction in the spring. One night a week, five of us played cards and drank beer. It was Jerry, Eddie, Jim, Forrest, and me. Forrest worked in the office. I don't remember his last name for sure. Three nights a week, we continued to work on the building. That was a fun winter. In the spring, Mishek hired several young girls. That was fun! It was the most fun job I ever had. I worked there for two years. But we didn't get paid much. In the spring, I sent a letter to every carpenter to apply for a job. Jerry and I decided to quit working at Mishek's. I got a job soon, but Jerry did not get another job.

I got hired by Stockwell Lumber. The owner had a small lumberyard in Owatonna. It was in a large barn just north of Owatonna. The city had grown, and now the barn was in Owatonna. They had a crew that built houses and buildings. I worked with his son. It didn't take his son long to realize that I was afraid to climb. I worked some in the lumberyard straightening everything up. I liked that job! I also waited on a few customers. But the customers always called ahead. They were all contractors. Some days there were none. In a month they let me go. There were not enough customers to keep me busy. I went to every millwork shop within thirty miles of Waseca and applied for a job with no luck.

I then got a job working for a small dairy. I don't remember the name. I had a job where I drove a delivery truck. I delivered milk, butter, cheese, and ice cream to grocery stores and other varied businesses. I started really early in the morning, and I was done before noon. Then in late afternoon, I had to go back and unload a truck to the coolers and the freezers. Then I had to load my truck for the next day. We left the truck inside the building, and I pugged the truck in so everything would keep. I got paid $300 per month for six days a week. I made almost as much at Mishek's. It was a lot more fun working there with all the girls. Was it a big mistake to leave Mishek's? I would work for the dairy for three months.

Then I got a job offer from Neubert Millwork Company. I started out working in the cabinet department making church pews. The first day I stained church pews. It was a dirty job. All my clothes were filthy. They would never be clean again. Billy Beal was the foreman. We had to install the pews, and that was fun. It usually took two days, and we stayed one night in a hotel. We made the pews for my church at that time, United Methodist Church in Waseca. One day we had to build fifty wardrobes for the college in Mankato. Billy showed me how to install something in the wardrobes. After I installed one part, I asked Billy to check on it. He said it was okay. After I was finished, Billy told me that I had done it wrong on all fifty. I had to do it over. I felt terrible! Then Billy went to the office and told them to fire me. Billy had made the mistake, and now he wanted to blame me for his mistake. Don Myers, the foreman of the window department, was in the office. He overheard the conservation. He heard that I was about to get fired. Don said, "I want Wayne to work for me." From then on, I worked in the window department. I wanted to be a cabinetmaker, but Billy was not a good person to work for. He was always good at blaming someone else for his mistakes.

Jerry Friedrich became a lifelong friend of mine. While still working at Mishek's, Jerry got a job rebuilding printing machines. He took a truck to Des Moines, Iowa, and picked up a whole load of worn-out machines. Jerry torn them apart and rebuilt them all. The machines were all full of ink, and it was a dirty job. When Jerry was all done with the first load, he went down to get another load. A man at the company asked Jerry, "What did you ever do with the last load?" Jerry told them that he rebuilt all of them, and Mishek sold all of them. In the next days, someone called him and wanted to interview Jerry for a job. Jerry asked me if I would ride along with him. We went on a Saturday. The company hired Jerry to work in their repair department. For a while, Jerry always came home on weekends. Jerry married Lois, a girl from Easton, Minnesota. My sister Sandy and I went to their wedding. Jerry advanced to become the head person at that department. He worked for the company until he retired.

I lived in a house in Mankato with five students that were going to college the first three months in 1964. Sandy came over one night in March to tell me that Grandma Larson had died. She was sixty-seven years old. She had a bad heart. The last weekend I was home, Mom told me that Grandma wanted to see me. I went down, and she told me that I should be a carpenter. I never shared with her that I was afraid to climb. Grandma said she didn't want me to be a farmer. In January, she talked about a cousin that had died. In February, she talked about another cousin that died. She told us that there would be a third cousin. On purpose, she wanted to talk to certain relatives, including me. I'm positive that she knew that she was going to die.

In March of that year, Don and Heather Myers bought a forty-seven-acre farm by Alma City. When I drove to work, I went through Alma City. I exchanged driving with Don the rest of the time I worked at Neubert. Neubert bought all the parts for the windows. We had to put the parts together to make a window. We had a large warehouse to keep the parts in. The parts were delivered by trucks. We had to unload the truck and then put the parts away on shelves. Then we had to go out and pick the parts to make various sizes of windows. Don usually got the parts ready, and another person and I put the windows together. Don was an easy man to work for, and I always enjoyed the job. The winter of 1965 was a bad winter. We had a record amount of snow. When the roads were bad when we were to go home at night, Don always had me stay with them. I slept in a bedroom down in the basement. We left early one day because of all the snow. We made it through several snowbanks. On some, we had to shovel. When we got close to Don's place, there was a huge snowbank. We got out of the car and walked over it. The snow was super hard. We could see Don's house. Maybe we should leave the car there and walk home. But it was still snowing and blowing. Don didn't want to leave the car on the road. Maybe it would get covered with snow and the snowplow would hit it. The snowbank was too big to shovel through it. What would we do? Don said, "Maybe the car will jump over the snowbank." We got into the car, and he backed up a way. Then Don pushed the foot speed down to the floor. We were over sixty miles an hour when we hit the snowbank. All of a sudden, we were on the other side of the snowbank. It never hurt his car. The snowplow never came until the next night. Don lived one mile north of Alma City. The next day, Don and I walked up to the store to buy some beer. The store is now long gone.

Neubert Millwork Company was right next to Minnesota River. In March, all the snow we had that winter started to melt quickly. The weather service warned us that there was going to be a flood. We had time to prepare. We moved everything on the floor at the warehouse up. Neubert's building was in a large brick building with two floors and a basement. It was really old. We had a large elevator in the building. We moved everything out of the basement and first floor to the second floor. The water was already coming in the basement. We had sump pumps in the basement. Someone had to watch them. Don volunteered to watch them. I said I didn't have anything better to do that night but to stay and keep Don company. There were many college students filling up sandbags to put along the river. I helped them several hours. Around midnight, we heard on the radio that the levees had broken. We went outside. Sirens were going everywhere. The light from the sirens lit up the sky. When we looked to the north, there was a two-foot-high wave of water coming toward us. We had to quickly leave. The towns of Mankato and North Mankato were flooded. That was a scary night!

Chapter 7

The Navy Years

Wayne

I was twenty years old; it was 1964. The Vietnam War was on. I knew that I would be drafted. For several months, I called the Waseca Courthouse asking what my draft number was. When I called in October, they said I was number 11. I didn't want to go in the Army because I would have to sleep in foxholes. If I went to Vietnam, their solders would be shooting at me. I didn't like the sound of that. I had the most respect for my Uncle Lyle, and he was in the Navy. He was making the US Navy as a career. My Uncle Duane was in the Navy from February 1956 to December 1957. My Uncle Cliff was currently in the Navy. He would later make the US Navy his career. All three had chosen the Naval Air branch of the US Navy. I joined the Naval Air Reserve in November. I could go to reserve meetings for one year if I chose and then go for two years' active duty. I could also go right away for two years' active duty. I was working at Neubert Millwork Company in Mankato. I was making $1.60 an hour. I said, "If you will give me $2 an hour, I will wait one year to go in the Navy. If not, I will go in the Navy right away." They gave me the raise. That was a huge raise at that time.

My first day of boot camp was my twenty-first birthday in 1964. I had to spend two weeks at boot camp in the naval air station in the Twin Cities. First, we were issued seabags with all our clothes. We had to carry it for a half mile. I didn't think I would ever make it. After only two weeks of training, I could carry the seabag for miles. We never had a swimming test since all the swimming pools were frozen in December. I still don't know how to swim. They said that the two best sailors would get a pass to go out on the town, and I won. There was one kid who was always screwing up. They said, "Do fifty push-ups." He could do them just like that. They said, "Do them one-handed." He had no problem. He drove everyone crazy.

After boot camp, I went to the air station one weekend a month. We were free on Saturday night. I always went to visit my Uncle Lenard and his wife, Carol. Lenard had a boy, Gary, who was two years old. Lenard and I tossed him up and down on a blanket. Gary really laughed. It was fun for everyone. Lenard was a cabinetmaker for the Richfield School District.

In July of 1965, I had to go to Yuma, Arizona, for two weeks where they had an air station. It was my first time to fly in an airplane. It was 140 degrees on the runway every day at two pm. We started work at 4:00 AM and got off at noon. I worked on a crew that put practice bombs on airplanes. These bombs were dropped in the desert. While I was there, we got to go to Las Vegas. We flew on a plane that carried paratroopers. We had to wear parachutes, and we had instruction on how to use them. All of a sudden, I didn't think this was such of a good idea. We stayed at the Stardust Hotel and Casino. There were ten of us in one room. We only used the room to change out of our uniforms. We stayed up all night and went back to the base the next day. We also rented a car one night and drove to the Mexican border. We walked across the border and then went to a Cantina. It was a bar. The whole trip was a lot of fun.

Right before I reported for active duty, my friends had a big party for me. On November 3, 1965, I reported for active service at the naval station in the Twin Cities. The first thing they did was to give me a physical. They said that my blood pressure was too high to pass. I could go home. I thought it would be embarrassing to go home after the big party that I just had. I said, "I want to go in the Navy." I had to lie on a bed for three hours, and finally my blood pressure went low enough to pass. The next day, ten other guys and I flew to Treasure Island, San Francisco. I stayed there for thirty days. I took a lot of tests and had to pick from various air stations in the United States where I would be stationed. My first choice was Whidbey Island, Washington. My Uncle Cliff was stationed there. In a week the orders came through, and I had my first choice. I don't remember what my other choices were.

I got to Whidbey the first week of December. Cliff had a leave to go home for Christmas. We made plans that Cliff would drive my car back to Whidbey. When he got home, my dad didn't want Cliff to take my car. I finally had to tell Dad, "I am over twenty-one. I'm in the Navy. You can't control my life." Cliff brought the car back. At Whidbey, I was assigned to Heavy Attack Squadron 123. I went to school for a month learning about bombs. After the school, I was assigned to Heavy Attack Squadron 8. I had now spent six weeks learning about bombs for nothing. I worked as a compartment cleaner. In a short time, we flew to Miramar, California, where the squadron did practice flying. I was still a compartment cleaner. I met an AMS first class. He was going to try to get me to work for him. He approved me to take the test for third-class structural mechanic. In two weeks, we came back to Whidbey. Then a short time later we flew to San Francisco and went on an aircraft carrier, The Constellation.

We went out to sea for two weeks on a practice mission. The pilots were practicing takeoffs and landings. I was again a compartment cleaner. A short time after we got back to Whidbey, I was transferred to Heavy Attack Squadron 2. This was really good for me.

Cliff and I often went to Tacoma, Washington, to visit Cliff's cousin, Keith Haushahn. Keith was my second cousin. Keith's wife was Carol, and they had three young kids. Tacoma was about a hundred miles from the base. Keith wasn't the best provider for his family. Cliff and I always bought a gallon of milk. In less than ten minutes, Carol and the kids drank all the milk. Keith took us grocery-shopping right away to a store his brother-in-law owned. He always charged everything. His brother-in-law didn't want to embarrass Keith, so he let Keith charge them. I doubt Keith ever paid for them. Keith played guitar in a country western band on Saturday nights. Cliff and I always went and sat with the band. A lot of people bought the band drinks, and we didn't spend anything. Keith was also on a TV show playing in a band every week for a while. We always stayed with Keith and Carol two nights. It was fun to get away from the military life and to experience family life.

Keith, Carol, and their three kids

Rumor went around the barracks that there was a sailor who wanted a ride to the airport in Seattle. I looked him up. He said, "I will pay you $20 for a ride to the airport." It was one hundred miles away. It would cost me $2.50 for gas. It would take me four hours to make the trip there and back. I would make money, so I said I would do it. Visiting with him on the way to the airport, I decided that I was not going to charge him that much money. I felt sorry for him. When we got to the airport, he told me that he didn't have any money. He promised me that he would pay me when he got back from leave. When he got back from leave, he told me that he wasn't going to pay me. How would I deal with this? We were waking up at six in the morning. I woke him up at five and asked him for the money. I kept him awake until six. I told him, "I am going to be here every morning at five until you pay me." I think the other men that were sleeping near him were also getting woken up. It took me fourteen days to collect the money. I think the other sailors were getting sick of waking up too. They put pressure on him. I had become so stubborn that I was willing to do this forever. By this time, I had invested eighteen hours in this. It wasn't a good deal. I got screwed. When other sailors wanted to pay me for giving them a ride, I had to see the money first. I had learned a lesson.

In Heavy Attack Squadron 2, I was a compartment cleaner in the aircraft hangar. I got to meet the officers and the other men. I convinced them that all businesses would have janitors work at night when no one was around. It would be much more efficient. We would work really hard, and we were allowed to leave when everything was done. I usually only worked three hours a night, so I had a lot of free time. There was a wooded area beside the base next to the seashore. I really enjoyed walking in the woods. I had this job only two weeks when they moved me to the maintenance office. I had to learn to keep the records for our planes. We also kept time records on everything. I had to learn how to make monthly reports on the time records. This was a time before calculators. I used a huge adding machine. It was about eighteen inches long, twelve inches deep, and twelve inches high. Right before I got out of the Navy, I asked, "How did I get this job?" I was told that I had a perfect grade on a math test I had taken at Treasure Island. I was never that good at school.

I didn't have any As anytime. I have often wondered if there was an angel helping me take the test.

Working close to the pilots and crew members, I really wanted a flight jacket. In the barracks where I slept, there was a guy who worked in supply. He was sleeping in the next bunk. He said, "I can get you a jacket for $25." I had in my mind, "I'm not stealing it, I'm paying for it." I should have known better. Right after I got the jacket, I had a leave to go home. It was July 1966; I was to be home two weeks. I drove the car home with four other guys. We made plans to go back together again. Three of the men lived a long distance from me. They had to take a bus from my place. I went out to the Pla-Mor Ballroom at Rochester with two good friends one of the first night's home. I met a girl, Marlys, that night. Being a sailor among thousands of other sailors, it was impossible to get a date around the base. Being a sailor in Minnesota, it was easy getting a date. I went out with her the next day. When I told her we had horses, she wanted to go riding. I took her home, and we went riding. I never did this before or again. To impress her, I stood up on the back of the horse I was riding. Mom took a picture of Marlys sitting on Tarzan and me standing up on Lady. I got a call from the base that I had to report back right away. I said that I drove, and that would take some time. They gave me five days to get back. The other guys didn't want to come back early, so I would be driving alone. I decided to fly, and that way I could spend more time with Marlys. I waited until the last minute. There was an airline strike going on.

I couldn't fly from Minneapolis to Seattle. They said that if I flew to Denver, maybe I could get to Seattle from there. When I got to Denver, they said, "The only place you can go is to Los Angeles." When I got there, they told me it would be impossible to get to Seattle. My leave was up, so I was AWOL. I called the base, and they said, "Take a bus to Oakland, across the bay from San Francisco." There was an air base there, and there was a plane flying to Whidbey at noon. I got on the bus, and there was no time to spare. I didn't have any money left. I prayed all the way that I could make it. I had no idea how I would find the plane from the bus. I would have to walk. It was noon, the plane was running, and it was about to take off. An angel was with me, and I got on the plane. It took me two days to get from the Twin Cities to the base at Whidbey. It took me less time to drive home from Seattle.

The next day at the base, they told me that I had stolen the jacket. I had to give it back. I had taken it home. I was really embarrassed to call my mother and ask her to send the jacket back. I would receive a captain's mast. That was the way for the Navy to deal with a minor violation. It was like going before a judge in a court. I got along really good with the chief. I had always done a good job for him. He said, "I will go to bat for you, and you will get off." The chief was right.

I was broke. Many sailors got money from home. They didn't want to stand night watch, so I stood night watch several times a week. They paid me $10 to stand the watch. I wanted to make enough money to go home again to see Marlys. We were going to go to Vietnam in a little more than four months. I was getting several letters a week from Marlys.

We were flying often, either to Miramar, California, or to San Francisco. We were flying in four engine props. They weren't pressurized, so we flew low. Often one of the engines caught on fire. Then they had to fly with only three engines. At San Francisco, we went out to sea on the carrier, USS *Enterprise*, the largest warship in the world at that time. I worked in the maintenance office. When the planes returned to the ship, the pilots wrote up a report on what was wrong with the airplane. My duty was the responsibility to get it fixed. I had to call the various shops, depending what was wrong. When the pilots came into the maintenance office at any time, I had to tell them when they could fly again. I didn't have time to call and check on the plane while they were there; I was supposed to know at all times. We were a tanker squadron. We filled the other planes in the air with fuel. I knew all the pilots really well. One night we had an accident. The plane we were tanking got too close, and they crashed. The pilots on the plane we were fueling were able to eject, and they were picked up in the water. Our tanker had two pilots and a crew member. They couldn't eject, and they were all killed. That was really hard for me. I knew them really well. I don't think they were able to recover any of the bodies. They searched for days.

In September, when we were back at the base at Whidbey, we could go on leave before we went to Vietnam. We got thirty days leave a year. We had to earn the leave. We couldn't take leave ahead of time. I took the maximum time when I went home in July. If I hadn't been called back because of the jacket, I wouldn't have enough leave left to go home. I called Grandma and Grandpa McColley to pick me up at the airport in the Twin Cities. I wanted to surprise my parents. I just walked into Herters where they worked. They were really surprised. That night I couldn't wait to see Marlys. She knew I was coming. As soon as I got there, she told me she had met someone else. She dumped me! I had spent an hour driving to Rochester and an hour driving home only to see her for ten minutes. My two brothers had grown so much; it was like I didn't know them. I wished I had stayed at Whidbey. The next night I called two friends, Butch Sternagle and Chuck Matz, and we went to the Pla-Mor Ballroom in Rochester. My friend Chuck and his girlfriend, Mary, introduced me to Ruth Borgen. I went out with Ruth the next three nights. We exchanged our high school graduation rings the third night. We talked very little that night. She was crying because I was going to Vietnam. If I hadn't bought that jacket and been called back from that first leave, I wouldn't have met my future wife. God and angels work in a strange way.

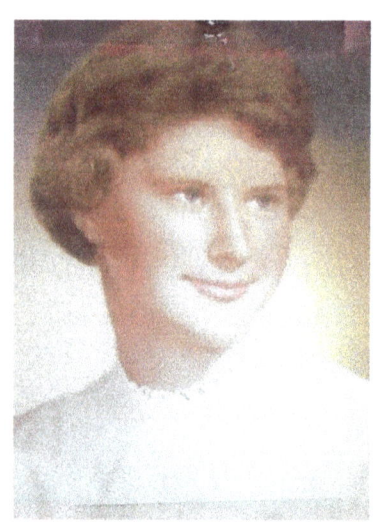

Ruth Borgen

Ruth wrote me a letter on November 17, 1966.

> Wayne, I don't want you mad at me, but I think it would be okay to have my ring back. If everything goes okay, I'll be glad to have yours back when you come home. I do want you to meet my folks and my family.

I think Ruth's mom and dad told her to get her ring back. They had paid for the ring. "How could you give the ring to a boy that you just met? Now he is going to war. You will never see the ring again." I sent the ring back to Ruth, but I told her to keep my ring. I thought, if we were going to get both rings back, then we would never see each other again. She wore my ring all the time and told everyone it was from her steady boyfriend.

In November 1966, our squadron left for Vietnam. We went on the USS *Enterprise*. It took us eleven days to cross the Pacific Ocean. We stopped at Hawaii for four days. Five other sailors and I rented a car to drive around the island. Steve Hibbert drove the car. Steve and two really good buddies, Bob Cunningham and Mike Sammon, were with us. I don't remember the other two sailors. Along the seashore was a grass-roofed bar. We stopped there to have a beer. There was an elderly couple there. They said, "Your money is no good." They bought beer for us all afternoon. Steve was driving, so he didn't have as many beers as the rest of us.

It took us fifteen days to get to Subic Bay, Philippine Islands. We would usually stay there for five days and then be at sea for forty days. Our squadron had five A3B Sky Warrior bombers. They used the bombers as tankers. When the other planes bombed Vietnam, they didn't have enough fuel to get back to the ship. We had to fuel them in the air, and jokingly, we also said that we would them give them green stamps. Back then, if you filled up your car with gas, they gave green stamps. You saved them for gifts. There was room for four crew members, but they only flew with three. Maybe when the planes were bombers, they required four crew members. The pilots were always trying to get me to fly with them. They were always flying over Vietnam. I was not afraid of getting killed, but I was afraid of getting shot down and being captured. My good friend, Bob Cunningham, who worked in the ready room with the pilots, went flying with them. We never lost any of our planes, and today I sure wished I had gone with them. When Ruth and I had visited Bob and his brothers were there, I always told them that Bob had flown a combat mission.

Navy Picture

In December, we had a contest. Every division on the ship submitted an enlisted man to be Man of the Month of the Enterprise. My squadron named me as Man of the Month. I didn't win, but it meant a lot to me to be named the Man of the Month from my squadron.

My responsibility was to always know when the planes could fly. I did this along with keeping flight records and time records. The crew chiefs had to turn these time cards in. They didn't like doing it. I had to take these cards to a division of our ship where they ran them through a giant computer. It made a report which gave the chiefs a grade. They usually had a failing grade. I was able to figure out how it was giving grades. I changed the cards so all the chiefs got a good grade. For my doing this, they always kept me informed when the plane could fly. In the service, it works like this: you rub my back, and I will rub your back. I had no calculator, so I did everything in long-handed arithmetic. I got really good at it.

On New Year's Eve 1966, at eight thirty in the evening, the general alarm went off. We were in general quarters, and enemy planes were spotted coming toward our ship. Everyone reported to their duty station, and the ship was sealed up. My office was under the water line. Every ten feet was a hatch you walked through. They were all sealed up, so we couldn't go anywhere. It was a weird feeling; it was really so quiet. The ship was made that way so if we got hit and started to sink, the water couldn't get into the whole ship. We sent up fighter planes, and the enemy planes turned around. It was a scary two hours. If water got into the ship where we were, we would probably die.

The third-class sailor who worked in the office next to mine wrote his hometown paper and said there were five thousand lonely men who needed someone to write to them. He was from Bingington, New York. They got mail bags full of letters. I always worked nights. When I had nothing to do, I went over to their office and read letters. One night I read a letter from Karen Covert. She was nineteen years old. I wrote to her, and she answered my letter. She wrote to me every day until the end of the cruise. We didn't get mail every day, so I got several letters at once. I always had something to look forward to. Ruth didn't write often; I asked her to send my ring back. I wrote several letters to her demanding her to send my ring back. She never did. At that time, I thought it was a mistake not to get my ring back when I sent Ruth's ring back to her. I started to write love letters to Karen. I don't know if she thought the letters were love letters. I thought I would see her one day.

Another time we were in a typhoon. The waves came over the flight deck, which was a hundred feet above the sea. The ship was partly sealed up; we could go through the hatches, but we could not get anywhere. We couldn't see out. This lasted for four days. The ship really rolled. We could hardly walk. It was impossible to work. Eating was a real experience because everything moved on the tables. All the planes were tied down. Ninety-six hours seemed like eternity.

One time an A4 plane was hit while it was dropping bombs. It was a small one-man plane. It was hit in the wing. They carried all their fuel in the wings. One of our planes was close by, and they hooked a fuel line to the plane. They tanked him back to the ship. When the A4 was close enough to the ship, they unhooked the fuel line. The engine stopped, and the pilot was able to land the plane on the carrier without power. The hole in the wing was so large the pilot stood in the middle of the wing with his arms stretched out, and he couldn't reach across the hole. He was one cool pilot. I wonder if an angel was with him.

Most of the time I worked nights. They had two twelve-hour shifts, seven days a week. They served food twenty-three hours a day, but the chow line was always one-hour long. They closed from three to four in the morning. Usually, after two, there wouldn't be a line. That was when I ate, once a day. The food was usually old by two o'clock. All in all, I thought the food wasn't that bad. Once in a while, they would have high up dignitaries come aboard. Then they would serve huge really good meals, and it was worth it to stand in line. My favorite meal was white rice covered with chili. It still is my favorite today. My favorite time was sunrise. I would go to the deck on the back of the ship. Most of the time it was fairly calm and the water was so blue. Sharks usually followed the ship because we threw the garbage overboard. If there were birds on the ship, we could see land way off. If we were really out to sea, we couldn't see any birds. It was about the only place I could be alone. In a twelve-by-twelve-foot space, eighteen men would sleep and have all their gear. My least favorite thing was picking up the time cards from the line shack, as they called it. I had to go on the flight deck, which was one hundred feet above the sea, and go down over the side of the ship on an open stairway. I could see though the stairway, and I had to go down one floor. I am afraid of heights. If the ocean wasn't perfectly calm, I just couldn't do it.

I took the test for aviation structural mechanic and passed the test and became third-class AMS. I worked as an AZ. I would have to pass a typing test to make AZ. No one knew I didn't know how to type. It was easy to get someone to do it. Being third class, I had someone working under me. Some of the others in my squadron liked to give Sam Mattern a bad time. They called him on the phone and really teased him. Sam became so confused he didn't know what to do. I decided I would put an end to this. Sam got a call, he didn't understand, and I thought they were teasing him. I took the phone and really gave them hell and hung up the phone. It was an officer of the ship. He called the Marines to arrest me and to put me in the brig. My squadron CO came in right away and asked what had happened. I told him that someone was always giving Sam Mattern a hard time. I thought this was it. He told me to get lost for two hours and he would take care of it. I was lucky that the CO was a pilot and he really liked me. No one ever gave Sam Mattern a bad time again.

We played a lot of chess and cards in our spare time, but I never played for money on the ship. My mother sometimes sent me something and packed it in popcorn. I always ate the popcorn; I was always hungry for that. I shared the cookies but didn't share the popcorn.

The USS *Enterprise* fight deck covered six acres. It was a hundred feet above the water. There were catapults that shot the airplanes off. There was an angle deck at the back of the ship with four cables across where the planes landed. There were hooks on the planes that had to catch the cables. If they didn't catch the cables, the planes had go up and come back to try again. Below the flight deck, there was a hanger deck which was thirty feet above the water. There were four elevators, two on each side, that would take the planes up or down. The hanger deck was 260 feet wide. There were eighty planes onboard and five thousand men. Above the flight deck was the operations center. It was fourteen floors tall. On the eighth deck was an observation deck where we could go up and watch the plane take off and land. I often went up there at night while they were bombing. You could see flashing from the bombs going off.

It was always really hot, so we didn't have to wear full uniforms. We wore dungarees, T-shirts, and no caps. They were afraid the caps would get sucked into the jet engines. All too often, we had to wear our dress white uniform to attend a funeral. Planes got shot down. If you have experienced war, you never get over it.

Two months before we came back home, Ruth sent her class ring back to me. In the last months, she started writing to me often. Ruth talked to her parents and her family a lot about me. They could see how sad Ruth was without me. She told me that she had made a big mistake when she asked me to send her ring back. Finally, her parents and her family told her to send the ring back. In her letters, she talked about getting married. She showed my picture to everyone and told everyone that she was lucky to have me as a steady boyfriend. She wrote to me that she was lucky to get me. I wrote my mother about this telling her that I thought Ruth thought I was going to marry her. That was not going to happen. We had only four dates. How could we get married after such a short time? How could Ruth make up her mind to marry me so soon? How could I make up my mind so soon?

We came back under the Golden Gate Bridge on July 4, 1967. Lucille Ball was standing on the bridge and waving at us. I had thirty days' leave. I had been home for two weeks. It was on Saturday night when I picked up Ruth and gave her class ring back and said I wanted my class ring back. Finally, she gave my ring back reluctantly. I made her think we were breaking up. I then handed her a diamond ring. I asked her to marry me, and she said, "Yes." We went to the Pla-Mor Ballroom in Rochester. She was thrilled to show off her ring. Her friends and mine played a terrible joke on us. They got Ruth really drunk. I think it was the only time I saw her drunk. I met her parents for the first time the next day. They were waiting to meet me. We got along well, and I could really feel that they liked me. I think it was in God's plan that we were going to meet and spend the rest of our lives together. I wrote Karen Covert and told her I was engaged. I would have to stop writing to her. The letters she wrote while I was in Vietnam had made my life more enjoyable. I would never forget her.

The next week we bought a brand-new Plymouth Satellite. It was a red, two-door hardtop with white interior. I got a loan from Otisco State Bank. I didn't have to make payments until December. The next day we went out to the Bernard farm to meet Ruth's sister and her husband, Eva and Junior. They were both unloading hay. I should have helped, but I would have gotten dirty. I have always felt guilty about this.

In the beginning of August, I drove my new car back to Whidbey. I took Steve Hibbert to look at a car. I think it was a 1962

Nash Rambler. Steve bought the car. All my friends were short-timers. Short-timers meant that you are going to get out of the Navy soon. We did as little work as possible. We could rent pup tents and cooking utensils. We did this often and went up in the mountains and went camping. I went with several guys, but most often I went with Bob Cunningham. We always cooked scrambled eggs in beer for breakfast.

Bob Cunningham

    I must have made a big impression on Ruth's folks and her family. On her August 19 letter, she told me that her mom was saying that her dad thought we looked alike. I don't know if we look alike so much. But I think her dad thought we were meant to be together. Everyone told her that she was getting a real nice guy. They were so happy for us. In her August 30 letter, she told me that her whole family and her folks wanted us to get married in November. How could I leave the Navy and be married right away? I would have to have time to adjust to civilian life. Her parents had a family before World War II. The baby boom started right after the war. I was coming home from the Vietnam War. They didn't want Ruth to get pregnant before marriage. Ruth signed her August letter, "Mrs. Wayne McColley." Our oldest child, Tammy, was born thirteen months after our marriage.

Every time someone was getting out of the Navy, we celebrated at the base bar. We always celebrated with flaming hookers—150 proof rum. The waitress lit the drinks, and you drank them on fire. We chased them with beer. Bob Cunningham got out a few days before I got out. He was going to stay in the barracks, waiting for me to get out. We were going to drive home together. When they gave me a physical, I had really high blood pressure. My Grandpa Larson had this problem too and had a stroke in his later years. He lived to ninety-one. They were going to put me in the hospital. I knew the corpsman well. I told him to mark the blood pressure low enough for me to get out, and he did. This was a big mistake for me. If I would have gone to the hospital, I probably would have drawn a disability check all my life. They would have worked at getting the high blood pressure under control. I never had it checked for thirty years. Maybe it was a cause of my stroke. I got out November 3, 1967.

Bob and I drove home together. There was no speed limit in Montana. We drove one hundred miles an hour most of the time. Oftentimes we saw only one or two cars in an hour. When we were getting close to Wyoming, it started to rain. Just like that, the car turned around, and we were going one hundred miles an hour in the wrong direction. We really slowed down after that. It really scared us. We got to Rochester to pick up Ruth at midnight. She had gotten her hair fixed, and she was afraid to lie down. She didn't want to mess up her hair. We picked her up, and we went back to my folks by Waseca. We got there about 2:00 AM. Bob stayed with us several days and then took a bus home. We went to the Pla-Mor Ballroom Saturday night. It was a sad day when Bob left. We had spent so much time together. We were together almost the whole two years.

I started getting orders to report to the air base in the Twin Cities. I threw them away. I would have to go to reserve meetings for three years. After a month, I decided I would have to go up there. When I reported to an officer, he really chewed me out. He said I was in big trouble. I let him go on and on. Then I showed him the contract that I had signed. It said that a person who lived more than fifty miles from a base didn't have to report. He studied the contact for a long time and then said goodbye.

Chapter 8

Marriage and Early Years

Ruth wanted to get married right away after I came home from the Navy. I felt it would be too big of an adjustment, getting out of the Navy and getting married right away. I felt I had to get settled in a job first. I went back to work at Neuberts Millwork Company in Mankato, Minnesota. The only job they had for me was driving truck. That was a job that I enjoyed. I had a route delivering millwork to lumberyards. I enjoyed visiting with everyone. I knew that I didn't want to do this for the rest of my life. The management at Neuberts said they were going to set up a new department making door units. I would be in charge. When I met Ruth, I told her I was a cabinetmaker. She told her parents. When we were visiting her parents, they were always questioning me about this.

I was living with my parents and driving to work with Don Myers. On Friday nights we always stopped at a bar on the way home and had two beers. Mom didn't like this. On Friday nights, she always had supper early so I would miss it. At Christmastime, I agreed to get married on April 6, 1968. My Grandpa McColley's birthday was on April 6. I was sure I would never forget our wedding anniversary. It would be a little more than three months away.

On Christmas Eve, Ruth and her family celebrated Christmas. She had two brothers and five sisters. This was the first time I would meet all of them. They were all full-blooded Norwegians. My Grandpa Larson would be proud of me. They served Lutefisk and Swedish meatballs for supper. They served me first. I didn't like lutefisk, but I took some to be polite. If they had served me last, I wouldn't have taken any. Some of my future brothers-in-law didn't eat lutefisk. We celebrated that Christmas at Palmer and Audrey's house. Palmer is Ruth's brother. I bought a pretty pink dress for Ruth's Christmas present. It cost $40, which was an expensive dress at that time. Ruth didn't like it; it was too short and the neckline was too low. I really thought the dress looked good on Ruth. I would learn that I couldn't buy any clothes for her that she liked. In fifty years, the only thing she liked that I bought was a pair of shoes.

    I started thinking more and more about when I was fourteen years old. I thought I was going to be a cabinetmaker. I had told Ruth that I was a cabinetmaker. On a Saturday in February, I applied for a job at Cabinet Craft in Rochester. It was now March. Cabinet Craft never hired me. We would need a place to live. I didn't think about renting; I was going to buy a house. On weekends we looked at different houses. We finally found a small, two-bedroom house in North Mankato. It would cost $5,500. The payments would be $55 a month. We signed papers to buy the house. When we got back to my parents' house, I had a call from Cabinet Craft. I called Cabinet Craft back, and they told me that I got the job. I would start April 15, one week after our wedding. We had to get out of the deal we had made to buy the house in North Mankato. We would now be living in Rochester. We could live another month in Ruth's apartment. Ruth could keep her job at the Methodist Hospital. She worked in the kitchen setting up trays for the patients. We planned for her to quit working after our first child was born. We wanted to have children right away.

    Ruth went to a Lutheran Church in Pilot Mound. It was less than three miles from their farm. It was too small to hold our wedding there. A few miles further on Highway 30 was another Lutheran Church. It was called North Prairie Lutheran Church. The same pastor, Percy Larson, served both churches. That was where we were married. It was a true country church. It sat by itself on the prairie with only a cemetery next to it. It was a warm day, and all the farmers were in the fields around the church. It was also very windy. Orville and Ruth Erickson were there. We had visited them when I was ten years old. I never forgot them. My Grandpa Larson came, and he visited with Ruth's Dad, Elmer Borgan. They talked Norwegian. Ruth's attendants were her sisters, Eva and Linda. My best man was Butch Sternagle. My brother Dallas also stood up with me. Ruth's two brothers, Howard and Palmer, and my brother Rick were ushers.

My mother had told me to pay the pastor $20. I did this right before we walked to a door right in front of the church. The pastor said there was a groom who asked the pastor, "What should I pay?" The pastor said, "Pay what you think she is worth." The groom gave the pastor a dollar. The pastor said, "Just a minute, I'll get you change."

I was really laughing when we went into the church. Maybe some of our guests would think I wasn't serious about getting married.

After the ceremony, we went to the back of the church and greeted everyone. My Grandma McColley walked out right after Ruth's parents. I heard Grandma tell Ruth's mother, Edna, how lucky Ruth was to get me. I could really feel how proud she was about me. The church ladies served lunch to everyone after the wedding. My dad opened the cards that we had gotten for the wedding. He gave me the money from the cards to pay for the honeymoon. We had a plan to go to the Missouri Ozarks. But we didn't have enough money to go until we got the money from the wedding cards. After the wedding, we went to visit Ruth's grandma at the rest home in Preston, about twenty miles away. Then we went to visit my Grandpa McColley at the Veterans' Hospital in the Twin Cities. We took two cars. Butch drove my car, and Eva's husband, Nado Jr., drove the other car. It was about one hundred miles away, and we didn't have enough time to go out to eat and make it to the dance. It was an extremely fast trip. I think an angel was looking out for us. It was Grandpa's birthday, and all the nurses were excited to see Ruth in her wedding dress. They really made a big deal for us to come. On the way back, we stopped at the Edgewood Supper Club to eat. I paid for everyone. We got to the dance at the Pla-Mor Ballroom at ten in the evening. I bought tickets to the dance for the close ones who came to our wedding. The total cost for the wedding dance was $80. Ruth sold her car to pay for the wedding. I think the total cost, including the wedding dress, was less than $500.

Ruth and Wayne's Wedding

After the dance, we stayed at the Holliday Inn in Rochester. I had a few drinks at the dance. I carried Ruth into the room. We couldn't see a bed. I called the front desk on the telephone. I said, "What kind of a deal is this? I reserved a room for my wedding, and you give me a room without a bed." They really laughed when they told me to open the large double doors in the wall and pull down the bed. In over fifty years, we have never had a room like this. For our forty-year anniversary, we stayed at the Holliday Inn again. I tried to get the exact same room. There was a regular bed in the room.

We had steak and eggs for breakfast late the next morning. We rented the suit I wore at the wedding. We dropped the suit off at Ruth's parents' home. They were going to return it the next day. The first thing Ruth's mother, Edna, asked me was, "How is married life?" I said, "Pretty good."

We made it to Decorah, Iowa, the first day. It was less than a hundred miles.

In Iowa, we crossed the Mississippi River into Illinois. They decorated our car at the wedding, and we didn't clean it off. The writing on the car said, "Do you know how it is done?" It rained a little one night. It then said, "So you know how it is done." There was a toll to pay when we crossed the river, and we got to cross free. We drove through Illinois and crossed the river into Missouri at Hannibal. We had no idea where the Missouri Ozarks were. We drove to Lake of the Ozarks. At Bagnell Dam, there was a restaurant with four rooms above it. That was where we stayed for three nights. Because we didn't clean up the car, everywhere we went, people were always looking and wondering where the newlyweds were. That was kind of fun. We made people think we were looking for the newlyweds too. We drove around, but there were no mountains. That was kind of disappointing. One day we went up in a small plane that landed on water. We rented a speed boat the next day. We went home Thursday. Right before we got home, we washed the car.

Friday morning, Ruth made me breakfast. She burned the eggs and the toast. I tried to make Ruth think I liked it. Ruth didn't eat anything. She spent the whole breakfast crying. She was trying to get out of eating. I wanted her to eat it too, but I had no luck. Cooking got better after that. The first year of our marriage, I couldn't wait to go home to eat my mother's cooking. After we were married five years, my mother was not such a good cook. Ruth was a better cook. My Uncle Cliff often bragged about Ruth's cooking. Her specialty has always been meatloaf. Everyone always compliments Ruth on it. Now after fifty years, Ruth doesn't like to cook.

On Monday morning, Ruth walked to work. I started working at Cabinet Craft. We belonged to a union. There was a four-year apprentice program. They allowed me one year for working at Neuberts. So I had to do three years before I would be a journeyman. Under the GI Bill, I got $100 a month for being an apprentice for two years. I always put this money in the bank to save up to buy a house. I started out making $3.45 an hour. Ruth's dad always questioned me about how come I was doing an apprentice program. He thought I was a cabinetmaker. I shouldn't have told Ruth that I was a cabinetmaker. It was something I would regret. Dick Brownlow taught me how to make kitchen cabinets. I really liked working with him. Because of my head injury when I was twelve years old, I couldn't nail straight. I always had to draw a line with a square.

Ruth's apartment was in the basement of a house. We could never see outside. We started looking for another apartment right away. We found an apartment by Silver Lake. They had two buildings side by side. Each building had four apartments downstairs and four apartments upstairs. We had a downstairs apartment. It cost us $95 a month. Ruth could take the bus to the hospital from the Silver Lake Shopping Center, which was close by. The only problem we had was that we had a bedroom window next to the parking lot. My brother-in-law Junior would knock on the window late in the night and scare us.

We started visiting Eva and Junior almost every Saturday. They lived on a farm, and I enjoyed helping Junior. I became bored easily and didn't like staying in the apartment on weekends. One time when I was there, Junior was taking feed into a pig lot. He said, "Watch the gate." I picked up a large stick, and when a pig tried to get out, I hit it hard. The pig went down. I felt terrible. Junior had never told me whether I killed the pig or not. I also helped him put a roof on a hayshed. I was afraid of heights, and I couldn't nail straight. We also baled hay. In the fall, I started working part-time for my cousin Judy's husband, Ted Deml, who was a farmer.

Our new home in Country Club Manor in Rochester

I wanted to have a house with a yard. We looked at many houses. My Uncle Duane and my Uncle Lyle were the only uncles to build a house. All my uncles have been a big influence in my life. Much later, my Uncle Dale would build a house too. We decided to build a new house in Country Club Manor in Rochester. Ruth's sister and brother-in-law, Phyllis and Allen Blazing, owned a house in Country Club Manor. I hired a contractor to frame up the house, insulate, and Sheetrock it. I was going to do the rest. The total cost was $20,000. I had to pay $4,000 as a down payment to get the loan. The work that I was doing counted as part of the down payment. The monthly loan payment was $110. It was only $15 a month more than we were paying for the apartment. My boss, Red, said I could cut out the materials for the cabinets, but there was not enough room in the shop to put the cabinets together. I had a blue print for the house, and I couldn't wait for the house to be built and to start on the cabinets. I cut out and machined the cabinets and took them to our apartment. I drilled and nailed them together in the apartment. I took a lot of time; I didn't want anyone to know what I was doing. I would work for a minute and then wait for fifteen minutes and then do it again. No neighbors figured out what I was doing. When I got all the cabinets together, there was barely room to walk through the apartment. Finally, the house was ready for the cabinets. When I pulled the truck up to the apartment and started to load the cabinets, the neighbors couldn't believe what they saw. About this time, Ruth quit working because she was pregnant. I sanded the cabinets and put them together. Red came out to see how the cabinets turned out. I had made them from the blueprints. I never measured the house. Red said I could start making cabinets by myself.

About this time, Dick Brownlow quit working at Cabinet Craft. His dad was a farmer, and Dick didn't want to be a farmer. He always talked about his dad and how bad it was to be a farmer. All of a sudden, his dad died. Dick quit to take over his dad's farm. He would remain a farmer for the rest of his life. I never met him again, but I often think about him.

We had to paint the house. Junior helped me. We left the paint in an unlocked house. One day I came over, and someone had painted

"Scab" on the walls. Rochester was a union town. Scab meant that a nonunion person had done this. It really made me mad. I designed the shutters and made them. Fifty year years later, they looked the same. I am sure they were replaced.

My foreman, Don Brakke, showed me how to hang doors. I borrowed the jigs and the router from work. Ruth's dad, Elmer Borgen, knew how to hang doors too. He helped me do this and helped me trim the house. Elmer was a farmer and a carpenter. Next to my Grandpa Larson, he was my favorite person. He was a Norwegian too. I was putting varnish on the cabinets the night before Tammy was born. I was all done with everything except sowing the lawn. We wanted to close the loan. They said I would have to sow the lawn first. It was way too wet. It was too wet to level the lawn well.

I said, "I'm not going to live in a house without having a lawn. When it gets dry enough, I'm going to do it."

They said, "You have to seed the lawn first." I did it the same day. One year later we rented a sod cutter and rolled up the sod from our lawn. I then leveled the lawn and put the sod back. Bankers have no common sense. They could have saved me a lot of work. We moved in the last of May.

I had too many bills to pay because of the house. I didn't owe so much money, but I had to pay it back now. I got a job at the grocery store at Silver Lake Shopping Center stocking shelves two nights a week. I also worked for Ted Deml weekends. We were busy at work, so I was working fifty hours a week, five days, ten hours a day. I didn't know how must longer I could keep working these hours. Ruth was shopping at Piggy Wiggles' grocery store. They had a bingo game. An angel was at work. The third time Ruth went, she won a $1,000. Ruth came to work to tell me about it. She had to go back to the store in an hour to claim the prize. Ruth left, but my foreman could tell how excited I was. He said, "You had better take the rest of the day off before you cut a finger off." I was able to pay up all the bills. I quit the job at the grocery store. A thousand dollars was a lot of money at that time. I made less than $8,000 at work in a year.

Ruth's Sister Donna and Husband John

After we paid off our bills from the house, we were able to go on a vacation. We went to Florida to visit Ruth's sister Donna and her husband, John. Ruth's parents went with us. I drove Elmer's car. The whole trip cost us $375. My cousin Judy watched Tammy. We stayed at Ruth's parents the night before we left. We got up in the middle of the night to leave. We were in St. Petersburg at noon the next day. Ruth missed Tammy so much she was often crying. My Uncle Lyle lived in Jacksonville, Florida. He was in the Navy. My Uncle Cliff was also in the Navy close by in Georgia. Elmer said we could take his car and go to visit Lyle. They would come up on the bus. Cliff came down to Lyle's while we were there. When Ruth's parents got to Lyle's, we went to tour an aircraft carrier. Ruth and her parents were really impressed with the ship. It was way bigger than they could imagine. When we started home, I said, "I have a Navy buddy, Steve Hibbert, who lives in Champaign, Illinois." Elmer said, "We will spend the night there so you can go to see him." The next day we stopped at Rockford, Illinois. Elmer's brother Ray and his wife, Alice, lived there. About fifteen years later, we started visiting Ray and Alice every year. Alice always said what was on her mind.

You always knew what she thought. I really liked Alice. She would live to be one hundred years old.

After the experience I had with too many bills to pay, I decided I would never live payday to payday again. We started writing down all the money we spent. We kept track of everything to the penny. We soon decided we didn't need everything we bought. We made out a budget and stuck to it. Instead of cashing my paychecks every week, I started saving them and cashing them once a month.

For Christmas 1969, we bought a new color television set. No one in my family had one before. Ruth had her family came for Christmas Eve supper. On New Year's Day 1970, my Grandma and Grandpa McColley, along with my folks and brothers, came for dinner. We watched the Rose Bowl Parade. None of us had seen it in color before.

They had started building Apache Mall. For six months, we had more work than we could handle. Red came out one day and said that he wanted me to build a concession stand for a movie theater. It was thirty feet long. Both ends had rounded corners. It was covered with Formica. I was still an apprentice. I had never worked on anything like this before. Red said, "I think you can do this." He also said if I got stumped, I could ask him to help me. It took about five weeks to build it and install it. Whenever I was at the movie theater, they would give me free tickets to a movie. We went to movies free for a long time.

The carpenters went on strike. We couldn't install anything. Soon the shop got so full there was no place to put anything. Everyone got laid off for a couple of weeks. It was the first time I would draw unemployment. I had been working a lot of overtime, so I had a little extra money.

Uncle Cliff teaching me to pour concrete

My Uncle Cliff came home from the Navy on leave at this time in the summer of 1970. He had been out of the Navy for a year or so before going back in. He had worked a while pouring concrete. He asked me if I would like a concrete driveway. I had never done this before. We poured the driveway together. I learned a lot, thanks to Cliff. All my life on the farm, I poured a lot of concrete.

Soon after, I bought a used 1964 Ford pickup. At one time it was a county truck. It was orange. I didn't like the color. Ted Deml helped me paint it. There was a new color that just came out, Cordova. It was a brown color. The pickup looked really sharp. The dash and the inside of the pickup were still orange. I didn't like that part.

I got a job making kitchen cabinets for a young couple. They wanted them made completely out of oak. They didn't want me to use any nails. I would have to glue everything. I made them on time and material. Time and material meant it wasn't a bid job. They paid for the materials and the time that I had worked. They didn't care how much the cabinets cost. They wanted everything to be perfect. They came to Cabinet Craft every afternoon to check on my work. They wanted to visit a half hour, and I was on their time. It took me six weeks to build them. It was fun to do a perfect job and not have to worry about how long it took. I was so proud of the cabinets. Then they ruined them. They had them stained green. They looked so terrible.

My Grandpa McColley died January 19, 1971. Cliff came back for the funeral from overseas. I had experienced a rifle salute before in the Navy at funerals, but this was so much sadder. Grandpa had a saying that he got from his dad, Emery McColley: "If someone can do something, you can do it too, but only better." Grandpa told me this several times while I was growing up. I've thought about this saying constantly. It helped me to be the person that I am today. Grandpa told me many times, "Your word and your credit are your most valuable assets you have. Always keep your word and keep your credit good." He was a smart person.

Soon we ran out of work. I was laid off. This was twice in a year. I now had a job I couldn't depend on. I always knew I was going to be a farmer. I still could remember the angel in the barn. It was now time for me to be a farmer. I went right from work to a real estate agent and listed the house for sale. I then went home and told Ruth I was laid off. I was going to be a farmer.

She said, "I didn't marry a farmer." She said, "I don't want to be married to a farmer."

Ruth finally agreed that maybe we could live in the country. Ruth wanted me to have a job with a steady paycheck. She had a good relationship with all the neighbor ladies. She would miss them. I wasn't working, so we had a lot of time to look for a place. I soon found something wrong with every place. I had $5,000 equity in our house. I wanted to buy a 160-acre farm. How could I buy a farm with buildings and start farming on $5,000? We found a 160-acre farm we could buy with the money we had. But it had no house. Maybe I could build a garage and live in it for a while. There was a good barn, but a family of skunks was living in the barn. I would have to get them out, but how? I went out to the farm several times. I didn't have the money to build a garage. Ruth wasn't going to be happy living in a garage. I still go by the farm once a while to this day.

I knew I would start farming. I know that an angel told me that I was going to be a successful farmer. I also knew it wasn't going to be easy. It would take a lot of hard work and determination to make it happen. After being off from work for three weeks, I went back to work.

Chapter 9

The Birth of Our Children

Tammy Lynn McColley was born on May 5, 1969, at 4:35 PM. We were building a new house. I finished the inside myself. The night before Tammy was born, I was putting varnish on the cabinets, and I worked until midnight. We had been in bed for only a couple hours when Ruth started getting labor pains. We slept off and on until five. At six, we decided to go to the hospital. We lived in town and didn't have far to go. Tammy was born at the Olmsted Community Hospital in Rochester. When we got there, they said the baby was going to be born, but it would take a while. We didn't know if it would be a boy or girl. I was planning on watching the baby being born. Ruth started to have terrible pain, but no baby. I was so tired from working so late that I went asleep between the labor pains. It took so long that I lost my nerve. I was not prepared for Ruth to have such a hard time. I waited in the waiting room with some other husbands. Finally, they come out and told me that I had a baby girl. I could go in and see the baby and my wife. She was seven pounds, seven ounces, and twenty-one inches long. I suppose I spent an hour with them. Ruth was getting really tired. I left the room to call everyone. First I called her parents and then my parents. I called Ruth's sister Eva next. It was fun the next day when everybody came up to see Ruth and the baby. I bought a box of cigars. It was sure fun showing Tammy off.

Tammy was baptized on July 13, 1969. Forty-five years later, on this same date, July 13, 2014, her granddaughter Jordan was born.

Ruth's sister and brother-in-law, Eva and Nado Jr. Bernard, were her godparents. My Grandpa Larson was born on July 13, 1886.

When Tammy was four years old, she had an operation. She was cross-eyed. The operation didn't turn out perfect, but we decided not to do it again. She was a big girl and didn't cry. She stayed overnight by herself. Ruth spent that night with her sister Linda in Rochester. We were so proud of Tammy. I was there for the operation and recovery, but I had to go home to do chores. My mom took care or Doreen and Bob.

Tammy Lynn McColley

Birth of Doreen

About three weeks before Doreen was born, Ruth started getting labor pains in the middle of the night. I got Tammy up and took her to neighbors, Joe and Carol Hennessey. When I got home, the labor pains had stopped. We didn't go to the hospital. Three weeks later, Ruth had labor pains around one o'clock in the early morning. I got Tammy up and took her to the neighbors. I got Ruth out to the car. She was having contractions close together. There was no traffic, so I drove fast. I went through all the red lights. I parked next to the hospital and helped Ruth in. I had to park the car and check Ruth into the hospital. I was sure that I would watch the baby being born this time. I went back to the birthing area. I said, "I want to watch." They said, "You are too late. You have a baby girl." Doreen Marie McColley was born September 2, 1970, at 1:46 AM. It was just fifteen minutes after we got to the hospital. That was fast! I had no time to spare! She weighed six pounds, seven ounces. She was 20.5 inches long. Her head measured 13.25 inches, and her chest measured thirteen inches. Ruth had an extremely easy delivery. Early in the morning, I called everyone and told them we had a baby girl. The next morning, I picked up Tammy from the Hennesseys' and took her to stay with Ruth's sister Eva. Tammy stayed with Eva until Ruth came home from the hospital. We lived in our new house in Country Club Manor in Rochester at that time. We had the names picked out. For a girl it was Doreen, and for a boy it was Chad. Marie was Ruth's middle name too. Jenna, Doreen's daughter, has Marie for a second name too. I bought a box of cigars to give out. That was a custom back then.

Ruth's brother and sister-in-law, Howard and Shirley Borgen, were Doreen's godparents.

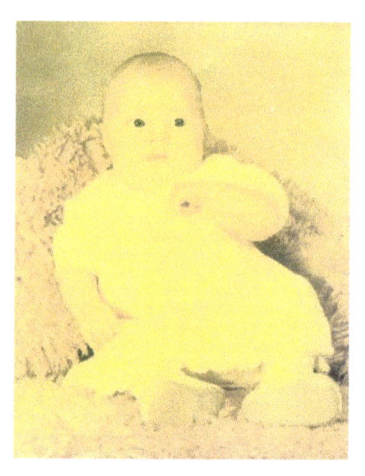

Doreen Marie McColley

Birth of Bob

Robert Wayne McColley was born on April 6, 1972, at 2:48 AM. It was the fourth anniversary of our wedding. It also was my

Grandpa McColley's birth date. He had died fourteen months earlier. We were living on the farm by now. Ruth had labor pains starting at midnight. We left for the hospital promptly with Tammy and Doreen. Going through Kasson, we stopped at Kenny and Norma Muhlbauers to drop off Tammy and Doreen. I checked Ruth into Olmsted Community Hospital. I then parked the pickup. We had a 1967 Plymouth, with only sixty-five thousand miles, but the transmission was out. I put on a gown and then went into the birthing room. They gave Ruth a shot in her right arm for pain, and she had a fairly easy delivery. I watched while Bob was born and then left to the waiting room while the nurses cleaned up the baby and gave him to Ruth. He weighed seven pounds, five ounces. His length was 20.5 inches. He measured at the head 13.5 inches and measured at the chest 13.5 inches. I called everyone and told them that we had a boy. I then went in Ruth's room and held Bob for a while. A nurse came in and told us that Ruth had a reaction to the shot in her arm and that there was nothing to worry about. I then went home to do the little chores that I had. I felt like I was on the top of the world! I owned a farm, had a good dog, and now a son. I would bring him up to be a farmer.

Next, I went to Norma's to pick up Tammy and Doreen. I was excited as I told Norma about Bob. I took the kids to my cousin Judy on a farm by Owatonna. When I got there, I had a message to call the hospital. When I called, they said Ruth had been taken to the Methodist Hospital and I had to go there immediately. I asked, "What's wrong?" All she said was to get there as soon as possible. I didn't know what was wrong! Maybe she was dying. I drove the pickup as fast as it would go. I ruined the engine. I made it to the hospital and made it back home, but it never ran good again. They didn't check the reaction that Ruth had to her arm until after eight. She was done eating breakfast. When her doctor saw her arm, he transferred her to the Methodist Hospital. He took Ruth in his Volkswagen. Ruth complained about how unconformable the ride was. When I got to her room, her arm was as black as a colored person's. They were getting Ruth ready for surgery. The nurse had given the shot directly to her artery. The medicine in the shot had eaten out the artery in her arm. They were going to try to reroute an artery to get more blood to her arm. After the operation, they said that she might lose her arm. Both her parents and my parents came up to the hospital and were there when Ruth got out of surgery. They did another operation that night. My parents were going to take off from work to take care of our girls. They brought the girls to the hospital the next day to see Ruth. They operated on her arm six times in four days. They saved her arm, but the end of her thumb had died, and they had to cut it off. They said they had to leave the end of the bone exposed for a month. When any air got to the bone, she had so much pain she could hardly stand it. Ruth was in the hospital for ten days.

Bob got out of the hospital in four days. Mom and Dad picked me up at the Methodist Hospital to go get Bob. Bob was still in the Olmsted Community Hospital. It was cold out, so Dad stayed in the car and kept it running. When Mom and I went to the desk, they said, "You will have to sign some release papers." I said, "I won't sign anything." They took the papers away and put up another set of papers and said, "You can sign these forms for the baby." I said, "No." They said, "You will have to sign these release forms before you could take the baby." The forms were blank. There were no names on either one of them. I never knew that Mom had left. I continued to argue with this woman. All of a sudden, Mom called out, "Let's go." Mom had walked into the nursery when no one was there and picked up Bob and left. We went to the car. When we got into the car, Mom said to Dad, "I feel like a gangster, and you are driving the getaway car. We just stole the baby." Mom never told anyone about this. Mom and I talked about this a short time before her death. My parents took care of Bob and the girls the first six days he was home from the hospital. Bob and my mother had a deep bond that lasted the rest of their lives.

I bought a brand-new blue Ford pickup for $2,200 in April. Ruth's mother, Edna, came to live with us for six weeks. Ruth's mother had our three kids in diapers. Edna had eight kids, and she knew how to train children. Tammy was trained just like that. At first Ruth couldn't do anything with her right arm. She had to learn to eat left-handed. They had taken skin from her left leg for skin grafting.

Her right arm and her left leg were extremely painful. When her young daughters wanted to be held, she had to hold them with her left arm and over her healing left leg, so she had pain from both sides. In a month, they cut off the bone from her thumb and sewed skin over the end of her thumb. We could never understand why they had to wait so long to do this. I had a great mother-in-law, and we always got along great. Ruth didn't have a pulse in her right arm. After about ten years, we could just feel a faint pulse.

Bob's godparents were Ruth's sister and brother-in-law, Phyllis and Allen Blazing.

If either the oldest babies were boys, the name I picked was Chad. After having two girls, I thought Chad wasn't to be. I picked Robert after my Navy buddy, Robert Cunningham.

When Bob started to lose his baby teeth, he would come to me with a pliers and ask me to pull his tooth. When Bob would notice a loose tooth, he would wriggle it for a while. When our kids lost a tooth, they put the tooth in a glass of water. In the night a tooth fairy would put a quarter in the glass. Bob could never wait long enough for the tooth to fall out.

Robert Wayne McColley

Birth of Brenda

I wanted to have six kids. Ruth didn't want any more. At first she only wanted two. I said we would compromise and settle with four. After the time she had with Bob, she didn't want any more. At Christmastime, 1975, I made a deal with Ruth. I would make an appointment to have a vasectomy done in March if she would stop taking birth control pills. If God wanted us to have another child, we would. If God didn't want us to have any more children, we wouldn't. I prayed that God would make the pregnancy easy for Ruth. By March, we knew she was pregnant. Ruth had an easy pregnancy. She wasn't ever sick.

In the early part of November, I was done picking corn, but I still had some plowing to do. After supper I went out to plow. I told Ruth if she went into labor, to turn on the yard light and I would come right away. All of a sudden, I saw a light. I pulled up the plow and went in road gear toward the light. I was really excited. A neighbor had just built a new house that fall. I was a quarter of a mile from our place. They turned on a yard light. I was very disappointed. It was false alarm. Ruth never turned on a light.

On November 13, we got up at six. Ruth felt a little funny. I quickly went out and did chores, and Ruth made breakfast. We ate breakfast leisurely. Finally, we called the doctor. We didn't know what to do. He said maybe we should go to the hospital. We went to the Rochester Methodist Hospital this time. We dropped the kids off at Adline Hrtaneks. She lived on a 160-acre farm four miles east of us. I would later rent the farm from her. I later bought the farm. We got to the hospital at nine thirty. At Methodist, they didn't allow the father in the room at that time so I couldn't watch. Ruth had an extremely easy delivery. Brenda Lee McColley was born November 13, 1976, at 10:30 AM. She weighed six pounds, three ounces. My prayers were answered. My mother and my dad took care of the three kids until Ruth got out of the hospital.

My brother and sister-in-law, Rick and Carol McColley, were her godparents.

After Brenda was born, all I wanted to do was to hold her. I knew I would never have any more children. I really wanted to enjoy her.

Brenda Lee McColley

Chapter 10

Buying the Farm and the Early Years

The house was sold. The buyers would have to get a loan on our house. The real estate agent told us that it wasn't going to be a problem. We would have to get serious about moving. Ruth wasn't happy. She didn't like leaving her neighbor friends or the house. I wanted to buy a farm big enough to make a living just from farming. We had been looking at places before. Every place we looked at was too small to make a living from just the land and livestock. I figured I would have to have at least 160 acres. But it was not going to be easy to find 160 acres with only $5,000. Finally, a real estate agent found 160 acres south of Dodge Center that we could afford. I wanted to deal directly with the owner. I met with Earl (Bud) Hoglund. Bud agreed to finance the farm with $5,000 down for five years. The farms total cost was $50,000. Bud had the farmland rented out already for that year. We made the deal that the rent was going to make the payment. Bud was responsible for collecting the rent. If the renter didn't pay the rent that fall, my payment to Bud was already paid. To make this deal, he wanted $500 down now. If I didn't carry out the deal, he wasn't going to give me the money back. The buyer's loan was approved on our house, and I thought that it was safe to give Bud the down payment. I was worried about getting the farm financed in five years.

A FATHER'S QUEST

The farm house, 1971

When I showed Ruth the house, she said she wasn't going to live there. Some of the windows were broken out. There was a barn built in 1950. There was a corn crib built in 1956. All the other buildings were shot, including the house. We went out to look at the house several times. At least whoever lived there last had left it clean. But there were leaves that had blown in the house. I promised Ruth I would build her a new kitchen and fix up the house. I promised Ruth, "We will eventually have the prettiest farm in the area." All these promises didn't matter. She didn't want to be married to a farmer. Ruth thought I had lost my mind. At least she never threated to leave me. I knew she really loved me. We had married for life.

I came home from work one night, and Ruth was crying. I thought she was crying about the farm. I didn't know what to do. We would be moving soon. I asked Ruth, "What is wrong?" Ruth always went to coffee every morning at a neighbor's house. She looked out the window and saw the neighbors leaving one house and going to another house. They didn't tell her. She thought they had cut her out of coffee. She said she was ready to move. Right away I threw my arms up and said out loud, "Thank you, thank you, God." The angels had been at work for some time. A big burden had been lifted off of my shoulders.

The next day the real estate agent called and said the buyer had signed the loan papers. But his wife wouldn't sign the papers. Time was running out for me. I had to close on the farm. I didn't have the money. There was not enough time to find a new buyer and go through the loan approval process. Ruth was now ready to move! I would lose the $500 down payment. I thought I had problems before. How would I get out of this one? I offered the buyer's wife $500 to sign the loan papers. I would lose $500 either way. She signed them.

I didn't have $5,000 left for the down payment. I didn't have enough money to fix up the house. I made a promise to Ruth that I would fix up the house. I made a list of everything we had, including the kitchen chairs. I went to a bank, and they gave me a loan on the full value. I would soon learn that I had a knack on how to deal with bankers. I agreed to make a big payment every month. The rent would make the payment on the farm. It wouldn't cost anything to live in the house. The angels and God had helped me get out of this one. We closed the loan on the house and on the farm. When I closed on the farm, there were people standing in line to get what was left of the down payment. The lawyer told me to make out a check to him. He would sort out the problems. Bud was in financial trouble. I got real nervous about how many people would put a lean on the farm. I would have to face that in five years. We had a month to move.

I built new kitchen cabinets and put in a new bathroom. I got new window sashes from Neuberts in Mankato. My old foreman, Don Myers, got the windows with an employee discount. I put some paneling on the walls. I had to do it as cheaply as possible. We moved to the farm on June 26, 1971. That was the same day that Ruth's sister, Linda, married Stan Scott. We moved in the morning, and Ruth stood up in Linda's wedding at six o'clock in the evening. That was a hard day for Ruth, moving in the morning and she had to be at the church in the afternoon for Linda's wedding.

The buyer's wife lived in the house for one month then moved out. The buyer and his new girlfriend lived in the house for one month. Then she moved out. The buyer lived one month alone in the house and then sold the house.

I had a plan on how to start farming. I would rent the farmland out in 1972 and 1973. I rented the farmland to Rodney Beckman. Rod was just starting farming. Later his dad would help my son to get started farming. I often wonder if God and angels are at work all the time. We received $23-an-acre rent. That was enough to make the payment on the farm. In 1972, I would start raising hogs. I could work at the cabinet shop and raise hogs. I wanted to quit working in the cabinet shop in 1974 and farm the land. Then I would be a farmer.

We had a new color TV, but we didn't have the money to buy an antenna. We went for two years without television. We didn't miss it. We were always busy, and we were in love. Ruth mowed the lawn with a walk mower that summer. I was always working on the house. Most times I had a second job working for my cousin's husband, Ted Deml, on his farm.

That summer I bought a 1944 John Deere A tractor at a sale about twenty miles away. Ruth's dad, Elmer, went with me to pick up the tractor. The tractor only went ten miles an hour. He said, "It will take you too long." He hooked a chain from the pickup to the tractor. I sat on the tractor, and he pulled it forty miles an hour. I was scared to death all the way home. Soon after, I bought an old John Deere manure spreader.

John Deere manure spreader

That winter we thought we would freeze to death! The house didn't have much insulation. The windows were drafty. It cost us $1,000 for propane in January. January was an extremely cold month. The furnace never shut off. The water pipes froze sometimes. The next year we bought combination windows for all the windows. We saved enough on propane to pay for the windows in two years.

A FATHER'S QUEST

Border Collie, we named her Sheba

In March, I bought ten gilts from Don Myers. I rented a boar. I bought a border collie. Her name was Sheba. Bob was born. Ruth was laid up and couldn't mow the lawn, so I bought a Massey Ferguson riding lawn mower on time. I always had too much to do. Elmer helped me make farrowing pens for the sows. I didn't want to spend any money, so we tore boards out of the granary for the material. The granary had holes in the roof. After we sold the first feeder pigs, I bought six sows from a neighbor. I bought a boar, and now I was in the pig business. Ruth would call me often at work. "The pigs are out." I said, "I can't come home. You will have to deal with it." Ruth and Sheba went out to get the pigs back in. Sheba worked until the pigs were all in. When I came home and if Sheba saw me fixing the fence, she would put the pigs back in again. If she didn't see me fixing the fence, she wouldn't put the pigs in again. By the end of the year, I was up to thirty sows.

Building a pole shed for hogs

In the spring of 1973, I hired workers from a lumberyard to build a pole shed. We would use it for hogs. I was ready to expand the hog business to sixty sows. I took out a loan to pay for the building for five years. I also bought a 4010 John Deere tractor. It was eleven years old. It had eighty-five horsepower. I bought a used four-bottom International plow. I paid cash for them from selling pigs.

Bob is sitting on the tractor, Doreen and Tammy standing

Then in July, I had problems. I didn't live from paycheck to paycheck. So after a month, I had some bills to pay. I went to the bank in Dodge Center and cashed the paychecks that I had saved. I paid off all the bills. The paychecks bounced. I had to take out a loan from the bank to cover the checks that I had written. The bank in Dodge Center told me not to bring them anymore paychecks. They wouldn't cash them. I had to take them to a bank in Rochester. Sometimes they were good and sometimes not. I never saved paychecks again.

In October, I had a lot of kitchen cabinets to make. I made a set of cabinets every week. I had two men helping me all the time. We got paid as cabinetmakers, at $5 an hour. For a carpenter, we made $7.50 an hour. When we installed the cabinets, we got paid carpenter's wages. The men helping me were doing the installing while I was starting a new set of cabinets. I had all the responsibility, and they had bigger paychecks. In the beginning of November, they installed a set of cabinets. The next day the contactor called and said the refrigerator didn't fit. If the men who were helping me would have measured it, then they could change it a little, and no one would have known the difference. Red said it was my fault. I had to go forty miles away to fix them. Afterward he said he wouldn't pay me for doing it. I quit. I went to the union office and said that Red owed me for the time and that I wanted carpenter wages. Red had to pay me.

I made $1,000 a month at Cabinet Craft. I made $1,000 a month on the hogs. After building the new building, we were going to raise many more hogs. It was time to be a full-time farmer. I had a young wife and three young children. Ruth wasn't going to work outside the home. I would have no certain income or paycheck. My dad really chewed me out. "What were you thinking? Why did you quit your job?" Ruth's parents didn't say a thing. Soon the price for pigs really went down, and I didn't make enough to live on. As much as Ruth didn't want to be married to a farmer, she helped me do everything. She was my partner. Behind every successful farmer is a good woman. The only thing I didn't like was, Ruth said I had to make all business decision by myself. I didn't ask her decision to sell our house in Rochester. She didn't want to be the blame for making the wrong decision. I have rented or bought farms without talking to Ruth. I wish it were different sometimes.

I would need machinery to farm in 1974. How much would it cost, and how could I afford to buy all of it? I was able to rent the machinery from a neighbor, Larry Peterson, who was quitting farming. I was able to get it all for $400 a year. I rented it all for one year. I got an H Farmall tractor, a disc, a digger, a corn planter, a sprayer, and an auger that I used. I got a Minneapolis Moline tractor and plow that I didn't use. The fertilizer boxes on the corn planter were rusted through. It took a whole roll of duct tape to keep them from leaking. I was thirty years old at this time. Larry Peterson was forty years old at this time. Larry had his eighty-acre farm for sale. He couldn't make a living from that small of a farm. I realized I couldn't make a living from 160 acres. Larry farrowed pigs, and he really missed it. Oftentimes he would walk over to my farm and sit with the sows while they were farrowing pigs. Larry sold his farm in June 1974. In the winter of 1974, I built twenty farrowing crates out of steel and put them in the barn.

When spring 1974 came, there were rocks everywhere. Ruth and I decided we were going to pick all the rocks up before we planted. My Grandma McColley stayed with us for a week watching the kids. We had to pick all the rocks by hand. We had a stone boat. It was a few planks bolted together that we pulled behind a tractor. Sometimes we had to put a chain around a rock and pull the rock onto the stone boat with a tractor. We spent too much time picking rocks. It started raining. I soon found out how wet the farm was. The quack grass got so bad I could hardly plant the crops. Right east of the house we, didn't plant the soybeans until July. It was the worst crop ever. The corn made sixty-five bushels an acre. The soybeans made fifteen bushels per acre. A neighbor, Dwayne Schmoll, combined the soybeans, and Ted Deml combined the corn and dried it. I had a lot to learn if I was going to be a farmer.

Future farm shop

Right after the crops were planted, we started building a farm shop. I poured a foundation out of cement. After the cement, we built the building in one day. My dad, Ted Deml, and Alan Runge helped me. I graduated from high school with Alan. Alan also lived on my farm and farmed for only one year in 1962. Alan worked part-time for Ted. We built the shop twenty-six by thirty feet. We had an eighteen-by-eight-foot door. It was big enough to get the biggest piece of equipment in it.

I converted the corn crib into a granary. I put in a used electric Mix Mill. I had a bin to store a semiload of soybean meal. I could store four thousand bushels of shelled corn, and I had two bins overhead to store premix. The granary turned out really well. I ground feed into a wagon with an auger and hauled the feed to the barn. I put two tanks up in the hay barn to store the feed. Ruth's cousin, Wayne Borgen, helped me the summer of 1974. Wayne was a schoolteacher in Hayfield. He lived on a farmstead three miles south of us. Wayne got feed and a pig from us to raise. His parents, John and Helen Borgen, visited us often that year.

I don't think I could have been a farmer if not for the Navy. I had a job where I put records together in a way they made sense. I used my farm records to convince the bankers to loan me money. When you learn the concepts of record-keeping really, well, it becomes easy to change these concepts to another business. I was successful. For years, the bankers said, "You don't have the best loan, but you do the best job showing us." In three years, my farm was now worth $100,000. I paid $50,000 for the farm. Only $5,000 as a down payment. Inflation had really settled into farm county. In September, I bought another 240 acres in partnership with Ted Deml. I also got a loan to pay off my contract for deed from Bud Hoglund. Land had really gone up. I was able to borrow enough on my farm to make a down payment on another one. We bought this farm really cheap. There was a lot of swampland. We also had to clear a lot of trees. There was a two-year-old house on the farm. There was a small barn that was falling down. There were no other buildings. It was four miles east of us. We sold the house, making the rest of the farm cheaper. I didn't show Ruth the house until after we sold the house. I didn't want to move there, but I was afraid Ruth would want to move there. I wanted the money from the sale of the house. I called this new farm the Kasson Farm. The farm was located five miles south of Kasson.

It was extremely late when the corn was picked on the new farm I had bought. It was almost Thanksgiving. The soil was freezing up. I wanted to get the land plowed. It was cold, and I was sitting on an open tractor. Ruth came out to the field ever two hours with coffee or hot chocolate. It gave me a chance to warm up in the pickup. She came out at eight o'clock at night and said it would be the last time. She had to put the kids to bed. It was now dark and cold. I had a lot left. At two in the morning, it started to sleet. I got wet and thought I would freeze to death. I was determent to finish the plowing. I finished the field at four in the morning. It was four miles to drive home. It would get even colder. When I got into bed with Ruth at four thirty, my whole body was so cold. I told Ruth when I woke up, "We are going down to Demmer Imp. and buy a cab for the tractor." I was never going to be that cold again.

With more land, I decided that I needed another tractor. There weren't a lot of used tractors for sale. I ordered a new 2030 John Deere from Demmer Imp. in Hayfield. I was to pay $8,900. When the tractor came, they wouldn't honor the deal we made. All tractors had gone up in value. Demmers said I wouldn't have to take the tractor. I took the tractor and paid $9,700. The tractor had sixty horsepower. I used it for planting and spraying corn. I bought a newer Oliver six-row corn planter and a new sprayer. I decided to raise only corn. I would have to learn how to raise corn before I could master soybeans. That would take a few years. Linda's husband, Stan Scott, worked for me that summer. Stan was a schoolteacher in Dodge Center. Stan worked for me eight years in the summer. We could read each other's mind. Both of us knew what to do ahead of time without talking. Stan was the best worker and the most enjoyable worker I ever had. John and Helen Borgen came up several times that summer. John liked to drive our new tractor. I hired Lawrence Scripture to pick the corn that fall.

While I was doing chores in December 1974, my legs gave out. I crawled from the barn to the house. Walking was impossible. The problem was my back and having pain go down into one leg. I went to a chiropractor. He did very little to help. He always twisted my neck, which caused me extreme pain. After four treatments I could hardly walk. I lay on the treatment table, and he started to reach for my neck. I said, "If you touch my neck, I'm going to get up and deck you." He didn't want me to come back again. I then went to the Mayo Clinic. The doctors said there were three vertebrae in my back that were too close together. There wasn't room enough for the disc between the vertebrae. The disc become inflamed and pushed on the spiral cord. That was what was giving me so much pain in the legs. They gave me some exercises to do, and that helped. The doctor said, "After you are forty years old, you will not have this problem again." He was right. I was too stubborn and never took time to do anything. I was always jumping off everything. When I had reached forty, I was starting to slow down. My back problems went away. Ruth did my chores throughout this time. I had to come up with ways to make farming easier. I think in the long run, the back problems made me change some of ways to make farming easier. This allowed me to expand.

In the spring of 1975, we put in a lot of tile into the Kasson farm. I hired Milt Bakken to do the tiling. While tiling through the wettest part of the swampland, they got the tiling machine stuck. They tried and tried, but they couldn't pull it out. They finally brought in another tiling machine and tiled around the first tiling machine. It took a month for it to get dry enough to pull out the tiling machine. I also put in a little tile at home in the wettest areas.

In August, I told Tina, my Uncle Dale's wife, that I had bought a second farm. Tina's dad started a chemical company and become a millionaire. Tina didn't think much of farming. She said I would never get rich farming. "You will never be a millionaire." Tina told me a joke that day that I never forgot. She was Catholic. She said there was a priest walking past a young boy sitting on a curb holding a box. The priest asked the boy, "What do you have in the box?" The boy said, "I have a box full of Catholic kittens." The priest was proud that this boy was a good Catholic. The priest looked at the kittens several days. On the next day, a bishop from the church was walking with the priest. The priest was proud to show the bishop what a good Catholic boy he had. The priest asked, "How are your Catholic kittens doing?" The boy said, "I don't have any Catholic kittens anymore." The priest asked, "What happened to the kittens?" The boy said, "They have their eyes opened now, and they are Lutheran kittens now." I really liked Tina. She had a good sense of humor. She could tell a joke against herself. Tina always said what was on her mind. I respected her for this. You always knew what she thought of you.

In March 1976, Don Musolf came up. Don came up to visit every week. He said there was going to be a farm for rent soon. My farm was next to Don's on the west. He said the farm for rent was next to his farm on the east. His wife, Verna, was raised on this farm. Verna's brother had died three years ago. This farm was sold to Palmer Dragsten from Faribault. I figured a lot of farmers were going to want this farm, and there were. "How would I get it?" Every neighbor had more money than I did. They all were better farmers than I was. I had to do something different. I wrote Palmer a letter telling him about my dreams. Palmer rented me the farm for $55 an acre. Palmer told me it was because of the letter that he had decided to give the farm to me. In three years of farming, I was up to five hundred acres. I would need more and bigger machinery. I rented the farm from Palmer for thirty-one years. In 2007, Bob and I bought the farm.

It was 1976, and I bought a 1971 tractor with 115 HP with a cab. It was a 4320 John Deere tractor with front-wheel assist. I also bought a 6600 John Deere combine. The combine was four years old. I bought this machinery from Demmer Imp. On the combine, I made a deal that they would go through the combine and fix everything free that they found wrong. I made the agreement to work with their employee, Alvin Gross. I needed to learn how to service and run the combine. At the end of the year, I traded the 4010 John Deere and the 2030 John Deere for a new 4430 John Deere with 125 HP and with a cab. The 4430 cost $21,000. They allowed me more in trade than I paid for these two tractors. I spent $80,000 that year. No other farmer spent that much money that year at Demmers. That winter they took me on a tour of several factories. There were two salesmen and four farmers on the tour. We flew in a plane out of Rochester to Waterloo, Iowa. In Waterloo, we visited the tractor plant and the engine plant. We then flew to Moline, Illinois. We attended a banquet at the John Deere World headquarters. The next morning, we had a tour of the combine plant. Then we flew home. The trip was free, but I had spent $80,000 to get it. Ruth did the chores while I was gone.

John Deere 1

John Deere 2

John Deere 3

Curtis Berg was an adult agriculture teacher in the Hayfield school district. I was enrolled in the program. I had to keep an account book on the farm's financials. We met once a month to discuss farming. I had a lot to learn. In January 1976, the University of Minnesota had an outreach program to teach farmers grain marketing. We met one afternoon a week at the Hayfield School. That was the smartest thing I did. It was taught by Warren Enevoldsen, a farmer from Waseca County. The class lasted three months. We learned every aspect of grain marketing. It would eventually make the difference if a person would be a farmer for the long haul or not. At the end, we went up to the Twin Cities and had a tour of the grain exchange. I really enjoyed and learn a lot from this class.

One day while I was trying to separate the sows, one sow got me down. I thought that I had a broken leg. Ruth left the kids with a neighbor. She took me to the emergency room in Austin in the pickup. Ruth went in to get an attendant to help me get in. I lay down in the cab because I was in so much pain. The attendant came out with Ruth. He asked, "Did you haul him in the back of the pickup?" When the doctor looked at the x-rays, he said I only have a bad sprain. "You have way too big and heavy of bones to ever break them." So far he has been right. They sent me home with crutches. I never made them work. I had too much work to do to walk on crutches. I went back to work.

My Uncle Stanley died of a heart attack on January 15, 1977. He was only fifty-three years old. His funeral was January 18. Stanley was twenty years older than I was. Ruth and I and our four kids were sitting in the pews of the church early the day of the funeral. All of a sudden, a terrible thought came into my mind. It seemed so real! I was going to die in twenty years or something worse. Was it an angel or the devil? This would haunt me for twenty years. I could never get this thought out of my mind. Uncle Stanley treated me like a son he never had.

Soon afterward, PCA—where I borrowed money—said they couldn't stick with me. PCA was short for Production Credit Association. PCA was set up by the government in the 1930s to loan money to farmers. It was now independent of the government. I had expanded way too fast. I would have to have more working capital. Working capital means the money and assets on hand that you can change to cash to pay your debts that are due in one year. They said if I could get a loan from FMHA for $50,000 to get my working capital better, they would stick with me. FMHA is a government agency to help farmers that were in trouble. FMHA means Farmers and Home

Association. I went to the closest office and applied for the loan. The banker turned me down. I thought I had a knack to work with bankers, but I turned him off. Soon he refused to even see me.

Wayne and Bob Cunningham, 1977

It was June, and I thought it was my last year farming. How could the angels and God let me down? About this time, I told Ruth about Karen Covert. It was now ten years since I wrote her. I was terribly depressed. Ruth said, "Why don't we go to finally meet her?" Stan could take care of the farm. My cousin Judy could take care of the kids. We had some equity in the farm, so I would have some money left after the sale. We could afford the vacation. Ruth recognized my depression. She knew I would have to get over it soon. I wrote a letter to Karen. She was now married to Tony, and they just had a baby. She gave me her phone number and said to call her the day before we arrived. Going to New York, we would be going through Pittsburgh. We could visit my Navy buddy Bob Cunningham. We planned the trip so we would get to Bob's on Friday night. We stayed at their place three nights. From what I had learned about Pittsburgh in grade school, it was a terribly dirty city. Was I surprised! It was a really clean city. From the fifties to the seventies, they cleaned up the city. We met Bob's wife, Pat. We really liked her. They didn't have any children yet. I met Bob's mother and his brothers. We had a really good time. We went on to Bingington, New York, Monday. It was a pretty drive through the mountains. We got there Tuesday afternoon. I called Karen on the telephone Monday afternoon. Karen said her baby was in the hospital now. We should visit her parents and they would come to their place and we would go out for supper. We got to their place at four thirty in the afternoon. It was a really awkward visit. We didn't know them. It had been ten years since I was in the Navy and was writing Karen. When Karen and her husband, Tony, got there, we went out to eat. They were a really fun couple, and we really hit it off. They kept us laughing. Karen said that Tony was always complaining about other men he was working with; their wives always wrote them love notes. So she wrote a love note and put in his sandwiches. Tony had started eating the sandwich before he found the note. Tony said Karen really complained that they had no house numbers on their door. She told him if he got the numbers, she would hang them up. At work the next day, he welded the numbers out of log chain. Karen couldn't lift the numbers. After two hours, they wanted to go back to the hospital to see the baby. We went back to the hotel. Ten years later, they were divorced, and she was remarried to Gary Trustler. He had an uncle who lived in Rochester, Minnesota. They visited his uncle and stopped at our farm one afternoon. Eventually, they moved to Arizona. We have visited them at least twice. The last time was 2013. We exchanged Christmas cards throughout the years. The next day we went to Niagara Falls. It was a fun trip. I wasn't depressed anymore. I made up my mind that I would get that loan and get the banker fired. I decided at that time vacations didn't cost anything. If you always stayed on the farm, you couldn't see past your problems. After a vacation, I always made better decisions.

 I think God and angels were directing me about what to do now. I decided to write to the US Congress. My representative was Al Quie. I did not know what to write, but if I was to get the loan, I had to write a really convincing letter. I think an angel helped me. A short time later, four men from the government visited our farm.

They looked at everything and said $50,000 wasn't enough. They wanted me to buy a new John Deere corn planter. They said I would have a better crop. The new John Deere corn planter came out two years ago. It was made completely different than planters of the past. They made me a loan for $65,000. In a month, the banker was no longer working for FMHA.

My Grandpa Larson died July 11, 1977. He was always happy when people came to his birthday party. We had his funeral on his ninety-first birthday, July 13, 1977. He died of a stroke. He had several smaller strokes the last two years. I still have a guilty conscience that I didn't spend more time with him at the end. When he was in the hospital at the end, I couldn't bring myself to go and see him. I always loved him more than anyone.

Grandpa Edward Larson

I planted oats east of the house that year. East of the granary, I planted corn. I don't know why I did this, but I planted a small area of oats next to the granary. We had a long chain of buildings east of the yard. I burned them down and had a cat bury the foundations. I don't know why I did these things. I had no plan, but maybe the

A FATHER'S QUEST

angels had a plan. We got done combining the oats. Corn got very cheap. If I didn't have to sell at harvest and had a place to store the corn, I could do better. I decided to put up a grain bin, a holding bin, and a corn dryer. I was glad I didn't have to destroy any corn. The corn price was a lot better the next year.

In September, I had a leaking hog waterer. I decided to install a new one. I would have to drill holes with a masonry bit to fasten down the hog waterer. The old waterer was really leaking, and there was water everywhere. I got an extension cord and a drill. As soon as I started drilling, I got a shock. I opened up my hand, but I couldn't let go of the drill. I tried to shake the drill off, but it wouldn't fall. The drill was stuck to my hand. My whole body started flailing. I was close to death by electrocution. I think an angel told Ruth to go outside and check on me. Ruth unplugged the cord, and I fell in the mud. It took me a couple of minutes to come to. I didn't suffer any damage. I got a rubber tire to sit on, and then I finished the drilling. Ruth was almost a young widow with a farm and four young children.

That fall I decided to do some custom work to pay for everything. I had five hundred acres to pick, and a neighbor that hired me had five hundred acres of corn. He had a corn dryer too. You only store and dry so many acres a day. I decided I would fill my holding bin full. I would then go to his place and fill his holding bin full. I would keep both corn dryers going every day. There was no time for sleep. Before we got done, we got snow. It never got warm enough to get rid of the snow. The snow pugged up the sieves on the combine. By ten o'clock at night, it was cold enough that the sieves wouldn't plug. The combine had a cab, but the wind got under the cab. My feet got so cold before morning came I couldn't feel my feet anymore. I got done on Thanksgiving Day. I never did custom work again for many years.

I got elected to the church council. I was on the Stewardship Committee. One Sunday, part of the committee gave talks. They set up a display to use in the talk. I was certain I would not have to talk. From high school, I got sick to my stomach get thinking about a speech. When they were done, they called on me to come up. What would I say? I never even thought of anything to say. I started walking slowly to the front of the church. I started praying, "God, you will have to put words in my mouth." They were taking down the display, and all of a sudden I asked them to leave the display up. I gave a really good speech off the display. Everyone gave me an applause. God had put the words in my mouth. From that time forward, I have enjoyed giving a speech.

That winter the Hayfield School had another class. It was an outreach program from the University of Minnesota. It was for three months, one day a week. The class was called Farm Management. The class was taught by a banker from Albert Lea. We had a lot of homework. We had to do a cash flow plan for our farm and keep books on our farm. I had always written everything in an account book put out by the University of Minnesota. I didn't like it. I devised a new bookkeeping program. I drew charts on sheets of paper on where to put in entries. I kept separate enterprise accounts on corn, soybeans, and hogs. I knew how much money that I made on each enterprise. The account book from the university didn't do this. We didn't have copy machines back then. Ruth and I have always had perfect handwriting. She was my copy machine. I become the teacher's favorite pupil. He gave me an A+ for the grade. I used this program until I got a computer. I was surprised to see the computer program was almost the same as the bookkeeping program that I developed. I guess I was ahead of my time.

In the winter of 1978, we decided to visit my Uncle Cliff in Poway, California. Brenda was still in diapers, so we left her with my cousin Judy. Ruth and the three kids and I flew to Los Angeles. Cliff picked us up at the airport. It was the first time for the kids to fly in a plane. We went to Knott's Berry Farm and to Disneyland. There were both amusement parks. We took Cliff's kids Kelly and Travis with us. We had five kids between eight and three. Several people gave us free tickets because we had so many young kids. All the kids were really good, and we had no problems.

A FATHER'S QUEST

Hog house

In the spring of 1978, a FHMA banker come to our farm. He told me I was going to build a hog house. I asked, "What are you talking about?" We were out in the yard. He said, "Show me where you are going to build the hog house." I couldn't believe what was happening. He came out every Wednesday for two months. He liked it the best if I wasn't home. He wanted to talk Ruth into building a new house. I wonder now how many farmers lost their farm in the eighties because of bankers in the seventies. We looked at prefab houses in Waseca. It would cost about $50,000. We decided against the house. What I really wanted was a machine shed. They made a loan of $150,000. We built a hog house 36×120 feet. We would be finishing our pigs to market size. We put a new roof on the barn, put in a barn cleaner and ten more farrowing crates. We were up to 150 sows. We also built a machine shed fifty-four by ninety feet. I also put up another grain bin. The whole farm was a lot different. I put the first pigs in the hog house on my birthday, December 21. I built the hog house just south of the granary. I put up augers from the mill to the feeders. I could now grind-feed without handling the feed.

Stan painting the granary

Year 1978 was finally a very good year. We made real money for the first time. Corn prices had really gone up. Putting up a corn dryer and grain bin had really paid off.

I decided I would hire a full-time man to help me. We would now have a lot of work to do. Jerry Paul was delivering propane for the corn dryer that fall. I hired him in November. We had a lot of work to do in the barn and the hog house. We got everything done by spring and were ready to go in the field. It started to rain for weeks. I had to think up things to do to keep Jerry busy. Finally, we got a break in the weather. Then Jerry wanted to take off three days to work on an old pickup he had just sitting. I told Jerry we had way too much to do now. I would give him time off in two weeks. Jerry took time off immediately. I fired Jerry. I worked ninety-six hours straight. I would sometimes go to sleep an hour on the tractor. I never took my shoes off in four days. I never hired another full-time man. Ruth and I did most of the work ourselves. Stan worked for me in the summer. I was really stubborn at this time of my life.

In September 1979, on a Sunday, we visited my parents. We got home late in the afternoon. It looked like we were going to get a storm. I had some chores to do and some feed to grind. Ruth said she would help me after she got the kids in the house. I set up the feed to grind, and just when I was turning on the mill, lightning struck. The whole mill lit up like an arc welder. It almost blinded me. If I had been touching the mill, I would have been killed. I would have to have someone come out to fix the mill. The motor was burned out. I was shaking so bad I good hardly walk. As I walked toward the house, I met Ruth. She was shaking worse than I was. Lightning had just struck a big maple tree. Ruth was right under it. We came close to both being killed. What would four young children do? How would finding their parents dead impact their lives? The lightning strike left a big hole in the tree. I think God was watching out for us. It wasn't our time yet.

This is the tree that Ruth was standing under when the lightning struck, 40 years later

That fall, Curtis Berg came out to the farm. He said, "You have way more work than you can do." He told me about the MAST program that the University of Minnesota had. I could get a foreign student live to with us nine months of the year. The student would be with you the whole growing season. He wouldn't go to school while he stayed with you. My job was to teach him American farming. I applied and got accepted.

In the fall of 1979, Alvin Gross sold his 240-acre farm for $3,000 an acre. It had an older house and no other buildings. Eight years earlier, I paid $312.50 for my farm.

We were all done with our work in the fall of 1979. A neighbor, Richard Finley, came up. There was water standing in his corn field. I had cane and rice tires on our combine. "Will you try to pick the corn?" I picked it. I didn't get stuck. After I finished it, he asked me if I wanted to rent the land. There was an eighty-acre farm two miles from us. There was a forty-acre farm eight miles away. He lived on the farm eight miles away. I would now be farming 640 acres.

I enjoyed reading history books. It is surprising what you learn. A famous naval admiral, David Farragut, while in a battle and one of his ships was sunk, instead of turning his other ships around, he cried out, "Damn the torpedoes, full speed ahead!" I have never forgotten this statement, and when things seem hopeless, I say, "Damn the torpedoes, full speed ahead!" That was how I got started farming and got through the farm depression. That is how I'm dealing with my stroke and cancer.

Tammy, Ruth, Brenda, Wayne, (bottom) Doreen and Bob

Chapter II

Farm Depression and the Exchange Students

We considered the farm depression to last ten years. It lasted all the eighties. Most of the things that caused the farm depression were the seventies. Inflation had gotten too high. Farmers, including myself, thought we could spend ourselves rich. Everything was worth more money the next year, especially land, rent, and machinery. Grain and livestock prices never got any higher than the early seventies. By the end of the seventies, we were growing a bigger crop. All farmers thought if we farmed more land, we would be okay. The rent costs and the price of land really went up. Interest rates had gotten higher, and several farmers sold their farms on contract for deed. Contract for deed means the landowner sold their farm with a small down payment to a new owner. The new owner was paying for the farm over a long period of time. The farmers that quit farming figured they could make a living on the high land prices and on the interest they got. Land prices really came down in the mideighties. Because of buying on a contract for deed, farmers turned the land back to the original owners. Land prices were much lower now than they owed on the farms. Some farmers kept the land but paid a lesser price to the owners. Land continued to be worthless until the late eighties. This caused a real nightmare to retired farmers. Not many farmers sell their land on a contract today. They had learned a costly lesson. In 1979, President Carter decided to punish Russia and put on a grain embargo. Grain prices really went down. He shot the American farmer in the foot. At the same time, the fed decided to tame inflation. They did it by raising interest rates. By 1983, interest rates were 22 percent. Up to that time, banks didn't set the interest rates for more than one year at a time. It made sense to borrow money at 9 percent, but when interest rates went up to 22 percent, farmers couldn't pay the interest on the loans. That was the cause of the farm depression. I never bought any more land after the second farm in 1974. The money that I borrowed from FMHA always stayed the same. The first loan stayed 5 percent. The loan I got to build the hog house stayed at 8.5 percent. That really helped me. I was lucky to be borrowing from PCA and not from a bank. PCA stayed with most farmers. Banks found it was easy to foreclose on loans.

We got our first MAST student on April 24, 1980. Johan Selenuis was from Finland. He was raised on a small farm in southern Finland. He come from a family of three brothers and one sister. One brother was raised to be a mechanic. One brother was raised to be a farmer. Johan was the smarter brother and was raised to get a good education. He had not done so much work on the farm. I think he was twenty-two years old at the time. He would stay with us until Thanksgiving Day. Then they had off December and went to the University of Minnesota for one quarter in January. He would not go to school while he was with us. I didn't consider Johan as a farm employee. I considered Johan as a student and I was the teacher. We had a lot of work to get done at the farm, but it had to be a learning experience. I would take him with me everywhere. I would teach him the financial aspects of the farm. I took him with me to meet with the bankers and discuss business. I didn't go in the relationship expecting too much. The year ended up much better than I had expected. I was extremely happy with Johan. We had built a relationship that would last our complete lives.

Johan Selenuis, MAST student

Johan got along really well with my four children and with my wife, Ruth. Brenda was three years old and became attached to Johan. She always sat on his lap. Bob was eight years old at the time. Bob was already a farmer, and he wanted to work with us. Johan and Bob worked well together. Doreen was nine, and Tammy was eleven. On a lot of nights, Johan played games with our kids. Everyone got along really well, and that made it easy for Ruth and me.

When Johan came, we had a quite a bit of snow. I thought we had a long time to get acquainted. Soon we had ninety-degree weather. We stated planting corn six days later on April 30. Johan caught on fast to everything.

We were required to give Johan two weeks' vacation. I needed a vacation too. By the middle of the summer, I thought Johan was able to stay on the farm alone for a week with Stan's help. My parents watched the kids. I took a trip completely around Lake Superior. We went through the locks at Sault Ste. Marie. It was our first time to go through a lock. It was fun. Afterward we visited Chester and Evelyn, my grandparents' foster son, at their lake home in Phillips, Wisconsin. My Aunt Myrtle and her new husband, Vince, were also visiting them. We all had a great time. We would visit Chester and Evelyn many times in the future years. Having a MAST student allowed Ruth and me to get away from the farm from time to time. That was always something that I looked forward to. We also started to visit Ray and Alice Borgen, Ruth's uncle and aunt, in Rockford, Illinois. We went every year for many years.

Having a MAST student caused me to think more about running the farm and having a hog operation. I became a better farmer. I decided to build an office unto the farrowing barn. Stan was working for me that summer. Stan, Johan, and I built the office by ourselves. We would have to keep many more records on the sows. I hired a veterinarian, Dave Blanna, to check the sows every week. I was to pay him for every pig we weaned. I had a clipboard over every farrowing crate to keep track of the pigs being born and the deaths. All the sows had a number. We took the temperatures of the sows the first three days after farrowing. We were to catch the problems that the sows had before they started to lose their pigs. The vet checked the clipboards on his weekly visit and made recommendations. He liked coming late Friday afternoon. We always had several beers, and he liked visiting with the students. The years when we were farrowing sows, Ruth the kids and the student went to bed around ten. I went to the farrowing barn to check on the pigs. Our dog, a border collie named Sheba, always went along. I usually went to bed at eleven. I decided that I would never give a job to Johan that I didn't want to do myself. I would do the bad jobs and give Johan the easy jobs. I had Johan clean the farrowing crates while I fed the sows outside. After about a month, Johan said, "Why are you always giving me the worse jobs when you always are doing the easy work?" I was surprised! We switched jobs. I had always liked cleaning the farrowing crates and looking at the little pigs.

Johan enjoyed being outside better. I had learned something. I should have asked Johan what jobs he preferred.

Most of the students went to Florida in December to pick oranges. The university arranged the jobs for the students. Johan wanted to spend Christmas with us. So I paid him to work for us the month of December. Johan went to the University of Minnesota January through March. The students had a special program for their hosts the end of March. All the students and their hosts had a ban-

A FATHER'S QUEST

quet together. Each country had a short play about something that pertained to their culture. We met many other farmers, and it was a fun evening.

(Top) Wayne, Ruth, Bob, Dirk, Brenda, (Bottom) Doreen and Tammy

In 1981, we had a student from Germany. His name was Dirk Steinhoff. I really liked Johan, but I knew I couldn't compare a new student to an old student. In some cases, Dirk was similar to Johan. He got along really well with Ruth and the kids. But other ways he was different. We always talked farming. He tested my mind. I had to keep a calculator at the table. Dirk always came up with the right answer in his mind faster than I could do it on a calculator. Every job we did, Dirk always kept track of the time on how long it took to do the job. He figured ways to do the job faster. Sometimes doing a job faster wasn't good. But other times we saved time. Dirk didn't come from a farm. His dad managed land for a company. Dirk came from a wealthy family, and he went with another student to Hawaii in December. When the students went to the university, they had a committee that worked with the new students for the next year. Dirk was on the committee, and he wanted me to come up to the university and give a twenty-minute speech to the new students and then take questions. I would have an hour of time. The topic of my speech was, "What can a student do to become a better student?" How could I talk on this topic or any topic for twenty minutes? How could I take one hour? I spent many hours coming up with the speech. I wrote the speech down, but I learned it by heart. I kept the written speech in my shirt pocket. After I gave the speech, many of the new students had questions. I had answered all their questions okay. I did a good job! Afterward I thought that was really something to give a speech at a university. I never went to school after high school. In high school, I always got a failing grade in giving a speech. That was something to be proud of! In April, Dirk's mother, dad, and his brother, Frank, came to Minnesota to visit us. They rented a large motor home to tour United States before Dirk went home.

Dirk Steinhoff, his father, his mother, and his brother Frank

In 1981, Dave Blanna, my vet told me that he was making so much money that he wanted to invest in a hog operation. He wanted me to be his partner. He wanted to build a large farrowing operation on our farm. We talked about it for almost two years. In the end, I didn't want to work for someone. I never took him up on his offer. In the future, I wondered if it was a mistake to not take his offer.

In 1982, Richard Finley wanted to sell his farm. I knew that I couldn't buy it. But I didn't want to lose the land. It was only two miles from our home farm. We rented the Dragsten farm from Hoysler Real Estate company. I called them and asked if they knew anyone that would buy the farm and rent it back to me. Don Rievers bought the land and rented it to me. He paid $1,800 an acre. Don was a big pig farmer in the Faribault area. He had to retire early because of health issues. He had money to invest after selling his home farm.

In 1982, we got a student from England. His name was Bill Toffs. He was a quiet student. It was hard to get to know him. We got in the field early. We got 40 percent of the corn planted, and then it started to rain. It rained the last week of April and all of May. Finally, the second week of June, we got back into the field. Even though we were in the field, it was still too wet. We mudded the crop into the ground. We set ourselves up to fail. The last week in June, I took my family up north fishing. When we got home from the fishing trip, Bill told me he was going home. He was homesick, and he really missed his girlfriend. I tried to get Bill to change his mind, but I failed. Bill went home the end of June. Bill told me that he only stayed until we could have a vacation. Otherwise, he would have gone home earlier.

Simon O'Louglan, Wayne and Ruth

The next week, the university sent me another student. His name was Simon O'louglan from Australia. He had first been sent to a farm in North Dakota. He lived in an old trailer house on a different farm alone. He spent a lot of time alone. He didn't get along with the farmer. I agreed to take him. But I had an uneasy feeling with him. What was I getting into? Ruth, the kids, and I hit it off really good from the start. Ruth and the kids never hit it off with Bill. Simon was a pleasant different situation for them. My Navy buddy, Bob Cunningham, and his wife, Pat, and their young daughter, Coleen, came to visit us. I think Coleen was three years old. Simon spent a lot of his spare time cracking a bullwhip. It made a loud noise. That was the only thing that Coleen can remember from their trip. She was impressed with Simon and the bullwhip. In the fall, the corn that we planted early went 150 bushels per acre and the corn we planted in June went fifty bushels per acre. The crop was a failure big-time, and we lost money big-time on the crop. But we made money on the pigs big-time, so I came out okay. The crop farmers in our area had a bad time financially. We again went to the banquet and the plays at the university. By this time, we knew several farmers, and it was fun.

I decided to hire some part-time help in the fall of 1982 to help take care of the sows and their piglets. I thought that maybe a woman would do a better job. I hired Connie Miller. She was from Dodge Center. In the winter of 1982 and 1983, Connie kept on saying, "I wish we would have a snowstorm, then I can have a day off." This made me mad! If we had a snowstorm, I would have a lot more work to do. Last winter was terrible. The snow was so bad that I had to shovel out the sow pens almost every day. We had to shovel off some of the roofs on the buildings. Ruth and I worked from first light until dark, and we never caught up. That was the reason to hire some help. Ruth and I never wanted to go through a winter like that again. I told Connie, "You can ask me for any day off. I'll let you have off." She never asked, but she said every day that she was praying for a snowstorm. This really affected my relationship with her.

At the end of 1982, I made a plan on how many pigs we would raise in 1983. Dave Blanna, my vet, told me that it would be impossible. "You don't have enough buildings to do it."

A FATHER'S QUEST

Jan Jonsson, Swedish student

In 1983, we had a Swedish student. His name was Jan Jonsson. When we first brought Jan to the farm and showed him around the farm, the first thing he asked, "Where is your torch?" I answered, "We don't have a torch." Jan said, "I'm not going to like it here." I knew that I would have to buy an acetylene torch. I took Jan to town the next day to buy a torch. I told Jan that I didn't know how to use a torch. I wanted him to teach me how, but he never did. The student we got the next year taught me how to use it. Crop prices were really cheap. We had a big harvest everywhere but Minnesota. The government paid us not to farm 25 percent of our land. We would make considerably more money not farming. Stan still worked for me in the summers. We put new windows in the house and new siding. Stan painted the house and all our buildings. One day while I was in the tractor, I lost my billfold. I looked everywhere and never found it. I had to get a new driver's license. I decided that we would not have as much work if we didn't farm all the land. We could stay up north fishing two weeks now. I invited Jan to come up one week to go fishing with us. I finally persuaded Connie and her family to spend the week on the farm when Jan was gone. Jan had a surprise for me when he got up north. He found my billfold under a seat in one of my tractors. I had several $100 bills in it. I gave him an award. When we came home, Connie said that she was never going to do this again. Soon she started to miss work. She never called; she just didn't show up. I fired her! I hired another girl. Her name was Lori Wolle. She had just gotten out of the agriculture college in Waseca. She was an excellent worker. She knew a lot about pigs. I really liked her! With Lori's help, we executed my plan on how many pigs we would raise. But I lost money on the pigs. I paid Dave so much money for every pig we raised. Dave made more money than he planned. He was always bragging about all the money he was making. Dave raised his rates to me when I was already losing money. Maybe that was his way to persuade me into gong in a partnership with him. I fired him! But in the end, I would really miss him. Soon afterward, he would move from Dodge Center. I never saw him again. Was I making a big mistake?

Our house

In the fall of 1983, I rented eighty acres of land from Adline Hrtanek. Her son was living in the buildings, and he was milking cows. He rented the other eighty acres from her.

Ivar Skrumsted, Student from Norway

In 1984, we got a student from a student from Norway. His name was Ivar Skrumsted. It was my dream to get a student from Norway. I wished that my Grandpa Larson was still alive. Ruth and her family were full-blooded Norwegians. Ruth's dad, Elmer, could talk Norwegian with Ivar. We sold all the sows, and I quit farrowing pigs. We took all the farrowing pens out and built pens for finishing pigs. Stan helped me do this, and then I had to tell Stan that we wouldn't need his help again. We lost money in 1983, and I felt that I had to make changes. I couldn't hire any extra labor. Don Reuvers told me that a farmer raising pigs in Faribault would hire Lori. At least Lori would have a job now.

We had to cut the fat out of everything, including me. I joined Nutri System, and I lost seventy pounds. I went from 240 lbs. to 170 lbs. Neighbors didn't recognize me. I wanted to get down to 190 lbs., but I just kept losing weight after I quit their food. That was a bad thing. Then all of a sudden, I wanted to gain weight for the first time in my life.

In 1984, everything was going against us. We couldn't service the debt that we had with the high interest rates. Land values had really gone down. My equity was all gone. Ruth's dad, Elmer, got lung cancer. What more could happen? Why did the angel tell me that I would be a successful farmer? I was a failure! How could this be even possible? How could God and the angels let me down? I had just gotten a young loan officer. His name was George Piechel. I met with him often. He would help me make up a plan to save my farm. We would make a three-year plan. If I followed the plan for three years, I wouldn't lose the farm. The first thing I did after harvest was to make out the checks to every one of my landlords, paying the rent in full. Then I called every landlord and said, "I need to come and visit you about rent." Many farmers at that time were not paying the fall rent. Landlords were talking among themselves. They already were expecting me to not pay the fall rent. They couldn't believe it when I gave them the checks. I told them, "In our agreement, I was to pay the second half of the rent in November. I'm a man of my word. But I cannot pay you this amount next year." I got every one of them to agree to a 40 percent deduction. They all accepted my offer without any argument. George had given me good advice. In the future, most landlords wanted all the rent up front. They wanted all the rent paid in the January-through-March period. George left PCA soon afterward and went to work for Christenson Farms in Sleepy Eye, Minnesota. He was from the Sleepy Eye area.

(Top) Tammy, Doreen, Bob, (Bottom) Wayne, Ruth, Brenda, and Ivar

When Ivar left, we had a party for him. We invited several of the other students in our area. All of my family really liked Ivar, but he was a quiet student. We had no idea if Ivar liked our farm or not. Several students told me at the party that Ivar had told them that he got the best farm. Ivar told us that when he got back to Norway, he would never leave. We didn't expect that Ivar would visit us. I wanted to visit him in Norway. It was a dream of mine.

I had a meeting with PCA in December of 1984 after Christmas. Ruth and I met in the basement with Tom Waters, my new loan officer. By this time, PCA got their name on all my checks. I couldn't cash the checks until they first signed them. I had already put my total crop under loan with the government and gave all the money to PCA, which George and I had agreed to under the plan we made. The first thing that Tom Waters told me was, "If I had my way, I would sell you out." At this time, I had a negative net worth of $25,000. I was broke! I started telling Tom about what George and I agreed to. He said, "I don't care what a lame duck loan officer told you." I really wanted to tell him off. Ruth could see this. Whenever I started to say something, Ruth kicked me in the leg under the table. At the end of the meeting, I could hardly walk. My leg was in terrible pain! But maybe Ruth just saved the farm. If she wouldn't have done this, I would have got into a terrible argument with Tom. How would have the argument turned out? Tom wanted all my income until they got $25,000. Under the plan that I made with George, I was to raise as much money possible before the end of the year. PCA would loan me more money as soon as the New Year came. At this time, I didn't have money to buy groceries. It would take two months to sell $25,000 of hogs. What would I do to live?

The first thing I would have to do was to go to the county and sign up for food stamps. Then I went to the school and arranged that the kids would get free lunches. For me it was the most embarrassing thing I had ever done. My grandparents never had to do this in the Great Depression, and they let me know that. They were proud people.

On January 4, 1985, I had a load of hogs to sell. I knew that PCA would take the entire check. We had a hog that looked like a deer. We had tried to load him for a month. He always jumped out. Ruth and I got him in the truck today. When I got the truck to the highway, I could see him in the rearview mirror. The hog was trying to jump over the box to the truck. I slammed on the brakes, and he fell back into the truck. When I backed up to the dock at Farmstead Foods in Albert Lea and took the end gate out of the truck, the hog ran out. I unloaded the rest of the load and moved my truck. When I got in the alleyway with my hogs, I could see him with the next batch of hogs ahead of me. He looked like a deer, and he was taller than the other hogs. I told the farmer ahead of me, "That brown deer looking hog is mine." The farmer said, "That isn't your hog, it's mine." We argued for some time. I knew he knew that it wasn't his. He was trying to steal a hog from me. What was I to do? How could I prove to everyone that it was my hog? Right then, the deer-looking hog helped me out. He was all of a sudden three pens ahead of us. Then the farmer said, "I guess it was your hog." Maybe this farmer was in the same case as I was in. Maybe he needed every dollar he could get. If it wasn't the time we were in, maybe he would have volunteered to help me. It took me a long time at the packing plant.

As soon as I got home, Ruth was waiting for me. She said, "What took you so long? My sister called and said that my dad was dying." I said, "Why didn't you just go to the hospital?" She said, "I was waiting for you." I changed clothes, and we left for the hospital. When we got there, someone said, "Dad just died." Ruth's mother and all her sisters and brothers were there. Elmer's brothers, John and George, and their wives were there too. If I would have not had all the trouble with this hog, we would have made it in time for Ruth to say goodbye to her dad. He was seventy-nine years old.

Ruth's family met at either Palmer and Audrey's house or at Phyllis and Al's house the next day. They all lived in Chatfield. I don't remember which house. At noon, Al asked me to go with him to pick up some food from a restaurant. I went with Al. I should have paid for half of the food. I had no money. I had no money in my checking account. We didn't have credit cards at that time. It was one of the most embarrassing things in my life. If George was still at PCA, I would have had some money. If I would have known what was happening I would have never given PCA all my money before the end of the year.

Ruth was too embarrassed to use the food stamps in Dodge Center. I told Ruth that we would have to cut the family living by 40 percent. How would she do it? I didn't go grocery-shopping with her. It wasn't fair to her if I had no idea how much everything cost. We decided to go to Cub Foods in Rochester. No one would know us there. When we had no money, we always went there. We watched the ads and bought as much as we could. Sometimes we bought enough of one item to last for months if it was cheap enough. In March of that year, we had some money, and we stopped getting food stamps. Ruth could now shop in Dodge Center. We still went one day a month to Cub Foods and bought a month's worth of groceries. Then we went out to eat. It was a time for just Ruth and me. We continued to go grocery-shopping in Rochester once a month and to go out and eat until the kids were grown. At the end of the year, we had cut out family living by 40 percent.

Tom Waters was not my loan officer for a long time, thank heavens. In 1985, I had nine different loan officers. Some I didn't even meet. It was a nightmare trying to do business with PCA.

We got a German student in 1985. His name was Dirk Heneroff. When he first came to my farm, he said, "I don't work with women or kids." I told him, "You are going to be working alone a lot." We had a neighbor that lived three miles from us that had a student. They went out drinking every night. Every morning he always had a hangover. He put no effort in trying to get along with Ruth or my kids. One day he asked me, "How do you get money?" I said, "That is why we raise hogs and crops." He told me that his dad died in a factory accident owned by his family. "Every month my mother just gets this big check." He imagined that I was getting a big check from somewhere. It was a long year! He was to stay until Thanksgiving. In early November, he was plowing a field of mine. The field had terraces. I told him how to plow them. When I came back several hours later, he had plowed the terraces wrong. I said, "Why did you plow the terraces wrong?" I thought that he would say that he didn't understand. I would have not been happy, but maybe it was my mistake for not explaining to him right. But he said, "You are wrong! I'm doing it the right way." We got into an argument. I said, "I'm renting this farm. The owner told me how to plow them." We argued more. Then I fired him!

Tammy, Dirk Heneroff, and Doreen

In late summer, Ruth and I got a job working at the Dodge Center corn-packing plant for the season. It ran from the middle of August until the end of September. No other farmers did this. My plan was to save for the farm. We couldn't be so proud not to work off the farm. Ruth and I both worked nights. That way I could work on the farm during the day.

That fall, my Grandma McColley's health had started to fail. I knew that I had made a big mistake for not going to visit with my Grandpa Larson at the end. I would not make this mistake again. I went alone to the St. Mary's Hospital to see her. We had a nice visit, and then she said, "It's harvesttime, and you have too much work to do to visit with me." My uncles, Lyle and Cliff, and their wives come up from Florida to visit with her. Grandma was putting on an act. Lyle and Cliff thought she was okay. They wondered why she was in the hospital. Lyle visited with me the next day and said that I was a millionaire. I said, "Where did you hear that?" Lyle said that his mother had told him. I told him that it wasn't true; I was broke. I wasn't worth anything. Over the next thirty years, he always asked me if I was a millionaire yet. He always wanted to know how much money I was worth. It didn't bother me. Grandma was soon in the nursing home in Waseca. I made a big mistake telling Grandma that I wasn't a millionaire. I told her that I wasn't worth anything. I was broke. She knew that I was farming several farms. We had a lot of new buildings. She didn't want to hear what I was telling her. She was proud of me. I had crushed her! The next time I took Ruth and my kids to visit her, she wouldn't talk to us. Sometimes it is better to be untruthful. I wished many times that I could do this over. I would prove that Grandma was right more than once! Grandma died on January 22, 1986. She was eighty-five years old. Her funeral was the same date as my Grandpa McColley and my Great-grandpa McColley.

At the end of 1985, I had exceeded the three-year plan that I made with George in just one year. George had helped me to save the farm. If Tom Waters had his way, PCA would have lost a lot of money. PCA never wrote off one cent of my loan. I was proud of that! PCA and banks wrote off a lot of money for farmers at that time.

In early 1986, the federal government and the state of Minnesota brought down the interest rate several points for farmers. But PCA didn't reduce my rate as much as the law required. That made me mad! But there was not anything that I could do about it at the time. I kept track of the extra interest they were charging me. In the end, I was going to get this money back.

We got a student from Ireland in 1986. His name was Johathan Craig. Ruth never like him. The kids got along with him, just so and so. This affected my relationship with him. I have often wondered if everyone had got along better with the previous student, if this would be different.

Johathan Craig and Doreen

I got a new loan officer from PCA in 1986. His name was Bob LeCox. He came out once a month and wanted me to have an inventory of everything. I believe it was March when he was out for the first time. I told him the numbers of pigs we had. Then he counted the pigs and said, "You gave me a wrong number." Was he calling me a liar? I told him, "My number was right. You made a mistake, you will have to count them again." When you count 1,700 pigs, it is easy to be wrong. But I was not going to admit a mistake. He never counted the pigs again. Finally, he took my word. The next month I made a diagram of the buildings with pens. I wrote the numbers of the pigs in each pen. Then when he told me I was wrong, we both counted the pigs in the pens over. Sometimes I was wrong, and sometimes he was wrong. I always gave him a can of Pepsi. When he was done, he always gave me to the empty can back. Pepsi had a contest where they had a symbol at the bottom of the can. Sometimes you had a winner. In July I gave Bob a can of Pepsi. When I asked for the empty can back, he wouldn't give it to me. Finally, he threw the can in the back seat of his car. I have often wondered what he won. I thought it was cheap of him to keep the can.

That summer we had some trouble with the John Deere 4320 tractor. I decided to trade it off. A dealership had four John Deere 4440 tractors in St. Charles. Bob and I went to look at the tractors. Three of the tractors had been repainted. One tractor was not repainted. Bob wanted me to buy one of the repainted one. He said, "If we buy one of the repainted tractors, it will look new." I said, "You'll never know what the tractor looked like before. Maybe they are trying to hide something. It's better to buy the unpainted tractor." It was a 1980 model. The other three were 1979 models. It was six years old. We traded it for $12,500 to boot. I got a FMHA loan. It was a loan from the government.

In 1986, Ruth and I again worked in the canning factory in Dodge Center during the corn pack. At that time, the government was paying $.25 a bushel a year to store corn. I found two six-thousand-bushel bins by Waseca for sale. I bought them. We took them apart and then put them together again at our farm. We did it all by ourselves. I hired a neighbor boy, Donnie Allan, to help us. We also bought a granary two miles from us and moved it with help from one person. The granary held seven thousand bushels. I got home from the factory at five in the morning and got up at ten in the morning to work on the bins. Bob always was done taking care of the pigs by ten.

In 1987, we decided not to have any more students. We had bad luck two years in a row. It was a time to end having MAST students. I hired Tim Thoman to help me that year. Bob became friends with Tim. That would last throughout their lifetime. The government came up with the PIK program. You could put corn under loan at $1.89 per bushel. Then you could buy the corn back at the local price. They set the price before the market opened in the morning. If the price for corn went up $.10, farmers went to the FSA office in the late afternoon and bought the corn back at the morning's price. Then you could sell it at the local price at a later date. Corn always got over the loan rate sometime during the year. You had to have corn harvest to put it under loan. About every three days, we put corn under loan. That fall corn got down to $.55 a bushel. If you did everything right, you could get well over $3 a bushel. We had corn to feed to the hogs at $.55 a bushel. There was more money farming the government than farming land.

On Thanksgiving 1987, Ruth and decided to visit Bob and Pat Cunningham in Pittsburg. We flew on an airplane out of Minneapolis. When we flew over Pittsburg, all we could see from the air was mountains. Was there a flat place to land the plane? We stayed with them for three days, and we had a good time. Then we flew back to Minneapolis.

Leslie Beckman asked me to custom his farm for $10,000 per year. Custom farming means that the owner of the land pays for the seed, fertilizer, and chemicals, plus a fee for farming the land. The owner gets all the crop. The operator pays for the fuel and repairs and then gets a set amount of money for farming the land. I asked him to hire my son, Bob, to do it. Bob was fifteen years old. Bob LeCox had too much control over me. I had to ask his permission to do anything. The only thing he didn't question was labor. So I paid my son, Bob, for labor, and he bought things that we needed. I told Bob, "If PCA sells me out before you graduate from high school, you have to sell these items and pay me. If I'm still farming when you graduate, you can keep these items." I had helped Leslie's son, Rodney, to get started farming in 1972. Now Leslie was helping my son, Bob, to get started farming in 1988. Maybe angels are at work in this. Maybe not. We'll never know for sure.

We were farming more land. I also rented an eighty next to my home farm. We had a six-row planter. I thought it was time to have an eight-row planter. We would be farming 1,025 acres. It was November 13, Brenda's birthday. I had all my loans paid up current. I had enough money to pay cash for the planter. I went to the PCA office in Blooming Prairie at three o'clock in the afternoon to talk to Bob LeCox about the planter. He wouldn't give me permission. I was not going to take a no. My parents were coming over for supper for Brenda's birthday. The staff all left at five. I wouldn't leave. I said, "I'm going to stay here until you give me written permission to buy the planter. We can stay all night." I knew he was stubborn, but I was also stubborn. Who would win? Finally, at eight at night, he gave me written permission. I had won! Would I win again? It was eight thirty when I got home. My parents were still there. At least I could have birthday cake with everyone.

I met with Bob LeCox in January 1988. I brought up the interest subsidy that the federal government and the State of Minnesota had made on my loan. I told him how much money they owned me from overcharging me. I told Bob that he was always looking so close to everything. "Why aren't you looking close to the interest?" He told me that I was wrong. I told him that I was positive that I was right. I told him, "If I don't have this money in one month, I will hire a lawyer and sue PCA for the money." I was taking a big chance. If I sued a bank, they would never lend me money again. But I knew that PCA was doing this to all the farmers. I knew that I would win the lawsuit. Then PCA would have to pay all farmers. Even if they thought they were right. If they were wrong, they would lose a lot of money. I'm sure they ran it by their lawyer. In a month, they gave me the money. Bob LeCox was still my loan officer. This problem didn't affect my relationship with him. I never told anyone. If they would never lend me money again, I would have told everyone. It could have caused them more trouble than they could take.

In January, I saw an ad in the paper. It said that if you bought a set of luggage for $250, you got free plane tickets and hotel for two to Las Vegas. I bought the luggage, and when they came, they looked cheap. If I went to a store, I'm sure the luggage wouldn't cost $25. They were made out of cheap cardboard. When I tried to get the plane tickets, they weren't available on any date that we chose. It was a sham, and we got taken. Finally, I told Ruth we would buy tickets and go to Las Vegas. That year we stayed at the Imperial Palace Hotel. We went every winter for six years. The second year, we stayed at the Riviera Hotel. We stayed on the fourteenth floor. The end of the room was all windows. One day we decided in the afternoon we would go up to the room and make love. When Ruth was starting to pull the blinds, I told Ruth, "Don't pull the blinds. We are up so high no one can look in the windows. There is no other building close to us. No one can look in." It was a nice sunny day. So we got naked and got on the bed. As we were making love, all of a sudden, a shadow came across the room. We both looked up. There was a man suspended on a harness washing windows. We both scrambled under the covers. Needless to say, the mood was gone! When the man moved on to the next window, we both went to sleep.

Steen Hansen, Student from Denmark

We would have more land to farm, and I really missed having a student. Ruth and I decided to give it another try. We got a student from Denmark. His name was Steen Hansen. He immediately got along with everyone. Everyone was happy. On May 5, 1988, I was planting corn. That day it snowed twelve inches. Then it turned dry. It was once-in-a-century drought. On our home farm and west of us, everyone got a fairly good crop. Our farms east of the home farm were terrible. A half mile east of our home farm was terrible. The farther you went east, the worse the crop was. The corn and the soybean prices really went up. A lot of the crops we bought back from the government cheaply in the fall of 1987, we could now sell at a high price.

Our first student, Johan Selenuis from Finland, came to visit us in the summer of 1988. He brought his dad. It was his dad's dream to come to America. His dream got stronger after Johan came to our farm and Johan wrote to his dad about his experiences. He really enjoyed his visit with us. A year or so later, he had a hemorrhage of his brain. He died after several days. Maybe it was like having a stroke. I think he was in his early sixties. At least Johan had made his dad's dream come true.

Johan and his dad

That fall, Don Rieuvers called me and told me that he was selling the farm. He wanted to sell it for me at $750 an acre. Soon afterward, Dick Finley called me. He had sold the farm to Don on a contract for deed. Don owed much more for the farm than it was worth. At that time Dick owed $800 an acre. Don was going to turn the farm back to Dick unless Dick settled for much less. Dick offered to sell the farm to me for $800 an acre. No money down. I would have to take over his loan. It would not cost me much more money than paying rent. I thought it was a no-brainer. Bob LeCox would not give me permission. I argued and argued with no luck. Was he still mad when I threatened to sue PCA over the interest? If my children were old enough to buy land, I would have had them do it. I even thought, if I divorced Ruth, she could buy the farm. Ruth didn't think it was a good idea. I could buy the farm and not register the deed with the courthouse. But maybe Bob LeCox would find out about it. In the end, I couldn't take the chance. Don Rieuvers sold the farm to Jim and Laurie Cory. I'm still renting the farm from the Corys in the year of 2020. It was the biggest mistake in my life not buying the farm. It would now be worth half a million dollars. I should have bought the farm from Dick and not have registered the deed. Bob LeCox would only be my loan officer for three more years. I should have taken the chance. That is one thing that I wished that I could do over.

New entryway off house

Everyone came in our house through the entryway into the kitchen. It kind of smelled like pigs. After harvest, Steen told me that I should build an entryway on the laundry room. That way, when guests came into the house, they wouldn't smell pigs. He would dig the hole for the foundation by hand. He would stay with us in December and help me build the entryway. He would be with us Christmastime. I had never thought about this before. It was a good idea!

Even before we got it done, I started planning on building a big addition to our house. I drew up the plans. I estimated the total cost would be $12,000. I would have a new office twelve by eighteen feet. We would add on to the living room. After the living room was done, it would be twenty-five by twenty-five feet at the longest point. Then we would take half of the old living room and turn it into a bathroom off our bedroom. This was a big project. We would do it ourselves.

Living room remodel

While Steen was at the University of Minnesota in the winter quarter of 1989, he was on a committee that worked with farmers. Steen asked me to give a speech to the farmers that were in the program. The topic was to be, "How can a farmer get the most use of a student? What can a farmer do to make the student happy?" I was to talk for twenty minutes and then take questions. I had an hour of time. Why did they pick me? We had two failures in 1985 and 1986. It was a lot more interesting to give the speech to the students in 1982. This was a harder speech. I started out with, "I was the teacher, and the student was just a student. It had to be a learning situation." Some farmers didn't agree with me. But the hour of time went fast. I got many farmers to engage in a conversion with me. It was an honor to give a speech at the University of Minnesota. It was my second speech. How many people have the opportunity to speak at a university?

Wayne's new office

In 1999, we got a student from Finland. He didn't get along with Bob, and he got in a fistfight with Bob. I knew that it wouldn't work. We had him leave. The first of July, we got a student from France. His name was Didier Cornu. He had a lot of experience in building and working with hogs. He was the perfect student at that time. Bob got along with Didier really well. They almost seemed like brothers. I put an ad in the paper advertising for help. I wanted to hire a student from high school that wanted to be a carpenter. I hired a kid from Kasson that was going to be a senior in the fall. He worked out well. So we had a crew consisting of this kid, Didier, Bob, and myself. Didier stayed with us through the winter. He helped me finish off the inside of the house. On the outside of the house, my estimate was right on. On the inside, my estimate was off 100 percent. The total cost was $20,000. I had a cost putting in the bathroom. I had to hire a plumber. I didn't figure that. Plumbing and I have never gotten along. We never had to borrow any money for doing this project.

House after remodel

We had two three-wheelers. Bob and Didier were riding the three-wheelers in the ditch and straight on the road. They were doing it over and over again. I knew this wasn't safe. I never saw them. A sheriff's deputy saw them. Bob and Didier headed for home right away. The deputy chased them. They ran into the house and told me. I could see the deputy coming up to the house. I told Didier, "Just speak French." The deputy came up to the door and asked to talk to the two boys. I invited the deputy into our house. When he started to question Bob and Didier, Bob wouldn't say anything. Didier only talked French. After several minutes, the deputy said to me, "You'll take care of it, won't you?" I said, "I will take care of it." The deputy left frustrated. I said to Bob and Didier, "I never want to hear about this again. You won't get by so easy next time."

Chapter 12

The Nineties

The farm depression was finally over, and the nineties were about to start. I thought better times were ahead. At the end of the nineties, I realized that living through the farm depression was the easier one. Stan Westin offered his home farm to me for rent at $95 per acre. I asked him to rent it to my son, Bob, instead. Bob was going to be eighteen years old. Stan said that Bob could have the farm for $85 per acre.

Georg Jacobson, MAST student

A FATHER'S QUEST

We got a MAST student from the University of Minnesota in March. His name was Georg Jacobson. I never was able to pronounce his name right, so I called him George. It was a really late and a wet spring. I bought a used mix mill at a sale. George completely rebuilt the mill by himself. I was really impressed with him. By summertime I started thinking about going to Europe. I knew that George was capable of running the farm by himself for three weeks. Ruth and all our children were going. We were first going to Norway to visit Ivar. Next, we were going to Sweden to visit Jan, and last, we were going to Denmark to visit Steen. It would be a vacation of a lifetime for our kids. George's last day in Minnesota, he met a girl. Soon afterward, she went to Germany and married George. Love at first sight!

We were going to leave my car at Uncle Lenard's house for the three weeks. There was no room for Lenard to ride in the car with us. My Uncle Dale gave Lenard a ride to the airport so Lenard could drive my car back to his house. I think both Lenard and Dale really enjoyed being at the airport with us and talking about the big trip we were taking. We flew on Sun County Air. We were to stop at a military airport in Newfoundland to refill with fuel before crossing the Atlantic Ocean. We arrived safely at the airport, but there was something wrong with the airplane. We sat on the ground in the airplane for hours waiting for them to fix the airplane. They opened up a door on the airplane where we could stand outside. There was room for six people to stand. The passengers were really good. All of us took turns, and there was no one that got upset. Finally, the airplane was fixed, and we left. As we got in the air, I could sense that there was a problem. I had flown a lot in the Navy, and I developed a sense when something was wrong. The airplane was turning around. All of a sudden, the pilot came on the intercom and told us that we had to go back to the airport. He told us not to get alarmed because they were dropping forty thousand gallons of fuel. He told us that the airplane was too heavy to land with that much fuel onboard. As we were approaching the airport, the pilot told everyone to put their heads between their legs and get prepared for a crash. I could not help but to look up. The whole runway was lined with fire trucks. It was a scary time for everyone. We breathed a sigh of relief when the airplane was stopped.

Soon someone came on the intercom and said the plane needed a new part and they would have to get it from Minneapolis. Another plane would have to bring it, and we would be there for some time. It was a very long wait. An hour went by before we got off the plane, and we were bussed to a mess hall on the base. Everyone was hungry, and we finally got something to eat. Ivar and his dad were to pick us at the airport in Oslo, Norway. We should be there now. Were they waiting? There was one couple that was really scared. They started telling everyone that we would die if we got back on the plane. They got everyone so worked up that it became a mob. It reminded me of a movie when a sheriff faced up to a mob and quieted everyone down. All of a sudden, a stewardess got up and told everyone that she was a grandmother and she would not get on the plane until she felt that it was safe. She then said she would get on the plane when it was safe. She had quieted down the crowd. Soon everyone was coming to me to see what I thought. I had told some people that I had flown in the Navy. I had stayed calm when the couple tried to get everyone worked up. Everyone could see that I was middle age and that I had a wife and four children with me. I told everyone that we couldn't get off the base without flying. There were no roads, and we would have to get on an airplane again. We had all dreamed a long time about going to Norway, and we were going to get on the airplane again and go. We were not flying back to Minneapolis. It would be a huge disappointment. After fifteen hours from the time when we first got to the airport, we finally left. Everyone went except the couple that said we would die. Another plane would take them back to Minneapolis the next day. When we left, the pilot took the plane straight up for what seemed like forever. He was doing a test on the airplane to see if it was safe to go across the Atlantic Ocean. It was now night, and a really weird thing happened. When the plane got close to the Arctic Circle, and we looked out the left side, to the north of the plane, it was light. When we looked out the right side, to the south, it was dark. We had just experienced The Land of the Midnight Sun.

When we arrived at the airport in Oslo, we expected that no one would be there to pick us up. What would we do now? Could I find someone that could speak English to help us? We got off the airplane outside and walked into the terminal, and Ivar and his dad were waiting for us. What a relief! They brought two cars for us. All our children rode with Ivar and Ruth, and I rode with Ivar's dad. I had called his number many times throughout the years. He answered in Norwegian, and when I talked in English, he hung up. Ruth and I sat in the back seat of his car. We were really tired from the trip. We were in awe just to be in Norway and to see the scenery. I thought it would be nice to just sit and not to carry on a conservation. All of a sudden, Ivar's dad asked me a question in perfect English. Evidently, I had the wrong number. Maybe this other man would feel relieved to not be getting any more calls from me. When we got to their farm, Ivar's mother told us that they came home from the airport and went to bed. She stayed up all night and called the airport every hour. When they told her we were in the air, she got Ivar and his dad up to come and get us. They lived two hours away from the airport. We couldn't believe that they had two big mansions on the farm. Ivar's mom and dad lived in one, and his grandmother lived alone in the other one. They all spoke perfect English. Each mansion had a large ballroom on the third floor. I told our kids they would have to eat everything and not complain. I was the one who had a problem. I didn't complain, but I didn't like anything. Ivar's mother made large and fancy meals that they would have eaten on holidays. If she had made ordinary meals that they ate every day, I don't think I would have had that problem. Our visit would have to be one day short in Norway because of the airplane's problems.

The next day they took us to Ringebu. It was a couple hours north of them. That was where the Borgens came from. There was a slave church build in the 1300s that had a cemetery that had Borgen names on some of the tombstones. There was a place to put your guns in the entryway. Ruth's Uncle John and Aunt Helen had visited Norway and this area several years ago. We had an idea where to go. We went up a long mountain road to a farm where one of Ruth's relatives lived. The lady that lived there had a rocking chair that

Ruth's great-great-great-grandmother had. She remembered John and Helen. She only talked Norwegian, so Ivar had to translate what she said to us. But she understood English, so Ivar didn't have to translate it to her what we said. She told us in World War II when the Germans came, they fled future up in the mountains. She had an old uncle that was sick in bed, so he stayed. The Germans didn't bother him. After we left this farm, we came up to a place where there was snow on the mountain. We stopped so we could see it. Bob and I have always wrestled. I got this habit from my foster uncle Chester. He always wrestled with his two boys. Bob and I got into a wrestling match in the snow. Bob won for the first time in his life. He pinned me in the snow. I never wrestled with Bob again. I thought it was appropriate for this to end in the snow on a mountain in Norway. Bob threw up his arms like he was king of the mountain while I just lay in the snow.

 The next day we went to the farm that Ivar managed for his employer, Johan Loken, the former secretary of Agriculture. Potatoes were the main crop. He served in the parliament of Norway. It was a four-hundred-plus-acre farm. We spent one night with Johan and his wife, Randi. We went to Oslo where I sat in Johan's chair in the Parliament. That was an honor for me! In the evening, we went up to their mountain farm. While there, we had strawberry shortcake at midnight. It was still light outside. It never got completely dark. We saw a moose while traveling in the car. The bed Ruth and I slept on that night was a true Norwegian bed. In the middle, there was a high board that kept us separate. Maybe that was a source of birth control years ago. The next day, Johan and his wife, Randi, along with Ivar, packed a picnic lunch and drove us to Jan's home in Sweden. We all stopped at the side of the road and ate lunch.

 Jan was married, and we stayed at his house. His wife had horses and the kids rode them. We never had any special meals, so eating was better now, or maybe I was just getting hungry. We toured the farm where Jan worked. It was quite a big farm, and they had several employees. Jan managed the farm work and the employees. Jan's boss, Staffan Gibrend, told Bob if he ever wanted a job, he should call him. We visited Jan's parents. One day we went on a tour where they were canning peas. We also went to the field where they were cutting the peas. They had a special guide for us that could speak English. She was a young lady. Her dad was a doctor that studied at Mayo Clinic in Rochester. She spoke English so well because she lived in Rochester for some time. She made the tour for us really fun. Jan and his wife took us to Denmark. We all crossed on a ferry from the extreme south of Sweden. Steen and his brother Palle picked us up at the ferry.

We first toured Copenhagen and then we went to Steen's farm. While in Copenhagen, we stopped at the office that arranged MAST students. Steen farm was named Bullerup Bjeiggaard. First, we toured a castle and a Dutch windmill. We could go up inside the windmill, and we climbed to the top. I have always had a fantastic feeling for windmills. Another day, we went on a tour of a factory that made farm equipment. They served all their employees and us lunch with beer. After lunch, we went to a dairy farm. As soon as we got to the farm, I had to use the bathroom. They had a bathroom in the basement of their house. It had an outside entrance. As soon as I got down there, I got sick to my stomach. Then I got lightheaded and fell down. They all could hear the commotion, and Ruth came down and helped me to get up. I think I had food poisoning. But I was the only one that got sick. How come? When we got back to their house, I spent the rest of the afternoon in bed. I had told them that I wanted to take them out for a meal. We went to an old part of town where Hans Christian Anderson was from. He was a famous author. There were ten of us. We all ordered the special, which was the cheapest thing on the menu. They dished up our plates from our table. They had several waitresses and waiters taking care of us. They told me that you never tipped anyone. The bill came to $480. It was double over what we would have paid at the Hubbell House at the time. When we left the restaurant, they all shook everyone's hands. I really felt guilty that I didn't give them a tip. I put the bill on a credit card. It was a lot of fun, but when I paid the bill, it didn't seem so much fun then. The next day we went completely across Denmark to the west side to visit Steen's sister and her husband. They had a dairy farm, and the house was connected to the barn. You went out of the kitchen directly to the cows. The last day, they took us by car an hour north. There we got on a train and went north to the sea. There we got on a ferry and went to Oslo, Norway. The ferry got there around four in the afternoon. We had a reservation at a hotel that night. I had no idea where it was. How would we find it? We decided to get off the ferry last. We went up to the top deck. Would we be able to see the hotel from there? All of a sudden, we could see Ivar and Randi standing on the dock! It was a relief! We flew home the next day.

Georg's parents visited our farm soon after we came home from Europe. Georg's dad was a MAST student himself when he was young. Georg's parents first planted the idea to go to Europe again next year. Also, I had a guilty conscience that we went to Europe and didn't visit Johan from Finland.

After our vacation in Europe, we decided to build a garage. It would be a double garage on the east side of our house. We would come into our house through the entryway and the laundry room that we had built in 1988. We would have to go up a small hill to pull into the garage. I poured the floor with a five-inch slope from the front to the back where we pulled in the vehicles. Water from the vehicles would always run out.

Either late in 1990 or very early 1991, we got a disease in our pigs called anomopolis pneumonia. We got it from the feeder pigs we bought. It was terrible, and it almost caused me to go insane. We had to give every pig a shot of penicillin for three days when it broke out. In early February, when I went out in the morning to check the pigs, I found forty-two pigs dead. I couldn't believe what was happening! I had been praying to God that he would help me out with this terrible disease. I would have to give seven hundred shots for three days. I was already busy. As I walked from the hog house to the granary to set up some feed to grind, I started to holler at God.

I shouted out loud, "God, get out of my life. I have been praying and praying, and now forty-two pigs are dead just this morning. You aren't helping me at all. I couldn't do any worse if you would just get out of my life and leave me alone. Get out of my life!"

All of a sudden, I heard a voice over my back. As I turned to look, the voice was always to my back. I believe it was an angel.

A FATHER'S QUEST

The voice said, "You have something much worse soon to happen. The thing you are going through now is to make you tough enough to get you through what's ahead."

Now I was hearing voices. Maybe I was going insane. I didn't know what to do. The disease didn't go away soon. But it was never this bad before or after this day. Maybe God was actually looking out for us. During this awful time, I was still making money on the pigs.

We got a student from Poland in 1991. His name was Leszek Jabubowski. He talked very limited English. We had never had this experience before. Shortly after Leszek came to our farm, his dad died in Poland. I tried my best to tell him that he should go home, but he didn't want to go home. I was able to send him to school in Dodge Center to learn English several afternoons a week. This helped some, but I would see that it would take time. When I showed Leszek one of our tractors, he was afraid to get into the cab. We were still losing many pigs, and all this death on top of his dad's death was getting to Leszek. I couldn't possibly see how he could work in the fields safely. Finally, I talked to the head one of the MAST program and told him that Leszek would do better on a mainly livestock farm. I saw Leszek at the university a couple of years later. He was going to the university as a full-time student. He thanked me for the help I had given him at our farm. We had a very nice visit. I never saw him again. I don't know if he went back to Poland or if he stayed in the United States.

Tammy met Garry soon after this time. Garry's sister was Tammy's best friend at that time. He was on vacation from prison. I tried everything to get Tammy to leave him. Garry completely lied about his past to Tammy. A young girl going out with a man ten years older and in prison was not a good thing. I don't think any parent would like it. I told Tammy that she would have to live under my rules or move out. I made a big mistake telling Tammy this. She moved to an apartment in Kasson. The husband of Garry's sister, Milo, told me that Garry would never beat Tammy. He told me that Garry would always treat Tammy nicely. He kind of talked me into this. Maybe I was responsible for Tammy's death. Maybe I was too strict. I perhaps was a dominating father. Maybe Tammy felt that I was having too much control over her. This was a way to show me that I couldn't control her. I only wished that I would or could have handled this differently.

We got a French student, Dominic Girlais, early in July. He would stay with us through harvest then go to the University of Minnesota for the winter quarter and then come back in the spring and stay until the first of July. We left for Europe right after he got to our farm. Ruth, Brenda, and I were the only ones going. Bob was staying home to run the farm, and Doreen was already in Europe. She would meet us in Germany. We flew into Amsterdam, Netherlands, and then transferred to another plane to go to Frankfort, Germany. Dirk, our student from 1981, picked us up at the airport. He was now married and had a little boy. His wife had a five-hundred-acre farm. She ran the farm and had two workers. Dirk worked in town at a computer company. The first day they gave us a tour of the farm in an old carriage from the 1800s pulled by two black horses. The farm had a mansion that burned down in World War II. They lived in a large barn that was remodeled into a house. It was nice. When Dirk was with us on our farm, he said his wife wouldn't cook or keep house. They had a maid who cooked the meals and did the housework. East Germany had just become a part of West Germany. Dirk took us into East Germany one day. Every building was the same color: a drab brown. People from the east didn't want people from the west coming over the border. They changed the street signs so it was impossible to find places. I thought it was a golden opportunity to see East Germany now. It would soon change not to be under communism. One night we went over to Dirk's dad's house. Dirk's mother had died. Dirk's dad was living with a nice woman, and we all liked her. We had a barbecue on their patio. Afterward we started drinking schnapps, a German liquor. His dad couldn't talk English, and I couldn't talk German. He was wearing a tie when we came. At the end of the evening, I was wearing his tie, and we were carrying on a conversation. I had a terrible headache the next day. I almost learned a lesson. Only once after this time I was so drunk. Dirk took us up to the Baltic Sea, where George picked us up.

Finally, we got to meet George's wife. She was from Minnesota. I couldn't believe that they fell in love after one day. I took Ruth out four nights in a row after we met before she decided on marry me. George's dad always put George down or made fun of him. When George was at our house and when we had visitors, George always showed them pictures of him working and me sleeping in my chair. This made Ruth mad, and it affected my relationship with Ruth and me with him. George's dad poured me and himself a big glass of schnapps, and he only poured George a little and then said, "Drinking liquor causes people to lose brain cells, and you have none to lose." He did this every time he poured a drink. I immediately recognized where George got this from. We could have gotten along better if I had known this while he was living with us. We enjoyed seeing their farm and some of the neighboring farms. George took us to Denmark and met Steen about halfway to the farm where Steen was living.

Both Steen and Jan were very busy at this time. We spent two nights at the farm where Steen worked. We spent one night at Bullerup Bjeiggaard. Then we went to Sweden where we stayed with Jan for two days. Jan was busy at work and his parents entertained us one day. Neither one of them could speak English. Jan's dad was a policeman. He had a new Volvo, and he wanted me to drive the car. But it was difficult for me to drive the car. The speedometer didn't work. I could never tell how fast I was going. Soon Jan's dad saw my problem. He had me stop, and he got out of the car and opened the trunk. He hooked up the speedometer. He had a new car, and he didn't want to put any miles on the car. We went to a large water tower. The way I remember, it was four hundred feet tall. We took an elevator almost to the top. We had to climb stairs on the outside one story. I'm really afraid of heights. But this was so high that it didn't scare me. There was a super-large, open platform at the top. We could see forever! When we looked down, the cars below looked like small toys. When Jan told us where his parents were taking us, I dreaded it. But it turned out being one of the highlights of our vacation.

The next morning, Ruth, Brenda, and I got on a train taking us to Stockholm, Sweden. It was cheaper to just ride the train and not having assigned seats. Jan got us assigned seats. When we finally found the seats, someone was already sitting in them. I told them they were sitting in our seats. They told me that the seats were theirs. They were not going to move. I didn't know what to do. I told them again that the seats were ours. They told me again that they were not going to give up the seats. I looked for a conductor, but I didn't see one. Finally, I showed them the tickets. Finally, they got up reluctantly from their seats and left. The train ride took a few hours. Most places trees were growing on both sides of the track. The train ride soon became boring. When we got to Stockholm, they put the whole train on the ferry. We had a berth or a cabin to sleep in. It was a small room with a super-small bathroom. Maybe we were going first class as most passengers just slept in their seats. It was really pretty as the ferry pulled out of Stockholm. There were dozens of small islands. We were getting into Helsinki, Finland, in the morning.

We stayed the first two nights in Helsinki with Johan and his wife, Carina. They lived in a townhouse. Helsinki was the capital of Finland. Johan worked for a large bank in Finland. He wanted me to go to work with him and talk to a rather large group of his coworkers about American farming. All of a sudden, I was an expert on farming, and none of them knew whether I was telling them the truth or not. It was fun talking as an expert. I was at a meeting one time when the expert told us the meaning of *expert*. An "*ex*" is from the past and "*pert*" is a drip of water. The definition of *expert* was "has been dripped." All of a sudden, you don't feel so important anymore. We went through an old church and walked the streets. There were a lot of people playing music, singing, and wanting money. It was fun!

Next, we went to Johan's farm and met his family. We really had a good time with Johan's dad in 1988. That was a goal for him to go to the United States, and he did it shortly before he died. I missed him when we were in Finland. They had a sixty-acre farm where they raised pigs. Their farm was a part of a huge estate in the age of feudalism. At that time, Johan's ancestors worked at the big farm during the day and worked on their small farms nights and the days they had off. Johan took us to the estate for us to see it. They had a large mansion, much like we had in the south on the plantations. Finland, in some ways, was the prettiest country that we visited. We drove through forests and then beside a lake and then farmland. They grow mostly wheat and barley. The grain was turning yellow. Every few minutes we were going through a forest and then beside a lake and then through farmland and then a forest again. Johan's family had a big house and a little house. Johan's younger brother and his family lived in the bigger house, and Johan's mother lived in the small house. We stayed in the bigger house, and Johan stayed with his mother. We found it awkward. We didn't know them at all. We had problems with the language. But all in all, they treated us well, and looking back at the trip, I thought we had the most fun in Finland.

We rode the ferry back to Sweden. This time it was during the day. When we docked at Stockholm, there were a lot of taxis. We were staying overnight at a hotel. We had gotten off the ferry, and we were standing on the sidewalk with our luggage. All of a sudden, a man came up to us and asked if we would ride in a black cab. I, at that time, didn't know what a black cab was. He loaded the luggage in the trunk, and Ruth and Brenda got in the back seat. I got in the front seat with him. As we left, he opened up the glove compartment and took out a bottle of whiskey and offered me a drink. I immediately declined. We didn't get in a taxi. We got into a regular car. I got really scared. Where was he taking us? I had a lot of money on me. Was he going to rob me? Was my family safe? What was he going to do to them? All of a sudden, my mind was going a hundred miles an hour. What had I gotten into? I was scared out of my mind. We didn't know where the hotel was, so we didn't know where he was taking us. Suddenly we saw a hotel in the middle of the city. The car stopped in the front of the hotel. What a relief! He got the luggage out of the trunk. I thought the fee he charged was reasonable, but I didn't give him a tip. If he hadn't offered me a drink, maybe I never would have known what a black cab was.

The hotel was really nice. By the time we got checked into the hotel, it was evening. We found a restaurant nearby. After we ate, we walked around the city a little. Stockholm was so clean we couldn't believe it. When we got up in the morning and looked out of our window, we couldn't believe what happened during the night. There were papers and beer cans everywhere. How could this get so bad during just one night? We got a regular taxi to take us to the airport this time. We flew from Stockholm to Amsterdam, Netherlands. The airport at Amsterdam was really easy to find where to go. We flew from Amsterdam to the Twin Cities. Bob picked us up at the airport. That night I had my thirtieth graduation party from high school. I had several classmates ask me what I was up to. I said, "I had breakfast in Stockholm, Sweden, lunch in Amsterdam, Netherlands, and now dinner with you." I had just eaten three meals in three different counties in one day. I was trying to get make my classmates to think that I was more important then I really was.

In the summer of 1991, there was a farm that had a for sale sign on it. It was one and a half mile south of us on the road to the west of our farm. It was the Renchin farm. I had known the Renchin' ever since we bought our farm. I had visited them many times. At the end of the seventies, they sold the buildings and ten acres and moved to Hayfield. There were seventy acres left. They both were dead now, and their children were selling the farm. If I remember right, they had eleven kids. On the radio station that I was listening to, there was a bank in Austin that wanted new loans. I met with a banker and talked him into giving Bob a beginning farmer loan with a little down payment. The farm was for sale at $ 1,100 per acre. Bob had just graduated from high school that year, and he had bought his first farm.

Jan and his boss Staffen visited our farm in September 1991. Staffen never combined corn before, and they wanted to. Corn was not really ready to be combined yet. They wanted to try it by themselves. Staffen wanted to learn how to set the combine. Jan had learned it when he was on our farm in 1983. It was really hard to set the combine when the corn was to wet. But I let them take the combine out to the field and play with it. I was working on getting the bins cleaned out for the crops we were going to harvest. At least, Staffen could say that he had combined corn. Staffen again offered Bob a job if he came to Sweden.

A FATHER'S QUEST

Tammy left her apartment and moved in with Garry in the Twin Cities. They both had jobs, working at the same place. I don't remember what they did. Tammy told us that she liked working there. Kayla was born on March 28, 1992. When Kayla was born, Ruth and I decided that we would have to accept Garry and make the best of the situation we were in. The next day, our whole family along with Dominic Girlais, a French student from MAST program, went to the hospital to see Tammy and the baby. Now we were grandparents. I had looked forward to being grandpa ever since Tammy was born. We took Garry out to eat after our visit with Tammy and Kayla. Every two weeks we went up to visit them unless they came down to our farm. On April 5, Tammy, Garry and Kayla came down to Waseca and had their pictures taken with the rest of my family. The picture was for my parents' fiftieth wedding anniversary. We had baby pictures of Kayla taken. I paid for them.

In July, I got another MAST student. His name was Garelt Perdoh, and he was from the Netherlands. Bob was going to trade school in Austin. He had to do a three-month internship somewhere. Jan's boss, Staffen, had offered Bob a job last fall when he visited us on our farm. So Bob went to Sweden. Bob never learned to talk Swedish, but he could understand most things. When Bob was disking a field of combined wheat, a spark from a rock started the field on fire. The fire got fairly large, but Bob kept his wits and was able to put the fire out. After that they called Bob the fireman. We were now farming all the Hrtanek farm. The building was sitting empty. In July 1992, I made a deal with Adline Hrtanek that Tammy, Garry, and Kayla could live in the house without paying any rent. I went with Tammy to Attorney Brian Weber's office to draw up a three-year lease on the house protecting Tammy and Garry. They could live in the house free for three years, and any improvements they put in the house, they could take them out when they moved. Adline didn't want to spend anything on the house. I paid the cost of having this lease drawn up.

Garelt and I took our big truck up to the cities and moved them down to the Hrtanek farm. Soon after they moved on the farm, Garelt and I took our backhoe over to the farm and spent several days burying all the junk that was there. Tammy went back to work in the nursing home in Dodge Center. Garry got a job at MTM in Dodge Center working nights. From July to the next January, we often watched Kayla.

We built a large porch unto the south side of the house. Garry helped us. There's nothing more fun than a farmer sitting on a porch in the summer and watching it rain, especially when you need rain.

Tammy and Garry had lived in the house for a few months when Garry's brother and his girlfriend moved in with them. Tammy didn't like this. Somehow Adline found out that they were living in the house. She had agreed that Tammy and Garry could live there free, but if anyone else was living with them, she wanted $200-a-month rent. I reluctantly went up to talk to Garry and his brother Terry about this. They weren't very happy about this. Terry paid Adline $200 and moved out before the next month's rent was due.

Year 1992 was not a good year for us. We had made a little money, but it was not enough. I was happy that Tammy and Kayla were close to us. But my relationship with Garry was up and down. I became really depressed about everything. I decided to get a night job working at Schmitt Printing in Byron in December. I went to work at three in the afternoon and got off at eleven at night. I thought that I could get up at eight and have plenty of time to get my work done. But I soon found that I couldn't get to sleep. I needed to unwind for a couple of hours after I got home. I was really tired when I got up at eight. The work was really monotonous. I worked with a man from Thailand cutting paper, and I could not understand his English. My job was to stack the cut paper on a pallet. I had worked with many students that I had trouble understanding. I could put up with this problem. But when I understood how to do my job, he changed the way he wanted it done. I was always wrong in his eyes. I soon got over my depression. If working here was something I would have to do forever, then I would really have something to be depressed for. This was a cheap way to get over depression compared to going to a doctor. I never cashed a paycheck until the end of January when I quit working at Schmitt Printing. I had enough money to go on vacation.

Sarah was born on January 15, 1993. She was born at home because Garry didn't want to take Tammy to the hospital. Kayla held Tammy's hand the whole time. When it was a breech birth, Garry finally called the ambulance. Sarah was born at home. Ruth called me at work that Tammy had her baby. The next day we visited Tammy in the hospital. Tammy's doctor told us that someone from above was watching out for Sarah. He said it was a miracle that Sarah didn't die at birth. I had questions why this happened, but I didn't ask. I supposed I didn't want to know. That was a huge mistake on my part. We watched Kayla at our home when Tammy and Sarah were in the hospital. We visited Tammy and Sarah at home on January 17.

Garry's mother was going to watch Kayla and Sarah while Tammy was working, but she did it for a short time. Sarah was really fussy for the first six months of her life, and she cried almost all the time while she was awake. It got so that Ruth was the only one that would watch her. We watched the girls almost every day that Tammy worked for some time.

We decided to visit Ray and Alice Borgen in Rockford, Illinois, in 1993. We were going to take Ruth's mother, Edna, and Ruth's Aunt Helen with us. Helen's husband, John, had died. We left very early and stopped for breakfast at Lanesboro. We then went to Galena, Illinois. It was a really neat town. The town reminded us being in a town in the 1800s. They had a large brick house that President Grant once lived. Helen was a schoolteacher, and she really liked history. She really liked the tour, and she talked about the trip to her family for the rest of her life. She thanked me over and over for taking her on the trip. When she died, her family wanted me to be a pallbearer at her funeral.

I had a lot of optimism after quitting at Schmitt Printing. I was over my depression. We got our second student from Sweden, Carl Cederstrom, in the spring. In April, I saw an ad in the paper with some slats for sale. Maybe we could put slats in our old barn. We would save a lot of work not using the barn cleaner. The slats were on a farm by Kellogg, Minnesota. I hauled them home in my two-ton truck. The load was too heavy. There was a long and steep hill going out of Kellogg. Five miles an hour was as fast as we could go, and it took forever. We were lucky that we never met a policeman. I was really overweight, and I can't imagine how much the ticket would have cost.

We had a hay mow in the barn. It had a lot of posts holding it up. How would I manage to hold it up after I built a fifteen-foot-wide pit under the barn? I hired Richard Finley, a neighbor teenager, to help us so we would have a four-person team plus Ruth. I rented a large compressor with an air jackhammer. I started out running the jackhammer, and the rest cleaned up the broken cement. They all told me that I had the easier job. When we got the first floor out, we found another one. When we got the second floor out, we found a third floor. I knew that a barn had burned down on this spot before, but maybe two barns burned down. By then everyone ran the jackhammer. Our wrists got so sore that it became impossible to run the jackhammer, but we had more concrete to bust out to. What had I gotten into? It was now a poor idea. But I had the slats, so we would keep on.

We decided to dig the pit eight feet deep. I rented a dirt conveyor to take the dirt out of the pit. We had a small skid loader, and Bob used it to put the dirt on the conveyer. I broke up the dirt with a pickax. Carl and Richard put the dirt from the skid loader to the conveyer. Soon water started coming into the hole we were digging. The year went down in the history books on the rain we had. What would I do now? I was at my wit's end. We got a long, heavy rope and hooked it on the skid loader, and we hooked the other end unto a tractor. Ruth ran the tractor. Bob ran the skid loader as far as he was able into the dirt. I shoveled the mud onto the skid loader. Ruth pulled the skid loader backward with the tractor so he could dumb it on the conveyer. The mud didn't dump, so Carl and Richard had to pull it off. The conveyor wasn't made to work with mud, so we had lots of problems. It took us five days to dig the pit.

Next, we had to pour a footing. We had a sump pump, but it didn't keep up with the water that was coming into the pit. We managed to form up the footings in the water and poured the concrete into the water. Next, we poured a two-inch floor in the water. The floor helped to keep the water out of the pit. But there was always some water. Next, we had to build walls out of concrete blocks eight feet tall. None of us had any experience with block-laying, and it wasn't pretty. But I was certain that the blocks would hold the slats and the pigs. Then we had to build a beam over the center of the pit. It would be an engineering feat. We would need an architect. I made a drawing where the pens would be. Then we went down in the pit and stacked twelve-inch tiles up to where the beam would be. Then we formed the beam out of wood to pour the beam. We had to build it strong enough that it would hold the concrete. Carl wheeled the concrete over the beam and also filled the tile. We were successful! Next, we sat the posts that were going to hold the hay mow floor up and took out the temporary posts that we had. Then we set the slats and built the pens. Finally, we were done, and we put pigs in the barn. We almost gave up several times. Maybe I was born to be too stubborn to ever give up. I would have to be stubborn many more times to get through life.

Brenda and Carl

We got along with Carl really good. He spent a lot of time with Brenda. At first I thought he was a slow worker. He never moved fast. But I soon learned that he got a lot of work done at the end of the day. When he went to the shop to get tools, he never had to go again. The work he did was always right the first time.

Lester Priebe had a sale. He had a collection of old John Deeres. He was a neighbor when we lived on the Frodel Farm. I knew him well. Herbert Hokanson had the AR John Deere tractor that I had first seen when I was six years old. It was the biggest tractor I had ever seen. At Herbert's sales, I went prepared to buy the tractor. I bid $850, and Lester bought it for $900. I was going to buy the AR this time. Gary Pittman, my brother-in-law, was standing next to me while the bidding was going on. Every time when the auctioneer asked for a bid, I nodded my head. Maybe I was bidding against myself. I had no idea what the bid was, but I knew that I was going to buy the AR this time. When the auctioneer said, "Sold," I looked to Gary and asked him, "What did I pay for the tractor?" Gary said that I had paid, $1,700. I had finally got the AR! In the end, we had a very bad year. But $1,700 didn't make much difference. I drove the AR forty miles home. Bob followed me in the pickup. Bob had to go home to get more gas for me. Ruth was really mad when Bob told her that I bought the AR. I was really lucky that Bob went home for gas. It gave Ruth time to cool down. I used the AR on augers so I got some use out of it. As Kayla and Sarah got older, I gave them many rides over the years. I have never used the AR after Tammy died. Suddenly I never had time to enjoy the AR.

In September, I knew I was in trouble. How would I ever get out of this one? Farming was bad for all farmers. I knew that some of the farmers were not going to make it. I would have to prepare myself to be able to take advantage of what could be ahead. I bought a three-year-old combine through a lease program. I didn't own it; I was just paying rent for the use of the combine. John Deere paid me cash for my old combine. I was able to completely pay for all my machinery loans. That way I could borrow money on my machinery to take advantage of anything that could come up.

We never had a summer in 1993. The weatherman said we were getting all the cold weather from a volcano that we had in Washington state in 1992. The corn stayed yellow the whole year. Once in a while, the temperature got into the low seventies, but not often. It was the worst year financially that we had. Looking back on it now, maybe it was the best year we had. The government come up with some programs that helped, but we lost money big-time. Much of our land needed tile, but the bank would never loan money for tile. They couldn't repossess tile. If we had a dry year, I made a little money. If it was a wet year, we went backward. Our profit was always up and down. In the fall, when I met with my banker, I said, "I'll give you two alternatives. Give me a loan to tile out all my land, or sell me out." They finally agreed to give me a loan to tile out all my land. Maybe an angel was with me. Ever since 1993, I've never lost money again. Every year since, we have always had a good profit.

On my birthday, December 21, Darrel Janes came up to our farm. Darrel rented the Sutherland farm just south of our farm. He said he was broke. He never wanted to go through a year like this again. He was having a sale and was quitting farming. He wanted me to rent the Sutherland farm. It was four hundred acres. He said he owned an eighty-acre farm next to the Renchin farm on the west side. He wanted me to rent this farm too. A few years ago, a neighbor called me and wanted me to go to the state capitol to lobby for a bill. There was six of us that went. Darrel Janes was one of them. I had known Darrel before but not good. Evidently, we really hit it off good on this trip. At the time I really thought the trip was a waste of time. Maybe I was wrong. I was able to rent the Sutherland for $95 an acre. Bob rented the Janes farm. I told Bob that we got in over our heads. He would have to get a job. Bob went to work at MTM at night. They agreed that Bob could have some time off in the spring and fall. Bob picked up Garry and took him to work. I had a $25,000 limit on a credit card that charged 9 percent interest. I used this credit card to finance Bob's farm money needs.

In 1994, we got a student from Denmark. His name was Fleming Rasmunsan. We got along with him great, and he liked our farm. There was another student from Denmark. His name was Rene Sorenson. He lived on a hog farm with a lot of employees' north of Dodge Center. Rene wasn't satisfied, and he wanted to go home. Fleming told me that if Rene went home, he was going home too. I told Fleming that I had work enough for the two of them. Rene moved to our farm. I really got in trouble with the people who were running the program at the university. I realized that having students was soon going to be over.

Fleming, Rene, and my father

The sheriff's office got a call from Tammy. Enclosed is a report from the deputy that was called.

> On 10-1-94 at approx. 02:27 hrs., I Deputy Trihey & Deputy Bentzen arrived at CA 29-01, The Tammy & Garry residence in ref. to a domestic between the two of them. While enroute, Dispatch informed me (via) radio that Tammy reported that she had been hit by Garry.
> Upon arrival, Deputy Bentzen & myself separated Garry and Tammy. At this point, Tammy was very upset & crying & Garry was very calm. Once they were separated, I interviewed Tammy. Tammy reported that Garry had been gone most of the evening & returned home approx. 01:50, grabbed a twelve pack of beer & was going to leave again. Tammy said Garry

would not tell her where he was going. She said she tried to make him stay home but he pushed her out of the way and got into his car. Tammy said she got into the car also & demanded he tell her where he was going & Garry would just reply "none of your business I have to take care of some business." Tammy then reported that Garry had hit her in the nose with an open hand; as she described, "pushing her nose up & into her face." I did observe that Tammy's nose was reddened and possibly swollen.

I explained to Tammy that I would be placing Garry under arrest for fifth-degree domestic assault and transporting him to jail or detox, depending on his condition. Tammy did not want Garry arrested or removed.

I then spoke to Garry, and he denied ever touching Tammy. I informed him that he was being arrested for fifth-degree domestic assault. I did observe that Garry was under the influence of an alcoholic beverage and transported him to the Rochester Detox Facility. Throughout the investigation, Garry was cooperative and well behaved.

On the Assault Release Form, Tammy wrote a statement:

> I want Garry to be at home with me and our two girls. He has never [then she crossed out these three words and signed her name and dated it, 10-3-94]

Garry was finally arrested on October 19, 1994, for beating up Tammy. I didn't find out about this until I got the report on Tammy's death in early 1998. If I would have known this at the time, maybe I would have checked into his past. Maybe Tammy would still be alive. Tammy reported Garry to the sheriff's office and filed a complaint against him. He was charged with fifth-degree domestic assault. Garry pleaded guilty and was sentenced to pay a $246.50

fine, to report to thirty days in jail, and was suspended for one year with the following conditions:

> No similar violations, meet with Julie, have a CD evaluation and follow recommendations.

State of Minnesota,
Vs. ORDER TO SHOW CAUSE
Garry, Defendant.

IT IS HEREBY ORDERED that the defendant above named show cause in this Court on the 9th day of March, 1995, at 9:00a.m. why treatment has not been completed.

You must appear and explain to the court why you have not entered outpatient treatment.

Failure to appear at that time may result in a bench warrant being issued which will result in an additional $50.00 costs.

Dated: February 16, 1995 BY THE COURT
LAWRENCE E. AGERTER
JUDGE OF DISTRICT COURT

This was something else I didn't know until I got the report on Tammy's death in 1998. But Tammy told me a few things eventually.

COMPLAINT

Your Complainant is David Bentzen, a deputy for the Dodge County Sheriff's Department. The Dodge County Sheriff's Department is under contract to provide police protection for the city of Dodge Center, Dodge County, Minnesota. Your Complainant bases his complaint upon facts obtained through his own investigation and from sources whom he believes to be reliable.

On December 2, 1994, at 0001 hours while eastbound on Main Street in the City of Dodge Center at 4th Avenue East, your Complainant noted a vehicle ahead on East Main Street next to another vehicle off the right shoulder of the road. The vehicle off the road was a van, license no. 079-BON. The van had hit and was resting against a utility pole at the left front corner of the van.

Your Complainant saw the brake lights go out and the driver cross over to the car on the road which was stopped alongside to the left. The driver entered the car on the passenger side. The car then left the scene of the accident and continued East on Main Street. Your complainant was able to stop the car at the intersection of Airport Drive South and 3th Street East. The driver of the van that was in the accident was identified as Defendant Garry.

Your Complainant noted the Defendant to have a strong odor of an alcoholic beverage on his breath and from his person while speaking. Defendant also had slurred speech while talking and watery and bloodshot eyes. Defendant was unsteady on his feet and swayed while talking. Defendant was advised of his rights under the Implied Consent Advisory and refused to take a test to determine if the Defendant was under the influence of alcohol or a controlled substance. A check of Defendant's driving record showed that his license had been suspended.

The above-facts constitute the Complainant's basis for believing that the above-named Defendant, on the 2nd day of December,

1994, at Dodge Center, Minnesota, in the above-named county, committed the following described:

The Complainant brought seven charges against Garry. One was for one year in jail. Several of the charges was ninety days in jail. They sentenced Garry to have treatment for his alcoholism. Finally, he went, but Tammy told us that he went directly from treatment to a bar. He was not allowed to drive without a license. That didn't make a difference.

Tammy was also arrested at the same time. Garry had the van in Tammy's name. She was charged for NO PROOF OF INSURANCE and ALLOW UNLICENSED DRIVER. This was something that Tammy never told me. I was really surprised when I read it in the report. When I read the report early in 1998 Tammy was given a court appointed attorney, Neil Simonson. He had the defendant enter a not guilty plea. On April 30, 1996, the tickets were dismissed.

Tammy and Garry got married in Las Vegas on February 17, 1995. Tammy thought that she could change Garry after they were married. At this time, we didn't know whether the marriage was a good thing or maybe it was a bad thing. Ruth and I were helpless to do anything about it. I said I would never walk Tammy down the aisle to marry Garry. At least I didn't have to decide at the last minute. The girls stayed with us from February 16 to 21. Finally, I had a wedding dance for them at the Stage Coach Ballroom in Mantorville and paid for everything. We saw Tammy in her wedding dress.

Sarah, Tammy, and Kayla

In 1995, we got a white student from South Africa. I never got along with him. All he talked about was that he was waiting for his parents to die. Then he was going to have a lot of money. He soon left. Bob quit his job and came home to farm. We never had another student.

In early 1995, a good friend of mine, Lyle Walker, was dying of lung cancer. Lyle was a member of our church. Ruth, his wife, and Lyle always came early. Ruth immediately sat in a pew, and Lyle always stayed in the entryway and greeted everyone that came to church. We always came to church later than Lyle, so he was waiting to greet us when we come. Lyle always came into church and sat next to his wife, Ruth, just when the services were starting. When Lyle was young, he lived in Waseca County close to my grandfather, Ed Larson. When we were together, he talked about my grandpa many times. This was always really fun for me. While living next to my grandpa, Lyle's dad decided to buy his first tractor. The dealer wanted his dad to try plowing with a tractor. When Lyle's dad came to the end of the field, he hollered, "Whoa, whoa," like he always said to the horses. The tractor didn't stop until it ran into a fence. When the tractor finally stopped, his dad refused to get on a tractor again. The dealer had to take the tractor back to the dealership. A year later, he finally bought a tractor, and Lyle always drove it. The day I visited Lyle, all he wanted to talk about was the shop that I was going to build. I told him that it would be impossible. I didn't have enough money to even think about building a shop. I tried to talk about different things, but Lyle only wanted to talk about the shop that I would be building. I never saw him again. I thought I had a bad cold, and I didn't want to visit someone with lung cancer. The cold never went away regardless of what I did. After Lyle died, I went to a doctor. I found out that I had polyps in my head. I didn't have a cold, and I wished that I would have visited Lyle more.

In July 1995, I made a deal with Adeline Hrtanek to buy the Hrtanek farm. Roads went through the farm. The buildings were on forty acres. There was another forty across the road to the east and an eighty across the road to the north. Garry was now my son-in-law. He was Tammy's husband and the father of our grandchildren. I had hoped that Garry would buy the entire forty that the buildings was on. I had encouraged Garry to save money to buy the place ever since they had moved there. After all, they were not paying any rent. If he could save enough to buy the forty, I was prepared to help him build a hog house, and maybe he could farm with us. It was a dream of mine, but it soon became clear that it wasn't a dream of Garry's.

Garry had threatened us that they would move far away if they had to move off the Hrtanek farm. I did not want this to happen. I was fearful for both Tammy and her girls if this happened. I then promised Garry sell him five acres and the building for $7,500. He promised me that he would save some money so he could buy it. He had told me this many times before, but he never saved any money. When I closed the deal in the fall, the county would not let me split off the five acres without putting in a new septic system. Adeline knew that I was going to sell Tammy and Garry the buildings. I got her to agree to pay one half of the costs of the septic system. The lawyer's fee was also much higher than I thought it would be from splitting off the buildings. I told Garry that I would still sell him the buildings for $7,500, but he would have to pay one half of the costs to put in a new septic system. The total cost would be $4,000. I had to pay Garry's share of the septic system on November 14, 1995.

When I bought the farm, I was planning on getting the money from Tammy and Garry before the end of the year. On December 20, I had to pay cash for the five acres, and I hadn't arranged any financing for it. Garry had trouble getting a loan. During this time, he bought an almost-new snowmobile and charged it at Commercial Credit in Rochester. He soon afterward bought two more snowmobiles. In January 1996, TCF bank in Rochester started to work on the loan application. Darrel Gentz called me several times about the loan. He wanted to know why I was selling the place so cheap to Tammy and Garry. They had appraised the five acres and the buildings for $50,000. I was having second thoughts about selling them the place. I really needed the money before the first of the year. Now I had to borrow the money to close on the farm deal and didn't need the money now. In a way, Garry had backed out of the deal we had by not paying me by the end of the year. I thought about backing out of the deal, but I had promised him, and I am a man of my word. I also had to think that Garry had told me that if they had to move off the Hrtanek farm, they would move far away. I didn't want this to happen. The bank made a loan for $36,000. After paying me off and paying for the snowmobiles, there was $19,000 left. I asked Darrel Grentz if they could hold the $19,000 in escrow until the house was fixed up, but he wouldn't do that. He said the appraised value was enough for the loan without fixing up the house.

Also in 1995, Darrel Janes wanted to sell Bob the eighty that he had been renting to Bob. He wanted $1,500 per acre or $120,000. He wanted a $30,000 down payment, and he would finance the farm on a contract for deed for twenty years at 9 percent interest. It was about the same interest as we were paying. Bob bought the farm and tore out the fence between the two farms.

Starting in early January 1996, Garry was in jail nights and weekends for the drunk driving accident he had in December 1994. One night when it was way below zero, Tammy took Garry back to jail in Rochester. Her car broke down, and she called me. I went to Rochester and picked up Tammy and the girls. They were all frozen stiff. The furnace was not working properly, and it was cold at their home. They stayed the night with us. The next day I went with

Tammy to Rochester and arranged with Moody Mobile to pull her car in and fix it. Garry was to serve three months in jail, but they left him out after one month. Tammy and the girls stayed with us during the month because their house was too cold.

Around this time, when I was in the barn doing chores, I started hearing voices. It was only in the south alleyway. How can this happen? Was I losing my mind? The voice said that I was going to lose a child. It couldn't be an angel or God. Why would God want me to lose a child? In my mind, I thought that it was the devil. The voice wanted me to pick which child it would be. I argued with the voice and told the voice why I couldn't lose any children. I had to go in the barn twice a day, and I started to hate it. I only heard the voice in the barn. Hogs were cheap at that time. The value of corn was really going up. Maybe I would make more money selling the corn instead of feeding pigs. I quit raising hogs when I sold the last one. I no longer had to go in the barn, so the voices stopped. It never left my mind, but I didn't think it would ever happen. I had heard voices several times in my life, but I have never heard voices again.

At the loan closing on February 16, 1996, I talked Tammy into giving me the $19,000. I would put it in funds held at Farm Credit where it would draw around 8 percent interest. That way the money would still be available when they started fixing up the house in the spring. Tammy and Garry both signed the check from the bank, and I immediately went to Farm Credit and deposited the money and got a receipt, which I gave to Tammy. Tammy, Garry, Ruth, and I went out to supper at Country Buffet. The next day Tammy came over and said that Garry was really upset. I had his money, and he wanted it back. I told Tammy it was her money. He never could have borrowed it if I hadn't sold the place to her so cheaply. On early Monday morning, Garry called me. He was really upset. He had to buy materials for the house right away, and he wanted the $19,000 back right away. I finally agreed to give him $7,000, and he had some materials delivered. The materials sat outside in the yard untouched until May and June.

Right after Garry got the $7,000, he started missing a lot of work. It was at this time that Tammy would call at five o'clock in the

A FATHER'S QUEST

morning to ask us if we could watch the girls. Garry was at home, but she didn't feel safe leaving the girls with him. I was really regretting that I sold the place to them. On April 12, 1996, Tammy called and said that Garry wanted the rest of the money now. I told her to come over. She came alone. We sat in our living room, and I had a long talk with her. I told her that the money was hers and not his. I told her that I had done a huge favor when I sold her the place for $7,500 when it was appraised for $50,000. I told her she had better be sure that Garry didn't blow this money and that she had better be sure that they didn't lose the place to the bank, because I was going to be really mad if that happened. I then gave her two checks made out in her name only—one check for the money and one for the interest.

She then left. Bob and I were working down by the grain bins loading some corn when Tammy's car came in the yard. It was Tammy, Garry, and the girls. Garry was really mad. He wanted his money, and he wanted it now. I told him that it was Tammy's money. He said he borrowed it so it was his. I told him that he never could have borrowed it if I hadn't sold the place so cheaply to Tammy. I told him that I did it for Tammy, not him. He then said, "Tammy had told me you wouldn't give her the money." I didn't know what to say at this point. The only thing I could say was, "I had given the money to Tammy." They then left. I had put way too much pressure on Tammy. I really felt sorry for Tammy when they left. What would he do to Tammy to get the money?

Shortly afterward, Tammy left Garry. The first night, she and the two girls spent with Doreen, who was living in an apartment in Byron. Garry came to the door and tried to break in. Garry shouted obscene words. Doreen was really scared and told Tammy that she couldn't stay with her anymore. The second day, on a Saturday, Tammy and the girls spent the day and night with us. That afternoon, we all went on a tour at the Al-Corn plant in Claremont. Bob and I owned shares in the plant. We spent money that we didn't have to buy the shares. I was president of the Dodge County Corn Growers. I had given speeches promoting ethanol. I couldn't live with myself if I didn't invest in the plant. Garry called early Sunday morning asking where Tammy was. I told him she was here and she was sleeping. I refused to wake Tammy. I then hung up on him. Late in the afternoon, he called again. This time he talked to Tammy. She then left the girls with us and went home. She came back an hour later to get the girls. I told Tammy not to go back. She said, "If I don't go back, he will take the girls away from me." I said, "I will hire an attorney, and he will never get the girls." I would never bring up the costs to her or to anyone. I promised Tammy that there was no way she would lose the girls. She was scared out of her mind, and she took the girls and went home. I have spent a lot of time thinking about all this after Tammy's death. I don't think that Tammy thought she could ever lose her girls to Garry, who had a criminal record. Maybe Garry had told Tammy that he would kill the girls if she left him? Maybe this was the time when he started planning Tammy's death?

Sarah, Brenda, Bob, Kayla, Tammy, and Doreen

Shortly after that, he lost his job. Also at that time, I was working in the field across from their house and a doll buggy that belonged to the girls had blown in the field. After Tammy came home from work, I took the doll buggy up to the house. When I got up to the house, Garry ordered me to leave.

I said, "Do you mean after the deal I gave you on this house, you are not going to let me come up to see my daughter and grandchildren?"

He then said, "You screwed me when you sold the place to me. I'm going to get a restraining order on you."

Tammy sat on the front steps of the house. She had a blank, scary look on her face. She never said anything. I just left. I didn't want to do anything that would make it worse for Tammy.

In June, Garry brought a $150,000 accidental family insurance policy. It pays 90 percent if Tammy died, or $135,000. He signed her name on the application. Garry didn't have a job, and he had no intention of getting another job. In light of what's taken place during the last preceding few months, I doubt that he was concerned for Tammy's security. If he was concerned for her security, why didn't he tell her? He should have had Tammy sign the application. By buying a family policy, he could say the policy was for him and not Tammy. I never knew about this until a year after Tammy's death. How could I have been so stupid about everything that was going on?

After quitting raising pigs, I would have ten thousand bushels more corn to sell. I had sold enough grain to pay off my operating loan and to pay all the bills due the rest of the year. If I was not raising pigs, I would have twenty thousand bushels of corn left to sell. Now I was certain that corn would go to $5 a bushel. I started thinking about building a shop. When corn got to $4.75 a bushel, I sold all the corn I had left. I could build the shop and pay cash for it. The size of the shop was getting bigger as the price of corn was going up. Now I could build a shop fifty-four by eighty feet. Corn could have gotten cheaper, and then I would have to build a smaller shop. Corn finally went to $5 a bushel. When Lyle told me that I was going to build a shop a year ago, I was certain that it would not be possible. Now I was paying cash for it. We didn't have to take out a loan. I started thinking, "Did Lyle have a part in this?" Then I was thinking about the Hrtanek farm. There was no way that I could buy it. Then after Helen died, I bought the farm. I was broke in 1985. Ruth's dad, Elmer, died in 1985, and my grandmother died in 1886. Suddenly, the farm started to prosper. After my Grandpa Larson died in 1977,

I built a large hog house, a machine shed, and two bins and put up a drying system in a short time. After my Grandpa McColley died, I bought the farm the same year. Did these people have an influence in these things? How could they? It was probably only a coincidence, or was it? That was something that happened that caused me to think about it a lot.

On July 15, Jan, our student from Sweden, and his wife came to visit us. It was really fun to see him again.

When we got the investigation report on Tammy's death, there was a report written to Deputy Rollie Spriegel from Sgt. B. Schei from Olmstead County. That was news to me. During early December 1996, this writer, B. Schei, was approached by Eva and Nado Bernard. They asked me if I knew a Garry who lived over in Dodge County as he had married their niece and they were concerned because he was not treating her very well and they were concerned for her safety. I told them at the time that I had known a Garry in the past and that if it was the same person, he would not come out very high on my list as a person that I would want to have around me.

Later on, I was advised by the Bernards that their niece had died in a fire and that they were concerned that there might be more going on than meets the eye. I was told that the family was not happy with the investigation that was conducted into the death, and they wanted to know what if anything could be done. I was told that the family had more information on the case and that they believed that the case was closed without further follow-up because of a threatened lawsuit by Garry's attorney.

I gave the Bernards the following information:

1. They should contact the investigator involved with the case and tell him about their concerns.
2. I contacted Deputy Spriegel and was told that there was nothing more to be done and the BCA had already looked the case over and it was fine.
3. That if they did not feel after contact with the investigator and their opinion had changed, they should request a

meeting with the Dodge county attorney and request that Sheriff Weber be present at the meeting.
4. That if they believed they were not being listened to, they could contact the Minnesota Attorney General's Office.

Now is the time to read chapter 1 again.

Chapter 13

The First Year after Tammy's Death

The nightmares were about to start and only to get worse. It would soon be hell on earth! We couldn't believe that Tammy was gone. It was almost impossible to sleep. As a man, I figured it was my responsibility to keep my wife and children safe. I had failed Tammy. I felt terribly guilty about this. I now felt I had to keep Tammy's two girls safe. For Tammy's sake, I felt it was my responsibility to provide Kayla and Sarah with as safe and as happy a life as possible Ruth and I had lived in fear since Tammy met Garry in the spring of 1991. He was on vacation from prison, and his sister was Tammy's best friend at that time. We did everything to discourage her, but it wasn't enough. We should have checked more on his past, but we didn't know how do to it. Maybe now I should fear for my own life. I fear for the lives of my granddaughters. We now know how it turned out. Tammy was dead.

Tuesday morning, January 14 after lying awake many nights thinking about all this and having many questions, Ruth and I went to the sheriff's office. We learned some shocking things that we didn't know. The main one being that Garry had beaten Tammy several times. We knew he didn't treat her nicely, but we didn't think he was beating Tammy. Garry's brother-in-law Milo, who was the husband of Sherry, Garry's sister, told me many times that Garry would never beat Tammy. I had always believed him. We knew that Garry had gone out Friday nights and came home Sunday many times. We also found out that Garry served 2.5 years in prison. We thought it had been only one year. We had been told that five years ago, he was

A FATHER'S QUEST

living with a woman and an older man. This woman had conned this man out of some money and that Garry had taken the blame for her and that he got only one year in prison. That was what he had told Tammy. We would find some time later that it was a lie. He didn't take the blame for her. We now had learned from several sources, including the sheriff's office, that Garry had been in trouble his whole life—theft, burglary, stolen goods across state lines, assault, drugs, DWI, etc.

Next, we were at the nursing home were Tammy had worked. They had called us to come up to see them. They had taken up a collection. As soon as we got there, they told us to close the door and they told some things that were extremely shocking. Tammy had come to work with black eyes. They absolutely didn't believe the reports of the fire in the paper. They thought that Garry was responsible for Tammy's death. They told us about the life insurance policy on Tammy. We contacted the sheriff's office. They checked the records and said that it was true. Kayla and Sarah were the beneficiaries. We then went to see a Rochester lawyer, Steven Youngquist, and hired him to look into this. When he checked into this, he said it was true. He said that we as grandparents had the right to petition the court to be appointed guardians of this money so we would be sure that our granddaughters would get the money. When we went to file the papers to do this, we were told Garry was the beneficiary. When we called the sheriff's office and asked them how they could be wrong about this, they said it had been changed January 1, 1997. Tammy died on January 5, 1997. He changed it five days before her death. This didn't seem right. Why were the girls blamed for her death? Three weeks later, we were told that Garry was always the beneficiary, and on January 1, the policy was raised from $40,000 to $100,000. How could Garry raise the policy from $40,000 to $100,000, and Tammy was dead five days later? Why didn't they arrest him for murder? How could so many people be so wrong about this? The more we found out, the more it was looking like it was a cover-up!

On our January 14 visit at the nursing home, we were told that Tammy had been coming to work with bruises and black eyes and Garry had been beating her. Afterward we went back to the sheriff's office and told Rollie Spriggle, who was the detective, about this. He said, "We know that he was beating your daughter. We have police records to prove it."

I then hired another lawyer in Rochester to check if Garry had a record of beating up any other women. I had to pay a $2,000 retainer fee to get her to work for us. She found out that Garry had been arrested and found guilty eight times for beating up women. One was for Garry beating up his first wife in California. We were starting to see how violent he was. We found out later that Brenda, our youngest daughter, was at Tammy's house in October visiting with her in the kitchen when Garry came in from the living room. He started swearing at Tammy and took his open hand and pushed on Tammy's chin so hard that she fell on the floor. If only I had known this earlier, maybe Tammy would still be alive. When a man beats up women, he is not a man anymore. He is simply a lowlife figure that doesn't deserve to live.

On Friday afternoon, Dorilyn Franko came to our house and spent all afternoon with us. I think she was from Victims' Services. She again told us that Garry had beaten Tammy. She painted a very clear picture of what kind of a person that Garry was. I told her that Sarah's birth had always bothered me. She was born at home. We were led to believe that there wasn't time to go to the hospital. I had always suspected this wasn't true, but I didn't want to admit to this. Tammy had said that someone came to the door to use the phone, and Garry had told her to be quiet. This never made sense. Anyway, when the baby was born breached, they called an ambulance. Sarah was born before the ambulance got there. Tammy told us that Kayla held her hand the whole time. The next day when we were visiting Tammy in the hospital, her doctor came into the room. When he found out that we were Tammy's parents, the doctor said that Tammy was really lucky to be alive. It seemed like the doctor wanted to tell us something more, but then he left the room. When I told Dorilyn this story and that Sarah was born one month early, she said that Garry had probably hit Tammy in the stomach. Why would Sarah be born one month early? That could explain why Sarah was born early and why they didn't want to go to the hospital right away.

That also explained why the doctor had said that Tammy was lucky to be alive. Dorilyn also asked if we had considered hiring a private detective. I said, "I have no idea how to do something like that." She said, "Lawyers and insurance companies usually have investigators." It was an afternoon that left Ruth and me really upset and mad. In our worst dreams, we had never expected this. What would we do?

On Friday night, January 17, I called Brian Nysteun at his home. He was the insurance agent that carried the insurance on Tammy's home. He was also a friend of mine. Brian worked for the CO Brown Agency in Kasson. I told him we had many concerns about the fire. Every time I told about one of my concerns, he said, "Oh, No!" When I finished, he said that Garry was always trying to get more insurance on the house. He wanted $85,000, but the insurance company would only write $40,000. Garry was very upset about this. After doing a little work on the outside of the house, the coverage was raised to $60,000, but Garry was still upset. He wanted $85,000. Garry always told me the house was worth nothing.

When Garry called on January 20 and told us we wouldn't be seeing the girls again because we were talking to the girls about the fire, I said, "None of us have talked to the girls about the fire." He said he heard Kayla on the phone saying something about the fire. I said, "She said something, but none of us said anything about the fire." It is hard to understand what a four-year old child says. We couldn't understand what she said. I then asked Garry about the fire. He said, "It is none of your business." Tammy was our daughter, and I think the fire was our business. What was Garry trying to hide? Garry asked about the cards we had gotten at Tammy's funeral. I said, "Ruth is working on the thank-you cards. All the cards we have were given to me personally." He accused me of stealing the money from the cards. I told him that we had learned some very disturbing news. "You have been beating up Tammy!" He said that wasn't true. I said we had heard it at the nursing home. He said it wasn't true. I then said, "It is on the record at the sheriff's office." He didn't deny it again. I then said that he was forcing me to get an attorney. He said he would get an attorney too, and he hung up.

Soon after this conversation, Garry's mother and two of his sisters went to the nursing home and threatened to sue anyone who talked to us about anything again! When I called the nursing home to see how they could have been so wrong about the insurance policy, the lady was extremely afraid. She said, "I can't talk to you or I will lose my job and I will be sued." Under the First Amendment of the US Constitution, we have free right of speech. I don't think they could have been sued. When I told Rollie Spriggle this, he seemed to think Garry's mother had justification to do this. I think they committed a terrorist act. But the sheriff's department didn't think they had done anything wrong. As parents who had lost our daughter, this was very disturbing and hurtful. People who we thought were friends were now afraid to talk to us. By now there were enough red flags that the sheriff's department should have investigated more. What was everyone trying to hide, including the sheriff?

I then went back to the sheriff's office. Rollie Spriggle, the detective, spoke to me. He thought Garry's mother was in the right. He said everyone was talking about Tammy's death. He said it had to stop.

I said, "I am not talking to everyone."

Rollie Spriggle said, "He didn't kill your daughter."

Ruth and I didn't believe him. We talked about the insurance, about the fire, and about Tucker. Tucker was a sixty-five-year-old neighbor who was retarded.

I then said, "Why aren't you looking into these things?"

He said, "Sheriff Bill Webber forbade me from looking into anything."

"Why is this?"

He then said, "Maybe you will feel better if we have Garry take a lie detector test."

I said, "It would help us to believe you."

He contacted Garry, and he agreed to take the test. When it came time, several months later, for Garry to take the tests, he refused! He then hired George Restovich as his attorney. His lawyer forbade the sheriff's office to question Garry or the girls again. I don't believe a lawyer can forbid anyone from investigating a crime. Maybe it was a false statement that came from the sheriff. He wanted us to believe he couldn't do anything. We couldn't believe Rollie, but he always would talk to me. That helped me.

I had only been on the board of directors of the Rochester's Farmers Mutual Insurance Company for six months. Duane Klingsporn was the president. He wanted Ruth and me to go to the convention in the cities in early February. Ruth didn't want to go so soon after Tammy's death. Duane's wife, Loretta, said she would be sure that Ruth had a good time. Jerry Clemons was also on the board, and his wife was Shirley. Ruth had ridden the school bus with Shirley, so Ruth knew her well. Ruth took the cards that we had gotten at Tammy's funeral. She spent most of her time writing thank-you cards. Ruth didn't want to go again. Afterward I realized that it was a mistake to go.

The convention was from Sunday afternoon until Tuesday night. The banquet was on Tuesday night, and the company paid for the hotel on Tuesday night so we didn't have to drive home after the banquet. We had Wednesday free. We decided to visit my Uncle Dale and Aunt Tina on Wednesday. When we got to their house, they told us that my Aunt Judy called them the day of the fire. Judy said, "Wayne and Ruth's Tammy died in a house fire." They understood that all three of us had died in the fire. They couldn't believe that Wayne and Ruth were gone. It was a sad day and night in their lives. Late the next day, my dad called Dale and told them when the funeral was being held. They both told us how relived they were that we were alive. I have always been close to my uncles and aunts.

I called Garry at seven o'clock in the morning of February 7 to see if we could get the girls. He said we wouldn't see them again. He was upset that our attorney wanted him to sign papers giving us visitation rights. I could hear someone talking in the background. Finally, he said we could get the girls if we came right away. He was going to go to the cities and get his driver's license back. He was staying with his cousin Shelly. I think Shelly was helping us. When we got there, Ruth, Bob, and I were invited in for coffee. He was upset that our attorney had said, "Tammy died screaming." He said we could probably have the girls three weekends a month if he didn't have to sign anything. I said, "We could wait six weeks to see how much trouble we've had getting the girls. If we never have trouble, we don't need anything signed." It was extremely hard for us to deal with Garry thinking that he had murdered Tammy. We had to do it for Tammy's daughters. It was terrible to lose Tammy, but now we were in danger of losing our granddaughters too.

We took the girls to church and Sunday school on February 9. About two o'clock in the afternoon, the girls finally got tired and took a nap. At six o'clock at night, we took them to the Burger King for supper. While we were eating, Kayla told us some things about the fire. Then she said, "Dad said we are going to leave her upstairs." We took the girls back to Garry's sister Bobbie Jo. The house was full of people. When we knocked, no one came to the door. I knocked again, and someone hollered to come in. No one got up or said anything. We took the girls' coats and boots off and gave them hugs. Then we just stood there for some time. No one got up or said anything. Finally, Garry got up and asked about Sarah's rash. Ruth explained that we had put on the medicine many times. Dean, Bobbie Jo's boyfriend, said that they were going to take Sarah to the Mayo Clinic. No one else said anything. They just sat and stared. We felt very uncomfortable.

We had received a card inviting us to come to a meeting in Rochester for parents who had lost a child. A cousin of mine, who had lost a son in a car accident, seemed to feel it was helping them. Ruth and I decided to go. The meeting was at Assisi Heights in Rochester. Assisi Heights was a compound where the Catholic nuns lived. The meeting was called Compassion Friends. We quickly found out we were not alone. Everyone told their story. The first night, I couldn't say anything. They said most men feel that a real man doesn't cry. That idea is wrong. After you have lost a child, it helps to mourn by crying. After the meeting was over, a man came over to me and sat down. We talked for a long time. I felt a little bit better. Ruth and I agreed to go back the next month.

In the next days, my cousin called me, and she wanted Ruth and me to come to a Compassion Friends meeting in Austin. If she would have called sooner, we wouldn't have gone to the meeting at

Rochester. Maybe God was at work, and we were supposed to go to both meetings. At the Austin meeting, we met several people who became close friends. They would remain our friends for life. We met at a Lutheran Church in Austin. There was a rather big group. The wife of one couple was a grandchild of my grandfather's brother Alfred. I didn't know her. Her name was Judi Schwab. She requested that I put her name in my book. She was also raised the first two years of her life by her grandparents. She was my age. We were together many times when we were young children. They had the loss of two daughters at separate times in car accidents. I couldn't imagine losing two kids. We would always remain close. Another couple said their daughter was murdered in California. She was working at a gas station. There was a robbery. Their daughter had two young daughters, and they went to California to bring them home and raise them. Jim's mother was a twin sister to Lillie, who was the wife of my grandfather's brother, Andrew. I became really close to Jim. We had something in common. I really had the feeling that I wasn't going through this alone. I was able to tell our story this time. There was also another couple that we met at the Rochester meeting. He was the guy who talked to me after their meeting ended. In both of these meetings, it was said that it helped mourning to keep a journal. I started writing a lot down. I didn't want to forget anything about Tammy's death. I kept the journal for six months. That is why my book goes into a lot of detail the first six months after Tammy's death. The meeting was the third Tuesday night. They also said on the first Tuesday of the month we would go to eat at a restaurant.

I had three dreams shortly after Tammy's death. The first dream was after Tammy's death, but in my dream, it was before Tammy's death. I was unloading feed from a wagon with an auger into a hog feeder outside in a hog lot. Tammy came up to me. We talked some. I told Tammy that I had terrible news for her: "You are going to die soon."

The second dream was soon after Tammy's death. She was in the dining room at our house. She was dressed in white. There was a glowing white light around her. She seemed to glow. She said that she wasn't dead. "I didn't die!" She said she was in a situation she couldn't get out of. She said she was so happy now. I told her that I had to call my mother and tell her that Tammy wasn't dead.

I don't remember the third dream as well, but it was similar to the second dream. The dreams seemed so real! I have never been able to get the dreams out of my mind.

I started to wonder if Kayla and Sarah would remember Tammy. I started to think about my Grandpa McColley. His mother had died when he was eighteen in 1916. His youngest sister was only five. Her name was Marion. Did she remember her mother? The only way I would know was to go and see her. Late one afternoon, I called Ray and Marion Wakefield. They now lived in Albert Lea. I said we would come to their house at 7:00 PM. We decided to eat at Trumble's Restaurant in Albert Lea first. We got there at seven o'clock. They said that they sat looking out the window ever since I called them, waiting for us to come. They had a hard time to figure how I fix into the McColley side. A lot of my uncles were so close to my age, and that confused them. Marion told us that she couldn't remember her mother at all. Her dad, Emery, had so much pain when his wife, Effie, died that he didn't want anyone to talk about Effie again. Marion told us to talk about Tammy often. She had to make a card for her mother on Mother's Day. She threw it away when she walked home from school. Emery was going to put the youngest children in an orphanage. Rudy, who was his oldest daughter, stayed home and raised her youngest siblings. Rudy never got married. She would stay single her whole life. Ray and Marion had lost a son, James, in a hunting accident. They knew how we were feeling. It really helped us!

On March 3, Garry called us early in the evening and said that he had some work to do on his new house. We could have the girls for the rest of the week. We were to pick the girls up at Shelly's. Ruth had to go to the doctor with Brenda the next morning. Bob and I went alone. Sarah met me at the door. As soon as I picked her up, I knew she had a fever. She really felt hot. When I asked Garry if we still had to put the rash medication on Sarah, he said that they had some medicine for strep throat. He said it was just a precaution. I asked if Kayla had to take any medicine, and he said, "No." As the day went by, it really became obvious that Sarah was really sick. Bob and Kayla went to the shop. When they were walking up to the house for supper, Kayla told Bob that her dad was kissing his new girlfriend. I couldn't imagine why he was doing this in front of Kayla and Sarah so soon after their mother's death. At seven o'clock in the evening, while we were watching TV, Kayla said, "I don't want you to take me back to my dad. If you do, I am going to cry."

We got the girls often, but Ruth and I were really happy to get the girls at a time that wasn't every other weekend as we had agreed. Sarah was so sick, and we now wondered if maybe he didn't want to take care of them when they were sick. We felt better when they were sick that they were with us. At least we knew that they would be taken care of.

On March 5, Sarah was really sick in the afternoon. I came in from the shop at four o'clock in the afternoon and rocked her until six thirty. When we had supper, she didn't have an appetite. She kept pointing to her throat. Finally, we got her to eat some pudding. We got a package in the mail from my sister Sandy. I made a big deal about opening the packages. It had two coloring books, some stickers, and small rulers. That really cheered her up, and Kayla and Sarah really played with it. Doreen and Brenda came out about eight o'clock. The girls were really happy to see them, and Doreen played with them until bedtime.

On March 7 at 5:15 PM, Steve McQueen, Garry's best friend, came to our house and told us many things. One thing was that he thought Garry killed Tammy. I then asked Steve, "Why would Garry go to Tucker's to report the fire when he told Rollie he didn't know Tucker and had neighbors living closer?" Steve said that Garry knew Tucker and that he and Garry had walked up there many times while hunting. Garry had talked many times how Tucker wasn't all there. Steve also said while they were in a bar several months ago, Garry told him about all the money he would have after the house burned down. Steve mentioned that he went to Frankenstein's in Byron with Tammy and Garry. Garry was drunk and was walking out, and he started beating up Tammy. Steve then said he beat up Garry. I was burning and very upset. I went the next morning to talk to Rollie.

They called in Steve and discredited him. They threatened him to not talk to anyone about this, including us. It seemed like the sheriff was protecting Garry. It didn't make sense! Why?

In the evening of March 8, Ruth took Brenda to the Methodist Hospital to have Brenda's baby. Ruth always slept with the girls on the living room floor. She made them think they were camping out. Ruth told me that I was not going to like sleeping on the floor. I slept in our bed with them. We slept with all our clothes on. In the morning, I made them breakfast. Afterward Bob and I took the girls to the hospital to meet Brenda's baby, Justin.

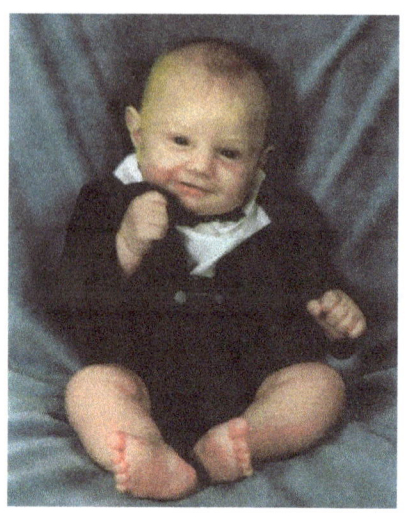

Justin Lynn McColley, 4 months old, July 1997

When Brenda got pregnant, Ruth and I weren't happy. She moved out of our house and went to live with Doreen. I never gave her hell. Doreen told Brenda that now she had to go home to live with her parents. I never blamed her for getting pregnant. It would do no good now. Justin was a really good baby. He was always happy and good-natured. Ruth and I felt we didn't have anything to get up for. We were in so must pain over Tammy's death. Justin helped both of our moods to improve. In a short time, we felt that Justin was a gift from God.

A FATHER'S QUEST

On March 10, Garry called midmorning to see why we hadn't brought the girls back Sunday night. I said, "You told us that you would call and tell us where we should take them." We waited all evening, and he never called. I then told him that we had promised to take the girls to see the baby, so it would be unfair to take them back now. He said Sarah's bed hadn't come in and we could keep them a couple more days.

We took the girls along to Rochester on March 11 to get Brenda and Justin from the hospital. We all went to Toys R Us and bought the girls doll beds. Shortly after we got home, Garry called and said his sister Sherry would be coming to get the girls. I asked if they could stay one more day. We had just got back from the hospital, and the girls were really looking forward to help take care of the baby. Finally, he agreed. The next day Garry called at noon and said Sherry would be coming to get the girls. I said we were just sitting down to dinner, and he said she would come at one o'clock. When she came, I never saw the girls look so sad. They wouldn't give any of us a hug. They just looked at us as like, "Why are you doing this to us?" Sherry took the girls to her house.

On Friday, March 21, Sherry's daughter brought the girls at 11:15 AM. She said that Sherry would pick them up at 3:30 PM Sunday. The girls had stayed with Sherry Thursday night. Kayla was sick to her stomach the next morning. By afternoon, she was okay. Garry called at 2:45 PM and said to have the girls ready in half an hour. Listening to him, it sounded like he was out of his mind! He was upset that his girlfriend had left him and it was our fault. We had talked to her parents. We had talked to Steve McQueen. He finally said he had a lawyer and I would find out what would happen to me, and then he hung up. We never went anyplace to talk to anyone. I had never met Steve McQueen before he came to our house. I knew his girlfriend's parents, but I never contacted them. They came to our house. They were worried that their daughter would end up like Tammy. We had company for Brenda's baby shower. I thought that he would be coming for the girls while the company was still at our place. Well, he never showed up or called back. We took the girls to church and Sunday school the next day. At 1:20 PM, Sherry's daughter came for the girls. Kayla and Sarah were planning on 3:30 PM like we were told. They didn't want do go, and Kayla cried and cried. Sarah had such a hurt look on her face. Finally, after fifteen minutes on the porch trying to comfort Kayla, Ruth went in the house. She was still crying when I went in the house minutes later. About fifteen minutes later, Bob and Brenda forcefully put Kayla and Sarah into the car. They went back to Sherry's home.

On April 4, Ruth and I picked up the girls at Garry's at one o'clock in the afternoon. They were ready and glad to see us. I then asked Garry if it would be okay if we brought the girls back at eight o'clock on Sunday night. He said it would be okay. A repairman from John Deere was working on the corn planter, so I was in the shop most of the day. That night Bob, Doreen, and Brenda went to a dance at the Pony Express in Manorville. Sarah's rash had gotten much worse. Kayla wanted to know when she had to go back home, and she wanted to know if she could go to church.

The next day Brenda told us that they had seen Garry last night. He said, "You should have the girls ready by noon tomorrow because I am going to come to get them." Bob stayed overnight with friends. When Bob got home, he said Garry's former girlfriend and Shelly talked to him about Garry. They told Bob that Kayla and Sarah were only happy when they were with us. They then said, "Garry is a terrible person when he is drinking." They were outside when they were talking, and when Bob went to go inside, Garry stopped him at the door. Garry was drunk. Garry said, "Tell your folks to have the girls ready at noon because I am going to come and get them." Doreen was going to take the girls shopping, so I gave her money and said to have dinner in town. If we were going to have a confrontation with Garry, I didn't want the girls around. They left at eleven thirty. I was waiting, but Garry never showed up. He was playing games with us. He liked to threaten us when he was drunk, and he couldn't remember when he sobered up.

Around five in the afternoon, Eric and Lori came over. Lori was Doreen's best friend. Eric told us that on March 22, he was running a pool tournament at Harold's Club in Dodge Center. Garry was there and wanted to play a game of pool with him for $100 a game.

Eric wouldn't play and said if he had $100 to bet, he would put it in a fund for Kayla and Sarah. He said Garry was drunk and buying drinks for everyone. He was also bragging about all the money he had. Eric said he overheard other people say, "That is the guy that killed his wife."

On April 6 we woke the girls and went to church. Doreen went along. After church we had lunch in the dining room. When Sunday school was to start, the girls ran into the Sunday school class room not waiting for Doreen. On the way home, Doreen said when she took Kayla into the bathroom, Kayla told her that she wished she could live at church. We had another baby shower for Brenda in the afternoon. Kayla and Sarah had fun playing with the other kids that were there. At seven forty, we started to get the girls ready to go back home. They didn't want to go and started crying. We tried to comfort them by telling them that we would see them in two weeks, but it didn't help. They cried all the way home. When we got to Garry's, he was waiting at the door. We carried the girls from the car. It was windy and cold. I was first, and when we got to the door, Garry tried to block the door, but we managed to squeeze by. The girls were still crying. Ruth came in too. Garry was in a bad mood.

He said, "Get the girls back earlier next time, eight o'clock is their bedtime."

Ruth said, "You said eight o'clock, and that is what time it is."

He said, "I know, but get them back earlier next time."

I then asked him if we could plan on getting them in two weeks at one o'clock on Friday.

He said, "Yes, but get them back earlier."

I said, "You set the time, and that is the time we will get them back."

He said, "I will call you."

I knew that he would be playing games with us again.

I said, "Sarah's rash is getting really bad again."

He didn't comment. We then left.

Garry brought the girls to our house on Friday, May 2, at twelve fifty. In the afternoon, while I was sitting in the living room, Kayla pointed up to my great-grandfather's gun which hung over the fireplace and said, "My dad bought a gun like that, but a toy gun. It is a small one." I was scared that Garry would be carrying the gun. Kayla and Brenda were in the bathroom that night, and Kayla said, "Don't tell, but I don't like my dad because he is always hitting Sarah and me." We knew that he was beating up our daughter, but now he was beating his kids. He was drunk most of the time or maybe using drugs. We would later find out for sure that he was using drugs.

Justin was baptized at the eight thirty service on May 4. My folks met us at church. My brother Rick and his wife, Carol, came over for dinner. They were Brenda's sponsors. Doris Nelson, our pastor's wife, also came for dinner. Doris was a registered nurse. We showed Sarah's rash to her. She wanted to see the medication. When Ruth showed Doris the tube, she said it was filled February 21, and it should have been long gone. Garry didn't call, but he came at two o'clock to get the girls. Kayla was sad and cried and cried. Bob tried to comfort her in the middle of the kitchen floor.

Ruth went down to Med Cap Pharmacy in Kasson at eight o'clock the next morning. She talked to Jay Harris, the owner. Jay told her the medicine had never been refilled and that it cost approximately $12.

I called Garry on the morning of May 16 to see what time we could get the girls. He was all upset. He said, "You had the cops out to talk to the girls at your house?"

I said, "That isn't true, it never happened." I asked, "Who told you that?"

He said, "Kayla did."

I said, "She must have someone else here mixed up with the cops."

He said, "Kayla knows what cops look like. Are you calling Kayla a liar?"

I said, "No, I'm not, but the cops weren't here."

I then asked him, "What difference does it make if the girls talk to the cops? Do you have something to hide?"

Garry's actions were making me think he was guilty. He said we could have the girls at one o'clock and that he would bring the girls over. I told him that we had plans Sunday afternoon and we would like the girls to stay until six thirty Sunday night. He said that if we got the girls at one o'clock Friday, we had to take them home at one o'clock Sunday.

I said, "Maybe we could get them later on Friday."

He said, "No, you wanted them at one o'clock, and that is when you are getting them."

I asked him if he had anything planned on Sunday afternoon.

He said, "No," and then said, "it is none of your business."

He then said that we could go to court and then we would only get them one weekend a month. "How would you like that?"

I said, "I guess we will have to do it your way."

He then hung up.

I was incorporating chemicals on the Sutherland Farm. I told Ruth to get me from the field so I would be home when he came at one o'clock. Ruth picked me up, and we drove into the yard at twelve fifty. Brenda was outside and said Garry was on the phone. I went into the shop and answered.

He said, "You aren't getting the girls because you are lying to me."

I said, "The cops were not out here. The only times someone from the sheriff office ever questioned the girls at our house or anywhere with us was the afternoon of the fire."

He was like a madman! He said, "I know the girls have talked to the cops."

I said, "That's not true."

He asked if I was calling Kayla a liar. I told him that the cops were never out at our house when the girls were here.

He then said, "You are not getting the girls again without supervised visitation, and my lawyer would be talking to you, and you would be sorry about this."

Ruth was listening on another phone and said, "Just try it!"

He then hung up. I was really upset, and I didn't know what to do. I went up to the house and called the sheriff's office. I asked to talk to Rollie Spriggle. He was out to lunch. I then decided it was best to go back out to the field and finish incorporating the chemicals. I knew I had only a half hour left.

In fifteen minutes, Ruth called me on the radio and said Garry had called and that I was to call him back. I finished the field and started for home. Just as I got to the corner west of our yard, Ruth called me and said that Garry was pulling in our yard.

I said, "I'm almost there!"

I told her to call Bob on the radio and tell him to get home right away. I was scared! I knew he had a pistol. He sounded like he was a madman when I talked to him less than an hour ago. I didn't know what he would do. I wished that I had a gun with me. Bob was out of the tractor cab filling the planter with seed so Ruth didn't get him. When I pulled into the yard, Garry was standing by his car in front of the garage. He was dressed up like a motorcycle hood. I was scared and asked Ruth on the radio to call Bob again. I parked the tractor and digger in front of the barn and got out. He walked toward me. We met by the old shop. He said that Kayla had told him that she told the cops about the lighter and going to the barn. If this was true, he would have wanted the girls to talk to the cops. I think this was a story that he had put in their minds. I then asked Garry how he thought we felt that whenever we had asked him anything about the fire, he had always said, "It's none of your business." I told him that Tammy was our daughter; I think how she died was our business. He then said, "You can have the girls until six thirty on Sunday." He then left. Maybe when Ruth threatened him on the phone earlier, it made him change his mind.

When I came in the house, Kayla and Sarah were in the dining room talking to Brenda and Ruth. Brenda told me that Kayla had said Grandpa had called her a liar. She covered her face and looked at me real sad. I then got on my knees and said, "I think Grandpa needs a hug," and they both ran toward me and gave me a big hug. I then went in the office and talked to Rollie. I told him that I wanted a permit to carry a gun. He told me to fill out the papers for the permit. I later did, but the sheriff wouldn't give me the permit. Next, I told the girls about the new kittens that we had in the shop. We all went out to the shop and played most of the afternoon.

On the next day (Saturday), we took Sarah to the Mayo Clinic Urgent Care. When the doctor saw the rash and learned that she had it for five months, she called in a Child Protection Social Worker. When I explained the whole story to her, I thought they were going to take the girls away, even from us. I had promised to take Sarah to a park and was wondering how I would explain this to her. They had someone else come in who took many pictures. The social worker finally came back in and said, "I'm really sorry, but I can't help you." She told me that she had been in contact with the Dodge Co. Sheriff's Office and the Dodge Co. social worker on duty and all they will do was to promise to go out first thing Monday morning and look at the rash and to follow up until it was gone.

She said, "You did the right thing to bring her in, and I'm very sorry."

I would find out that Dodge County would always protect Garry and never protect the girls. Doreen, Sarah, and I had been in the doctor's office for three hours. We then took the girls to a park by the Silver Lake Swimming Pool.

We took the girls on Sunday to church and Sunday school. We all went down to Kevin and Kris's after dinner. We got home at five o'clock. Kayla kept asking if she could stay over one more night. When she had to put on the clothes she came with, she cried and cried. At six twenty, I told her that I would have to take them home. I didn't know if I was to take them home or if Garry was to pick them up.

She said, "I want to stay until my dad comes."

A few minutes later, he came. I was really afraid of what he would say when we told him about taking Sarah to the doctor. His cousin, Shelly, was with him. That really helped us. If Garry would have come alone, he would have exploded. When I told him about taking Sarah to the doctor, he got a terrible look on his face. Just then, Shelly said, "What did they say it was?" I then told her it was scabies, but I don't know if they can tell it from just one visit. I think there will have to be some follow-ups. I then gave him the medicine and instructions, and they left.

We went to Olmsted County Courthouse late the next morning. They told us there was nothing they could do now. It was up to Dodge County. We went to the sheriff's office in the afternoon.

Gary Thompson, Child Protection Officer, was called into the room. He told us that Social Services would not do anything until they had written orders to do something. What's wrong? Several people have told them about the problem several times. The Mayo Clinic had called them. They still refused to act! Why did Dodge County even have a Social Services office? Who would write the orders? No one was going to go out to Garry's house or contact him about Sarah's rash. I would later learn that the second-in-command at Social Services was a childhood friend to Garry. Nothing was ever going to be done. I told Rollie that maybe Garry thought someone from the sheriff's office was out to our place. When the pastor's wife was out for dinner for Justin's baptism, the car she was driving looked like an unmarked sheriff's car. I saw a car drive by that day that looked like Sherry's car. She was Garry's sister. That was why I got blamed for having the sheriff out.

Garry called us a little after nine o'clock Saturday morning, June 7, and asked us if we wanted the girls for the weekend. Bob and I went to get the girls right away. He said we should bring them back at six thirty Sunday night. In the afternoon we went to visit my parents. My brother Dallas and my parents had two houses on the same place. My sister-in-law, Marsha, gave the girls a ride on one of their horses. That night Doreen and her friend Jenny saw Garry at the Pine Island Cheese Fest. He was drunk. By his probation, he wasn't allowed to consume alcohol.

Later in the afternoon, we went to a park in Austin. The park was by a small lake, and the girls played in the water. We went to two other parks where they played. We then went to an A&W Root Beer Stand, where we all had root beers. Kayla and Sarah also had ice cream cones. Both girls were very unhappy when we got them ready to go home. They wanted to stay at our house until their dad came to get them. I said, "No, I have to take you back." When I gave Kayla a hug, I told her, "I will talk to your dad and ask if you can come again next weekend." She then asked Brenda if she would come along to show Brenda her new bicycle. On the way over to Garry's, Kayla told Sarah, "Grandpa is going to talk to Dad to see if we can come over next weekend." When we got there, Garry wasn't home.

We waited about five minutes, and I said we would have to go back home. Sarah and Kayla were really happy! When we got out on the road, I could see a car coming up behind us. I started to slow down. Kayla asked, "Why are you driving so slow?" Soon I could see it was Garry, so I pulled over to the side of the road. Garry backed into the driveway in front of us. We got the girls out of the car. Garry got out of his car and leaned beside it. It was obvious that he was one of these different people like he was sometimes. He had to be on drugs. He wouldn't have acted the same if he was just drunk. The girls got into the car by themselves. I asked Garry if we could have the girls again next weekend. Doreen was working this weekend, and she had not spent much time with them. He said, "Yah." He never moved from leaning against the car. I was positive that he would have fallen down if he would have moved away from the car. He got in the car and left. As he left, we could hear the girls crying. What kind of a grandparent was I? How could I let our granddaughters get in a car with an impaired driver? I'm positive, if I had called the Dodge County sheriff, he wouldn't have done anything.

I asked Don Gray, who was a Dodge County commissioner to go with me to talk to Social Services. We had talked to Brian Hartung, who was in charge of Social Services before about Sarah's rash. It didn't do any good. I thought it would help to have a commissioner there with us. He said they wouldn't do anything. We talked about Garry driving impaired while the girls were in the car with him. I then asked Brian, "What would you do if Garry is picked up by the police, driving drunk with the girls in the car?" He said, "As soon as he is sober, I will give the girls back to him." I then asked, "God forbid if one of the girls dies due to Garry's neglect, what would you do?" He answered, "I would give the other one back to him." I couldn't believe his answers. He wasn't doing his job, and the commissioner wasn't doing his job. Why was this? It didn't make sense. Doris Nelson, our pastor's wife, contacted Dodge County Services. Nothing was done! My sister Sandy Pittman talked to Brian Hartung. He told her that he wanted her to know that he cared, but he wasn't going to do anything.

We then went to the sheriff's office with Don Gray. While at the sheriff's office, Gary Remine, Dodge County assistance district attorney, was asked to sit in on the meeting. I had brought along court records that we had on Garry. The sheriff's office had led us to believe that Garry could be arrested for having guns. Ruth and I had hoped that Garry could be put away long enough for the girls to get professional help to deal with their mother's death. I showed them numerous places in the court records where it was a disgrace that there was no follow-through and sentence not served. I said that Ruth and I had gone to support groups that some parents had lost their children to drunk drivers. "How do you think they would feel if they had read this?" Gary Remine got up and said, "You have no damned business being here telling us how to do our jobs. All of us workers at the courthouse are hard workers, and I don't need to listen to this." He then got up and left the room. He was the one that was responsible for giving the order to follow up on Sarah's rash. He wasn't doing his job, he knew it, but why? I told this to Dodge County Victim Services, Dorilyn Franko. She said she had similar happenings several times. Gary Remine was a public employee and a professional. I can't believe we have a person in his position who makes a habit of acting like this. It was all a waste of time, but we learned what we were up against. It was going to be hard; how would we do it?

I think some of Garry's actions were soon going to help us. They would help us, but it was going to take a long time. On June 15, the sheriff's office got a report of a vehicle accident from Sara Marquardt. She stated that on June 14, at approximately 20:30 hours, she was heading southbound on Central Avenue and making a left-hand turn into a driveway of a residence when a motorcycle stuck her vehicle just behind the driver's door. She then stated that when the motorcycle hit her, it then proceeded to slide under her vehicle. The driver of the motorcycle was Garry. He told her that he wasn't hurt and didn't want the cops involved. He convinced her to go to a friend's residence to exchange information. He told her he had insurance with CO Brown Agency. When she contacted the police, she found out the insurance didn't start until June 16. Garry bought the insurance after the accident. Garry didn't have a motorcycle endorsement. The motorcycle was recently purchased and was not yet titled in his name. Judge Agerter issued a warrant for his arrest with a bail of $500 before they could release him. Finally, something was being done. I figured Garry would hang himself, but I didn't know it would take so long.

Rollie told Bob that if he saw Garry drinking, they would arrest him. Bob told Rollie that he knew he would see Garry drinking at Centerfest on Saturday night. I asked Bob the next day if he had seen Garry drinking. He said he had but didn't call Rollie because he knew a member of the sheriff's posse. He talked to him, and he said he was going to pick up Garry. He also said there was a fight between two girls that Garry became involved with. The next day Bob and I went to talk to the member of the sheriff's posse that Bob had talked to on Saturday night. He said they hadn't picked up Garry because they couldn't get orders from anyone to do so. When they called Rollie at his home, he didn't answer. Was Rollie protecting Garry? Why? When Garry left Centerfest, he was with a woman, carrying a beer, and he said, "See yah, officers," real smart aleck like. Somehow he knew he could do anything, and no one was going to do anything.

On Thursday, June 19, I noticed that I had forgotten to pay Brenda's car insurance. As it was due that day, I got a check ready and told Ruth to take it to Brain Nysteun's office. When Ruth came home, she told me that Brian had told her that Garry had run into a car with his motorcycle Saturday night. I then called Brian Nysteun, and he told me that Garry had come in Monday morning and bought insurance on the motorcycle. He had the motorcycle for about a month. If Garry was so concerned about having insurance on Tammy and the house when he couldn't afford it, why didn't he have insurance on the motorcycle when he had all this money? Brian told me that in that afternoon, a sheriff's officer came in to check on Garry's insurance. He told Brian that Garry had run into a young girl's car on Saturday night. Brian told me that Garry insured the motorcycle for $9,000. I told Brian that it must be fraud to buy insurance after an accident. I then went to see the member of the sheriff's posse that I had talked to Monday. At first he was reluctant to say anything. Then I told him that I knew about the accident that Garry had with his motorcycle. He told me that it had happened about eight o'clock Saturday evening. Garry had talked the girl into not reporting it. They found the motorcycle hidden in one of Garry's relative's garage. He also told us that the paperwork had been done and sent to the district attorney's office, charging Garry with disorderly conduct, concerning his actions with the two girls fighting at Centerfest on Saturday night. He said, "If he is found guilty of this, it would break his probation, and Garry could get some jail time." It went to Gary Remine, and Garry never went to court. I don't understand this. Why? Garry did go to court regarding the accident that he had with his motorcycle. He was fined $284.50. He paid $500 bail, so he got back $215.50.

On Friday, June 29, we got the girls at ten o'clock in the morning. Ruth had bought a small pool that we set up in our yard in front of the house. The girls played a lot in the pool over the weekend. Sarah's rash was coming back. We stayed home Saturday, and the girls played a lot in the pool. Sunday we went to church. In the afternoon, the girls didn't want to go home. We met Garry by the bridge west of their place.

Bob and I went to get the girls at ten o'clock on Friday morning on July 11. They were happy to stay home and play. When we were getting ready to go to the fair on Saturday, Kayla was concerned that they would have to go home after the fair. We assured them that they could stay another day and go to church and go to a park. She was happy then. Both girls rode on many rides and saw the animals. When we got back home from the fair, the girls played in the pool again. Sarah's rash was worse than the last weekend. She was solid red in the genital area. She said several times over the weekend that the rash didn't hurt. I had to question if Garry told that she better not complain because we would take her to the doctor and she wouldn't see us again. I knew it would cause trouble for us. We tried to get some help, but we had failed.

On July 27, at approximately 1:00 AM, Dodge County Sheriff's Deputies James Trihey and Loring Guenther were dispatched to the scene of a one car accident one and a half mile east of Co. Road

Nine on Co. Road Six. Upon their arrival, the deputies found a car lying on its side in the south ditch. It was in a creek. License check revealed the car was registered to Garry. The vehicle was unoccupied at the time of their arrival. The deputies conducted a search of the area for persons who were in the vehicle. Approximately twenty minutes after the deputies' arrival on the scene, Garry walked up to the scene. Garry was dirty and smelled of alcoholic beverages. Garry was read the Implied Consent Advisory and consented to a blood test. Garry admitted to drinking. Garry told the deputies that he was a passenger. Garry was not able to say who the driver was. He told the deputies that the driver had walked to Austin by now.

We had the girls on this weekend. On Sunday, we took the girls to Chatfield to see their great-grandmother. On the way back, we drove by their place to see if Garry was home. His car wasn't there. When we came to the bridge west of his house, we could see the railings broken. Soon we saw his car was in the water. As soon as we got home, Garry's mother came to get the girls ahead of time. She had never come before to get the girls. I asked where Garry was. She didn't answer. After they left, I called the sheriff's office. I found he was in the hospital. The next morning, I went down to the bridge. There hadn't been much traffic that had gone by. The tire tracks were still plain on the road. Garry was going west from his house, and it looked like he stopped just before the bridge. He must have pushed the pedal to the floor. It appeared that a lot of gravel was thrown up. It appeared to me that he turned right into the railing of the bridge. He must have felt guilty about killing Tammy that he was trying to commit suicide. It would have been better if he would had succeeded.

On Monday, July 28, Ruth, Doreen, and I went to the sheriff's office. We found out that Garry was in the hospital and we were told that they were charging him with DUI. We showed the pictures that we had taken of Kayla's bruises and the statements that Ruth and Doreen had written concerning how Kayla got them. The sheriff's office called Social Services and told them we would be coming down to see them. We met with Candis Astoff and Carol Trup. We showed them the pictures. We again expressed our concerns about Sarah's rash, and most importantly, we expressed our concerns about

Garry's accident. If the girls had been with him when he had the accident, they could have been killed. They said they would take this information before their board of review. They wouldn't promise they would do anything, but they would call us with their decision at four o'clock in the afternoon. They called at four fifteen and said they were opening up a full investigation. Garry had made too many mistakes. If this went on, more of the people that were protecting him were going to get into trouble. I also knew that we had to keep the pressure on Dodge County.

At the Omnibus Hearing, Lois Hollst, a friend of Garry's, now a resident of Nevada, testified that she was driving the vehicle at the time of the accident. Ms. Hollst testified that she got Garry into the car about 11:00 PM. The defendant was semiconscious at the time and was unable to give clear directions to his home. Ms. Hollst testified she missed a turn, lost control of the vehicle, and the accident occurred. Because the defendant was very belligerent toward her, Ms. Hollst testified she walked to her parents' home in Byron. At the time of the accident, Ms. Hollst held a current competition license for drag racing in the state of Nevada. Testimony was taken from Eric Fosberg at the hearing. Mr. Fosberg testified that he believed Ms. Hollst was the driver of the car when she and Garry left to go home. Mr. Fosberg was legally blind. What a laugh! The bridge was three eights of a mile from the nearest corner. It would be impossible to miss a corner and run into a bridge three eights of a mile away. Garry was always getting someone to take the blame for his actions. Later, we would learn that Tammy took the blame for one of Garry's car accidents.

Shortly after this time, when we went to get the girls, Garry's mother was there. She told us that we wouldn't get the girls again. "Kayla and Sarah want to stay with you all the time. How do you think Garry and we must think about this? The solution to this is to not have them visit you. They will forget about you eventually." If Garry didn't beat them and she and her family treated the girls better, maybe they wouldn't feel this way. But then they couldn't see that.

I knew it was time to get our rights as grandparents established. I went down to the sheriff's office to talk to Rollie. He told us that there was a different lawyer from the cities in the courthouse now that we should talk to. We stayed in his office, and he brought the lawyer in. She was a female lawyer, and we felt she would do a better job for us than a man. I felt that a woman would care more for the girls. Her name was Roxanne Heinrich. She didn't have an office. No one worked for her. We thought it was unusual that she worked alone. Maybe we were getting into something that would hurt us. But in the end, she was a Christian, and she felt that God sent her to help us. We felt the same way. She helped us for almost five years. She never sent me a bill. Once in a while, I gave her $1,000. She went to court several times with us. Maybe I gave her $25,000 in all. It would have cost us real money to have a lawyer working for us for five years.

At this time, Bob and I decided to make a change on the farm. Bob built a thirty-six-thousand-bushel grain bin. We poured the foundation and the floor by ourselves. We had the bin built, but we put the ventilation floor in by ourselves. The bin was too tall to reach with an auger. We put in an air lock system, which would blow the corn in the bin with air. We bought everything from Sommers in Waseca. I had known them from the time I was a teenager. They made me a good deal if we paid for everything upfront. Fifty thousand dollars was the total cost, and we had the cash to pay for it so we didn't have to borrow any money. They did everything as they agreed to do it. Dave Sommers's dad, Buddy, helped. I really enjoyed that. I went to dances with Buddy before I went in the Navy. We always had a lot of fun.

On August 27, 1997, the above-entitled matter came before the undersigned judge on the application of Monumental Life Insurance Company for appointment of a guardian ad litem for Sarah and Kayla. Eric Thompson was appointed as guardian ad litem. Judge Agerter signed the order. We found out about this, but we thought it was the insurance policy that Tammy had at work. Steven Rolsch was appointed as attorney for Kayla and Sarah. Rolsch shouldn't been appointed attorney for Kayla and Sarah because he worked for Restovich in the past. Soon afterward, we found out that Garry had taken out a quarter million insurance policy on Tammy through the mail. It was two policies that someone had signed Tammy's name.

One policy, we were sure that Garry signed her name. But we had no idea who had signed the other policy. On one of the policy, it was unclear to whom they were to pay. Maybe it was to Garry or it was to Kayla and Sarah. Also, one of the policies was bought right before Tammy's death. Evidently, the sheriff didn't think it was wrong to buy a policy on his wife and have someone sign her name shortly before her death. What's wrong?

That fall, we went to a wedding dance for our neighbor's son. Ruth talked to Donna Thomson, who was a coworker of Tammy. Donna told Ruth that Becky Sullivan had told Tammy at work the night before she died that she was having an affair with Garry. Tammy was observed at work that she was crying. Later at work, Becky told everyone that she was going to live with Garry in his new house.

We went to court on October 29, 1997, to have our grandparent right established. The Conclusions of Law were number 1. Insufficient evidence exists to adequately assess the best interests of the children with regard to proposed grandparent visitation request. An independent guardian ad litem should be appointed on behave of the children to conduct an investigation and make recommendations to the court. Because of the current role as guardian ad litem for the children in an independent matter, it was not appropriate for Eric Larson to serve as guardian ad litem in this case. Number 2 was following the investigation and the report by the guardian, an evidentiary hearing should be held for determination of the best interest of the children. Later, Judge Agerter would appoint Barb Pike.

Around this time, I would use my Uncle Lyle for advice and support for what to do. His son was on drugs, and they went to court, and Lyle and Kathy had won custody of their two granddaughters. I would talk to him often. Whenever something come up, I would call Lyle. Ruth and I didn't feel so alone with Lyle for support. Most of our friends didn't want to know. When we talked about this at the support groups, many of the men told me that I should shoot Garry. That was no help to me. If Lyle and Kathy could get custody of their granddaughters, we could get custody of our granddaughters too. We would never give up! If I was to shoot Garry, I then would go to prison, and his family would get custody of the girls, and we would lose.

On November 1, Ruth was taking the pickup to pick me up at the Dragsten Farm, one half mile east of our home farm. Bob had gone with the combine. I had taken a tractor and wagons up there, and I needed a ride home to pick up another tractor and wagons. When Ruth got to the intersection, another pickup came from the north and went through the stop sign. He never slowed down, and I don't think he saw her. Leslie Colburn was so drunk he didn't know anything. He hit her on the door where she was sitting. She wasn't wearing a seat belt, and Ruth turned the steering wheel to the right as she slid across the seat. When you looked at the door, I couldn't imagine Ruth being alive if she had stayed next to the door. It helped her to be wearing insulated and baggy coveralls. Our pickup swung around, and he hit her again on the passenger side, then our pickup went in the southeast ditch. He must have slammed on the brakes so hard that his pickup didn't move. An angel must have been with Ruth. She could have been killed. Our pickup was totaled. Ruth called Brenda on the radio, and she came up and got me. When I saw the pickup in the ditch and how bad it was wrecked up, I couldn't believe that Ruth was alive. Ruth was standing beside the pickup. Leslie was lying in his pickup with his hands hanging out the window. We called 911, and a police car and the ambulance soon came. An ambulance person checked over Ruth. She had a leg that really hurt. He told us that we should go to the emergency room to get it checked. We went, but God was looking out for Ruth, and it wasn't broken. Bob said, "I wish you had taken my pickup, I want to get a new one." I bought Bob's pickup, and he bought a new one.

I hired Timothy Braatz from Atlas Investigations from Rochester to look into some things. I had him look into Ruth's accident. Mr. Colburn was charged with failure to yield, no proof of insurance, and open container in a motor vehicle. The officers noted that he had two bottles of Southern Comfort in the vehicle and that he had a strong odor of alcohol. They took a sample from him that came back from the BCA at only 0.02 percent, which was far below the state-mandated 0.10 percent level at that time. I talked to people that had seen him at the bar. They told me that Les had been drinking heavily all day. Who changed the reading? Was it the sheriff? He could have killed Ruth, and now he would get off. I also had him look into Rebecca Sullivan, who was found guilty of felony fifth-degree controlled substance possession on December 2, 1997 in Dodge County Court after she was found sitting in a car in Canisteo Township with a razor blade and white rock and powder substance that was later found to be methamphetamine. A presentence investigation had been ordered in the case; however, she had agreed to seek chemical dependency treatment. The actual Dodge County sheriff reports were not in the court files. They were suddenly missing. She had a passenger in the car when Deputy James Trihey stopped her on September 11, 1997, and the passenger was Garry. Who pulled the file? Was it the sheriff? Maybe it was someone that worked in the sheriff's office. We would later find out there was a woman that was working in the sheriff's office that was looking out for Garry. The sheriff was responsible for what happened in his office.

Bob bought a new pickup in December from Clements Chevrolet in Rochester. As soon as we got home, Garry called Bob and told him that he knew that Bob had got a new Chevrolet pickup and he knew how much Bob paid for it. Garry told Bob that he knew all our business. It really burned me. Whenever I asked Garry anything, he would say, "It's none of your business," especially about Tammy's death. I called the salesman and told him what had happened. I said, "Neither Bob nor I am never going to buy another vehicle from you." He told me he would find out why this happened. He later called back and told me that a cousin of Garry's worked there. Clements then fired her. We never bought another vehicle there again.

Barb Pike got Garry to agree in writing, on December 17, 1997, on Christmas visitation. In the written agreement, it said, Wayne's son, Bob, would pick the girls up at 10:00 AM on December 24 and return them at 2:00 PM the same day. He would pick them up again at 4:00 PM on Friday, December 26, and return them at 7:00 PM on Saturday, December 27.

I would soon see that this whole thing was going to get very expensive between the lawyer and having a private investigator work for us much of the time. I really thought that God was helping the farm to pay for this. Most of our lives, we were just getting by, but now we were making enough money to pay for this.

Chapter 14

The Investigation into Tammy's Death

On January 22, 1998, Rollie called me early in the morning. He said that he had given the investigation to Garry's attorney, Resovich. He thought I deserved to get it too. He brought it to our house at 10:00 AM. I had to sign for it. I sat up to the kitchen bar right away, and I started to read it. I didn't eat dinner and never got up from the bar until 6:00 PM. It was so lengthy that it took me that long to read and study it.

In Deputy John Snaza's report on the day of the fire, he spoke with Kayla and Sarah. He indicated that they went out to the barn with Garry and, while in the barn, looked out and saw smoke coming from the residence and told Garry, who went running to the house. In Deputy Dave Bentzen's report, he said,

> I went to the McColley farm and stayed with the family while the ambulance crew checked the girls and Garry. The girls both said that they were not in the fire but saw the smoke from the house and told their daddy in the barn about it.

He then asked Garry what happened with Deputy John Snaza present.

> Garry said that he was in the barn trying to warm up some water equipment, and the girls came

running in for him, telling him there was smoke coming from the house.

Garry said that he went in the kitchen from the back door and could not see anything because of the smoke. Garry said that he went outside and propped a ladder against the side of the house to try to get to the bedroom window where he knew that Tammy was sleeping. Garry said he broke the window which was near the bed, and he could not see her or reach her when he tried to go in.

On the morning of January 6, 1997, Garry and the girls were called to the sheriff's office. I believe that they had done the interview with Garry first. I am not going to copy Garry's interview. If I were to copy the whole investigation, my book would be a thousand pages or more from just the investigation. I believe that they did Garry's interview first. At the start of the interview, Garry didn't know the birth dates of the girls. When they asked him what the spelling of Sarah's name, he answered, "S-a-r-h-a." That is why the spelling of her name is wrong in the interview with the girls. They asked him, "What happened?" He replied that Kayla had told him that she had seen smoke from the house. He said that he tried to go in the house, but there was too much smoke. He then set a ladder up against the bedroom window, broke out the window, and tried to find Tammy but couldn't. He then put the girls in the car and went to a neighbor, who was Tucker, and told him to call 911. His next answer was,

> I opened the door up to him and told him to dial 911 because my house is on fire and I saw him looking through the phone book for the phone number and I just left.

After some time, he then went to another neighbor to report the fire. They then asked several questions about the electrical and the heating system. They then asked if his wife smoked. He answered that they both smoked. They then asked, "Is it common for your wife to be up in the bedroom smoking?" He answered, "Yes." The next question was, "Is it possible that she may have fallen asleep smoking?" He answered that she was always leaving cigarettes lying around. They then asked if she left matches lying around. He said that they only used lighters. When they asked him how much he paid for the house, he tried to make them believe that he paid a lot more than he did. He said that he took out a loan for $40,000. After asking more questions about the loan, he said that he paid me $10,000 and $4,000 for the septic tank. They then asked, "What was the total cost for the house and the property?" He then answered, "$7,500." He admitted to having a problem with alcohol and drugs. They asked him, "How did you get along with Tammy?" He answered, "Really good." They asked, "Would the kids have access to the lighters?" He answered, "Well, I suppose Tammy laid her cigarettes down or lighters, or there could have been lighters lying around." He then told them he couldn't get into the house. They asked Garry if he knew Mr. Tucker. He answered, "No."

A person from the sheriff's office and two fire marshals next interviewed the girls. The whole interview with the girls doesn't make sense. They were not qualified to interview young children. When you read the interview, you will realize that these men shouldn't have done this interview. They wanted the girls to say what they told them. Why did they want to talk to Sarah first? Evidently, they had talked to Garry off the record first. Garry had to blame the fire on someone else. That was what he did in the past. He always tried to get someone else to take the blame for his actions. These men all should have lost their jobs. I am going to copy the interview exactly as they did the interview. In some places in the interview, I am going to express my opinion, and I am going to enclose them in square brackets. The girls told the truth at first, but when they were trying to create something that never happened, everything went wrong with the interview.

> Q: This is Tom Neudahl from the State Fire Marshall's Office. We're going to begin interviewing ah Sarha and she's 3 years old and we're gonna ask Sarha about what happened

yesterday at ah…they had a fire at their house. Sarha, my name is Tom okay. Do you understand what I'm sayin' to you? Okay. I'm sure you're a little scared cause you don't know who we are but we're not gonna hurt you or nothin'. We just want to ask you some questions about what happened yesterday at the house when you had the fire. Okay? Do you understand. Sarha can you tell me… maybe if I can get down to your level it will make it a little bit easier. Can I hold your hand or don't you want me to? Hmm…Sarha can you tell me yesterday when you guys were playing with the toys in the dining room. Do you remember that yesterday? Huh? And you had some kind of a fire in the house. Do you remember that you went out to the barn to tell your Dad about what was goin' on? Can you remember that at all Sarha? Hmm? (pause) What I think what we're gonna is we're gonna stop and we're gonna bring the other child in here.

Q: Let's get Kayla in here.

Q: Yup yup.

Q: Do you want Kayla in here too Sarha?

A: Kayla

Q: You're Kayla? Oh. I'm Dave.

Q: And I'm Rollie.

Q: And I'm Tom. Okay. I know we're strangers but we're we're here to help you okay? We just want to ask you a few questions about what happened yesterday at the fire at your house. Okay? Do you remember the fire yesterday at your house?

A: Last time we started in the barn and the smoke just came inaudible [*sic*] and…

Q: Okay. But can I ask you. Daddy went out to the barn to work on the pipes and and you and Sarha were in the house playing?
A: We was out in the barn with my Dad.
Q: Were you down in the barn right away with Daddy? When Daddy first went down to the barn or were you in the house and then came down and told Daddy about the smoke?
A: Daddy was waking Mommy up. [Sometime after the fire, Kayla told her grandma, right before we went to the barn with our dad, Dad went upstairs to talk to Mommy.]
Q: It was after the fire was discovered, right?
Q: Daddy tried to wake Mommy up after the fire was discovered? Yeah. Okay. But how about that? Kayla can you tell us what happened?
Q: Were you and Sarha playing with the toys in the house for a while?
A: Picture of fire I saw too [When they said the picture, it couldn't have come from their house. They were watching a fire on TV at our house the afternoon of the fire.]
Q: Did you see the fire?
A: I thought I did.
Q: Okay.
A: I saw the fire smoke and then went and told Daddy.
Q: And then you went and told Daddy after you saw the fire right?
A: (both talking)
Q: I'm sorry
A: My Mom just died.
Q: Yeah your Mom died in the fire. We're sorry about that. But can you tell us about the fire in the house? How did the fire...where was the fire in the house?

A FATHER'S QUEST

A: The fire was upstairs. (both girls talking)
Q: The fire was upstairs?
A: Hmm hmm.
A: Hmm hmm and in my Mom and Dad's room.
Q: Okay but how do you know the fire was upstairs in Mom and Dad's room? Did you go up there and see it?
A: Nuh nuh I didn't run in the house. I inaudible [*sic*] out but my Mom is. My Mom's sleeping. Her not dead.
Q: Your Mom was sleeping up in the bedroom right?
A: Huh huh.
Q: And then you guys were downstairs in the dining room playing with your toys? Right? Is that right? Okay? [The girls have now told them several times that they were in the barn when they saw smoke. Why don't they believe them?]
Q: What were you playing with?
A: I was playing with inaudible [*sic*] not playing with it now. But I was playing with inaudible [*sic*].
A: I got a rabbit.
A: And I was was watching t.v. [Maybe it was at our house.]
Q: I see. Were you awake when Mommy came home? When Mommy came home from work? Did you have breakfast with Mommy? Did you? What did Mommy have for breakfast?
A: Eggs and sausage and toast. [There was less than five cc of anything in Tammy's stomach according to her autopsy. Why?]
Q: Did she drink coffee?
A: Nope. Chocolate. Chocolate milk.

Q: Chocolate milk. Oh

A: I inaudible [*sic*] my Mom brought me chocolate milk. Inaudible [*sic*]

Q: Did she?

Q: And did she talk to you a little bit? What did she tell you?

A: inaudible [*sic*] I don't know.

Q: Did she say you were a good girl?

A: She said I love you.

Q: Did she? Pretty.

Q: When you were at home and you were talking with Mommy at the table ah Mommy and Daddy say anything or do anything? Did Mommy then have to take a nap? Was she tired?

A: Yeah.

Q: Okay and when Mommy got tired were you playing in the living at that time? What were you doing in the living room?

A: Playing with my bicycle.

Q: With your bicycle and what about your sister. What was she doing?

A: Sarha was playing with a car.

Q: What kind of a car.

A: That purple one.

Q: Oh. Inaudible [*sic*]

A: inaudible [*sic*]

Q: Four cars?

A: We were playing four

Q: And while you're playing with this stuff, what else did you do?

A: Hmm…

Q: Do you remember finding Mommy's lighter? Did you see Mommy's lighter? Did ya? [In Tammy's autopsy, there was no nicotine in her body. Garry had tried to blame the fire on Tammy's smoking in bed. Tammy didn't smoke! Why did they bring up Mommy's lighter?]

A: Its Pink

Q: Its pink.

A: My Daddy's got purple.

Q: Daddy's is purple huh?

A: Purple and blue.

Q: Purple and blue. And where did you find the lighters?

A: In the living room.

Q: And when you found the lighters in the living room, what did you do with them?

A: We just fired 'em on the glass table.

Q: on the glass table? Oh… And this you break the table.

A: inaudible [sic]

Q: Did the lighters make a fire?

A: Nuh nuh.

Q: No? What do you think made the fire?

A: I don't know.

Q: Did you see the fire start? You did? [Now they are putting words in the girls' mouths.]

A: I did too.

Q: Did you? Where abouts was the fire when you saw it?

A: In the house.

Q: In the house.

A: Upstairs

Q: It was upstairs in the house.

A: Hmm hmm I saw it.

A: inaudible [sic]

A: inaudible [sic]

A: There was lots of them.

Q: There's what?

A: Lots of fires. Upstairs outside. [They told you again, they saw the fire from outside. You are trying to make up something that never happened.]

A: outside

A: and it broke a window.

Q: Who broke the window?

A: The fire. [Either this was what they saw at our house on TV, or they were outside at their home.]

Q: Oh. But inside the house…were you inside the house when the fire was there?

A: inaudible [*sic*] inside.

A: I sit in the car and the other car…a gray car. [Garry put the girls in the car after they told him about the fire in the barn.]

A: inaudible [*sic*] gray car and Daddy.

A: inaudible [*sic*]

Q: When you first saw the smoke in the house and went to see Daddy… Do you remember where you saw the smoke? Was that in the living room?

A: Hmm hmm. It was inaudible too [*sic*].

Q: And do you know where about in the living room?

A: By the t.v. And inaudible [*sic*] chair. Off the table and inaudible. [If they were in the house when the fire was at the TV, it would have been impossible for them to get out. They would have died!]

Q: and was the smoke over by the t.v.?

Q: Were your blankies on fire? Your blankies were burning? [You were trying to put words in the girls' mouths! You brought up blankets first. You told them that the blankets were burning.]

A: Mine was.
Q: How did your blankies get on fire?
A: My blankie's inaudible [sic]
A: (both children talking)
A: car
Q: Your blankie's in the car?
A: inaudible [sic]
Q: Kayla...are you telling me... I want to be make sure I understand you correctly that when you were in the living room and saw the fire... Your blankies were on fire in the living room. Is that correct?
A: Hmm hmm.
Q: Okay. Was the sofa on fire too? Okay. But... but were you guys playing with the lighter and that how the thing caught on fire?
A: I didn't.
Q: Is that what happened...Sarha?
A: (both talking) They burned somewhere. Inaudible [sic].
Q: Where you playing with the lighter or your sister?
A: My Daddy's
Q: Did you play with Daddy's lighter? Okay
A: I inaudible [sic]...purple
Q: Dad's purple lighter? Okay.
A: inaudible [sic]
Q: Is that the one that caught on fire?
A: Uh huh.
Q: Okay.
A: Daddy's lighter is the purple one.
Q: Okay. Were you playing with Daddy's purple lighter?
A: inaudible to him [sic]
Q: Kayla do you remember that's what happened? Was Sarha playing with the lighter

and maybe accidentally the blankies caught on fire? Is that what happened? Are you saying yes?

A: Yup.

Q: Okay. But you need to tell me what happened. Okay? I don't want to put words in into your head or anything or in your mouth. You need to tell me what happened. Okay? Can you tell me? Was Sarha playing with Daddy's lighter and then accidentally something caught on fire?

A: Hmm hmm.

Q: Okay. But can you tell me that.

A: inaudible [sic] lighter.

A: I don't know.

Q: Did she get burnt on her cheek?

A: Nmm nmm.

A: inaudible [sic]

A: Sarha keeps picking on it.

A: I had an owie.

Q: Oh you had a scratch on your face and she's been picking at the scab?

A: Hmm hmm

Q: Oh okay.

A: I keep bleeding.

Q: Yeah.

A: inaudible [sic]

Q: Where did you find Daddy's lighter?

A: On the Counter. [Before they had just established that the lighter was in the living room. In the past the lighter was in various places in the house. It didn't mean that the girls were in the house when the fire started.]

Q: On the what?

A: On the Counter.

Q: On the counter.

A: Hmm hmm.

Q: Oh. Daddy's lighter was on the counter in the kitchen?

A: Hmm hmm I got it from my Dad. You remember my Dad?

Q: Yeah I met your Dad. He's a nice guy isn't he?

A: We love Daddy.

A: inaudible [sic]

Q: Your Daddy loves you very much I'm sure.

A: Hmm hmm

A: Mommy too.

Q: And your Mommy loves you very much. Okay? Kayla I have to make sure I understand you correctly that what happened. Okay? So you need to make sure and tell me what happened Okay is that Sarha was playing with the lighter and your blankets caught on fire and that's when and told Dad?

A: Hmm hmm.

A: My blanket caught on fire too. [When you can tell a lie often enough, they will believe you. Blankets are treated so they won't burn easily. How does a three-year-old, with a lighter, set a blanket on fire without burning her hands or her own clothes?]

Q: Yeah. Your blankie caught on fire didn't it?

A: Hmm hmm I dropped it.

Q: Okay

A: in the house. Inaudible [sic]

Q: But Sarha was playing with the lighter and not you or both of you were playing with it?

A: I was not.

Q: You were not so Sarha

A: I was sleeping.

Q: You were kind of laying around and sleepin' on the floor. Is that what you were doin'?

A: Uh huh

A: I was sleeping upstairs my Mom inaudible [sic] died inaudible [sic]

A: inaudible with my Mommy yesterday [sic]

Q: Yeah. You're pretty sad about Mom dying aren't ya?

A: Hmm hmm

Q: Yeah

A: I like my Mom.

Q: Yeah. You guys are tired aren't ya? You didn't sleep much last night huh? Did you go to Grandpa's and go to sleep last night?

A: Hmm hmm

A: Nmm nmm

Q: No

A: Daddy picked us up

Q: No but you slept at Grandpa's last night?

A: Yes. [They didn't sleep at Grandpa's. Garry and his mother picked them up at 9:00 in the evening. Now they are getting the girls to lie!]

Q: But that's what happened. You guys…Sarha was playing with the lighter and the blankies caught on fire and then you got your jackets on and then you ran out to tell Daddy about the fire? [They were three and four years old. They got their jackets on and ran to the barn?]

A: inaudible [sic] fire inaudible [sic] fire…that purple one…my Daddy's.

Q: The purple was on fire? Huh?

A: inaudible [sic] I have a race car.

Q: You have a race car?

A: I got names for my inaudible [sic] I got a blue coat.

Q: Okay. Do you know its very important for us to tell the truth about what happened? Okay?

A FATHER'S QUEST

We need to know. Hmm would you be willing to tell Dad about what happened? Have you told Dad? Has Daddy asked you about what happened?

A: I did it. I tell inaudible [sic] my grandpa.

Q: Did you tell grandpa and grandma about what happened?

A: 'Uh huh

Q: Yup

A: inaudible quiet [sic]

A: inaudible too [sic]

A: inaudible [sic]

Q: But you told grandpa and grandma about playing with the lighter? [The girls didn't tell us about the fire or anything. They never talked to us about playing with a lighter anytime. Why didn't they question us to see that it was true?]

A: inaudible [sic]

A: inaudible [sic] grandma inaudible [sic]

Q: So you told grandma about Sarha playing with the lighter? Okay.

A: inaudible]

Q: Let's shut the tape off. We're gonna stop the tape and bring Dad in so they…we're understanding the kids correctly.

Q: We're back on tape. (pause) A little more or? Mine's cold, I won't throw it out…inaudible [sic]

Q: Well we had a little talk with the Kara…Sarha and Kayla and we named the teddy bears. [That is the first time they talked about the teddy bears. I think the three stooges were conducing this interview.] So we got the names for 'em and they told us they were in the house playing…and that they found a lighter and their blankets caught on fire. (pause) And that when they got their coats on and came out to tell Dad there was a fire.

Q: And basically this is Tom Neudahl talking… Basically Garry, Kayla is telling us and Sarha has told me that she found you're your I believe it was purple… I'm sorry that's the color of the car…she found your cigarette lighter.

A: Like these?

Q: And she found it in the kitchen on the counter…is what she's telling me.

A: inaudible [*sic*]

Q: Okay. What we would like to do is we're not familiar with the kids so what we would like for you to do is we're gonna ask them again to tell you because maybe they will be a little more honest with you being familiar with you hmm…ask them to tell Dad about what happened and see if can just make sure that you know you can tell better than we can if the kids are being honest with us. Okay? And we realize it's hard cause they are talking about kinds of different thing but hmm I basically Garry to be honest with you I really believe…I have a pretty good idea that's what happened.

A: inaudible [*sic*]

Q: Oh no no and that's what we're saying and we just have to make sure that's what happened and so hmm Kayla can you tell Daddy hmm what happened yesterday before you came out to the barn you and Sarha we're playing in the house. Can you tell Daddy what happened.

A: inaudible [*sic*] smoke inaudible [*sic*]. [She told the truth. She didn't say *fire*; she said *smoke*.

A FATHER'S QUEST

She was out in the barn and saw smoke from the house. How many times does she have to tell you what happened?]

Q: You saw smoke in the house and then you went out and told Daddy but remember you told us about you and Sarha were in the living room and Sarha was playing with the lighter and accidentally some how the blankets caught on fire.

A: inaudible [sic]

Q: is that what happened?

A: inaudible [sic]

Q: Sarha do you remember where you found the lighter?

A: Hmm hmm

Q: Where was it?

A: In the kitchen. [By now they have the girls so confused from telling them about the lighter and the kitchen and what color it is. How does anyone know the truth?]

Q: In the kitchen? And it was on the counter? Is that what you told me? Okay. And was it like Daddy's lighter that it is now?

A: Hmm hmm.

Q: It's the same type but different colors on it?

A: Hmm hmm.

Q: Like that?

A: Our car is gray.

Q: Is that the kind of lighter that you had yesterday? Something like that?

A: No.

Q: What color was it?

A: Pink one.

Q: Pink one huh?

Dad: Did you have the pink one?

A: inaudible [sic]

Q: Can you show Daddy what happened? Can you take the lighter and show what happened? [Pause.] It's okay. You can show us. You were playing with the lighter, is that right? Remember that's what you told me was that Sarha was playing with the lighter? And that maybe accidentally you started the blankets on fire. Is that what happened Kayla? [Kayla didn't answer; she knew this was a lie.]
Q: Do you know how the lighter works? When you push it down what happen?
A: Then it's on fire.
Q: Then it's on fire.
A: Do like this. [The girls didn't learn how to use a lighter by themselves. Garry must have been playing with a lighter with them.]
Q: Oh do like that huh?
A: Hmm hmm inaudible [*sic*] do that yesterday inaudible [*sic*] used it. It was pink inaudible [*sic*]
Q: I think we'll go ahead and we'll stop the tape' You know we're not.

These three men had never met Kayla and Sarah before. It's hard to understand three-and four-year-olds talking. I assume that a woman employee typed this report. Most women can understand young kids better when they have kids themselves. I don't know if this is the case. When you type the report, you can study the inaudible parts and try to understand what they were saying. There were way too many inaudible parts to determine what happened. In a courtroom, even a dumb lawyer could make these men seem foolish.

Didn't the sheriff read this report? It doesn't make any sense that he would believe the report. We have shown our friends this report, and every one of them has said that it doesn't make any sense. Rollie told me that there was a fire that started in Hayfield. Some kids were playing with matches, and that was how the fire started. They must think how this fire started. How could they blame the girls from this investigation? How could they put on Tammy's death certificate that the girls started the fire that killed her? Sheriff Bill Weber told Rollie not to investigate **anymore**. Why would the State Fire Marshall Tom Neudahl stand for this? I knew I had a big job ahead of me. I was not going to stand for this!

Next, I looked at a report that we got from the Office of the Medical Examiner, County of Ramsey, State of Minnesota. It was quite lengthy. It was not easy to read an autopsy when it was for your own daughter. I started, but I couldn't read it. I did discover two things. There was no nicotine in her system. It was a complete lie when Garry told the investigators about Tammy smoking. There was also less than 5 cc of anything in Tammy's stomach. How could this be if he had made Tammy a big breakfast? Becky Sullivan had told Tammy that she was having an affair with Garry at work the night before. Tammy was upset, and that would explain why she didn't have anything in her stomach. If anyone from the sheriff's office would have read this, there would have been many more questions for Garry. But they wanted the girls to be held responsible for the fire, not Garry.

From this investigation, we found out that Garry had more insurance on Tammy than we realized. There was a policy that Garry bought on Tammy shortly after Kayla was born. The policy was for $100,000. It was bought through the mail. It was an accidental death policy. Someone else signed Tammy's name on the application. Who signed her name? There was another accidental policy on Tammy for $135,000. It was again bought through the mail. The signature was not Tammy's. It was obvious to us that Garry signed her name. Garry bought this policy five months before her death. Garry also had an accidental death insurance policy on both of them on the mortgage amount of their house. It was almost $40,000. Tammy also had a policy at work for $100,000. It had been raised from $40,000 five days from Tammy's death. Garry collected $125,000 on the house and their personal goods. He also collected $11,000 from the policy that I had bought for Tammy. All in total, he collected almost $511,000. He received about $600 Social Security for each child from Tammy working. He never put any of this money away for the girls. On the insurance policy for $135,000, they couldn't tell from the application if Garry got the whole amount or if the girls were going to get part of it. It went through court, and the girls each got $35,000.

Looking though the investigation, I came across an anonymous letter written on January 8, 1997. I am going to copy the letter as it was written.

To whomever it may concern.

The story of the rural Kasson woman who died in a house fire Jan. 5, 1997 bothers me because I don't understand a few things. First, was her husband cleared on any involvement? It just sounds strange that she came home at 8:30a.m., ate breakfast and went to bed. Her cigarette caused the house to burn down 5 hours later? Why were her young daughters left unsupervised while she needed to sleep and her husband was out in the barn? I myself have a 3 year old and a 4 year old daughter and let me tell you there is no absolute way you can sleep in the daytime especially if they weren't used to her having that schedule!!

The paper said the 4 year old daughter went outside to inform the father she smelled smoke? You mean he didn't smell or see it? Nor was he the one who called the fire department?? Usually daughters go to their mother instinctively when something isn't just right. Did the home have working smoke detectors? I just think it sounds fishy and that it needs to be further investigated! I feel terrible sadness for this gals family. Someone has to make sure all actions are taken to investigate all causes! Her daughters will live with this the rest of their lives, how sad. Are you sure they weren't outside with him? It's awfully hard to believe they didn't wake their mom while they played (or whatever) let alone stay quit when the house was burning!

There was just a story last week in the Post Bulletin about a husband that was responsible for a house fire that resulted in his wifes death. Sometimes they try to get the life insurance policy! I wish you could respond to my letter but I wouldn't dare sign my name. It's a cruel world and I wouldn't want someone coming after me. Anyway I just felt I had to write, it just really bothered me. If the case has been 100% investigated, then that is good and that lady can Rest IN Peace. If not, well then it is owed to her to be.

Thank You

I went to talk to Rollie about this letter. "Why aren't you looking into some things that she brought up?" Rollie told me that she didn't sign the letter and it didn't mean anything. I wish I knew her. I would thank her for writing the letter. If she had signed the letter, I know that Rollie wouldn't have looked into anything. He then told me again, "Sheriff Bill Weber told him not to look into anything."

I went to the sheriff's office often or called Rollie the first three weeks after Tammy's death. I questioned Rollie every time about the clothes that Garry was wearing. He wasn't dressed to be outside on a very cold day. I would learn much later that when someone was on meth, they were always hot. I had questions about the insurance. Reading the report, I never realized that there was so much insurance. Finally, Rollie had another interview with Garry on January 27, 1997. The interview is so long that I'm not going to copy it. There were pages of Rollie questioned Garry about the clothes. He said he couldn't remember. His story always changed. He finally told Rollie that he had just bought a new pair of Carhartts after the fire. It proved that I was right about what he was wearing. Rollie again questioned Garry about going in the house and looking for Tammy. He said that he never went in the house. He broke an upstairs window and reached in. When we were at the house the day of the fire, he told me that he went in the upstairs bedroom and couldn't find Tammy. When I said to Garry, "You told me you went in the house," he said "You are a fu——ing liar." Rollie asked about Tucker. Garry didn't know Tucker. He said he went to the house and told Tucker to call 911. When he saw Tucker looking for the phone book, he left. Why would you need a phone book to dial 911? Did Garry actually tell Tucker to call 911? Rollie asked Garry, "How did you and Tammy get along?" Garry answered, "We've been getting along real good." That was a lie! When Tammy came to our house on the Friday before her death, she told us about how bad she was getting along with Garry. Rollie then questioned Garry at length about Bill Akinson. He was a known drug dealer. Garry denied buying any drugs from Bill. Why wasn't Garry dressed warmly the day of the fire? Rollie then questioned Garry about the insurance. Garry had insurance if he got hurt working around the farm. It cost him $50 a month. He would draw $700 a month if he got hurt. Rollie then asked Garry, "So if you got killed, who would have been the beneficiary on that policy?" Garry answered, "Tammy would have been." Rollie said, "Would you ever set it up so someone else would have been the beneficiary on that?" Garry answered, "Well, it would be Tammy or the girls." Rollie then said, "If I told you that I saw a copy of that particular insurance policy, and it's got your mother listed as the beneficiary, would that sound right?" Garry answered, "That's possible." That was the policy that Garry bought on himself for $150,000 with a rider giving Tammy $135,000 insurance. Garry made it seem like he was buying insurance on himself and not Tammy. He bought the policy on August 1, 1996, five months before Tammy's death, when he didn't have a job. Rollie asked Garry about a $100,000 policy that he had. Garry told Rollie that he didn't know but would have to look into it. In the investigation report, it showed that Garry applied for the money on January 14, 1997. Rollie then asked Garry if the girls would need counseling about their mother's death and the fire. Garry agreed, but he thought it should not start for a couple of years. He was counting on that girls that young would forget by then. He didn't want anyone talking to the girls now. They then talked about all the rumors that were going around about Becky Sullivan. Rollie then said, "Yeah, I mean, jeez give us a break. You know, we didn't need that either, and we don't need this crud that's going around." Garry had now lied about almost everything, but Rollie wasn't going to do anything. Rollie was okay with blaming the girls.

Rollie did an interview with a lady that worked with Tammy at the nursing home from Brownsdale on January 29, 1997. He didn't list her name on the interview. Rollie asked if Tammy liked her job. She replied, "She seemed to enjoy her work. She was sad about working with these older people that are terminal and the way they were, but she really enjoyed her job." About six months ago, Tammy had told her that she wanted to leave her husband. She was afraid to leave because Garry had told her that she would never get custody of her girls. She then said that Tammy was so emotional that she would start bawling in a minute. Tammy had showed her the bruise on her arm. She asked Tammy if Garry had done it in front of the girls. She said, "Yeah, he did it right in front of the children," and then one of the girls had said, "Daddy's being mean. Why is he such a bad man?" Rollie asked about the bruises. She said, "There was a really bad bruise on her arm last October, it was all over her arm. Tammy was always crying at work." Rollie asked if Tammy ever drank. She answered, "She doesn't drink." Rollie then asked, "Do you think someone hurt Tammy?" She replied, "Well, that's a good thing, well, it's something to think about because he abused her." Rollie then asked about work. Tammy was working a lot of hours. She needed the money because they were behind on their debts. Garry wasn't working! Rollie then asked her, "Would you say that she was depressed?" She replied, "Yes, she was. I'm not sure. But I mean, she was crying almost every day. I'd say she was very depressed." Rollie asked her, "Did you talk to other employees about what you saw?" She answered, "Yes, we have been before her death, we talked about it too you know. We always or we don't always know what was concluded, but it was because of Garry." Rollie then tried to discredit her. Rollie then said, "And you really can't prove that he beat her, right?" She replied, "No, I can't, I'm just saying what she told me." Rollie then said, "And this is what I'm getting at is basically that you really don't have firsthand knowledge what you're telling a story that she said to you? She could have fallen down and bruised herself, or she could have been trying to handle one of the calves or something at home." Then she hesitantly answered, "Yes." Rollie then said, "Right? So you really don't know what was going on, right?" She then answered, "Right." Rollie then said, "Okay, and if I told you that we went through a complete investigation and we find that we have an accidental house fire, would you believe me?" After a long pause, she finally said, "Yes." Rollie finally told her it was carbon monoxide that killed her.

Rollie was good about putting words in mouths of people he talked to. He made the lady feel like she shouldn't have come in. Why didn't Rollie take her word about the bruises? Garry had been convicted eight times in court for beating up women. They had on record that Garry beat Tammy. Why did Rollie now believe Tammy caused the bruises herself? Reading this interview made me really mad and disgusted! Why didn't I do more to help her? I had failed Tammy. Thinking about the investigation, I should have killed Garry. I would be in prison, but Tammy would be alive. Why did Garry purchase all the additional insurance on the house and on Tammy when they were behind on their bills? Tammy was working all these extra hours to catch up on the bills.

There was a copy of a court summons in the investigation report dated August 4, 1997. *Monumental Life Insurance Company vs. Garry*, and on Sarah and Kayla by and through their guardian ad litem, Eric Thompson, was listed in the summons. There was an issue on the policy that Garry bought in 1996 on himself for $150,000 with a rider on Tammy for $135,000. The designated beneficiaries on Tammy were Garry or the decedent's children, Kayla and Sarah. Tammy was not listed as a beneficiary on his policy. It said that detectives of the Kasson County Sheriff's department were also investigating the cause of the fire that killed the decedent. Although the sheriff detectives refused to comment either way regarding whether they suspect Garry of intentionally causing the fire and or the death of the decedent, they requested Garry to submit to a polygraph examination regarding the fire, but he refused. Upon information and belief, the Kasson County Sheriff's department had not made a determination regarding the cause of the fire nor had it closed its investigation of this matter. Kayla and Sarah had potential claims to the proceeds of the policies, which were averse to Defendant Garry's claims in that they might be entitled to a portion of the proceeds as alternative beneficiaries or as the decedent's heirs if Garry was found to have intentionally caused the fire or the death of the decedent.

> WHEREFORE, Monumental respectfully requests this court judgment as follows:
>
> 1. Finding that Monumental is or may be exposed to multiple liability by the adverse claims of the Dependents
> 2. Allowing Monumental to deposit the proceeds of the Policies with the court and requiring Defendants to interplead their claims to the proceeds among themselves;
> 3. Discharging Monumental from further liability to the Defendants and dismissing it with prejudice from this action upon depositing the proceeds of the Policies with the court;

I then called the company. I told them I was certain that Garry started the fire. I tried to get them to investigated the fire. We had a long talk. I told them that they could save a lot of money if they didn't have to pay. They said it would cost them less money to pay the claim than fight it. Maybe if Garry was guilty, they would still have to pay Kayla and Sarah. It could get very expensive for them!

There was also another investigation report written by Kevin L. Dunkin. The fire didn't get reported immediately because Garry at first went to the Tucker farm. After waiting until the fire got going good, Garry then went to another neighbor whom he knew. The fire then got reported. The fire occurred on Sunday, January 5, 1997, between 12:45 and 1:00 PM. Garry stated that at the time of the fire, he was in the barn located approximately forty feet from the house.

He said that Tammy was asleep in the upstairs bedroom as she had worked the 11:00 PM–7:00 AM shift. She got home at approximately 8:30 AM and then went to bed. Garry stated that he had gone into the residence to fix lunch for the children then left them inside and traveled to the barn. He advised that his daughters later came to the barn, and Kayla stated that there was smoke in the house. Garry stated that he was last in the house at 12:30 PM on the day of the fire. He advised that his daughters were the last persons to leave the house at 12:45 PM. He wrote the conclusion of the report:

> On the morning of January 5, 1997, Tammy returned to her residence after working an eleven to seven shift at her job in a nursing home. She then went to bed. At approximately 12:00 to 12:30 PM. Garry fixed lunch for their three and four-year-old daughters. He then left the children inside of the house and traveled to the barn to thaw water pipes. Shortly thereafter the children came to the barn and advised Garry that there was smoke in the house. The fire department was notified, and they responded. Tammy perished in the fire as a result of smoke inhalation. After interviewing Garry, it was learned that during his conversation with the Minnesota State Fire Marshal, the children indicated to him that they set a blanket on fire. Due to the amount of destruction from the fire I was unable to determine the exact point of origin for the loss. Furthermore, I was unable to eliminate all accidental causes and I was unable to eliminate incendiary. Therefore, the fire remains undetermined.

It seemed like Kevin Dunkin didn't buy the investigation that the sheriff's department did. The sheriff's office had always taken Garry's word for the fire regardless how much he changed his story. Why? How could the girls stop what they were doing, find a lighter, start a blanket on fire, get the jackets and boots, and go to the barn in fifteen minutes? Why wouldn't they go upstairs to their mother and tell her? Why didn't the girls smell of smoke, if they were in the house? Why didn't Sheriff Weber pay no attention to this report?

Chapter 15

The Second Year after Tammy's Death

Ruth was cleaning out a cupboard in November 1997 and found an invitation to a baby shower given for Tammy in 1992. I was working in the office when Ruth brought the card in for me to see. I looked at the card and said, "The person that wrote this card is the person that signed Tammy's name on the insurance application." We got out the application, and the signature matched. There were four women on the card who were giving the party for Tammy. "Who was it?" I gave this card to Timothy Braatz, who was from Atlas Investigations. On January 23, 1998, I got a reply from him.

> Enclosed, please find certified copies of the most recent MN DOT driver's license application for Bobbie Jo who is Garry's sister. As you can see, Bobbie signature appears to be very similar to the writing on the baby shower card you provided.

He also found another criminal case.

> Case #89-50906 for 9/11/89 stated that Garry damaged Linda's apartment door, threw a beer can at her, hit her arm and threatened to kill her. Linda his girlfriend, alleged that Garry became violent when he was drinking. Garry called her six and eleven-year-old daughters, "Bitch" and other cruel names. He was arrested and the offi-

cers found 5.8 grams of marijuana in his jacket. He was convicted on the drug charge. I then took the letter from Atlas and the card to the sheriff's office and talked to Rollie. He sent the card to the BCA. They checked out all four signature on the card and didn't find a match. I still didn't know who signed Tammy's name.

Invitation from Tammy's baby shower

On January 7, 1998, Ruth and I went to the courthouse in Grant County to find out why Garry was in jail when Tammy met him. We couldn't control our emotions when we asked two women that were working there. We told them that our daughter Tammy had died. We wanted everything that they had on Garry. They looked up everything and copied it for free. There were more than one hundred pages. The arrests on Garry were fifty-two pages. They bent over backward to help us. They told us that the sheriff's office was in the courthouse. "You can't leave before you talk to Sheriff

Dwight Walvatne." We had to sit in his office for almost an hour waiting for him. When the sheriff came in, he talked to us for two hours. Garry, along with Linda, had met James Olin in California. While living with him, Garry talked him into selling everything he had and moving to Minnesota. James had $90,000 when they first met him. They bought a farmstead outside Barrett. James thought it was his, but Garry had it in his name. Garry then didn't feed Olin and gave him a lot of laxatives every day. He became very sick in bed, and they didn't clean him up. Olin had a friend in California that called the sheriff's office in Grant County to check on him. When he went out to the farmstead, he found Olin almost dead on a bed that was smelly and full of feces. Sheriff Walvatne said it was Garry's plan that the old man would die and then they would bury him. Then the farmstead would belong to Garry. In the fifty-two pages that they had on Garry, they accounted for the $90,000. Garry's mother got $20,000 of this money. She had gone to Barrett at least once. Garry's mother was in on this crime. When it came time for it to go to court, Olin had Alzheimer's and couldn't testify. They had to plea bargain with Garry, and he only got one year in prison. Linda got off free. When we told our story to the sheriff, he said, "Garry was capable of murdering Tammy. If I was the sheriff in Dodge County, Garry would be in jail."

After we left the courthouse, we went to Jackpot Junction Casino in Morton to spend the night. We got there about 4:30 PM, and when we got to our room, we wanted to read the information that we got at the courthouse right away. After we read the report, we never left the room. The report was so upsetting that we had no appetite to eat.

While James Olin was living in Barrett, everyone left him alone for a short time. He managed to call Guy Bates in California. On March 28, 1990, Guy Bates of Grover City, California, phoned and requested a check on the welfare of James Olin, who had recently moved from California to near Barrett in Grant County, Minnesota. Bates reported that Olin had left California with approximately $48,000, and now he told Bates that he had no money left and the people with whom he was living in Minnesota had somehow gotten it all. Bates provided the name of Pam Loge, who had knowledge of the situation. She was contacted and reported that she formerly lived in California and provided care and a place for Olin to stay. Olin stayed there several months and sold some real estate and placed the proceeds in one or more banks in California. Olin then met Garry, Linda, and Michael. Linda and Michael were Pam's siblings. Olin, along with the three of them, had moved to a farmstead near Barrett in Grant County. None of them had a job or any money of their own. Garry then conned Olin into giving him his money. The money was used by the three of them to live on, to acquire the farmstead and to purchase a motorcycle, a car, some guns, a new engine for an old pickup truck, numerous household goods and appliances, and other items. Pam stated that she had attempted to phone Olin to inquire into his welfare, but the three of them wouldn't let her talk to him.

Bates was then able to call Olin back and to tell him that the police would be there within the hour. Olin was found to be in need of medical care. He was undernourished and dehydrated and suffering from pneumonia. He was taken to Grant County Hospital for immediate treatment and remained hospitalized at least through April 2, 1990. Garry, Linda, and Michael were arrested and taken to jail. Olin was confused at first but became more lucid as his condition improved. He stated that Garry had been very abusive to him. He further stated that he had purchased the farmstead on which he had been living for about $18,000 and that he owned it. A check of the records in the office of the Grant County Recorders showed that the deed had been placed in Garry's name. Olin had no legal ownership by deed, mortgage, promissory note, or otherwise in the farmstead. Olin further stated that Garry and the other two had gotten all his money, which he estimated to be $48,000 or $49,000, and he didn't know how they ended up with it. It was not a gift or loan. He told them what they bought with his money, all without his permission. He said they refused to feed him or take him for medical care. Additional investigation showed that Garry had obtained from Olin, while in California, cashier's checks for well in excess of $20,000. Garry then converted those cashier's checks to cash and traveler's checks in his name, without having consent or permission from Olin. Garry's mother got $20,000 out of this money. Garry bought a motorcycle, which he brought to Grant County when he moved here. Garry's mother visited them at Barrett and met Olin. She had to know what they were doing. Was she in on the crime? I started thinking that maybe she signed Tammy's name on the insurance application. Was she in on Tammy's murder? How much money did she get from the insurance? How could I prove that she signed Tammy's name?

On April 11, 1990, the sheriff interviewed Michael because he wanted to talk. He described the beating he had received from Garry. Michael said the following:

> Garry had first started with a heart punch to my ribs and then I went down a little bit and then he punched me in the kidney and I went down a little more and then he came back and kicked me with his steel toe boots and in the same stop he hit me with his fist and I fell over and then he came back and kicked me in the kidney. I got back up and said, "What's wrong with you? What are you doing?" Then he kicked me in the groin area. Garry was very drunk when he did this. Another time Garry had Mike set up bottles or cans for him to shoot at. As soon as he would set them up Garry would shoot them with a shotgun. Mike said that he wasn't even a foot away. When Garry had gotten into a fight with Linda he put a gun to Linda's head and threatened to kill her. Linda then left in a car and Garry fired several shots over the car as she was driving away. Then the sheriff had a doctor examine Mike to see if he was telling the truth. The doctor found bruises in the groin and kidneys areas.

Ruth and I couldn't believe how someone could be so cruel to another person. When Garry told Tammy he was taking the blame for Linda, it was a complete lie. We both wished that we had gone to Grant County while Tammy was alive. Tammy was living with a madman! We left early the next morning because we were certain that the sheriff would do something now. We went to Rollie's office as soon as we got back. Rollie told us that it didn't make any difference. They had seen the investigation report a long time ago. We told him to call the sheriff in Grant County. He said that wouldn't do any good. He refused to call the sheriff! Rollie said, "Garry didn't kill your daughter. You will give up on this in six months and get on with your life." I told Rollie, "I will never give up on this. Tammy was our daughter. How could I give up on her?"

We then went out to supper with Ruth's cousin Glen Borgen and his wife, Barb. We talked about our trip to Grant County and the card Ruth had gotten inviting her to the baby shower. I told them that I suspected that Garry's mother signed the card. Glen told me that he used to drive to work with Garry's mother's third husband. They were now divorced, and she had really taken her third husband. Glen said he would contract him and ask if he had anything with her signature on it. Glen called me sometime later, and he told me that he had an old driver's license belonging to Garry's mother. We looked at it, and we were sure that she was the same person that forged Tammy's signature on the insurance application. I told Rollie that it was against the law to forge someone else's name. I said, "Put pressure on Garry's mother, and Garry will confess." Rollie said he would have to send it to the BCA first. I kept asking Rollie if he had got the driver's license back. He kept saying, "No." Finally, he said he got the license back, and Garry's mother didn't sign the card. I said to him, "Show me the report." He refused. If the report had said that Garry's mother didn't sign the card, he would have shown me. Why? All he said was, "Garry didn't kill your daughter."

Barb Pike, the appointed guardian ad litem, wrote a report on January 15, 1998.

1: Recommendation:
   A. It is my recommendation that Kayla and Sarah have regular visitation sched-

uled at the home of their grandparents, Wayne and Ruth McColley, the first weekend of every month from 4:00pm on Friday until 4:00pm on Sunday. They should also have one-week vacation during the week that includes July 4th of each year. Christmas visitation should be allowed from noon to 6:00pm on Christmas Eve Day with their grandparents and either the weekend prior to Christmas or the weekend following Christmas. The girls should be allowed visitation from 2:00 to 4:00 pm with the McColley's the first Saturday afternoon immediately following Sarah's birthday, which is January 15th. Garry should continue to contact the McColley's at other times to arrange visitation for the girls with their grandparents whenever agreeable to both parties.

B. The McColley's son "Bob" should continue to pick up and return the girls to their home at the start and end of each visitation period, if he is willing and able to do so. If he is not able to do so, Wayne should be allowed to pick the girls up for their regularly scheduled visitation. If Garry is not agreeable to Wayne picking the girls up at his home, when Bob is not available, he should meet Wayne at the Sheriff's Office to facilitate the transfer of the children.

C. There should be no travel out of state with the McColley's unless they have obtained prior permission from Garry, and he is informed of the location and phone number where they can be reached while out of state

D. Garry should provide a duly signed release to allow the McColley's to seek medical care for Kayla and Sarah in the event that a medical emergency should arise while the girls are in their care.

E. Both parties should refrain from making derogatory comments about the other party/parties or about the girls not being able to see their grandparents.

F. Kayla and Sarah should be evaluated by a competent child psychologist to determine to what extent they have been able to deal with the tragic loss of their mother. The recommendations of the outcome of the evaluations should be followed.

G. On their weekend of visitation, the McColley's should provide transportation on Sunday mornings for the girls to attend Sunday School at Byron United Methodist Church at their usual class time.

The girls have had some history with bad dreams and worries that they may not to be able to see their grandparents again. All parties involved should reassure the girls and strive to ensure that they will be able to continue this relationship. Kayla and Sarah have not had any counseling to date to help them work through their feelings about the circumstances leading to the untimely loss of their mother. I feel, as do the McColley's, that it is imperative that they be giving the opportunity to fully deal with those issues, so that they do not lead to bigger problems in the future. Even though Garry does not feel it is necessary at this time. It was a very emotional trauma for them, and an evaluation of their needs in the matter is certainly indicated.

At Faith Lutheran Church, Dorothy Norman approached me and asked me to be on the church council. Pastor Nelson had spent a lot of time with me. I didn't really want to be on the church council, but I found it was impossible to say no.

We took the girls to the Byron United Methodist Church once. Soon afterward, Garry's mother told us to never go to her church again. She gave us permission to take the girls to our church.

At this time we got a feeling that we just needed to get away. Ruth and I felt so sad from losing Tammy. I wanted to visit with my Uncle Lyle. After this visit, I would turn to Lyle for support. We didn't have much time but we would visit Lyle in Milton, Florida. Then we went to St. Petersburg, Florida to visit Ruth's sister, Donna, and her husband, John. On the way home we decided to go to Plains, Georgia. Plains was the home of President Carter. We went to the Carter Museum on a Saturday. A lady working there invited us on go Jimmy Carter's church. Jimmy would be teaching Sunday School. We went early. Sunday School was first. Jimmy went out of his way to find everyone a seat. At church services, Jimmy and Roselyn sat four pews ahead of us. Jimmy had his arm around Roselyn the whole time. After the services the pastor said, "Everyone can have their pictures taken with the President. Maybe our Guardian Angels were with us. We were the last to have our pictures taken. We just sat in awe, just to be with President Carter."

Ruth, Rosalynn, Jimmy, and Wayne

Being a director on the Rochester's Mutual Insurance Company, the company sent me to a school in St. Cloud on fraud. They had a form that said if more than four items are checked, you should investigate for fraud. The items that I have checked were the following:

- Recent increase in coverage, occurs at night or holiday, shortly after insured leaves
- Poor financial condition
- Domestic turmoil, during renovation
- Condemned or run down
- High evaluations
- Application misrepresentation
- Exaggerated contents
- Blamed on smoking
- Loss of job
- Notes coming due
- Construction changes

I checked fourteen out of forty-six. Why didn't the insurance company investigate? I have now been on the board for over twenty-two years. It helps to have a sheriff's report pointing to fraud or having a fire marshal saying fraud. For a small company to fight fraud, it gets really expensive and hard to win.

Around this time, I got a call on the phone from Garry. He was really mad at me. He seemed that he was out of his mind. He said, "Why was Tammy buried? I wanted her cremated." I asked, "Why are you bringing this up now? It happened over a year ago. You agreed that Tammy was to be buried." He then said, "I know, but I wanted her cremated." He then told me that I was the fault for all his problems. I said, "I am not causing you to do these things. I do not make you drink. You have to get help with your addictions." He then went on and on in a slurring voice. I couldn't understand most of what he said. I finally said, "Maybe we should dig up Tammy." He then hung up the phone. Maybe he had a fear that they would dig up Tammy. What would another autopsy show? I didn't need this phone call! It left me very upset. From that time on, whenever the phone rang, I got cramps in my stomach. Garry didn't call me often, but I got cramps whenever the phone rang. I would have to put up with this for years.

I was digging the field next to Garry's place in April. The girls were playing on the trampoline in their yard. I stopped the tractor and went up to talk to them. Garry came up and said, "You are talking about me." I said, "I'm not talking about you. I never mentioned your name." He said, "Get off my property." I then left. It was a real mistake to sell the property to Tammy. If they had gotten divorced, he wouldn't have gotten anything. Tammy could prove that her dad had practically given the property to her. He had to know that sooner or later they would get divorced. Maybe it was the same with the Barrett farmstead. He had to get rid of Olin so he would own it. He had to get rid of Tammy so he would own the farmstead. Maybe I was guilty of Tammy's death. Suddenly I felt terrible. I went back to digging. When I came up to the buildings, Garry had the girls picking up sticks in the yard. I waved to them. I know they saw me, but they didn't wave. Every time I came up to the buildings, the girls were right in front of me. I waved, but they only looked sad. I'm sure that Garry had told them not to wave at Grandpa. When I got past the buildings, Garry took the girls in the house. When I got done with the field, I moved across the road, north of their house.

A FATHER'S QUEST

Around 11:00 AM, I came to the end of the field by their house. Their building was on the corner. A car came from the east and turned south past Garry's house. It went really slow past the house, and then it speeded up. It turned around at the corner and then came back and stopped on the road in front of Garry's house. Garry came out and handed them something. Then the car turned east at the corner and then stopped. He threw something out of the window and then sped away. I thought that Garry had just made a drug sale. I folded up the digger and went up on the road to see what he threw out. When I got up there, I saw a plastic bag. I had a dinner bucket in the tractor. I had already eaten my lunch. I know there would be fingerprints and maybe residue from the drugs. I opened up the dinner bucket and used two pencils to pick up the bag. I was careful not to destroy any evidence. I then went back to the field. I called Ruth on the two-way radio and told her to call the sheriff's office. "Tell them that I just witness a drug sale and I have evidence." Before anybody came out, I finished the field and went to the field south of Garry's house. About 3:00 PM, a sheriff's deputy came out. I described to the deputy what I had seen. I opened the dinner bucket and showed him the bag. He picked up the bag with his hands and roughed it up. He destroyed any evidence on the bag. He then said, "I will go up to Garry's right now and tell him he has to be more careful." He left and went up to Garry's. Why did Ruth call the sheriff's office? Why was the deputy so dumb to tell me what he did? I went up to Rollie's office and told Rollie what happened. Rollie dismissed it. Something was really wrong in the sheriff's office and Dodge County. What would I do? But I knew I would have to try to do something.

When Ruth and I went to Companion Friends meeting in Rochester and Austin, we told them about going to Grant County and when I had witnessed the drug sale. Several of the people there told me to run for county commissioner. Maybe I could change Dodge County. We had several people say, "If you want to get away with murder, do it in Dodge County." I decided that I would try. The commissioner in our district was not going to run again. It would be easier to win if I didn't have to run against a commissioner in office. The election was in the year of 2000, so I had some time to wait.

Garry appeared in court on April 15, 1998. Garry pleaded guilty to careless driving. All other counts in the complaints were dismissed. Garry was fined $246.50.

On May 18, 1998, Deputy Chris Hansen was patrolling in the City of Hayfield when he received information from dispatch that Garry was leaving Rochester on a Harley Davidson motorcycle en route to his residence in Kasson. It was further reported that Garry's current driving license status was canceled. Evidently, everyone from the sheriff's department wasn't corrupt. After driving by Garry's residence, the deputy turned onto County Road 6. Upon coming to a stop at Dodge County Road 6 and Dodge County Road 13, the deputy observed a Harley Davidson turn from County Road 13 unto County Road 6. The deputy stopped the motorcycle and identified the driver as Garry. Garry admitted he did not have a driver's license. In addition, Garry was unable to provide proof of insurance. The ticket was sent to the prosecuting attorney. Gary Remine finally signed the ticket on August 14, 1998.

We went to court to have our grandparents' rights established in the spring of 1998. It was the only time that I didn't buy a transcript of the court proceedings. The judge said that we couldn't get more visitation than we had when Tammy was alive. Ruth has always had several calendar that she kept track of things. Ruth had a calendars of every year since the girls were born and when they were staying with us or visiting us. When the judge saw this, he gave us the most visitation as the law allowed. Garry's lawyer, Restovich, brought up that the girls were sleeping on the floor at our house and they shouldn't have any overnight stays. We have one bedroom downstairs and three bedrooms upstairs. Brenda had a fear that Tammy died upstairs, so she wouldn't sleep upstairs. Brenda and her baby slept downstairs in the living room. Brenda had the girls believing that they were afraid to sleep upstairs too. I told the judge that I would build two more bedrooms on the house soon. That ended Restovich's argument. As we thought about the court case and what happened, we couldn't remember everything. We decided to buy the transcript in the future. We also decided that we would ask someone to go to court with us. It would help us greatly to hear what they understood about the hearing.

In the beginning of August, I started to build an addition on the house. I hired Lee Loppnow to help me. He was a carpenter who worked alone. I had hired him before and would hire him many times in the future. We became friends, and I really enjoyed working with him. The addition was twenty-four by twenty-six feet. The addition was off the living room. We would make our bedroom bigger and add on two more bedrooms and a bathroom. Our bedroom had a door off the dining room. This would remain the same, but off the new addition of our bedroom, we added a door to the rest of the bedrooms. This created a runaround to the house. The girls really enjoyed running around the house. They came in one door in our bedroom and went out the other door. The girls would share one bedroom and had their own beds. Brenda and Justin would have the other bedroom. It would free up the living room. We built a wood foundation. The total cost was $30,000. Justin was one and a half years old. He liked to be with us. Bob and I had gotten two boxer puppies that spring, and Lee and I enjoyed watching Justin play with the puppies. Lee didn't have grandkids yet. I kept telling Lee, "You are getting grandpa training."

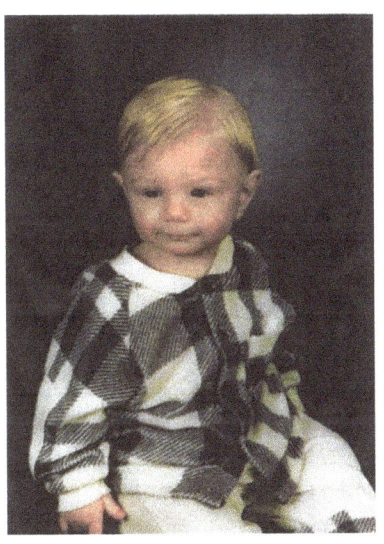

Justin Lynn McColley—1 year old

Craig Benndix heard that I was thinking about running for commissioner. He called and said he wanted to come over and talk to Bob and me. I had bought sows from Craig's dad years ago. When Craig came over, he told us that if I became commissioner, we would have to hire more help. He wanted Bob to build a hog house for him to raise his pigs. It would enable Bob to hire a full-time person. I told Bob, "You would have to decide on your own. I won't express my opinion either way." Bob, after much thought, decided to do it. It ended up being very good financially. The hog house was 42×408 feet in size. It would hold two thousand heads.

We were back in court on August 10, 1998. Garry was not obeying the court orders. Garry told us that the court couldn't tell him what to do with his kids. Restovich tried to make the judge believe that we wanted only one girl at times. Restovich said, "The McColleys have to take both girls every time." This was absolutely not true! We always wanted both girls at the same time. I would find out that you would never learn the truth in a court of law. Lawyers, especially Restovich, would often tell lies to make his client seem better. He would turn the truth around. Rolsch was the attorney for Barb Pike and the girls. He then said, "Okay, I wanted to make sure, Garry, you continue to contact the McColleys at other times to arrange visitation for the girls with their grandparents whenever agreeable to both parties. Sherry has agreed to provide transportation, and if she is unable to do so, then Bob McColley will provide transportation." Rolsch then told the court, "The father shall see that the girls should have access to counseling and support service to assist them in dealing with the loss of their mother." Then the judge said, "Okay, Garry, you understand the terms of this order?" Garry said, "Yeah, once it's done, it will work. That's the end of it." The judge then asked me, "What are your plans for vacation with the girls?" I answered, "Well, because we couldn't plan anything for a long trip, we are planning on some short vacations like going to a hotel over in Waseca and staying overnight so they can go swimming there. And that's where their great-grandparents live. We will go to see them. We will also go down to visit their great grandmother in Chatfield and maybe go to Lanesboro and rent bicycles for two." The judge then said, "Well, spend a week and enjoy the girls. Okay."

When we had our visitation with the girls in September, we found out that Sarah had a cast on her arm. She told us that her arm was broken twice. One break was between the wrist and the elbow, and one break was above the elbow. We asked her, "How did that happen?" She told us that Wendy was giving her a ride on the pony, and she fell off. She told us she was riding bareback because they didn't have a saddle and that Wendy was running the pony. There was not much to hang on to without a saddle, and a five-year-old was much too young for this type of ride. We have taken Sarah to fairs and watched her on rides. Sarah has never been too brave. This was very careless behavior on Wendy's part. I would have to find out who Wendy was and why she was there.

On October 8, I got a letter from Minnesota Life. I decided that I would have to search everyway for help. I wrote a lot of letters. Some didn't help; some did.

>Dear Mr. McColley
>
>I have been asked to respond to your correspondence regarding the claim for Tammy. I apologize for the delay.
>
>We have performed a thorough review of the material you sent. We have also been in contact with a Monumental General representative. Our Law Department has also reviewed the file.
>
>Unfortunately, without a conviction there is little we can do. We are writing to the Sheriff's Department to inquire if further investigation is occurring. I am enclosing a copy for your review.
>
>We regret we are unable to assist you at this time. If anything new should occur regarding this case, please let us know.
>
>Sincerely,
>Nancy Brinkman
>Claim Specialist

I would find that everything I would do would not help. But I figured I could leave no stone unturned. Mourning Tammy and the situation we were in was eating me alive. I had to be doing something to keep me busy.

I got a letter from Tim Braatz of Atlas Investigations on October 19, 1998. We had learned something about Wendy, and we wanted to know why she was with Garry. In reviewing a recently filed motion by Wendy's husband's attorney, it was that the Wendy and her husband had separated on August 30, 1998, when Wendy left the family home without notice and moved in with Garry. She abandoned her children, ages sixteen and fourteen years old. Wendy's husband claimed that Wendy had a gambling addiction, which caused the couple to incur considerable debt over the past several years. He went on to state that her gambling debts were the main reason the couple had to obtain a home equity loan in February 1998 for $50,000. He reported that they owed over $122,000 on the home in Kasson, which only had a market value of $100,000. He asserted that he was totally shocked by his wife's decision to leave the family and move in with another man who already has children of his own living with him. In fact, he included a copy of a wedding anniversary card that she gave to him on July 31, 1998, in which she stated that she loved him and always wanted to be with him. A month later, she left him a long rambling letter in which she claimed that the reason she was leaving was not his fault and that it was something that she had to do for herself. He should not be mad at her. She signed the letter, "Your confused wife."

I learned in October that Garry had bought a rifle. Garry had prior convictions of domestic violence, so it was against the law for him to have a gun. I put pressure on Rollie to do something. He knew that I would not stop, and eventually, I would go over their heads. Local law enforcement officials became aware that Garry had purchased a firearm and notified the Bureau of Alcohol, Tobacco, and Firearms. Subsequently, ATF Special Agent William S. Baudhuin applied for a federal warrant to search Garry's property in order to locate the weapon. A search warrant was granted, giving investigators the authority to search for numerous items, which included firearms, ammunition, photographs, literature, and receipts.

On October 30, 1998, at approximately 9:30 AM, federal agents and members of Dodge County Sheriff's Department executed the federal search warrant. Garry and Wendy were present when the officers arrived. Garry and Wendy were handcuffed and told to sit at the dining room table. In response to questioning, Garry disclosed the location of the gun and explained that it was intended to be a gift for Wendy's son. The officers found the gun and continued to search the premises. The officers recovered some ammunition and came across a substance which the officer suspected may be contraband drugs. An officer tested the substance, which was negative for illegal substance and turned out to be a compound for fixing walls. As the search was proceeding, the officers found drug paraphernalia and what they suspected to be methamphetamine in the bathroom. As the officers were searching the bathroom, an officer found a can of Aqua Net hairspray which contained baggies of illegal substance. When the drugs were found, the search was stopped while Dodge County Investigator Rollie Spriggle left to get a state search warrant to look for drugs. When Officer Spriggle returned, some of the substances found in the bathroom were tested, and others were sent to the lab for tests. Defendants Garry and Wendy were arrested and charged with a controlled substance crime in the fifth degree. I always had trouble figuring out Rollie. At times, he would look the other way and refuse to do anything. And now this? How did the federal agents get involved? Maybe the crime had gotten bigger than they imagined. Maybe they were looking for drugs in the first place. This arrest left me with a lot of questions. What should I do now?

At five fifteen Sunday afternoon, November 1, 1998, Sherry and her husband, Milo, came to pick up the girls. Sherry stayed in the car, and Milo came to the house. I met him on the porch and told him that our monthly visitation was to be the night of November 6–8. Halloween was an extra time that Garry had arranged with Bob. The court order says that Garry was to arrange extra visitation from time to time. This past weekend was not good for us. But I would never refuse to take the girls. Ruth's sister Eva and her husband, Nado

Jr.'s son, Nado James (Jim), had died, and his funeral was when we had the girls. We took the girls to the funeral. The girls were upset that their dad was in jail. They didn't do anything fun. We had to comfort them, but they weren't happy.

Friday, November 6, 1998, at 12:45 PM, Bob took my place working in the field. On the way home, I drove by Garry's house. The girls were playing outside. Sarah was riding her bike toward the house. As I was driving by, Kayla saw me and came running. I stopped the pickup and backed up to their driveway. It was obvious that they were really happy to see me. I asked them if they were coming to our house tonight. They both said, "Yes." I said, "Grandpa had better get going so he has all his work done before you come." I said, "See you tonight." They both said, "See you tonight." I then went home. Sherry was to bring the girls. She never came. No one called.

On Saturday at eight in the morning, Bob and I went to Sherry's house. Sherry didn't have a phone. Sherry's son answered the door as soon as we knocked. He went to get Milo. I asked, "Why didn't we get the girls last night?" I handed him the court order that said when we going to get the girls. The court order said that Sherry was going to arrange the transportation. He told us that he didn't have anything to say in this. He didn't want to get involved. He then said, "I don't know why Sherry gets involved in these things. We aren't always home." Finally, Sherry came into the living room. She said, "What are you doing here at eight o'clock in the morning?" She used a tone in her voice that implied it was way too early to get up. Already, I was in a bad mood. I said, "We could have come at five when I got up." I told her that we were being considerate waiting until eight. She said, "You just got the girls last weekend." I told her that we were supposed to get the girls this weekend. The court order said that Garry was supposed to arrange extra visitation. I then told her that we had a terrible weekend with them last week because we had a close family member that had died. She then said in a really loud and nasty voice, "I'm getting really sick of you, and there are a few things I could say to you." Bob and I turned around and left. I didn't want to get in a fight with her. Milo followed us and said, "I will call Garry to see what was going on." We never heard from him.

A FATHER'S QUEST

On November 22, 1998, at approximately 2216 hours police time, Officer Metz of the Rochester Police Department, observed a white pickup truck driving northbound on Broadway. He then stated:

> I was behind the truck at Center Street and Broadway. The truck swerved in the lane of traffic, then the truck swerved to the left approximately five times touching the fog line next to the median.

The officer put on his lights planning on stopping the truck. The truck made a sharp left turn into a parking lot. Garry then changed places with Wendy, and the truck went on. The officer chased the pickup truck through several parking lots, and then they stopped. When the officer went up to the pickup, he could smell alcohol and noticed two male occupants and the female driver. It was typical for Garry to get someone else to take the blame for his actions. When the officer attempted to get Wendy out of the vehicle, she lost her balance and almost fell. He then did a test on Wendy, and she failed everything. Then the officer told her the next test was a preliminary breath test. She said, "Okay." Garry then got out of the pickup and told Wendy not to take the test. She then refused to take the PBT test. The officer then told Wendy she was under arrest for DUI. She was handcuffed and placed in the back of the police car.

Now we had learned that Wendy had been arrested for drugs. In the sheriff's report, Wendy stated that the drugs could have been hers. Maybe she was trying to take the blame for Garry. She had also been arrested for DUI, so evidently she had a drinking problem. Now we wonder what state of mind Wendy was in when she was running a pony with a five-year-old girl, sitting on the pony with nothing but a mane to hang on to. What should I do? I had let Tammy down; should I do it again with Tammy's girls too? It was a very difficult problem for me. Where would I get help?

Because husband and wife could not testify against each other, Garry and Wendy were married at the end of 1998.

At several meetings at the Compassion Friends in Austin, we had a discussion about whether we should forgive someone for causing our child's death. We had one couple who really knew the Bible. The Christian law of forgiveness in Matthew 18, verses 21 and 22, states:

> Then Peter came to him, and said, "Lord, how often shall my brother sin against me, and I should forgive him? Till seven times?" Jesus saith unto him, "I say not until thee, Until seven times: but, until seventy times seven."

When you read the Bible, there are many ways that you can interpret it. Everyone at the meeting interpreted it a little bit differently. We discussed this at several meetings, and finally the majority agreed that someone had to ask us to be forgiven. If they didn't ask, we didn't have to forgive them. I said that I could never forgive Garry. A lot of people there agreed with me. Finally, we agreed that if someone who had caused our child's death and asked us to forgive them, we had to forgive. If Garry would confess what he had done to Tammy, I should forgive him. A couple there, Lester and Marion, agreed with me. Their son was killed by a drunk driver. He was sent to prison. They could never forgive him! When he got out of prison, he came to them and asked to be forgiven. Lester and Marion forgave him, and they became friends with him for the rest of their lives. Garry had never asked me to forgive him. I don't know if I could be as good of a Christian as Lester and Marion were.

When the Austin chapter of the Compassion Friends had their monthly meeting to go out to eat the first Tuesday of November, we ate at the Kernel Restaurant in Owatonna. They had sour cream raisin pie on the menu. It is my favorite pie. Several people ordered the pie. I said, "The pie is not as good as the pie Ruth makes." Several people got into an argument. We had the Christmas meal at the Hubble House. Ruth and I invited everyone to our house for dessert. Several days before the meal, Ruth made a sour cream pie for me. Ruth didn't like the pie so good, and I had my kids thinking that they didn't like the pie. So I got the pie all to myself. Ruth asked me if she got it right? I told her that it was really good. Ruth made sour cream pies for dessert at our house. I won the argument we had at the restaurant. Ruth made enough pies that she sent a pie home with every couple. There were eight couples there.

It was established in open court on December 22, 1998, that there was a tray on the bathroom floor with residue of cocaine and methamphetamine. If the children would have played with the tray and put their fingers in their mouths, they could have died. What should I do now?

Chapter 16

The Third Year after Tammy's Death

Sarah and Kayla, January 1999

In January, Ruth saw an article in the paper which told about Parents of Murdered Children. The meeting was the fourth Tuesday of the month at Assisi Heights in Rochester. Ruth and I went to the meeting in January. Lois Hackbarth was the leader of the meeting. She worked for Social Services in Preston. She never lost a child but had lost a son-in-law in an airplane crash. She became a really good friend of Ruth and me. She helped us more than anyone else.

Wendy's sister Susan called me on the phone. She was concerned about Wendy being married to Garry. She was afraid that the same thing would happen to Wendy as it did to Tammy. She wanted my help. I told her that there was nothing I could do. I made a mistake telling her to give Wendy support and to not abandon her. In her affidavit to the court on March 25, 1999, she stated this whole thing was my fault. I was harassing Garry. She wanted my help, but then she turned on me.

At our January meeting of Compassion Friends in Austin, it was suggested that I contact a representative in the Minnesota legislature. George Sierakowski said that he had been in contact with Senator Dick Day before. He volunteered to go to the capital with me. Senator Day recommended that I should file a CHIPS petition in court. The definition of CHIPS is "CHILD IN NEED OF PROTECTION." Our attorney cautioned us on doing this. But I had asked Senator Day for advice. If I didn't do it, the visit to the capitol was worthless. He never helped me. When I went to the capitol months later, he wouldn't see me. He also told me to call the attorney general's office. When I called and talked to receptionist and told my story, she transferred me to another person. When I got through telling my whole story to another person, she said I should talk to someone else. I was on the phone over an hour. When they transferred me the tenth time, I hung up the phone. I was emotionally drained. I couldn't talk anymore. I just sat and cried! It was one of the worst experiences in my life.

On February 5, 1999, at ten minutes to five, Garry's white pickup came into our yard. They were bringing the girls over for their monthly visit. Wendy was driving the pickup. Kayla and Sarah got out the back door of the pickup and ran to the house. As they were leaving, Wendy had a big smile on her face, and she waved. Wendy didn't have a driver's license. She got a DUI in Rochester in the past November and lost her license. It was very disturbing that our granddaughters were with people while they were breaking the law. We were helpless and could not do anything about this. Garry knew through experience that he could keep breaking the law and odds of anyone doing anything about it were almost zero.

We decided to file a CHIPS petition with the court. We started the process in early December of 1998 by talking to the Dodge

County Social Services. They denied the application and answered "Unknown" on the form. Reasons the Social Services agency denied protection or services was also answered "Unknown." They gave no explanation on why they didn't approve the application. Social Services didn't have a reason for deny our application, so they just marked in "unknown" on the form. I knew that we would get no help from them.

We checked the box marked:

> Subd. 2a (3), because the children are without necessary food, clothing, shelter, education, or other required care for the children's physical or mental health or morals because the children's parent, guardian, or custodian is unable or unwilling to provide that care.

We also checked the box marked:

> Subd. 2a (9) because the children are one whose behavior, condition, or environment is such as to be injurious or dangerous to the children or others. An injurious or dangerous environment may include, but not limited to, the exposure of the child to criminal activity in the child's home.

On item 6 on the form was the following:

> The facts upon which petitioner relies for the assertion that the children are in need of protection or services are as follows; On October 30, 1998 a search warrant was issued on the two granddaughters' home. Drugs were found in the bathroom area of the home with residue on the trays. The drugs were methamphetamine and cocaine. Garry and his live-in girlfriend Wendy

was handcuffed and arrested. Our youngest granddaughter, Sarah, witnessed this whole scene. I believe under Subd. 2a (3), the care of the children's physical or mental health or morals is not being done by the father. Also, Subd. 2a (9), where the children are exposed to dangerous illegal drugs in their own bathroom. What would happen if the children ate these chemicals like candy? Furthermore, the father was convicted of domestic abuse and lied on his application. That is how the federal warrant was issued. Their father has a long history of alcoholism and severe violence to women. Wendy who lives in the home was arrested for DUI in Rochester since.

We filed the petition on March 2, 1999. Social Services should have filed the CHIPS petition. But Garry's childhood friend wouldn't do it. Why? If it would have been a stranger, she would have done it.

Judge Agerter immediately answered our petition and issued a summons with a court date set for March 22, 1999. He signed the summon on March 5, 1999. Finally, maybe someone was going to do something.

We got a letter from Parents of Murdered Children dated March 15, 1999.

REMINDER:

The next POMC (Parents of Murdered Children) meeting will be March 23rd at 7:00pm at Assisi Heights in the Christian Community Center on the north side of the building in the "Water Center" Room.

The Honorable Judge Lawrence Agerter from Dodge County will be the guest speaker.

>Any questions call me at 507-281-9418 or 507-765-2341 or Sue at 507-634-4767.

>Sincerely,
>Lois Hackbarth

Lois invited the judge hopefully to help us. My good friend Jim from the Austin group, who had his daughter murdered, came to the meeting. Jim questioned the judge on why the orders were never followed. He asked the questions I would have liked to ask. Ruth and I acted like we didn't know the judge, and the judge never acknowledged us. This was a way to make Judge Agerter seem more comfortable. I knew it would do me no good to get into an argument with the judge. I would fail.

The end of March, I wrote a letter to Roxanne Heinrich, our attorney.

>Dear Roxanne.

>Your call about the letter you received from George Restovich has been very disturbing to us. I don't understand how George can decide that we are getting the girls on Thursday and Friday instead of the weekend. I don't see how he has the authority to decide this unless he has talked to the Judge. I thought that protocol was that if he talked to the Judge, that you had to be notified. It seems to me that if he is making deals with the Judge without our knowledge. Both of them should be brought on charges. If he hasn't talked to the Judge and that he is coming up with this by himself, then he is telling his client to break a court order. I would think that is unlawful and charges should be filed against him. Maybe I missed something in our conversation, but it

seems like both Garry and George Restovich think they are above the law.

I don't see where we should have the cost of the going to court to change this so soon after the order for visitation was signed. I think it was April 9th, that you said we should go to Court. That was not a good date for us. That was the game George played with us for ten months. Ruth and I are really too busy in April for this. May is planting time. June is vacation time and etc. All through this, he keeps changing his mind. Sherry Walters is supposed to pick up and bring the girls to our house. This doesn't happen. First we were to take them to church in Byron, then we were not. The Judge hasn't responded to your letter that we missed our November visitation. We have never received the Medical Care form. Have the girls ever had counseling. Kayla and Sarah are brought to our house by an unlicensed driver. The Judge said that he didn't need to put in the order. It was a given that the girls were to be driven by a licensed driver. Because not to be, would be breaking the law. I think all of these things need to be addressed long before we have to go back to court to change the visitation. Garry keeps breaking the law and harassing us and he wins on the visitation. We are honest hard working citizens and try to follow the court orders and we are the losers. What's Wrong???

Sincerely
Wayne McColley

P.S. 8:50am March 9, 1999, the sheriff's office called and said that Garry was served the order on the CHIPS at 4:20 pm March 8, 1999.

I didn't know what to do. I knew that I had to look for help anyplace I could. I decided to write to Governor Ventura on April 13, 1999.

>Dear Governor Ventura,
>
>Our lives have been a nightmare for the last two years. I don't know where to start.
>
>Wayne served in the US Navy during the Vietnam War. We have been farmers for the past twenty-five years. We started our farm from scratch and have built a large operation with no family financial help. During the farm crisis of the 1980's, we took no write downs on our loans, even though we had a negative net worth. We borrowed the money of our free will and therefore we were responsible to pay it back. We do not say these things to brag, but only to indicate what kind of people we are and what our values are.
>
>On January 5, 1997 our oldest daughter died in a house fire. She was 27 years old and left behind two daughters, age 3 and 4. In the days following the funeral, we learned that her husband had been beating her. Tammy was an employee of the county, working as a nurse's aide in Dodge Center Nursing Home. We learned that in October of 1994, she had her husband, Garry arrested for beating her. He was found guilty in the County Court and sentenced to get treatment for his abuse to women. The County never followed through on the treatment. Even though Tammy was a county employee in a job where she changed diapers for the aged and cried out to the county for help, Dodge County didn't

care enough about her to see that the court order was followed.

When a child dies in a fire, all parents question whether their child was awake. The Fire Marshall told us that Tammy probably woke up and stood up and then died from the smoke immediately. This was not true and the investigation proves it. It took us over a year to get the investigation report.

We were told by the Dodge County Sheriff's Office that there was $150,000 worth of life insurance on her life. In October 1997, we learned that there was an additional $236,000 of life insurance. We called the Sheriff's investigator out to our home. He made a report of this that Wayne believes that there is $450,000 to $500,000 of total insurance, when the Sheriff's Office believes there was only $250,000 of total insurance.

In a January 27, 1997 interview with Rollie Spriggle, the Sheriff's investigator, and Garry. Garry tells Rollie about this insurance. When Rollie asked who the beneficiary is, Garry says he doesn't know. We have a signed copy of Garry signing to get this money on January 10, 1997, seventeen days before he says he doesn't know who the beneficiary is. The Life Insurance Company wrote to the Sheriff's Office about the fire and Tammy's death, but they still didn't know that the insurance existed in October 1997. These were two separate polices and someone forged Tammy's signature on both applications. Tammy didn't know the policies existed. The signatures were sent to the Bureau of Criminal Apprehension and we have a report saying the signatures are not Tammy's.

The Fire Marshal and Rollie Spriggle did an interview with our granddaughters on January 6, 1997, where they state that the youngest, Sarah, started the fire. On January 5, 1997 (the same day as the fire) two separate Sheriff's officers interviewed our granddaughters and state in their reports that Kayla and Sarah were outside when this happened. On January 6th, Kayla and Sarah tell the Fire Marshal that they were outside, but the report is twisted to show that Sarah started the fire. We have a February 1997 insurance report, where the fire marshal lists Garry as a suspect in the fire.

Now, Garry has been arrested for drugs in his home. It was established in open court on December 22, 1998 that there was a tray on the bathroom floor with residue of Cocaine and Methamphetamine. If the children would have played with the tray and put their fingers in their mouths they could have died. Under Minnesota Statute Section 260.015, subd. 2a(9), we reported this to the Dodge County Social Services. They investigated it under a different statute and claim there is no evidence. A high-up individual in Dodge County Social Services Department is a childhood friend of Garry's. Senator Dick Day's office recommended that we file a CHIPS petition, so we have. Now Garry is taking us to court asking that our grandparent's visitation be stopped because we are harassing him.

Garry is also on probation for DWI and have broken his probation two times, and probably three times if the current case ever goes to trial. This case is a separate case from the drug arrest. Dodge County officials have always looked the other way and done nothing.

We know you are a busy person, but hope you take time to read this letter. We have documented evidence to back up our claims. I feel that you are a compassionate person, who doesn't believe in politics as usual. I hope and pray that you will be able to schedule us an hour of your time, so that we can give you the details of this nightmare and that you can give us some guidance in how we should proceed. Thank you very much.

Sincerely,
Wayne McColley Ruth McColley

We were in court again May 6, 1999. We had taken Garry to court for not living up to the visitation order in the court orders. We could never plan on anything. Garry let us have the girls if it suited him; otherwise, we didn't get them. The judge again spelled out everything to Garry. We had a feeling that it was a waste of time.

We got a letter from Charles Weaver, a commissioner, on May 27, 1999.

Dear Mr. & Mrs. McColley:

Governor Ventura asked me to respond to your letter, which was received by his office on April 16, 1999.

Let me begin by offering my sincere condolences on the death of your daughter. I have reviewed your letter with State Fire Marshal Tom Brace and Bureau Chief of Investigations David Bahma. A copy of this letter, and your original letter, will be forwarded to the BCA and the Dodge County Sheriff's Office.

The fire marshal investigation revealed that, due to the location of the victim's body and the debris found in the area, the victim was not in bed during the building collapse. The superheated air at the upper level of the bedroom, coupled with the toxic by-products of the burning taking place downstairs, is consistent with her standing up and being overcome by carbon monoxide, which is also consistent with our findings.

The interview with the children, done by Deputy State Fire Marshal Neudahl, clearly states that the girls said they were in the house when saw the fire and went outside to tell their dad. There is nothing contained in the report to indicate that the girls were outside before the fire.

It appears that a criminal investigation into who may have signed the insurance applications is in order. Because the State Fire Marshal expertise is the fire only, any investigation or subsequent charges in this matter would have to be brought by Dodge County or the BCA.

Sincerely,
Charles R. Weaver

This letter made me really mad! Either he didn't read the interview with the girls or he outright lied to me. I suspect he didn't read the interview with the girls. When Neudahl said the girls were in the house when the fire started, that was a lie. The girls never said they saw fire. If they would have been in the house, they would have said fire. They only said smoke. That goes with them being outside and just seeing smoke. I would soon make Neudahl admit that the girls were never in the house. Weaver said that an investigation was in order on the insurance applications. He sent it to the sheriff, and nothing was done. Why?

At our meeting with Parents of Murdered Children the fourth Tuesday of May, we shared the letters that I had written to the governor and the letter we got from Weaver. Lois Hackbarth said she worked in Fillmore County as part of a three-county program service, servicing Dodge, Fillmore, and Olmsted Counties. She said she would have Jerianne Gonser, who worked in the same position at Dodge County, come out to our house and help us. Jerianne Gonser came to our home on June 7. She said she would help us and stick by us. She said, "I will not abandon you."

June 17, 1999

Dear Mr. Weaver

My name is Jerianne Gonser; Victim Services Staff Advocate in Dodge County. I am writing this letter on behalf of Ruth and Wayne McColley who lost their daughter Tammy in a house fire on January 5, 1997. They had written a letter to Governor Venura in April of this year. In turn the Governor's Office referred the matter to you. In your response you stated that the Fire Marshall's interview of Tammy's two daughters, Kayla and Sarah 'clearly' stated that the girls were in the house at the time the fire started and then when went to the barn to get their father Garry. I met with the McColleys' on June 7, 1999 when they showed me the letter and a copy of the interview. During the first part of the interview it clearly states that the girls were in the barn with their father. Throughout this interview conducted by Deputy State Fire Marshal Tom Neudahl and investigator Rolland Spriggle of the Dodge Co. Sheriff Dept. many conflicting statements are made. Ruth and Wayne have fought long and hard for someone to take another look into this matter with no luck. Also during my June 7th meeting with the McColley's they showed me copies of reports conducted by Deputy Dave Bentzen and

Deputy John Snaza of Dodge County. In their reports it 'clearly' states that the girls went out to the barn with their father and while in the barn saw smoke coming from the house, at which time Garry went running to the house.

While you may have just been giving a small portion of the investigation surrounding this matter, numerous inconsistencies are apparent. I was not in this position when the fire occurred but was put in contact with the McColley's in or around February of this year. After the initial meeting I spoke with investigator Spriggle about this in which he stated "If I had to do it over again, I would have had the girls interviewed by a psychologist or another professional who specializes in interviewing children." In the eyes of the Dodge County Dept. this matter is closed. I am enclosing copies of the interview done by Deputy State Fire Marshal Tom Neudahl and also copies of the reports filed by Deputies Benzen and Snaza and ask that you review these. If you wish to see any additional documents, you may contact Ruth and Wayne McColley and they would be more than happy to send those along to you. I will enclose their address and phone number for you as well. The McColley's would like this matter reopened and perhaps another agency conducts the investigation. In my mind there is just too many conflicting statements made that a new investigation is needed.

With Garry's prior charges/convictions of serious domestic assault in or around 1985 and a matter involving Garry and a female swindling an elderly man out of property/money, my gut is telling me that he was the one who started the fire. There have also been reports to Dodge

County made by Tammy involving domestic abuse on her by Garry. If you could give any further recommendations and/or names of people with the BCA, I could contact on behalf of the McColley's regarding the fire as well as the insurance matter, it would be very much appreciated. The McColley's just want some answers one way or another. If mistakes were made during the investigation an, "I'm sorry," would be nice.

I want to thank you for taking the time to read this letter and review the enclosed documents. If you have questions, please feel free to contact me at the Dodge County Victim Services Office at the following number 507-635-6266. Thanks again and I hope you can help the McColley's put some sense of closure to this knowing that everything has been done to find out the truth.

Peace
Jerianne Gonser

Our pastor, Larry Nelson, wrote a letter to Commissioner Weaver on July 1, 1999. I was not at first going to put this whole letter in my book. I debated for a long time. Here is the whole letter.

Dear Mr. Weaver

I am writing on behalf of Wayne and Ruth McColley with whom you have corresponded concerning the death of their daughter Tammy in a suspicious fire 1/5/97. You responded to them in a letter dated 5/27 99 in which you write that the interview with the daughters, Kayla and Sarah, conducted by Deputy State Fire Marshal Tom Neudahl "Clearly" states that the girls said they were in the house when they saw the fire and then went outside to tell their father.

After reading the interview it does not appear so "Clear" that they were inside. In fact, it often seemed that during the interview certain theories or assumptions had already been made and words were put in the girl's mouths or questions asked in ways to prove the assumptions. In the interview the first time the girls were asked where they were they said they were outside with their dad in the barn, even though the interviewer had already suggested to them that they were in the house playing. And, when the interviewer first asked the girl's if the lighters made the fire. They said no. The interviewer on page 5 questioned them about their "Blankies." This seems to be the theory that they were trying to prove, that the girls started the fire with the lighters and then their blankies started on fire.

However, my wife and I were there at McColley's soon after the fire. Neither we nor a number of others could smell any scent of smoke on the girls. It seems unlikely that girls this young could start a fire, not get burned themselves, nor have any scent of smoke on them, then put their boots on and their jackets on by themselves and go out to their dad.

Another example of inconsistency is on page 7 when the interviewer asked the girls if they had spent the night at Grandpa's One said yes and the other said no. The interviewer again, repeated the question about sleeping at Grandpa's. Then the answer at the bottom of the page was "Yes." The truth is that their father's family picked them up that night and they did not sleep at Grandpa's.

This is just one example where the interviewer did not get the real truth from the girls.

I could go on but I just want to say that I am not satisfied that the real truth is known. I believe that girls this young should have been and even now should be interviewed by a child psychologist or psychiatrist who specializes in helping children who have experienced traumatic events. Mr. McColley mentioned that in the evening while the girls were still at his house they were watching TV in another room. Unfortunately, when he discovered what they were watching it about a fire. He speculates and I find some credence in this, that the next day when the girls were interviewed they may not have been able to separate the fire in their house from what they saw on TV.

I think that the girls need to talk to someone who specializes in dealing with deep trauma in children. Their father, Garry resisted this for a long time. He has become angry with the McColley's if he has heard that the girls talked to them about the fire. What is he afraid of? Shouldn't these girls be able to talk about it and hopefully heal from this terrible memory? The very fact that he seems to know whatever they talked about indicates that he is a very controlling person and may "coach" the girls on what to say.

I have known the McColleys for twenty years as their pastor and have found them to be very responsible and honest people. I was at their farm within an hour of the fire and have spent a great deal of time with them as they have sought to recover from this tragedy. I believe they cannot lay this to rest because of their lingering suspicions regarding the cause of the fire. They want to know the truth. And there are many people in the community who share their suspicions.

Thank you for your attention to this matter.

Sincerely,
Pastor Larry Nelson

A short time later after Weaver received the two letters, I got a call from his office. They made an appointment for me to see the attorney general. We would have to go to St. Paul, and Jerianne Gonser would go along with us. I would really have to prepare for the meeting. I would have to convince the attorney general that Tammy was murdered. I spent hours the next few days studying the reports of the fire and the drawings that I had on the house. I would have to learn everything by heart. I couldn't make even one mistake. This was my big chance, and I was not going to fail. The day before the meeting, I got a call from his office. The attorney general had broken his leg. He would be off from work for a month. They would call me when he got back to work. I felt terrible! I had prepared so much, and now it was for nothing. I thought if he missed work for a month, he would have a lot of work to catch up on. Maybe he wouldn't see me at all. Then they said that I could meet with the head of the BCA at the scheduled time instead. I quickly agreed! BCA means Bureau of Criminal Apprehension.

It really helped us that Jerianne came along. His office was not in the capitol, and we would have trouble finding it. Jerianne was sitting in the back seat of the car, and she heard me taking to Ruth. I said, "Before now I have never told you to not talk, but now I'm saying, do not interrupt me for anything. I can't forget anything." I knew this was the biggest thing I have ever done. I prayed over and over that I would be successful. When we walked into Mancel Mitchell's office, the first thing I saw was Tom Neudahl sitting there. My first thought was that I was going to fail. I never thought he would be there. He never allowed me to express my opinion before. How could I, with no education, go up against him? He appeared to be much smarter than I was. I was lucky that I had done some public speaking before, but not much. I prayed again! I don't think I heard anything they said at first. Finally, I got my chance to talk. I was lucky that I had learned it by heart. I had parts of the investigation with me. I showed them parts and talked about that the girls were not in the house. I showed them the drawings of the house. "Tom, your drawings show that the fire started at the south side of the room. The TV was on the east wall, a long way from where you said the fire started. I want to ask you, if the girls saw the fire at the TV, which you say they did, how did they get out of the house?" They didn't say anything. I was done, and I didn't have a comeback. At least five minutes of silence went by as they studied the drawings. All of a sudden, both men said at once, "The girls were never in the house." I had won the battle, but I would lose the war. They agreed that they would have a cold case unit investigate Tammy's death.

In July, I decided to build a new holding bin at the dryer. We had a 2,200-bushel holding bin with a cone bottom. We had built it twenty-two years ago. The farm was now much bigger. The combine was bigger, and we were pulling two wagons at a time. We had it full in less than three hours. We decided to build a ten-thousand-bushel bin with a flat bottom and a power sweep. Sommers from Waseca built the bin. Dave Sommer's dad, Buddy, helped every day. We had gone to dances years ago, and I really enjoyed him.

We had vacation with the girls in July. We went to Wisconsin Dells. We asked Garry for permission to take the girls out of state. For once, he didn't refuse. We stayed in a motel. Our whole family went, including Ruth and me, Kayla, Sarah, Doreen, Bob, Brenda, and Justin. We went horse riding more than once. I made a fool of myself getting on the horse. I jumped so hard that I went over the horse and fell on the ground. At least everyone had a laugh on me. We rode the duck boat and went on many rides. Everyone had a good time, and they all wanted to go back again next year.

Judge Agerter signed an order on July 29, 1999.

> The above entitled matter is before the court with a hearing set for trial commencing August 9, 1999. The juvenile file is a Child in Need of

Protection or Services petition filed by Wayne and Ruth McColley, the maternal grandparents to the children. The McColley's are represented by Roxanne Heinrich, Attorney at Law, Landfall, Minnesota. Barbara Pike is the Guardian Ad Litem who is represented by council Steven Rolsch. The natural father, Garry is represented by council George Restovich and the Dodge County Department of Human Services is represented by Assistant County Attorney Gary Remine.

The court has deep concerns about the matter that will be presented starting August 9, 1999. The counsel for the petitioner has requested four days of time and indicated that she wants to proceed on the child in Need of Protection or Services petition first and then the visitation file, which is in the family court. The court thinks the hearing ought to be combined because the witnesses and issues ought to be very similar. The court is concerned that the deep hostility between the parties is only going to be exasperated by fully hearing all the witnesses out on both sides.

Now therefore, This Court is hereby ordering that the parties and their respective attorneys be present on August 9, 1999 at 9:00 am for a pretrial and settlement conference. The court intends to take Monday afternoon off and the court is assigned to Steele County on Tuesday morning. If the matter stills go to trial, we will start trial on Tuesday August 10, 1999 at 1:00 pm The attached memorandum may be and hereby is incorporated by reference herein.

MEMORANDUM

Minnesota Statute Section 260.131 Subdivion 1 allows a private party to file a Child in Need of Protection or Services petition with this court. The court has found probable cause, although it is minimal, to proceed at this point. However, the statute indicates very clearly that the court may allow a petition to proceed under this paragraph if it appears that the sole purpose of the petition is to modify custody between the parents. In this case, the maternal grandparents have brought the petition and it appears to the court that the petitioners' attorney is confused as to the purpose of the CHIPS proceeding, and Garry's attorney is equally confused as to the CHIPS proceeding.

If the court were to assume jurisdiction of the CHIPS proceeding, then the ODERS out of the CHIPS proceeding file would cover the conditions Garry and his present wife would have to meet in order to satisfy the requirements of disposition. At the same time, there is probably not enough evidence to remove the children from Garry's custody. Therefore, the maternal grandparents would be allowed whatever visitation the court will allow in the CHIPS proceeding file. As long as the court had jurisdiction of the CHIPS file the visitation file will be put on hold.

On the other hand, if the petitioner fails to present evidence to satisfy the court that it ought to assume jurisdiction over the children in the CHIPS proceeding, we still have the visitation question that has to be decided between dad and the maternal grandparents.

I anticipate the maternal grandparents are going to present a lot of negative evidence regarding Garry. They may even show that Garry is truly a jerk, but it seems to this judge that if the petitioners cannot show by clear and convincing evidence one of the statutory grounds for the court to assume jurisdiction, then the petitioner's petition may well fail. The petitioner's attorney at the previous hearing indicted that there might be might be something where the court will assume jurisdiction and change custody. The statute would prohibit this and if the court assumes jurisdiction it would direct the Department of Human Services to prepare a case plan for Garry and Wendy to meet. A case plan at this point would seem to be with the children still in physical custody of Garry and Wendy.

At the end of all the negative testimony on both sides and the hunt feeling, it is going to be that we still have a visitation order where the maternal grandparents are foster proper respect of the children towards the natural dad and his new wife, and where Garry is to respect the visitation rights of the maternal grandparents. We may be expecting too much out of these parties. I know that the McColley's have lost a daughter and they cast the entire blame on Garry. Somewhere, somehow, the maternal grandparents may have to let go of this and treat Garry as the father of their grandchildren.

In conclusion, I expect the parties to be fully prepared at the pretrial to discuss all the issues, and if there are any motions to be filed, that they will be heard on the morning of August 9, 1999. As I have indicated, if we get to trial on these matters, it will still have three and a half days of time during that week to get the testimony into evidence.

L. E. Agerter

I felt that the memorandum was written for just us. I didn't like it at the time. Now, twenty years later, as I read the order thinking about the book I'm writing, maybe Judge Agerter was truly looking out for us. When we got to the courthouse on August 9, we were put in a room by ourselves. We never went into the courtroom. The judge never wanted this to go to trial. The attorneys met by themselves, and our attorney came into the room from time to time where we were sitting. We would have to give up the CHIPS petition. Ruth and I had to decide what we really wanted. Maybe if we went on with the CHIPS petition, we would lose everything, including the visitation with the girls. Ruth and I had really felt that God had sent Roxanne Heinrich for us. But we knew that she wasn't good enough to go up against Restovich and Human Services. Restovich had planted custody change in Roxanne's mind, and she had fallen for it. Restovich had won, and she would lose. We were caught between a rock and a very hard place!

Lois Hackbarth wrote and sent a lot of information about Tammy's death to The National Organization of Parents of Murdered Children. We got a letter from Second Opinion Services. Second Opinion Services is a program of the National Organization of Murdered Children. The letter was dated August 9, 1999.

> Second Opinion Services
> Parents of Murdered Children
> 100 East 8th Street
> Cincinnati, Ohio 45202
> Re: Tammy
>
> I have reviewed all of the materials sent; although the past history makes the death suspicious, the absence of an autopsy report and findings limits

by ability to do anything meaningful. An autopsy would help determine whether or not she was already dead at the time of the fire as well as if she had suffered any serious injuries before the fire.

Perhaps we could refer the file to an arson investigator or criminalist

Sincerely,
Harry J. Bonnell, M. D.

Mancel Mitchell sent me a letter he had gotten from Randy Stricker.

DATE: September 21, 1999
To: Mancel Mitchell, Commissioner Department of Public Safety
FROM: Randy Stricker, Special Agent Bureau of Criminal Apprehension
PHONE: 651-643-3048
Subject: Case review of Tammy's Death Investigation

At your direction the Bureau of Criminal Apprehension Cold Case Unit conducted a review of the case file in reference to the death of Tammy. The review consisted of SSA Evertt Doolittle and SA Randy Stricker meeting with Sheriff William Weber and Investigator Rolland Spriggle of the Dodge County Sheriff's Office. Agents also met with Wayne and Ruth McColley, parents of Tammy, who expressed their concerns in reference to the original investigation. Agents further reviewed the autopsy report and did meet with Dr. Michael Mcgee and discussed the final autopsy report. Court documents concerning Garry and his two children were also reviewed.

A discussion with the State Fire Marshal was also conducted in reference to has report concerning the fire.

As a result of this review certain areas of concern were discovered and will be discussed in the following text. First and foremost, the children should be re-interviewed by a specialist to obtain a factual accounting of their activities and observations with respect to the fire. A court order, file number F-2-97-455, signed by the Honorable Lawrence E. Agerter does allow for counseling and support services for the children. These very critical interviews could resolve this matter or bring this case forward.

A follow-up interview and possibly a polygraph should be conducted with Steven McQueen to verify has original statement. Becky Sullivan needs to be located and interviewed in regards to her involvement with Garry. Were there any relevant conversations between her and Garry about a future together? An interview should be conducted with Sheery Wolter, sister of Garry and best friend of Tammy to obtain any insight she may have in regards to this matter. The insurance agents should be interviewed, particularly the agent who insured the dwelling. It appears Garry was adamant about increasing the coverage of the residence.

An effort should be made to contact Garry and his attorney in an attempt to solicit their cooperation in trying to clear up some of these unresolved issues.

Based upon our review of the case file and interviews conducted, we have made the forgoing recommendation which will aid all parties in making any determinations.

In discussing the foregoing details with SAIC John Fossum, a decision was made that the matter will be referred to SA Herman Dybevik in the Rochester Field Office to assist the Dodge County Sheriff's Office in the following our recommendations.

I thought something would be done now. It was a joke! How could the sheriff have so much power? Wasn't it just last year when I witnessed a drug sale and the deputy destroyed the evidence and warned Garry to be more careful? Was Herman Dybevik in with the sheriff? I would later find out there was a lot of corruption, and I still suspect that it is going on today. They never followed up with any suggestion that Randy Stricker made. The investigation into Tammy's death was dead on arrival. Why?

Dodge County Court Services did an unannounced UA on Garry on September 28, 1999. The result of the test was a high positive for cocaine. A confirmation test requested and paid for by Garry also produced a positive result. Garry had denied the use of cocaine; however, court services strongly felt that Garry did use cocaine and was not being honest about his chemical use. They had requested a court hearing for probation violation and recommended that Garry serve 120 days in jail. Wendy was not present, so she could not be tested when the unannounced UA was performed on Garry.

Doreen was going to marry Alan Nelson on October 2, 1999. We were picking corn at the end of September. For some reason, I started having cramps in my stomach. I was happy for Doreen and Alan. I shouldn't feel this way. I was driving the tractor, pulling two wagons, one night the end of September. Suddenly, I got a cramp that doubled me up in the tractor. I couldn't control the tractor! The second wagon went in the ditch and tipped over, spilling the corn. The wagon was ruined, and it was a big job cleaning up the corn. On October 1, we were combining soybeans. I had just taken two loads to town. I knew we would have to quit at noon to go to the rehearsal for Doreen's wedding in the afternoon. She was getting married in a Lutheran Church in New Richland. They would be living on a farmstead close to New Richland, and they would be going to church there. Pastor Nelson was a friend of the pastor in their church. They were both going to marry them. I felt really bad that the farmers were going to be able to combine when I couldn't. On the way home from town, it started snowing. Everyone had to quit. I felt better!

Doreen and Alan

We had the rehearsal in the afternoon, and then we went to the Creamery restaurant in Otisco, which was a few miles north of New Richland. When I was a boy, my dad took milk to that creamery. When they closed the creamery, it was made into a restaurant. It was special to me. Bob took his pickup and took the girls. We went in our car and took Pastor Nelson with us. Pastor Nelson's wife, Doris, joined us at the creamery that night for the rehearsal meal. Doreen and the bridesmaids were going to stay overnight in a hotel in Waseca and have their hair done the next morning. Kayla and Sarah overheard them talking about it. They wanted to stay too. Doreen said they could stay. I was to call Garry if they stayed somewhere else. I knew they weren't home, and I didn't have a number to call them. The girls really begged me. They would have their hair done too. I knew they would have a good time, so I reluctantly agreed. Going home from the rehearsal supper, it was snowing so much we could hardly see. After the wedding we had the supper and the dance at the Oaks Golf course by Hayfield. It was seven miles from our home. Sarah was tired from the wedding and went to sleep in the back seat of Bob's pickup. When we got to the Oaks, we had to carry several things in from our car. Soon, I realized that I couldn't see Sarah. We looked all over, and I became afraid. What happened to Sarah? A thought came into my mind: maybe someone had taken Sarah. I asked Bob, "Did Sarah come in with you?" Bob said "Yes." I then asked Bob to go out to the pickup and look. He said, "She isn't there." Finally, Bob went out to the pickup. Sarah was still sleeping! Everyone had got so caught up with the excitement of Doreen's wedding that no one noticed Sarah. Garry somehow found out about this and tried to end our visitation.

Kayla and Sarah at Doreen's wedding

Barb Pike sent her monthly report to Judge Agerter on October 29, 1999.

On Friday October 22, 1999 I visited the Garry and Wendy residence in rural Dodge County. Kayla and Sarah spend the weekend with Wayne and Ruth McColley while Garry and Wendy assisted her parents with their move up to northern Minnesota. They also attended and were part of their aunt's wedding at the time of their regular monthly visitation with the McColley's. This resulted in an impromptu stay overnight at a motel following rehearsal. This was due to the girl's early appointment to have their hair done the next morning. Garry was upset as he hadn't been informed of the overnight stay. Ruth McColley has been advised that they need to make a phone call to Garry any time they plan to have the girls stay overnight any place other than their own residence.

Kayla and Sarah have their next therapy session on Monday November 1st with Dr. Mary Hennessey of Zumbro Valley Mental Health Center. Garry has visited Zumbro Valley Mental Health for his CD eval; however, it has been reported to me that he was guarded and defensive during the interview process, which resulted in an invalid evaluation. Wendy had a CD assessment at Charter Behavioral Health System on 8/10/99. Their recommendations were: 1. She should have ten sessions of IOP followed by re-evaluation to determine the extent of further treatment, if any. 2. She should avoid any use of mood altering chemicals. 3. She should attend NA with a sponsor once a week throughout probationary period. 4. She should obey all court mandates. Wendy has informed me that she currently setting up the ten sessions and is attending AA.

Barb Pike was talking about what Ruth and I had requested for in giving up the CHIPS petition. Maybe it was going to work for Wendy, but we had no hope for Garry. In fact, we had no hope for Wendy while she was living with Garry.

I decided to write a letter to Judge Agerter on November 11, 1999. It was a mistake to write the letter at the time, but maybe in a few years, it would help us. It was hard to tell.

To: The Honorable Lawrence E. Agerter

From: Wayne McColley

Subject: The welfare of Kayla and Sarah

I feel the need to write to you at this time to express my concerns about Garry and its effects on my granddaughters. I realize this should be kept short and to the point, but I also feel some background information should be heard.

We were not happy when our daughter Tammy met Garry. He was on furlough from prison visiting his sister, Sherri, who was Tammy's best friend. After Tammy and Garry's daughter was born, my wife and I decided to make the best of the situation. We arranged with the owner of a farm we were renting to let Tammy and Garry live rent-free in the house. Three years later, we bought the farm and sold Tammy and Garry the building site for $7,500. The property was appraised at $50,000 and they got a $40,000 loan. Garry has since told me that me that I took advantage of him on the deal.

When Tammy died, Garry and his family assured us that we would be able to see the girls whenever we wished. We agreed that we would have them every other weekend. Shortly after the

A FATHER'S QUEST

funeral Kayla phoned us and Garry overheard her saying something about the fire. We didn't understand what she said. Garry accused us of initiating talk about the fire and that we would not be able to see our granddaughters again. Naturally, we had a number of questions about the fire that took our daughter's life. Whenever we asked Garry anything about it, he would tell us that it was not our business. What happened to our daughter is our business? We have been told in court that we are to treat Garry as the father to the girls, but he has never treated us as parents of Tammy.

At the time of Tammy's funeral and shortly afterwards, several area people told us that our daughter was murdered. The sheriff's office assured us that they were only rumors. We also started hearing other things about Garry. We had been told that Garry was in prison because he took the blame for someone else's actions. We felt the need to know the truth and hired an investigator. The results were very shocking.

We were brought up to be honest, hardworking people and believed that our court system was fair and honest. Our faith in that system is fading fast. I was never as humiliated as when we were in court on April 29, 1999. George Restovich said many things against us that were either half-truths or total lies. It was not easy to just sit there and listen. On page 19, line 15 of the transcript, Mr. Restovich says "Just briefly, the typical problem for those of us, who seek the truth in courts with motion practices that people will up and say why, and it didn't happen, it's a lie, it's a whole bunch of lies, and then the court kind of throws up its hands you know, a lot of times just won't make a decision because you can't tell what the truth is."

From our standpoint, this pretty well summarizes Mr. Restovich's strategy. He wants to confuse the real issues, so that the court cannot make a decision. When we filed the Chips Petition, we believe that Mr. Restovich felt Garry didn't have that strong of a case, so he confused the issue. He was the first to mention, "change of custody." I shook my head no. We knew under the law that one can't use a Chips Petition to change custody. Miss Heinrich accepted Mr. Restovich's comments and everything after that point was focused on change of custody. With that being the issue, Garry's case was much stronger.

Here is another example from the court transcript of August 9,1999, page 24, line 20 to 25:

Heinrich: There was an unlicensed driver that took the children and transported them.
The Court: Who was the unlicensed driver?
Heinrich: Wendy
Restovich: She had a license.

Mr. Restovich represented Wendy in court for DUI. He knew she didn't have a license and I am submitting proof of this with the letter.

Garry is still driving on Oct. 25, 1999 at approximately 4:30 pm, as our son Bob was working in the field around Garry's house. Garry's white pickup came into the yard from the road and went by the barn. Garry got out of the pickup on the driver's side and he was alone in the pickup. On Nov. 2, 1999, I was working in the field in Ashland Township, Section 25. I was doing the headland right next to the road. Garry drove by in his pickup. He was alone in the vehicle. Just days before he appeared in court for his DAR, Vitim Services officer Gerry Gonser saw Garry drive his motorcycle down main street in Kasson. The first weekend in November, Kayla told our son Bob that Garry has a job working on a house in Austin and that she has to help him sometimes. Who is driving her? Bob didn't ask. That is only one example about how often we ask them things. It is far different than George Restovich would have you believe.

I would like to address some of the statements Garry made in his affidavits. Affidavit of April 1, 1999, item 13: "In his affidavit, Wayne McColley apparently quotes a sentencing order from 1985, though he doesn't attach a copy for my reference. The sentencing was almost 15 years ago. The fact that the petitioners have gone to the courthouses and searched through the records to find out my criminal history is more proof of the fact that they simply do not like me, never have, and never will. I certainly believe that I am much more responsible and mature than I was fifteen to twenty years ago. Isn't everyone." Is going from DUI to Cocaine use, Garry's example of being more responsible and mature?

In Garry's affidavit of Oct. 7, 1999, item 10, "Mr. McColley also states in paragraph 15 of affidavit that I am an alcoholic, have a history of abusing women and refused to seek medical care for the girls. Mr. McColley appears to be questioning my fitness to have custody of my children. I have had problems with alcoholism in the past, but I have since received outpatient treatment at Zumbro Valley Mental Center in Rochester. It is true, there was one incident of assault involving my wife Tammy and one incidence with a former girlfriend, Linda. These were isolated incidents." Garry would like the court to believe that on Oct. 7, 1997 that he had no problem with alcoholism. In July of 1997, he was in a car accident and had .17 blood alcohol on his test. His outpatient treatment with Zumbro Valley Mental Health was shortly after his 1994 DUI in Dodge Center, from which he is still on probation. Our daughter Tammy told us he went immediately from treatment sessions to a bar. Garry has been arrested at least eight times for domestic assault and I am enclosing the reports. The girls have told us about the violence that goes on in their home. Experts say that domestic violence is a learned behavior children learn in the home. I have a great fear that the girls will also learn this behavior.

Many times in his affidavits, Garry and his family have said that the girls have come back to their home crying. This is true, especially at first. They begged us to let them stay with us and not to send them back home. The reason they were crying and were unhappy with us was that they didn't want us to send them home. We also have a 2 ½ year old grandson who lives with us. Sarah once made a comment that Baby Justin is the lucky one. He gets to stay with Grandma and Grandpa all the time.

All parties were also told in court to try to foster a relationship with each other. In October, Garry filed a nuisance complaint against us. According to the report, his attorney told him to do it. It seems odd to us that every time Garry is in trouble, George Restovich wants to cause trouble for us. I will enclose the Sheriff's Report.

Garry wants us to pay half the costs of building a fence around his house. He states he had the same problem last year. Last year, we only had soybeans on the farm so no corn stalks could have blown in his yard.

Susan Osborn called us one-day last spring. I had never met her. She is Wendy's sister and was concerned about Wendy. She said that Garry's mother had told her mother, Karen, that Wendy would have to take the rap for Garry on these drug charges. She also told me that Garry was driving the night that Wendy got the DUI. They were able to lose the police long enough to change drivers. She told us that Garry was going to make a deal to move away if these charges disappeared. It seemed odd to me that one week before he goes to court on the charges, a for sale is by his home and the charges seem to disappear. The whole question in all of our court cases is what is best for Kayla and Sarah. In light of everything, I surely don't see that it could be in their best interest to move away.

We are now told that Garry has violated his probation. We feel that it is actually at least the fourth time that he has violated his probation. In June 1997, he had an accident in Dodge Center with his motorcycle. His probation had states that he should not operate any motor vehicle without a license. He had no motorcycle endorsement on his license. In July 1997 he had a DUI with .17 blood alcohol. He got a witness, Lois Holtz, to say she was driving. She said the accident happened because he was unable to give clear directions to his home and she missed a corner and hit the bridge. We observed Lois Holtz at Garry's house many times from April to July

1997. She didn't need directions. The bridge is also ½ mile from the nearest corner. He pleaded guilty to careless driving. His probation says no alcohol related driving offences. Careless driving with a .17 blood alcohol is an alcohol related driving offence. In September 1999 he was found guilty of driving without a license, again breaking his probation. The court system has laid these rules down for him and then gives a clear message that they will never follow through with any punishment. In his domestic abuse against our daughter, he was to have an evaluation and follow through. The last note in the file was that he never showed up.

In our Court Order of October 18, 1999, it states that Garry and Wendy will have chemical dependency evaluations and follow through with recommendations. According to Barb Pikes October 29, 1999 report Garry did not pass his testing. He tested positive for cocaine on two tests, but still denies it. I imagine George Restovich will arrange for Garry to take another test and this time Garry will con them and pass the testing. Both his and Wendy probation state that they are not to be using alcohol, but 1 1/2 cases of beer and a bottle of hard liquor was confiscated from their house.

The Court now has to make a big decision, and it will affect all parties involved. If Garry spends some time in jail, perhaps the proper messages will be send to everyone. Wendy doesn't appear to have any problems with the law until after she met Garry. Her chemical dependency evaluation of August 29th, she is just setting up appointments. I feel with Garry living with her and his record of alcohol and cocaine use, and with alcohol still in the home, Wendy stands little chance of a successful treatment program.

Our ultimate concern is for our granddaughters, Kayla and Sarah. If no actions is taken on Garry's alcohol and cocaine violations, their lives became even more dangerous. When Tammy was living, she would often call us at 5:00am and ask us if we would watch the girls. Garry was at home, but she didn't feel safe leaving the girls with him. I would hope that the court would give us temporary custody of the girls. We have never said anything about Garry in front of them and never will. We won't do anything to turn them against their father. If Garry can truly get his problems under control, it would only be proper that the girls should be returned to him. In our opinion that doesn't mean, that as soon as he is released from jail, that the girls are retuned. He needs to prove that the problems are truly under control for the welfare of the girls.

When the Chips file was dismissed in court, I was really upset. As Barb Pike stated in her report there was enough evidence. The more I read the transcripts the less upset I have become. To have proceeded with the Chips file, we would have had to use Dodge County Social Services. When we went to Dodge County Social Services to report the Chips case we met with Deb Dibler. She told us she was a childhood friend of Garry. I think that speaks for the investigation. It is a clear conflict of interest. I would hope that Olmsted or Steele County Social Services could be used in the future.

I appreciate your time reading this. I swear that everything I say is the truth. I would like to be questioned about all of this and all of the affidavits and would have no problems taking a polygraph test. I wonder if George Restovich or Garry would do the same.

I have already spent $20,000 in attorney and legal fees. With the farm economy as it is, I can no longer afford these legal bills. A year ago, the Court stated that Garry was to give us a signed statement giving us permission to take the children to the doctor, if necessary. We were told in Court, August 9, 1999, we would get this. We haven't received none of this. Also on the order signed October 18, 1999, Motion 2, sub paragraph d, we have received none of this. Do we have to go back to Court to make this happen? Why should we have the extra expense? We would like to meet with you and would appreciate your advice on what we can do before we incur more legal expenses on this.

Sincerely,
Wayne McColley

We got a reply from the judge written on November 22, 1999.

Mr. Wayne McColley
20213 680th St.
Dodge Center, MN 55927

RE: Material You Filed on November 11, 1999
Letter to the Court on the Same Date

Dear Mr. McColley:

Please be advised that a Judge cannot meet with you individually, and the Court certainly cannot give you legal advice on how to proceed. A Judge has to remain impartial, and if the Court were to meet with a party privately, the Court would have to remove himself from the proceedings.

I know this has been a terribly traumatic and costly proceeding for you and your wife. However, you must allow the prosed to proceed under the rules that we must all follow.

Very truly yours,
Lawrence E. Agerter
Judge of District Court

I then realized that I should not have written to the judge. Our attorney had prepared for a trial, which we didn't have. I wanted to testify, but it never happened. I never got to express my views. Restovich lied about us so much in court. It was more than I could take. I didn't know how to express myself without writing to the judge. At first I thought that it was a big mistake. But maybe in the next three years, it would help us some. I would never know for sure. I knew that the judge and Restovich met socially at times. I didn't trust either of them.

On the seventeenth day of November 1999, Garry appeared in court in front of Judge Agerter. I can't figure out why Restovich wasn't representing Garry. But he appeared alone without an attorney.

> THE COURT: And are you going to admit or deny the violation?
> GARRY: Well, yes, I'll admit.
> THE COURT: And what did you do?
> GARRY: I took some pain pills.
> THE COURT: You did what?
> GARRY: Right, for my back. I got a fractured back that happen a few years back.
> THE COURT: Okay. Now, the drug test came back on September 29, 1999 which was high pos-

itive for cocaine. Now, is that the pain killer you are talking about?

GARRY: Well, that's the only thing I took, Your Honor.

THE COURT: Well, pain killer doesn't show up cocaine, do they?

GARRY: Right.

THE COURT: And, Brenda Koppy, I will accept the admission to this violation. Brenda Koppy recommends you serve the 120 days in jail. And, Miss Koppy, do you stand on that position.

Ms. KOPPY: He has been on probation for four years, and he actually has three other legal charges that he could have violated on. And I feel we have done everything we can. And I was thinking 120 days, and actually for three new offences and a cocaine charge would be the appropriate number.

THE COURT: It's a lot of days, but the court gives you 120 days

Brenda Koppy was Garry's probation officer. After always looking the other way, finally Garry was going to pay the price for something.

At the end of November, Bob wanted to buy a semitruck. Since a young kid, Bob dreamed about owning a semitruck. Bob bought a 1996 Kenworth truck with a sleeper.

In December, I got a copy of a letter that Barb Pike, GAL, sent to the judge. I am going to print the total letter except the questions that she asked the girls.

TO: The Honorable Lawrence E. Agerter
SUBJECT: Guardian ad Litem Monthly Report for November

On Tuesday November 30, 1999, I visited the Garry and Wendy's residence in rural Dodge County. I made the appointment, so the family was expecting me. Kayla and Sarah arrived home from school just as I got there. They were clean, neat and dressed appropriately for school. Sarah had fallen and had a huge run in her hosiery, but was not afraid to disclose that fact to Wendy.

During the month of November Garry was sentenced to jail for 120 days and Wendy was sentenced to 27 days on electronic home monitoring with 5 years' probation. Garry has not been able to begin serving time as yet, because there was not any space available for him. Both of these convictions were due to chemical abuse, which substantiates the need for both Garry and Wendy to face up to these issues. Apparently Wendy is on a wait list for outpatient treatment at Charter Behavioral; However, they do not have any opening until February. They have suggested that she access treatment though some other facility such as Zumbro Valley. I am not sure of the current status of Garry's treatment. Subsequent to Garry's recent conviction, Dodge County Human Services and assistant Dodge County Attorney Gary Remine evaluated the case with regard to any child protection issues. They have determined that there are not presently any reasons for filing a CHIPS petition in the matter.

The McColley's have still not received a medical release for emergency care from Garry. Wendy stated that if the McColley's attorney wished to prepare one they would have their attorney review it. There is some concern as to who should be receiving what information relative to the court ordered CD evaluations and counseling for the girls. The order states that releases should be signed and all attorneys should receive this information; however, it is questionable as whether complete discloser to all of the parties would be of any benefit to the girls. Perhaps the court could clarify this matter.

The girls were seen by Dr. Mary Hennessey of Zumbro Valley Mental Health on November 1st. She would like the opportunity to meet personally with Garry. Dr. Hennessey has recommended that Kayla and Sarah be seen by her on a monthly basis foe supportive reasons; however, Garry and Wendy have refused to allow these visits to take place during school hours. The next available appointment outside of school hours is the end of December, which Dr. Hennessey feels is too long of a span. Perhaps the court could address this issue.

The questions to the girls were left out.

I only submit these questions and responses to indicate that the girls do indeed have the normal routine one would expect for children of their ages, other than the turmoil that is brought about by some of the poor choices Garry and Wendy have made in the past, plus the ongoing dissension that occurs between Garry and Wayne.

Respectfully Submitted,
Barb Pike

I think that Barb did a good job with our grandchildren. It was hard for her to work with Garry. He was very intimidating to

A FATHER'S QUEST

all women. I really felt sorry for her. I had really fought for the girls to get counseling. Garry had really fought against it. He said, maybe they could go to counseling in two years. The girls were so young at Tammy's death. His plan was to brainwash them. In two years they couldn't remember. He was right. I was hoping the truth would come out on Tammy's death. It never happened.

In early December, I was reading the newspaper. North of the Twin Cities, there was a Dodge dealer who had a really good price on a new Dodge van. We had been renting a van when the girls were visiting us. That way we could all go in one vehicle. I told Ruth, "Maybe we should go up there and buy a new van?" Ruth said, "No, why would you go so far from home to buy a vehicle?" I said, "It's a good deal." The next morning we left. Ruth was unhappy. She said, "What are you thinking about?" We drove two hours away from home. Ruth was mad at me, and it only became worse. I thought the trip would take forever. When we got there, we drove the van. Ruth didn't like it. Then we went in a room with the salesman. Ruth didn't like the van. The salesman said, "Ruth, what can we do to make you happy?" Ruth said, "I want to go home." Then Ruth really chewed me out. That was the first time for me, and I couldn't believe it. The salesman started to feel sorry for me. He offered to sell me the van for less than they had advertised it. All Ruth said was, "Let's go." Then the salesman left to talk to his boss. Soon the salesman came back with a cheaper offer. Ruth got up and left. I didn't know what to do but to follow her. The salesman and his boss caught up with us. They made me an offer so good that I couldn't refuse it. Finally, Ruth thought it was a good deal. Ruth drove our car home, and I drove the new van home. We kept the van for six years and never had any problem with it. It was the best deal I ever got on a vehicle.

Our Christmas holiday with the girls was Christmas Eve. Bob picked them up at 4:00 PM. Garry was to pick them up at 10:00 PM. Garry called me on the phone at 5:00 PM. He said, "When I pick up the girls, I'm going to take care of you." I felt threatened, and I was afraid of what he was going to do. He must have been drinking or maybe on drugs. He was like a madman! I called the sheriff's office. The deputy said, "We cannot sit in your yard waiting for him. When he starts walking up to the house, call 911." I was nervous about how long it would take for them to get here. I didn't enjoy Christmas at all. I was afraid that Bob would get in a fight with him. I knew from reading the reports on Garry, he wouldn't fight fair. I had cramps in my stomach the whole time. When Garry started to walk up to the house, Bob went out. I called 911. In seconds two sheriff cars drove in our yard. They told Bob to go back to the house. Then they told Garry to get back in the car. Then one officer said, "I will get the girls from the house and bring them to the car." Garry had ruined Christmas Eve for us. That was his plan.

Chapter 17

The Turn of the Century

I had several conversations with Wendy prior to New Year's weekend of the year 2000. She expressed to me that she wished this conflict between Garry and me would end. I told her that it could end anytime Garry wanted it to end. We would like some questions answered concerning Tammy's death. Garry had always told us that it was none of our business. She expressed to me that if something happened to her daughter, it would be her business and she would have to know. She said she would talk to Garry about this and try to get him to sit down and talk to us. In the next conversation, she said that she had talked to Garry but had got nowhere. He was not happy with her. She was finding out that Garry was not very easy to deal with. I expressed to her that if he had nothing to hide and he wasn't guilty of anything, he would want to get this resolved. She said he told her that I wouldn't believe him anyway. That was when I suggested that he take a lie detector test. My attorney and the guardian ad litem both told me to warn Wendy that she would be facing contempt of court charges if she didn't follow the court orders.

Barb Pike sent her December monthly report to the judge on January 5, 2000.

> My last report indicated several issues that I felt needed to be resolved in this case. I was not able to get what I felt were satisfactory resolutions to these issues so a motion was filed on my behalf by Attorney Steve Rolsch. These matters will be

heard before the court on January 18, 2000. Two of the issues have been addressed as I write this report. #1. Garry and Wendy have both had a visit with Dr. Hennessy and have agreed to allow the girls to miss school for one visit per month. It is important that they also stay in contact with Dr. Hennessy as issues arise that she feels are important to discuss with them. #2. Wendy has an appointment with Charter Behavioral for a reevaluation regarding her CD issues. It is extremely important that she follow through with whatever plan they recommend for treatment. To my knowledge, Garry has still not satisfactorily addressed his CD issues. The matter of who is to receive reports from Dr. Hennessy is still not technically resolved, although I believe all parties are in agreement that the girls do need privacy relative to matters they may discuss with her.

With regard to visitation, it appears that a visitation expeditor should be appointed to this case to work out visitation problems on a timely basis. My services and authority in this area are limited by state statutes, and it is bound to be upsetting to the girls when conflicts arise surrounding visits.

There was a matter of dissension surrounding the regular monthly visit the first part of December. The girls were unsettled due to the fact that Garry had recently checked into jail, and wanted to call and/or go home. I believe they did call Friday night; however, McColleys did not perceive any problem on Saturday night. When they got home the girls apparently related to Wendy that they were not allowed to call. These types of incidents are perfectly normal for children staying with grandparents; however, if there is better communication between the individuals the problems can be worked out between the adults to everyone's satisfaction. According to Wendy, Dr. Hennessy has recommended that a notebook be passed back and forth to try to address some of these issues. There was also a disagreement as to which weekend was the correct one for the regular January visit.

> Respectfully Submitted,
> Barb Pike

Maybe we were guilty for not allowing the girls to call their dad on Saturday night. When they called Garry on Friday night, he made the girls feel guilty that Wendy had to stay alone. They wanted to go home. We never tried to use the girls against Garry, but he always tried to set the girls against us.

After Garry threatened me on last Christmas Eve, I started having nightmares that Garry was coming in our house to get me. I put a shotgun under our bed with a box of shells on the bed stand. I kept having nightmares every two or three nights. This went on for almost a month. Suddenly, I realized if I was having a nightmare at the same time when Bob was coming home in the middle of the night; I could shoot Bob. It was a dumb idea! I put the shotgun and the shells away. When I put the shotgun away, the nightmares stopped.

The girl's counselors recommended that we would have a tablet that we would write in it. The girls would give it to us. We were to write in it, and they would take it home with them.

Wendy wrote on January 7, 2000:

> This is the tablet we are to transfer back and forth in hopes to open communication. The girls Therapist has suggested this. So I told Ruth, Sarahs rash is on her tummy and neck. Please make sure to apply lotion 2 times daily. We have a birthday coming up the 15th. So the girls will

see you on the 22nd. We will see the Girls at 5:00 Sunday.

Thanks,
Wendy

Ruth answered her:

I did put on the cream on Sarah's spots. Had a nice weekend, hope to see the girls again the 22nd.

The notebook was a good idea. Wendy always wrote and most time I wrote. I always liked writing letters, so it was usually a long one.

On January 12, 2000, I wrote a letter to Dr. Hennessy. By then, I would search anywhere for help.

Dear Dr. Hennessy

I have given much thought to this and I don't know if it is proper for me to write to you or not, but feel that I must. I am the grandfather to Kayla and Sarah and I understand that you cannot share any information with me and I don't ask you to do so. I am very concerned about their health and safety. I am concerned about how they will deal with their mother's death as they become older and start asking questions. I am deeply concerned about the environment they are living in, especially the domestic violence in their home that they have told us about. It is pretty well documented that domestic violence is a learned behavior in the home. I have a deep concern about the kind of people they will grow up to be living in this atmosphere.

There is an ongoing police investigation into Tammy's death and I am fearful of their safety as this progresses. I am enclosing some reports that I hope will help you in their consulting and to better understand what they have went though and what they have to go through in the future.

I thank you for your time and understanding in reading this.

Sincerely
Wayne McColley

I sent Dr. Hennessy a copy of the interview that Rollie Spriggle and Tom Neudahl had with the girls the day after the fire. At the time I wrote this letter, I thought there was an ongoing police investigation taking place. As I think about this twenty year later, there was no police investigation taking place. The sheriff was covering up Tammy's death. I wish I knew why.

We got a letter from the court that Judge Agerter signed on January 18, 2000.

Wayne and Ruth McColley.
Petitioners, ORDER TO
SHOW CAUSE
And
Garry Respondent,

To: Garry, Respondent above named and his attorney: George Restovich:

YOU WILL PLEASE TAKE NOTICE: that upon the attached Notice of Hearing on Motion and Affidavit of Petitioners, and all files, records and proceedings herein, on the motion of attorney for the petitioners herein, and the Court being duly advised in the premises.

It is hereby ordered that you, Garry, the above named RESPONDENT, PERSONALLY APPEAR AND SHOW CAUSE, if any you have, before the above-named Court at the Dodge County Courthouse, in Mantorville, Minnesota on the third day of February at 3:00pm, or as soon thereafter as counsel can be heard, why the Court should not hold you in contempt of court and grant the petitions the relief as set forth in the attached Notice of Hearing on Motion.

IT IS FURTHER ORDERED that all responsive pleadings shall be served and mailed to or filed with the court administrator no later than five (5) days prior to the scheduled hearing. The Court may, in its discretion, disregard any responsive pleadings served or filed with the court administrator less than five (5) days prior to such hearing in ruling on the motion or matter in question.

Let a copy of the attached pleading be served on Garry. Respondent in these proceeding.

BY THE COURT
Lawrence E. Agerter

Judge Agerter issued an order on January 20, 2000. The matter was originally scheduled for hearing on January 18, 2000 at 9:00 am in the city of Mantorville, County of Dodge, upon the motion of Steven E. Rolsch, attorney for the Guardian Ad Litem, Barbara Pike. Prior to the hearing Roxanne Heinrich, attorney for the Petitioners, indicated she had no objections to the motion as did George F. Restovich, attorney for the Respondent. As such the court makes the following Order:

1. Garry shall fully cooperate with Zumbro Valley Mental Health Center, including allowing the girls to have appointments at Zumbro Valley Mental Health Center during school times.
2. Garry shall meet with the staff at Zumbro Valley Mental Center and cooperate fully with them in counseling of the girls.
3. The sessions between the girls shall be confidential and records and notes of these sessions shall be released only to the court and the Guardian Ad Litem as it is the best interests of the girls to be completely frank and open with the staff at Zumbro Valley Mental Health Center.
4. Wendy shall get into treatment as soon as possible instead of waiting for Zumbro Valley Mental Health Center to have an opening in February of 2000.

The above is hereby ordered: BY THE COURT
Dated: January 20, 2000 Honorable Lawrence E. Agerter

On February 3, we appeared in court. There was a lot of talking by the attorneys, but there wasn't much settled. The judge had made a big mistake on the visitation issue. It should have been spelled out so there could be no mistake. It appeared that the court had an order on visitation that could be interrupted by Garry. It wasn't totally fixed; I still had a lot of doubts.

Ms. Heinrich: Your Honor, I'm just going to say one thing.

The Court: Sure.

Ms. Heinrich: Ignorance and stupidity of the law is not an excuse. Thank you.

The Court: I'll review this. I'm not going to take any testimony today on this. I'll review it and issue a written order. Okay? Have a good day.

The court issued a written order on March 2, 2000.

ORDER

1. Petitioner's motion to find the Respondent in willful civil contempt for violations of paragraph 2(f) of Court Order dated October 18, 1999 and Paragraph (6) of the Court Order dated November 3, 1999, is hereby GRANTED.
2. Petitioner's motion for compensatory visitation to be granted to Petitioners is hereby DENIED.
3. Petitioner's motion to amend the order to include an enforcement clause is hereby DENIED.
4. Petitioner's motion to award Petitioners their attorney's fees and costs incurred in having to bring this motion is hereby GRANTED.
5. Petitioner's motion imposing a civil penalty of $500.00 on Garry is hereby DENIED.
6. Petitioner's motion ordering Garry to post a bond to ensure compliance is hereby DENIED.

The way the court left the order meant that Garry could still play games with us. I thought an order meant something. When I'm writing this book, I think an order is written so both attorneys can ague both ways against the order. At least Garry suffered a conscience and had to pay our attorney's fee. I thought this would teach Garry a lesson, but I would soon realize that I was wrong. We also learned in court that Garry took a $45,000 mortgage on his house. How could Garry go through a half of a million dollars in three years? He was drawing $1,200 a month from Social Security from the girls. It would be easier to deal with him now that he didn't have so much money.

I wrote a letter to Social Security on January 28, 2000.

> Social Security Admin.
> 401 16th Ave. N.W. Ste. 104
> Rochester, Minn. 55901
> Dear Mr. Ocstreich.
>
> Early in 1997 we had some correspondence concerning the death of our daughter Tammy and the benefits paid to her children. I do not remember where I learned this information, but it is our understanding that the children's father Garry is receiving $600 a month social security for each girl. It is also our understanding that Garry is receiving another $600 a month for staying home and taking care of the girls.
>
> Garry has been in jail since Dec. 1, 1999. He is out on work release, so he must have a job. I am enclosing the court transcript showing this. On Dec. 3, 1999 Garry got a mortgage on his home for $45,000 from Northwest Mort. Company. This on record at the Dodge County house. To receive a mortgage one has to have a source of income to make the payment.

The girls are in custody of Garry's new wife, Wendy. Eighteen month ago Wendy abandoned her children. She is also on probation for using drugs. As grandparents this is of deep concern to us.

The investigation of our daughter's death has also been reopened by the Bureau of Criminal Apprehension.

Garry has a long history of abusing the system. As a concerned citizen who pays into the system, we hope you will look into this future.

Sincerely
Wayne McColley

The letter did no good. There are thousands of people like Garry who are abusing the system. Why aren't they checking into things like this?

On February 14, 2000, Rollie Spriggle and Herb Dybavik from the BCA called in Deputy John Snaza. They wanted to know what he had written in his report on the day of the fire. John had written in his report that the girls had gone to the barn with their dad the day of the fire. They saw smoke from the house and told their dad. It was a long interview. They tried over and over to confuse John to make him change his story. They tried everything they could, but John never changed his mind. When I went to St. Paul to meet with Mancell Mitchel and Tom Neudahl; I convinced them that the girls were never in the house at the time of the fire. They were trying to prove something different. They weren't successful with John. By this time, the sheriff knew he was wrong, but he wasn't going to admit that he was wrong under any circumstances.

On February 24, 2000, Garry appeared in court. It was for a pretrial hearing. Garry was brought from jail, so he had an orange jumpsuit on. I was in the court room, and it felt good to see Garry

A FATHER'S QUEST

dressed up like a prisoner. There was nothing decided. Garry pleaded not guilty to the charge of using cocaine.

> THE COURT: All right, we will put it back on the jury calendar then. You will stay in touch with your attorney then. Okay Garry.
> GARRY: Okay

Wendy called me in the early afternoon of March 3. I was out in the shop, and she caught me by surprise. She asked if we would take the girls on Wednesday to Friday night (March 31 to April 2) instead of the first weekend of April as that was Easter.

I said, "I don't know about that. When they are here, we like our whole family to be together, and Doreen and Brenda have to work on Thursday and Friday."

I asked, "How about Wednesday to Saturday night?"

She said, "You can't have them Saturday because we have an Easter egg hunt planned."

I said, "We have plans too."

She said that George told her that Easter was Garry's holiday.

I said, "There is no mention of Easter in the court order. All it says is that we are to have them the first weekend of every month." I said, "I'm out in the shop, and I can't make a decision on this alone."

She said, "Call me back tonight."

I went in the house to look at the calendar and talk to Ruth. I saw that we had a meeting Thursday afternoon that Ruth and I both had go. Ruth said she knew that we were getting them on Easter and that Doreen, Brenda, and she had made plans on this. We talked about how when we were in negotiations at the courthouse the day of the hearing on visitation, we had asked for every other Easter, and we had to give this up knowing that Easter would only fall once in a while the first weekend of April. That would be the only time we would get the girls on Easter. I called our attorney about this for advice. At nine on Wednesday night, Roxanne called me. She told me, "It doesn't say anything in the court order or the transcript about Easter. It only says that you are to get the girls the first weekend of

325

every month." She said, "The way Garry is treating you, there is no reason you shouldn't enjoy your granddaughters on Easter." I told her that Wendy had said that George had told them they were going to have the girls on Easter.

At seven thirty Thursday morning, March 4, I called Wendy. I told her that we talked this over.

"On Thursday Ruth and I won't be home. I am a director of an insurance company, and there is a meeting that Ruth and I are required to go to on that day."

She said, "Someone will be at your home that day, won't they?"

I said, "Someone will have to be home to watch Justin, but Ruth and I won't be home, so we aren't going to have this be one of our visitation days."

She then said we could have them on Saturday. What was this? She wanted them on Saturday for an Easter egg hunt. Was Garry playing games with us again?

I said, "Everyone was planning on Easter Sunday. My parents are in their late seventies, and this may be the last time they have to spend Easter with the girls. The court order says we are to have the girls on the first weekend of April, and that's what we are planning. It also says we are to get the girls for two hours the following Saturday after their birthdays, and that Saturday is after Kayla's birthday."

Wendy said, "The order will have to be changed. You get them every holiday."

I said, "No, we don't. We get them every other Fourth of July and Labor Day." I said, "We don't get the girls on Labor Day this year."

Wendy said, "No, but it is a three-day weekend. Those are family weekends."

I said, "No one at your house works, so you can have three-day weekends anytime."

She said, "I work."

I asked her where, and she told me, "Rochester."

I could hear some discussion in the background. I told her that we would have to stay with the court orders, and we both said goodbye.

Garry called about five minutes later. His first words were, "How come you are asking Wendy where she works? That's none of your business." He then told me, "You aren't getting the girls on Easter."

I told him, "The court order says we are to get the girls the first weekend of April."

He then told me, "You can't tell me what to do, I'm the parent, and I will decide what to do. You are trying to act like a parent."

I said, "No, I'm trying to act like a grandparent."

He then said, "I'm the parent, and I have rights. The grandparents don't have any rights."

I then told him, "The grandparents have rights too. The court has given us rights."

He then said, "I don't care what the court says. No one can tell me what to do. What I say goes, and you aren't going to get the girls on Easter."

I then told him that we would have to go back to court.

He said, "Good, you are not getting the girls on Easter."

I then hung up the phone. I didn't care to get in a fight with him. The court had never held him responsible before. The court had issued orders over and over, and when Garry didn't obey an order, the court didn't enforce it. Garry felt he was above the law. I was so stubborn that I was not going to let this go.

On March 3, 2000, Barb Pike submitted her monthly report to the court.

> I visited Garry's home on 2-28-2000. Kayla and Sarah were dressed appropriately when they arrived home from school, and were both anxious to share their school papers. They are doing well in school; however, Garry and Wendy feel Kayla may need to attend summer school again this year for help with math. They would like to be sure that scheduling can be worked out to facilitate the girls summer vacation with their grandparents, Wayne and Ruth McColley, as well as the

summer school schedule if need be. Garry and Wendy stated they have checked with the school regarding speech therapy for Sarah, and were told that the school isn't concerned at this point. They will continue to monitor her progress.

    The notebook is working well for exchange of information between the parties, and they are sticking to appropriate subjects regarding the girls. Garry and Wendy are hopeful that the girls will be able to bring pictures home to share with them when they do special activities with their grandparents. These types of communication should help bridge the exchanges between the two homes, and improve the relationships all around. I understand the girls are free to call home whenever they wish when visiting in the McColley home. The emergency medical release has been prepared by George Restovich, signed by Garry and should be in the McColleys possession by this time.

    Wendy was approximately half way through her outpatient treatment at Charter Behavioral when they closed their program. She is presently making arrangements to continue her treatment through Zumbro Valley. Garry stated that he is still on a wait list at Fountain Center; however, I have not been able to make contact with them at this point to verify that information. Garry, Wendy, Kayla, and Sarah are keeping their once per month appointments with Dr. Hennessy. She feels these appointments are extremely important for the girls, as do I. Dr. Hennessy and I are hopeful that both parties will consider the information in these court reports as being a useful tool to work toward the best interest of the girls, and not as information to be used against one another in court or otherwise.

Respectfully Submitted,
Barb Pike, Guardian ad Litem

I didn't feel that Garry was going to change. We could tolerate Garry when he wasn't using drugs and while he was sober. But this often was not the case. I thought Wendy was good for the girls and she was trying to clean up her act. I hoped that she would be successful. We never saw any information from Dr. Hennessy, so there wasn't any information that I could use against Garry. It took Restovich over two years to act on the court order to give us the right to take the girls to a doctor in an emergency. He was helping Garry to disobey court orders. I had started to hate George and was praying that God would take care of him.

On April 12, 2000, our attorney wrote a letter to Restovich and Rolsch.

Dear Mr. Restovich and Mr. Rolsch:

Enclosed and served upon you by United Stares Mail, please find the Clerk's Notice of Filing Entry and Order in the above reference matter.

I Have enclosed a bill for services for this motion hearing that Judge stated That Garry is ordered to pay. I have submitted to the court and you have a rough estimate of my attorney fees and did not include the time I spend working on February 3th.

I understand that the medical release has not been done as promised in open court and on record.

Truly,
Roxanne Heinrich
Attorney at Law

I had learned the hard way that I couldn't write to the judge, but maybe I could write to the court. I wrote the letter on April 16, 2000. The court received the letter on the seventeenth day of the month. They sent a copy of the letter with a stamp from the court on it back to me. We got the medical release almost right away. It did help some.

Statement by Wayne McColley

In a court order signed Nov. 3, 1998, it states that Garry shall provide a duly signed release to allow the McColley's to seek medical care for Kayla and Sarah in the event that a medical emergency shall arise while the girls are in our care.

In court on Aug. 9, 1999 this medical release is brought up. The court states, we are going to get it now.

In court on Feb. 3, 2000 this issue is brought up again. The court tells Mr. Restovich to take care of it. Mr. Restovich says he will. As of April 16, 2000 we have not received this release. Is this some kind of game? Are we to come back to court again about this? There seems to be no respect for these court orders. Garry and Mr. Restovich have lied, twisted the truth and disobeyed most of the things we got by the court. Someone has to have respect for laws and court orders if this system is going to work and it has to start at the top, the court itself.

In the court order of Oct. 18, 1999 our attorney is to receive Garry and Wendy's C D evaluations. This was discussed in court Feb. 3, 2000. When the Court made the ruling this was not addressed, so we can only assume the order still stands. Why hasn't our attorney received these? Is this going to be like the medical releases?

Must we spend money to come back to court for something that is in another court order.

This has been an extremely emotional and tragic event in our lives. Now it appears everyone is playing games with us.

Sincerely
Wayne McColley

On May 10, 2000, our attorney got a letter from Barb Pike's attorney Rolsch.

Dear MS. Heinrich:

Enclosed please find a copy of the letter your client wrote to Judge Agerter. Also enclosed please find a copy of the medical release Mr. Restovich provided our office. If you have any questions, please feel free to contact me.

Very truly yours,
Steven E. Rolsch

Also on May 10, Rolsch sent a letter to Restovich.

Dear Mr. Restovich:

Enclosed please find a copy of the letter that I wrote to Ms. Heinrich. Also enclosed is a copy of the letter to the Judge written by Wayne McColley.

I have been informed by my client that your client has removed the girls from the care of Zumbro Valley Mental Health Center. This is in direct violation of paragraph 2b. of the Court's October 18, 1999 Order. Please instruct your client to obey the Order so that we do not to have further Court proceeding in this matter. Also, pursuant to the same Order, I have not received Garry's chemical dependency evaluations. Please get them over to me as soon as possible.

Very truly yours,
ROLSCH & ANDERSON LAW OFFICES
Steven E. Rolsch

On May 14, 2000, our attorney wrote to Judge Agerter.

Dear Honorable Judge Lawrence Agerter

This letter in response to Mr. George Restovich letter dated May 9, 2000 for Garry. I have enclosed a letter from Mr. Steven Rolsch, attorney for Barb Pike, GAL. As you can see Garry still is not obeying the Court Orders.

Mr. Restovich did not dispute my attorney fees at the February 3th hearing as to travel time and at that time the estimated bill was $1,000 without the costs Mr. Restovich bill was for travel time was for $819.50 and he only came from Rochester. Garry's behavior caused the hearing to occur and it looks like I will be up there again based on Garry's behavior.

Some of the reasons I did not have the sheriff serve the papers are 1) the time limit, 2) I did not know how busy the sheriff's office was, and 3) I felt I should be there in person in case your honor had any questions about the papers. I was not going to sit by the phone and wait for either your call nor the sheriff's office.

The time limit issue was the papers had to be served at least 14 days prior to the hearing scheduled February 3. By serving them January 18 in person I did not miss time period. Since there was a hearing already scheduled for this day which was cancelled and I had my schedule available that I could personally serve the papers I felt this way the most reasonable and safe way to serve these papers so they would not be untimely and have to schedule another hearing date.

As for 4 hrs. to prepare for the hearing based on Mr. Restovich's papers it took him that long to prepare for the hearing. I don't see my 4 hrs. as excessive. To be paid travel time back and forth was one of the reasons I reduced my attorney fees with my clients. So if I do not receive travel time my fees will go up. I do not charge for phone call, copying, and mileage expense wish are costs.

Furthermore, your horror I would like to order Garry to pay me within 5 days after you order the amount of attorney fees and costs I am to receive from Garry. I do not want to wait for Garry to wait for Garry to pay me at his own time.

Thank You.

Respectfully submitted,
Roxanne Heinrich

Shortly after Lois Hackbarth got a letter from Second Opinion Services, which was a part of The National Organization of Parents of Murdered Children, she called me. She and another woman wanted to come out to our house. They received a letter from Parents of Murdered Children. I had given a copy of Tammy's autopsy to Lois some time ago. When they got to our house, they said that Tammy had been given a severe beating shortly before her death. Kayla had told Ruth that shortly before they went outside the day of the fire with their dad, Garry went upstairs to see Tammy. That made perfect sense. That would explain why Tammy was unable to get out of the house. I got sick to my stomach thinking about this. I am going copy part of the letter that they got.

> Tammy was certainly alive at the time of the fire as evidenced by smoke inhalation and the carbon monoxide level. However, I do not understand how the spleen and lung can be described as dark red to burgundy in color with such a high carbon monoxide level. She also has 100 cc (7 tablespoonful) of blood in her right chest and 300 cc (more than a half-pint) of blood in her abdomen with no source of bleeding identified. Since there is no other reason for her to be incapacitated and unable to try to escape the fire, the probability of ante-mortem blunt force or sharp force trauma needs to be considered.

I immediately took this letter to Rollie. I felt that now we finally had proof that Garry had murdered Tammy. He said he would contact Dr. McGee, who was the person that had done the autopsy. Dr. McGee said, "How dare someone question my work?" The sheriff wouldn't question Dr. McGee's work either. My letter didn't mean anything. That was the end of it.

I then called Mancel Mitchell on the phone. I said, "We have just gotten more evidence into Tammy's death. Can I come up to see you?"

He said, "I think it's time I come down to see you. I will call you soon."

Now, finally, we were going to get somewhere. I was so happy and excited!

The next day I got a call from the sheriff's office. They said, "Come in right away."

Now something was going to be done! When I got there, I met with Sheriff Bill Weber, John Fossum, and Herman Dybevik. They were both from the BCA.

John Fossum told me right away, "You have no business starting at the top. You have to go through the chain of command. You have to start at the bottom first. I am at the bottom, but before you can come to me, you have to start with the sheriff." Then they threatened me. "If you want to keep seeing your granddaughters, you better give up on Tammy's death."

I felt like they had just kicked me in the stomach. Then they said they didn't want to see me again. Why was this? Threatening me was not going to fully work. I did not want to lose my granddaughters, but I figured that they would have to go through court to do it. How could they take away my grandparents' rights? They were using fear as a way to intimidate me. Fear was never something that I would give in to. Mancel Mitchell never called me. Why? But I didn't feel that I could call him now. Why did Mr. Mitchell take orders from someone at the bottom? Evidently, the BCA was in it with the sheriff. I started to hate the sheriff and was praying that God would take care of him.

The notebook was going well. I enjoyed getting a letter from Wendy every month. I suspected that Garry was still using drugs, but by the way her letters were written, maybe she wasn't using drugs. I hoped so.

She wrote on June 2, 2000:

> The girls are so excited school is out and this year they do not have to go to summer school so they may have swimming lessons! Sarah's rash is so much better this month. We didn't go to any chlorine pools. Maybe that's one problem with her rash, besides metal. Are you planning on the second week in August for the girls, if so from what date to what date? Report cards were really good! Smart girls. Kayla need to practice

her math but excellent in reading. Have a nice weekend and we will see the girls Sunday at 5:00

Wendy

On June 4, 2000, I wrote in the notebook:

Friday night Kayla, Sarah, Justin and I went to the park in Hayfield.

Sat. afternoon everyone went to the pool in Hayfield and to the park. We ate supper in Hayfield.

Sunday, what a gloomy day. We all went to church. Afterward the girls played in the playroom for a while. We went out to dinner.

Our Aug. visitation with the girls is the first weekend of the month should be from Friday night, Aug. 4th until Sunday night Aug. 13th. Because the girls are going to girl scout camp the weekend before we understand that you would want some time with them between camp and their visit with us. So Sunday night at 6:00 Aug. 6th till Sunday night Aug. 13 will be okay. We have reservations made in Wisconsin Dells at a resort so we hope this won't be a problem. Because we are giving up Aug. weekend it would be nice if the girls could come up for a day now and then during the summer.

Wayne

That summer we decided to build two more bins. Bob now had a semitruck. To make it pay, we needed more storage so we could get a better price by hauling the grain further away from home. We built two thirty-thousand-bushel bins. We now had room to store most of the corn crop and some of the soybean crop.

We again took the girls to Wisconsin Dells. This time I rented a three-bedroom condominium. Bob had to sleep on the sofa. Doreen slept with the girls. Brenda and Justin had another bedroom. Ruth and I had the third bedroom. The condo was on a lake. We again went horseback riding, rode on the ducks, and went to a nearby town and rode on a train. Justin was fascinated by trains. We okayed the trip with Garry.

State of Minnesota, Plaintiff,-vs-Garry, Defendant.

Date of sentencing hearing: August 14, 2000

APPEARANCES: Mr. Gary Remine, Assistant Dodge County Attorney, appeared as counsel on behalf of the State of Minnesota; Mr. Restovich and Gary Gittus, Attorneys at Law, appeared as counsel on behalf of the defendant. The defendant was personally present in Court.

Pursuant to defendant's plea of guilty entered August 14, 2000, the Court hereby enters judgment of guilty of the following charges:

Controlled Substance Crime in the 5th Degree, a felony, in violation of MSA 152.025, Subdivision 2 (1) for which the maximum penalty is five years in prison and / or $10,000 fine.

The Court makes the following disposition:

It IS HEREBY ORDERED that execution of sentence be stayed for the period of one (1) year on the following conditions:

1. That the defendant shall pay a fine and surcharges amounting to $930.00.
2. That the defendant shall serve six months in jail at a facility as selected by the Dodge County Sheriff. However, the defendant

shall be given credit for six months jail previously served in this matter.
3. That the dependent shall cooperate with a polygraph examination to be conducted by the Bureau of Criminal Apprehension and under the auspices of defense counsel and approval of the County Attorney's Office.
4. That the attached memorandum is made a part of the sentencing order herein.

Dated this 17 day of August, 2000.

BY THE COURT:
Lawrence E. Agerter

MEMORANDUM

The above matter came on before the court for jury trial on August 14, 2000. Counsel and the court met in chambers for two hours to discuss this case. This court is very familiar with the defendant and his background, having dealt with him in court in criminal matters over the years.

Based upon the discussion in chambers, the court's review of this file, and plea negotiations between the parties, the court find that a presentence investigation is not necessary in this particular matter. The Court, therefore, waives the presentence investigation and proceeded directly to sentencing.

The disposition ordered in this particular case is a downward departure from the sentencing guidelines. Based upon a thorough review of this matter, the court has decided to follow the plea negotiations which would essentially call for a downward departure from sentencing guidelines. The defendant is amenable to local sanctions and been cooperative in this matter.

Garry was sentenced to have a polygraph test. We never heard anything about the test. Did he take the test? Did the sheriff want him to take the test? Are typical orders not followed? Why? "The defendant is amenable to local sanctions." Why? How long will it take before Garry's in court again?

On September 26, 2000, the girl's attorney, Steven E. Rolsch, wrote to the judge.

> Dear Judge Agerter:
>
> I've receive Mr. Restovich's September 5, 2000 letter and I've also received Ms. Heinrich's September 15, 2000 letter. I refer the Court January 20, 2000 Order, a copy of which I attach. Paragraphs one and two require Garry to fully cooperate with appointments and the counseling of Sarah and Kayla. Because of paragraph three of that Order, which states that the records and the notes of the sessions will be released only to the Court and the Guardian ad Litem, I refer to the Court only, Dr. Hennessy's July 11, 2000 letter. Without quoting you, it certainly indicates that Garry has not cooperated and because of threating behavior, Dr. Hennessy refused to see Garry back in her office. As such, when Mr. Restovich says in his September 5, 2000 letter that his client has cooperated with Dr. Hennessy he is incorrect. Certainly Mr. Restovich has not had the opportunity to review this letter as the Guardian has or I have as the Attorney for the Guardian, however, I'm certain that his client could have informed him that the meeting with Dr. Hennessy on

March 22, 2000 did not go well and that he was told that he could not come in her office. If that is not the case, then Mr. Restovich needs to have a conversation with his client about the facts of the meeting.

As the Court also knows, the July 14, 2000 report of Dr. Mary Anna Miller stated that she does not provide a comprehensive psychological evaluation but she offered to provide referrals for that to be done. As such, I have not seen any further progress on the part of Garry with regard to this matter. If there is some type of counseling through Lutheran Social Services in Rochester, I request Mr. Restovich have his client sign a release for my client immediately and sent it over to my office. Now Mr. Restovich states his client simply sees no reason to continue to pay for professional counseling services for his daughters when the only people who believe they need it are their grandparents. Again, this seems to be quite a statement to make given the facts of the case. Finally, Mr. Restovich suggested Associates 2000 or Associates in Psychiatry would be alright if the McColley's would want to pay for the counseling. It is my client's position that follow through by Garry with Mary Anna Miller was lacking and that his inability to follow the Court Order requires a review hearing. As such, we would greatly appreciate a review hearing at which Garry can explain why it is he fails to follow Court Orders.

Very truly yours,
ROLSCH & ANDERSON LAW OFFICES
Steven E. Rolsch
Attorney at Law

A FATHER'S QUEST

I immediately called Mr. Restovich's bluff. I volunteered to pay the girls' counseling. Paying would give me a part of it. Garry didn't want me to be involved.

We were back in court on October 19, 2000. Garry had to explain why he threatened Dr. Hennessy.

> MR. RESTOVICH: Wait a minute, wait a minute. My client will tell you…and I think it's only fair to say…that you don't feel as though you "threatened" Doctor Hennessy.
>
> GARRY: No, I did not.
>
> MR. RESTOVICH: But you understand that apparently there…she indicated that there was some kind of threatening behavior, Garry. That's what she interpreted it as. Do you understand that?
>
> GARRY: Wait a minute…
>
> THE COURT: Let me tell you, Garry, my observation of you over the years is that even when you are right sometimes, you can come across as being be very threatening sort of individual to other people. Okay?
>
> GARRY: Well, see, I was trying…
>
> THE COURT: Just accept that, okay, because that's probably where it's at, okay. And I can assume what happened with Dr. Hennessy probably happened, okay.
>
> GARRY: All right.

Then there was a lot of discussion. Restovich tried to put the blame on me. It was all my fault. Garry was blameless. Every time I saw Restovich, I would hate him more and more. I continued to pray that God would take care of him.

THE COURT: Now, we have made some progress in this case, but the expectation is you follow the court order. Okay?
GARRY: Yes, Sir.
THE COURT: You got me?
GARRY: Yes.
THE COURT: We will give it another shot.

Why did Judge Agerter think Garry would obey his orders now? Garry never had.

Garry had lost his driver's license. He thought he could take the State of Minnesota to Court and get his driver's license back.

Garry, Petitioner
vs. ORDER
Commissioner of Public Safety,

Respondent.

This matter came on before the Honorable Lawrence E. Agerter for hearing on the 30th day of November 2000.
    Petitioner appeared in person and was represented by Attorney Gary A. Gittus, George F. Restovich & Associates 117 East Center Street, Rochester, Minnesota 55904. Joel A. Watne, Assistant Attorney General, 525 Park Street, Suite 500, St. Paul MN55103-2106 represented respondent.

Based upon the information presented to this court, IT IS HEREBY ORDERED AS FOLLOWS:

Petitioner's Motion for Reinstatement of his license is hereby DENIED.

BY THE COURT
Honorable E. Agerter
Judge of District Court

Chapter 18

The Elections

It was time to file to run for commissioner in the spring of 2000. I had waited for two years to run. Two other people filed, so in the summer, there would be a runoff. I really campaigned hard. My district was Ashland Township, Canisteo Township, and the town of Kasson. I tried to call on every house in Kasson. Ruth helped me. I took one side of the street, and Ruth took the other side. I called on most places in both townships, but it was hard to catch people at home. I felt fairly confident on Election Day. I won 48 percent of the vote. The other two candidates each won approximately 26 percent each. Rodney Peterson was slightly ahead, so I would be running against him.

A couple of months before the election, I started to attend all the commissioner's meetings. I was sure that I would win, and I wanted to know what they did. I wanted to be ready when I won. I always went out to eat dinner with the commissioners. I seemed to get along with all of them really well. The county auditor invited everyone who was running for election to come to the courthouse to see how the election was held and how the votes were counted. I went, and just a few other people were there. I told the auditor that I was unhappy that I would have to run again in two years because of the census being held that year. The auditor told me that I didn't have to worry because I would lose. What did he know before the election? I knew that I had made enemies in the courthouse. Could the sheriff and certain people control who won the election?

On the night of election, Jim, my friend from the Austin group, and his wife came to our house with a bottle of champagne. Jim said all of us should go to the courthouse and listen to the election results as they came in. When we knew I had won, we would go to our house and celebrate with the champagne. At the end of the night, it was a bitter disappointment. I won just 48 percent of the votes. Rodney Peterson got 52 percent of the votes. Jim said that we should keep the bottle of champagne in the refrigerator until I won the next election. I lost by fifty-two votes. It was strange that the auditor resigned in six months. He finally went to work for the town of West Concord. He had a secure job for life. Why did he quit? Was it because of the election? I don't know how someone can change the results of an election. But it left Ruth and me in doubt. I had hopes that I could tattle the corruption in Dodge County. Jim talked me into running again. I now felt that I should have spent my time campaigning instead of attending the commissioners' meetings.

In 2002, the districts were changed. Ashland, Ripley, Vernon, Westfield, Hayfield Townships, and the town of Hayfield were my district. Dave Erickson was a commissioner in this district, and he was a retired popular schoolteacher. He taught in Hayfield and Vernon Townships and the town of Hayfield. I knew it would be almost impossible to win. I won in the townships of Ashland, Ripley, and Westfield Townships, but I really lost big in the town of Hayfield. But I had promised Jim I would run again. I didn't campaign much. I won 35 percent of the votes.

At the Ashland Township annual meeting in March of 2002, someone asked me if they elected me as a treasurer if I would serve. It would be a write-in vote, and the election was already going on. I would be running against Dave Moenning. I think I got ten votes. Dave got eleven votes. If Bob and Ruth would have voted, I would have won. Next year, Cliff Oehlke asked me to be a supervisor on the board. I would not have to campaign. He would campaign for me. I won easily. It was a three-year term. After serving one year, we got a call from Garwin McNeilus. He wanted the whole board to come to his office at eight o'clock the next morning. When we got to his office, he told us that he wanted to build a new town hall for us. We were to come back at four o'clock in the afternoon with plans for the town hall. I was chosen to write up the blueprints. Ruth and I went to the Westfield Town Hall. It was a newer town hall. I wanted to know how they had the voting booths set up. In some ways, I copied their plan. Garwin wanted a sixty-foot-wide building. I knew from experience that a fifty-four-foot-wide building would be much cheaper. I talked Garwin into a fifty-four-foot-wide building, but he wanted it longer. We built it bigger for a grader and a truck for in the future. In three years, Dave Livingston ran against me. I campaigned this time, and I easily won. Most people that did these jobs stayed on them for life. I thought everyone should serve in a government job for a short time. I thought six years was long enough. Someone else should have a chance. I didn't run again for the township.

In 2006, I ran for the commissioner seat again against Dave Erickson. A large number of people didn't want Dave to be elected again. I had a dozen people who volunteered to help me. We held many meetings, and several people went with me to campaign. A few people gave me money to be used for ads and to pay for the campaign. I didn't like this. I could afford to pay for everything myself. I had the feeling that if I got elected, I would have to vote their way. In a way, they were buying me. I thought it was helping me to have this committee. They were pushing me to run and helping me to meet people. When I went out in the morning to campaign, I always had cramps in my stomach. At the end of the day, I always thought it was a good day. I enjoyed meeting new people. I got 45 percent of the vote, so I lost. But I gained 10 percent of the vote from the time before. Maybe I would get 55 percent next time. But I didn't run.

In 2012, the districts were different. Ashland, Canisteo, Vernon, and the city of Kasson south of the railroad tracks were in my district. I decided to run. Rodney Peterson was again running against me. This time I didn't have volunteers helping me. I put ads in the paper and sent letters to everyone living in my district twice. I campaigned hard. I again got 48 percent of the votes. I again won in Ashland Township where I lived. I almost won in Canisteo. I did fairly good in the city of Kasson, but I lost. I did poorly in Vernon Township. Rodney Peterson called me the day after the election and thanked me for running a clean campaign. It seemed in the elections in our county, if you ran a dirty campaign, you would win. Maybe I should have, but I wasn't going to sink this low. I told him that if I would have won, I was going to use my influence to look more into Tammy's death. He told me as soon as he was commissioner, he was going to look into Tammy's death. He promised he would call me soon after he was in office. He broke his promise; he never called.

Jim Jensen ran for sheriff in 2012. He won. Jim told me that he really thought that Tammy was murdered. Tammy was a friend of Jim's wife. He would look into it. He gave the case to Scott Rose. Scott Rose never looked into Tammy's death. I think that Jim was trying to end the corruption that was in the sheriff's office, but he wasn't successful. Too many people in the sheriff's office were against Jim. Scott Rose ran against Jim Jensen in the election in 2016. Scott Rose won. People that worked in the sheriff's department, including Scott Rose, didn't want the corruption to end. Why?

Chapter 19

The Fifth Year after Tammy's Death

Barb Pike turned in her monthly report to the judge on December 28, 2000.

> TO: The Honorable Lawrence E. Agerter
>
> Judge of District Court
>
> FROM: Barb Pike. GAL
>
> Kayla and Sarah enjoyed their visit with you, and would like to do it again some time – they enjoyed the cookies. The visits have been going well, according to both parties, and the grandparents Wayne and Ruth McColley were able to attend the girls Sunday School program. Their other grandchild, Justin had a program the same day that they were unable to attend. They may alternate and go to each one every other year, if they happen on the same date again.
>
> The girls have been meeting regularly with Kristi Meyer of Associates in Psychiatry since their initial visit on November 1st 2000. She was not available in her office this date; however, I left a message and will attempt to speak with her

tomorrow. She hopes to also confer with school counselor Karen Besch, according with Wendy.

> Respectfully Submitted,
> Barb Pike
> Guardian ab Liten:

Garry wrote in the journal that is taken back and forth with the girls on February 2, 2001.

> Well im sorry the girls forgot there cap's & gloves, but if it was cold out, then maybe you shouldn't of takeing them to the park, don't you think?
>
> —Common Sence-
> Garry
>
> P.S. we have Plan's March 24th

We took them to the park, but we bought them caps and gloves. Garry wrote in the journal on March 2, 2001.

> Kayla tell's me that Ruth is still washing her in the tub is this true? What Part don't you understand. My daughter's are old Enough and big Enough to take bath's by there self. If this happen's again, im going to have charge's brought up! Is that Clear Enoght! And when you leave town you are suppose to let me know where my daughter's are, before you leaves.
>
> Read your Paper's
> Garry
>
> P.S. I still want proof where the money went, that you say are in the girl's account

Ruth did not wash the girls in the tub. Ruth got the water ready so the girls wouldn't get burned from the hot water. Ruth sometimes washed their hair if the girls asked her. Why did Garry insist that the girls had to take a bath at our house? Ruth and I suspected that he wanted the girls to get burned. Then overnight visitation would stop.

Our attorney wrote letters to the GAL and the girls' attorney and Garry's attorney on March 20, 2001.

> Dear Mr. Rolsch and Mr. Restovich, Esq.
>
> It is my understanding that Garry is transporting the children in a car without a licensed driver, mainly himself. Secondly, I have enclosed written statements written in the journal carried back and forth by the children. As one can see my clients are trying very hard to communicate with Garry. Garry makes accusatory statements about my clients. These statements are false and made with the purpose of harming my clients. This is inappropriate for Garry to be doing. (see journal entry of 3/2/2001)
>
> Garry wants all of us back in court and that is where this case is heading if Garry is not stopped from doing this behavior. My clients have contacted Barb Pike, GAL.
>
> Lastly, how is the children' counseling going?
>
> Sincerely,
> Roxanne Heinrich
> Attorney for Ruth and Wayne McColley

A FATHER'S QUEST

March 29, 2001

TO: The Honorable Lawrence E. Agerter
FROM: Barb Pike, GAL
Re: Guardian ad Litem Monthly Report

The issue of therapy for Kayla and Sarah is now in place. I have attached documentation from Kristi Meyer to that effect. I have conferred with Karen Besch at K-M Elementary School, and she is comfortable with this arrangement. She has known the girls for a long time, and is familiar with the family dynamics involved. She is aware of the Court Order of 10-23-00 which states that the court will quickly get involved if problems arise with counseling.

    I would normally feel that this would put an end to the need for my services in this matter; however, a couple of issues have arisen that should be addressed. A problem has been presented around the girl's bath time while at the McColley residence. Garry has requested that the girls be totally responsible for their own baths, while Ruth has been getting the water ready& sometimes helps wash their hair. I suggest that Ruth continue to get the bath ready & then leave the room while the girls take their bath. Wendy and Garry will then have to understand that the girls may sometimes not wish to bathe or wash their hair while at their grandparent's house.

    There has been a question as to what notification Mr. & Mrs. McColley have to give Garry when they leave the farm with the girls. The McColleys have agreed to notify Garry when they are going to be away from the farm overnight. It would also be great if the parties could communicate civilly when daytime activities occur. I don't know of any court order that requires notification ahead of time other than when they leave the state for a vacation. The request for this type of vacation was not to be unreasonably denied by Garry.

Both parties have assured me they do not wish to appear back in court regarding visitation with their grandparents. I wholeheartedly trust they are sincere in this wish.

> Respectfully Submitted,
> Barb Pike
> Guardian ad Litem

Garry again wrote in the journal that was carried back and forth by the girls on April 6, 2001.

> Just letting you know ahead of time, that in the first week of August is Summer School, and the Second week they have girl Scout Camp.
> And Just a Reminder the girl's are to take baths by themselves
> I Still haven't heard from you, about the girl's trust account.
> I truly hope there is'nt a Problem, it has been over four years, you Surly should of gotten a statement by now.
> This is a communication tablet, So let's try to Communication!
> Thank you
>
> Garry

In our May visitation with the girls, they told us that Garry had told them that he was going to kick them out when they turned

A FATHER'S QUEST

eighteen. That was when he could no longer draw Social Security on them. It appeared that drawing Social Security was more important to him than the welfare of his own children. The girls were concerned about where they would live. They wanted to know if they could live with us. Ruth and I told them we would be happy to have them live with us.

I wrote a long and rambling letter to Roxanne. I was getting really depressed. The doctors couldn't control my blood pressure. I wrote in this letter:

> I am so tired of this that I have even thought about giving up the visitation. It just not worth it anymore. I have even thought about going away and disappearing. But what kind of a grandfather would I be then. And would I be able to live with myself. It is not easy to talk to Garry. I'm completely convinced that he murdered my daughter. What kind of a person am I, to look the other way on that?

I wrote in the notebook on June 3, 2001.

> We had a nice weekend with Kayla & Sarah. Brittney Edgar came and stayed Friday till Saturday night. We went out to supper Saturday night and to a park for a while, then took Brittney home. Sunday went to church, then to a park in Hayfield. Then to a new A&W. The girls had a lot of fun with the puppies. Now that school is out it would be nice if they could come up and play with the puppies once in a while. In a month to six weeks we will be selling them. Before we go to the Dells I will give you the phone number. Ruth & I hope to go there soon and make reservations, If the weather will co-operate so we can ever get our farming done.

I will answer Garry's letter, but not this weekend.

Thank You

Wayne

Roxanne got a letter from George Restovich on August 8, 2001.

> This letter is to advise you that I no longer represent Garry in regard to the above-reference matter.
>
> In light of the fact that the case is essentially closed. I do not believe it is necessary to file a Withdrawal of Counsel as this letter should suffice as notice to the Court and opposing counsel. If the Court feel otherwise, I trust it will so advise.
>
> All future correspondence should be sent directly to Garry at 68073 240th Avenue, Kasson, Minnesota 55944
>
> Very truly yours,
George F. Restovich & ASSOCIATES

This was really good news to all of us. He wouldn't be telling lies anymore about me in court. Garry had run out of money, and he couldn't pay Restovich. It gave me some satisfaction that Garry was not living on money he collected in Tammy's death. All parents look for closer in their child's death. This was just the start.

I wrote in the notebook on August 19, 2001.

> Had a great vacation. It was raining one day, but still found things to do. The girls went swimming every day at the Dells. We went horseback riding four times. Kayla is a really good rider and Sarah went three times also. We were really proud of

them. Went on the ducks twice. Went to a water park one day. Went to a County Western Music show one night. We went on a boat ride one day and watched Bob go Para Sailing. Everyone could have stayed longer. We are already looking forward to next year. Looking forward to see the girls again, August 31.
 Thank You

Wayne

Roxanne wrote a letter to Garry on August 27, 2001.

Dear Garry:

My clients have informed me you want to punish them by not following court orders. You state that my clients cannot see the grandchildren on their weekend visitation on the first weekend of the month.
 There is nothing in the court orders that state that they have to inform you when they leave Dodge County. They informed you when they went out of state as requested by the court order.
 You are put on notice that if you do not allow visitation this August 31st, 2001, my clients have no other alternative then to take you back to court for contempt of court orders.

Sincerely
Roxanne Heinrich
Attorney for Wayne and Ruth McColley
dc: clients
The Honorable Lawrence E. Agerter

One time when I called the operator for a number, Jim answered. The phone company was going start having a recording doing his job. He was sixty-two years old, and he was going to retire. He didn't want to retire. I could tell that Jim was really depressed. It was harvesttime, and I offered Jim a job. The farm was making enough money that I could hire some help. It would be easier for me. It was too far for Jim to drive from his house in Clarks Grove. He would come on Monday morning and stay with us until Friday night. That way, he wouldn't work weekends.

Jim run the ripper and worked up the fields. He always dressed as a motorcycle hood with a pigtail. All our neighbors asked me, "Who do you have in your tractor? I can't believe how good of a job he is doing. It's better than what you do." We always quit at 8:00 PM and had popcorn and Pepsi and talked. He liked to play with Justin. Ruth and Brenda got along terrible. Jim could sense it. He had just sold his home on a lake in Albert Lea and bought a new double-wide trailer in Clark Grove. He told me that they had a used double-wide trailer there for sale. It was in tuff shape. We could put it in my shop during the winter, and he would help me fix it up. Then Brenda and Justin would have a house of their own. Ruth and Brenda would get along better if they didn't live together under one roof. When harvest was over, Ruth and I went down to look at it. They would deliver the home to us, put it in our shop, take it out of our shop, then set it up on the yard where we chose. It was twenty-four by forty feet. The total cost would be $15,000. I bought it. We spent the afternoon visiting with Jim and his wife, CeCe. When we left, I told Ruth, "This was the most fun day we had in a long time."

Early the next morning, we got a call that Jim had a heart attack. We prayed all day that Jim would make it. In the afternoon, we got a call that Jim had died. I was an honorable pallbearer at his funeral. We had become so close it was really difficult for me. I missed him so much. I was going to back out of the deal on the trailer house. Jim wouldn't be helping me. Finally, Jim thought it was a reasonable price. Ruth and Brenda would get along better. Only because Jim thought it was the right thing to do, I carried out the deal. Soon afterward, I wrote "A Tribute to a Friend."

A FATHER'S QUEST

A Tribute to a Friend

The old saying out of every bad thing in life comes some good. Five years ago when our daughter Tammy died, I couldn't see how this could possibly be true.

Then came the first compassionate friends meeting. I don't think Jim was there. I remember meeting C C. Her daughter had been murdered. We had suspicions that Tammy was also murdered. C C's daughter had two daughters, Tammy also had two daughters'. My first thoughts, we have a lot in common with this lady. Sometime later we met Jim. I don't remember exactly when. Over time Jim taught me so much. That's it's OK for men to cry, for men to give men hugs, for men to show emotions, and to be compassionate. Jim truly taught me how to be a much better person and a better friend than I was before.

Jim helped us during harvest of 2001. He stayed at our place overnight, so we had breakfast together many morning and popcorn and diet Pepsi many nights before going to bed. Jim was a person that had lived a full life. He had done many more things than the average person. He truly enjoyed being useful and he wasn't looking forward to retirement. When I talked about retirement, Jim would say, you will never have to retire. You will be able to farm forever. Jim loved little children and our grandson, Justin truly adored Jim. I am so thankful we got to spend so much time with Jim. We were all at Jim's house the last afternoon he was alive. We had such a good time. It's so hard to believe he is gone. I will treasure this day forever.

I know that Jim looked forward to being with his daughter, Linda again. I know that he looked forward to meeting all of the children of his friends he had met through compassionate friends. I know that Jim is with our Lord in heaven and that he looked forward to that more than retirement. The hard part is for us the rest of us left on this earth.

I feel truly blessed to have had the opportunity to have met Jim and his family. I only wish it could have been under different circumstances.

Jim will always live in my heart and mind.

With Love and Compassion, Wayne

Garry again wrote in the journal on October 5, 2001.

I want to know when ever you leave the farm, when you have my daughter's in your care, if you Can't do this I'll have you back in Court, and another thing I don't want my daughters going anywhere this Week End, they are both Sick.

I'm Sorry Wayne but its about time for you to grow up and Start acting like a grandparent

And another thing I want Proof of where that money is, Yes I feel if you Can't Prove of where you Say it is, that you spend it, and another thing, as far as I'm Concern you Stole that Money & Cards

Thank's

Garry

At the same time that Garry wrote in the journal, we got a letter in the mail from the courthouse. Garry was taking us to court October 11, 2001, at 9:30 AM. The things he wanted was a change in the drop-off and going back home changed to three o'clock instead of five o'clock. He also checked on the form:

> Directing the other party to pay me for my Court fees and costs that are a result of having to bring this motion."

He also checked:

> Directing the other party to pay to the Court a civil penalty of up to $500 as allowed under Minnesota Statutes section 518.175 subdivision 6 (c)

I felt that I had to answer what he wrote. The journal was something that the girls could see. The notebook wasn't made for something like this. I wrote Garry a letter and sent it in the mail.

> Garry
>
> I don't know how to answer what you wrote in the journal without upsetting you and that's why I have been putting it off. I don't want to have another big fight.
>   Being in court all the time was never my choice. Your problems with alcohol & drugs caused all these court cases. This caused a very unsafe environment for Kayla and Sarah. The only way we could think of to help them and you was to put enough pressure on, that you would change your ways. I hope this was somewhat successful. I would have liked to discuss these and some other issues with you as adults, but your answer to us has always been, it none of your business.

I don't think you understand how memorials work. First of all, if the people giving the money designate where they want the memorials to go, it is the responsibility of the family to send on the money on to these places. If there is no designation, then the family can use the money as they please. You, yourself sit up a fund at the bank for people to donate money to you. People who wanted to do this had every chance. I was totally surprised at Tammy's wake when people started to hand these cards to me. I have never seen this done before. Maybe you should look deep in your heart and life and ask yourself how come this happened. If these people would have wanted this money to go to you to spend as you wished they would have never handed it personally to us. Others who gave large gifts to us stated that they didn't want you to know how much, or to ever be able to get your hands on it. I am going to keep my word on this. I don't understand why you don't trust me on this. It is very insulting to me for you to imply that I would have spent this money.

I may have many problems in life, but money isn't one of them. I could retire right now and have plenty of money to live the rest of my life. I am only working because I enjoy it and want to leave enough to my children and grandchildren that they can enjoy life.

So for you to imply that I spent a few thousand dollars of my granddaughter's money is an insult. Also for you to imply that we were not part of Tammy's immediate family shows no respect for us. We were her parents, as you are Kayla & Sarah's. Are you saying that after they marry you will no longer be part of their family?

Think about this awhile! If they were injured or died, I'm sure you would want to know what happened. Pastor Nelson knows where the money is. I don't think he will tell you how much, but he will tell you that's it set aside for Kayla and Sarah. If this is such a big deal to you, maybe you should contact him.

The bath issue has been very difficult for us. First of all, you said in court that we shouldn't have overnight visitation because we didn't give them baths. I believe that at one time you told them not to take a bath at our house. Ruth will never help them with their baths again. We are concerned though that the water may be different at our house than yours and they could get burned. Hopefully they are old enough now that this won't happen. We are not going to send them to bed dirty or take them to church dirty and we go almost every Sunday. They may come home dirty from Sunday afternoon play. I hope this is the end of this issue.

On your third issue. Maybe you stated earlier in your letter the main issue is Trust! We have never made a habit of telling people when we are not going to be home. You have demonstrated in your past that you can be trusted. You have not only been in Prison once, but twice. You have received drugs from Criminals. These people are not to be trusted. When we go on vacation we hire someone to stay here. We can't do every time we go somewhere. Also usually when Kayla & Sarah are here our whole family goes places together. That makes a lot of ideas on what to do. Often when we leave we change plans and go somewhere different. I hate to think about the trouble I would be in if we were somewhere different than where I said we would be. Bob always has his cellphone, so you can get in touch with us if there in an emergency.

I would like to think that it's the best interest of the girls that we should "Both" have in mind. It is very troubling to me that when I'm working the field around your house that I'm not allowed to stop and say Hi to the girls. It also has to be upsetting to them that they can't wave to me or talk to us when we are up there. If we were both thinking what was the best for the girls and not ourselves this situation would be different. This upset me so, that I have sold the land right around your house, so I won't have to deal with this after we harvest the corn.

I hope this answers your letter and hope you will read it with an open mind and think about both sides.

Thank you

Wayne

We were in court on the eleventh day of October 2001. Garry didn't have an attorney, so it was just Garry and Wendy against us and our attorney.

> THE COURT: And Garry brought this motion essentially to reduce child visitation right, of the girls?
> GARRY: Yes
> WENDY: Basically we brought it as to have it added to the court order to have the grandparents let us know when they are leaving town and the whereabouts of the girls. We feel safer knowing where they are at, and they refused to, because they wanted it court

ordered. And the other thing was to see if they could bring them back at 3 o'clock on Sunday instead of 5:00 for homework issues, bath issues and supper time. It's just rushed. That was it.

The Court: And how many weekends a month?

Wendy: Once a month

The Court: It's just one weekend a month?

Wendy: Yes.

The Court: Unfortunately I take it we dropped the guardian out of here? Our Guardian ad Litem was discharged.

Ms. Heinrich: They were ordered not to put anything in the notebook about derogatory statements. That not allowed. But it is okay for him to do it. He had accused them of theft. He has accused them of abuse, sexual abuse. He submitted this.

The court: Oh, where did this come from now?

Garry: I'm sorry, Your Honor there is no accusing nobody of nothing.

Ms. Heinrich: Touch is underlined on abuse.

Garry: That is something I wrote, Your Honor

Ms. Heinrich: That has to do with the bath.

The Court: I'll give you a chance to respond.

Ms. Heinrich: That has to do with the bath. He is accusing Mr. McColley of abuse in the bath. That is a derogatory statement.

The Court: Well

Ms. Heinrich: And we get accused all the time, and the notebook is supposed to be for positive things. Wendy puts positive things in there. Garry…accuse, accuse, accuse, threats, threats, threats, threats. That why I'm asking for attorney's fees. That notebook was supposed to be…

THE COURT: How much are you asking for?

Ms. HEINRICH: 500.

THE COURT: Well, does Garry write some derogatory stuff in that...

GARRY: You can look at it, Your Honor. You are more than free to look at this. There is nothing really...nothing...

THE COURT: Okay. Can I review it for a day or so.

WENDY: Yes.

GARRY: Yes.

THE COURT: Well, you have seen the letter by Miss Besch. Apparently she talked to the girls about this.

WENDY: I don't know if she has talked to them about the two hour difference or if it was a whole weekend thing.

THE COURT: Now wait a second. She said, "In speaking with Kayla and Sarah they expressed concern over a shortened weekend visitation." I thought it really reflected right back to that two hours.

We all had a long discussion about notify Garry whenever we left the farm. Telling Wendy was not enough. I had to tell him personal. If we changed our plans, we were to call him. What should we do if he didn't answer the phone. He wanted to have total control. We couldn't change any plans without Garry's permission.

THE COURT: Can I suggest this, on the notebook, on a day—long event you will let them know if you are going somewhere. You can notify the sheriff if you are worried about the farm. Okay? I'll review the notebooks. Do you think you have written anything derogatory in there, Garry?

GARRY: Have I?

THE COURT: Yes.

GARRY: That he wrote anything?

THE COURT: That you wrote anything derogatory?

GARRY: No, I don't, Your Honor.

THE COURT: Well, I'm going to review it.

GARRY: On the trust account, I thing Wayne, he went…because she had already taken that money.

VOICE: The money was given to them.

Garry: Oh, was it really? When Miss McColley put a box out there for…

THE COURT: Can I suggest this on that damn trust account…forget about it. Okay?

GARRY: Well, I got this…I want to make sure…if they can prove it to you, that's fine.

THE COURT: What?

GARRY: If they can prove it to you that it's in the trust account. You know, what's so hard about that.

THE COURT: He will confidentially tell me what's there, and you will accept that it's okay?

GARRY: Sure. But he will refuse to answer my questions.

THE COURT: Can you agree to that? Just let me know confidentially. I'm not going to even let him know. Just tell me how this got established and what's in there, and it's for the girls, right?

WAYNE: Okay.

GARRY: Because I got a letter here somewhere, and I can't find it, but I think you got it. He wrote in there if it's not designated where the money is supposed to go, that he could spend it as he pleased. Well, highlight that part.

THE COURT: Well, I'll take a look at it. Give it to me.

GARRY: And that's what I mean about how I think he spent the money.

THE COURT: Okay. I don't think this is a big issue. Okay. But Wayne McColley will just give me the information on it, and if I'm satisfied, I'll let you know I'm satisfied, and let's drop it. Okay?

WENDY: Kayla must…she had a question about why she needed to take a bath because we're going to have her take one anyway when she gets home, and she has said that grandpa said, "You have to take a bath, otherwise you won't be able to come here again."

WAYNE: That what you brought up in court before. You said that over and over again.

GARRY: But you tell that to the child?

WENDY: But you really shouldn't be saying that to Kayla.

WAYNE: I told Kayla, Sunday, I says, "You don't have to take a bath. Just drop it."

WENDY: But still, you shouldn't have said that, because then she is going, "Why?"

WAYNE: This bath business, it went way too far. Just plain should be dropped. If they are dirty and they need a bath, they take a bath, otherwise forget about it completely. And that's the end of it.

GARRY: Eight and nine year old daughters, you know, Your Honor, that they are giving baths in the sink. That should be dropped? No, it shouldn't be dropped.

WAYNE: Who gave who a bath in the sink?

GARRY: Kayla said she had a bath in the sink, the kitchen sink.

Wayne: Oh, you're crazy.

The Court: Now, wait a second. I know where this is going to go fast, you know.

I was now to the blame for telling Kayla that she had to take a bath. Garry brought this up in court and now it appears that what you say in court means nothing. He told me in court that the girls had to take a bath before they came home. How was I to explain this to the girls. There was a lot of discussion on this matter.

The Court: Now wait a second. Everybody calm down. Let's just calm down. Any way that Wendy and Wayne and Ruth can talk a little bit once in a while?

Wendy: Yes, we have... Well, it probably won't now.

The Court: Why don't we leave that communication door open, and if you guys have some questions about it, just feel free to call each other.

Garry: Well, they're my daughters, but I can't communicate with them?

The Court: That's the way it appears to me.

Ms. Heinrich: I just want to... I know this is a tough issue, but it's a bad situation. That's where that touch thing came in.

The Court: Yes.

Ms. Heinrich: Does Garry truly believe that Ruth abusing or touching his children?

Garry: I do believe, Your Honor.

The Court: Sexually inappropriate?

Garry: They don't need to be washed. They are old enough to wash their own bodies. That's all I'm trying to say. I didn't say nothing about touching or sexual.

THE COURT: Let me tell you this, Garry, we have grandmothers who will be grandmothers, okay?

GARRY: And where's my rights as a father then, saying, "I don't want you guys touching my daughters when they're in the bathtub." They are old enough to take baths by themselves. Do I have the right to do that anymore or…? You know, I have had enough of your lip, too.

THE COURT: I agree with that one, Garry let's just back off a little bit. Okay? I want to see us through this, okay?

GARRY: Well, I would like not to even be here, you know, fighting over this, but they are old enough to baths by themselves, Your Honor. I'm sorry.

THE COURT: I might respect that, but you know, grandmothers will be grandmothers, too.

GARRY: You know, if it was me, you know, they would have me in court for sexual or something, you know.

THE COURT: Probably, but that's different.

There were forty-four pages in the transcript that Michael Crawford, court reporter, wrote. There was a lot of fighting that went back and forth. I tried to pick the main things out of the transcript for my book. It should have never taken this long. Maybe Tammy gave Kayla a bath in our sink when she was a baby. I don't remember. How could you give a nine-year-old child a bath in the kitchen sink? The longer this went on, the deeper of a hole Garry dug for himself. I suspected that Garry was on drugs and maybe Wendy too. I looked forward to write a letter to the judge. I got in trouble the last time, but now the judge ordered me to write a letter.

A FATHER'S QUEST

The Honorable Judge Agerter

I am writing this as you requested in court to explain this money. Perhaps I am writing to much but I don't want any doubt about, weather I stole anything from Garry. In fact, the opposite is true. I have helped him greatly financially.

The day after the death of our daughter Tammy our Pastor, Larry Nelson told us that a number of people and organizations in the community had approached him. These people wanted to do something to help Kayla & Sarah, but did not want Garry to be able to get the money. Pastor Nelson suggested that we set up a trust fund at the Security State Bank in Dodge Center. He also suggested that we pick someone to be in charge of this fund. We chose Tammy's God Parents, Nado & Eva Bernard.

The night of Tammy's wake, just as we were leaving our house, a young lady from the Snow Mobile Club came to our door. She had a large check. She wanted it to go to Kayla & Sarah. She made me promise I would never tell Garry how much or that he would ever get this money. Normally when one goes to a wake, you sign the quest book and put your card in the box provided. At Tammy's wake, people were there handing cards to me as they were giving us sympathy. After a while I had so many cards I had no place to put them. These are cards Garry has accused me of stealing. If these people had wanted Garry to have these cards, they would have put them in the box provided in the funeral home.

The week after the funeral the Dodge Center Nursing Home where Tammy worked called us to come in. They had taken up a donation for Kayla & Sarah. They again made me promise that Garry wouldn't get the money.

This money all stayed in the original fund until Jan. of 2001. We had two problems with this original fund. Because Nado & Eva Bernard were listed as the main people of this fund they had to declare the interest on there Tax returns and pay tax on this interest. We didn't feel this was fair for them. Also the bank was paying a low interest rate. In Jan. 2001 we purchased a C D with the money. It was right before interest rates starting going down, so we have a good rate locked in for four years. Ruth and I as well as Nado & Eva are owners of this C D with my Social Security listed. That way I will declare the interest on my tax returns and pay the tax.

Kayla & Sarah will receive all this money after they graduate from High School as the four of us decide when the proper time will be. Hopefully it will be to help them in college.

In the summer of 1992 I was renting a 160-acre farm from Adeline Hrtanek. Adeline has been a good friend of mine for many, many years. The house became vacant. I arranged with Adeline that Tammy and Garry could live there free, with no rent to pay. They lived there with no rent until the end of 1995. In the summer of 1995 Adeline wanted to sell this farm. I at that time told Garry that if I could buy the farm for $200,000 I would sell him and Tammy five acres and the building for $7,500. That would be per acre the same as I was paying for the land plus a little for attorney's fees, and I would be giving them the house, and the other buildings. I also expressed that they should try & save some money so this whole transaction could take place before the end of the year. By the end of the year they had saved no money. Garry had run up a debt buying snowmobiles and our relationship had deteriorated. The sales contract I had with him expired at the end of Dec. 1995. By the end of Jan 1996 they were able to get a loan. By that time, I knew it was a mistake for me to sell then the property but I have always been a man of my word and I went ahead with the sale. Garry has since expressed to me that I screwed him in this deal. The property was appraised for $50,000 by the loan company. I am enclosing Part of an interview between Garry and the sheriff's dept. only to prove what I am saying here.

Now Garry has accused me of Stealing. I would think at the very least I deserve a apology in writing from Garry.

There also seems to be another standard in all of this. We have Kayla & Sarah one weekend a month and Garry wants to know our every move ahead of time even he knows his daughters will be returned on Sunday at 5:00. Our daughter Tammy died, she will never return to us in this world. When we asked Garry questions about the fire, he has told us it's none of your business. He hired an attorney who forbid law enforcement from every questioning Garry about the fire. I would think we deserve the same from Garry as he wants from us.

Sincerely
Wayne McColley

I wrote a letter to our attorney, Roxanne Heinrich, on December 3, 2001.

Dear Roxanne.

When Bob took the girls back Sunday night Garry was there. He came outside to Bobs pickup and told Bob he was no longer allowed on his property for what Bob said in court. Bob said he was only there because he was bringing the girls back. Garry then said, "Get out of the pickup, let go at it." Bob then backed up the pickup to leave and Garry flipped Bob off with both fingers. Bob returned the gesture which was the wrong thing to do, but Garry isn't a very easy person to deal with. Kayla & Sarah were right there and witnessed everything. When Bob got back on the road he stopped for a second and Garry gave him the finger again. Doreen went along and was crying when she come into our house. Bob never came in our house, he just dropped Doreen off and left.

Wendy called shortly afterwards and was upset that Bob gave Garry the finger. She seems to think that Garry has problems and because of that it doesn't matter. What he does doesn't matter, but no one should do anything to Garry. I told her that Garry started it and if Bob had got out of the pickup, Garry and Bob would be in jail now. She said that she would be bringing the girls back and forth from now on. I guess this is just another example of Garry breaking the court orders and every one looks the other way. Is there something that can be done about this?? She said that she hopped the judge would say that Garry and I would have to have mediation. I said, "I hope so to." She said she was trying to arrange Mediation though her support group and that Garry had agreed to go. I said I would go. We both agreed that Garry needed to talk about Tammy's death. I said I believe that Garry had beaten Tammy severally before the fire started, and that I had a report from an expert to show this. She said she never saw that. I told her that I offered to show it to her before but she didn't want to see it.

She became upset and said maybe she should see it. I told her that I prayed for her often and didn't think she realized what a dangerous situation she was in.

About three weeks ago I went up to see a neighbor of Garry's on another matter. This neighbor's wife is a school teacher in Kasson. He told me that Garry has wolfs and that the girls are afraid of them. I believe that this comes from school. He led me to believe that a County Human Service van had been up to Garry's just days earlier. He also said, you won't believe how often the Sheriff's car goes by their place. It's at least a dozen times a day.

We are wondering if this has anything to do with why the judge hasn't made a decision yet. Ruth has called the court house a few times. She was told at first that the judge was working on it. The last time she called she was told rudely that the judge had 90 days and not to call back again.

We also have some very sad news. Jim the motorcycle man that went to court with us had a heart attack and died last Friday.

Sincerely
Wayne McColley

PS Maybe this is the wrong thing to do, but Garry tried to get Bobs pickup door open to start this fight. I called the sheriff's office and they are sending out an officer to investigate this.

The judge issued his order on December 3, 2001. Reading his whole report, we could see that he spent a lot of time.

The above-entitled matter came before the Court on October 11th, 2001. The Petitioners appeared personally, represented by their attorney, Roxanne Heinrich, 8 Ivy Lane, Landfall, Minnesota 55128. The Respondent appeared personally, representing himself.

The Court, having heard and considered the evidence presented, as well as legal arguments made on behalf of both parties, make the following:

FINDINGS OF FACT

1. The Respondent, Garry, is the parent of the following minor children:
   Kayla
   Sarah
2. These minor children live with the Respondent.
3. The children's grandparents, Wayne and Ruth McColley are the Petitioners.
4. As per the original visitation order, the Petitioners are entitled to visitation with their two granddaughters, Kayla and Sarah, every other weekend from Friday to Sunday at 5:00pm.
5. Kayla and Sarah enjoy and look forward to regular visitations with the McColley's.

A FATHER'S QUEST

6. Kasson-Mantorville Elementary School counselor, Karen Besch, who counsels both Kayla and Sarah, believes it is in Kayla and Sarah's best interests to remain with their grandparents as long as possible on their designated weekends.
7. The court also believes that the settled visitation with the McColley's satisfies Kayla and Sarah's best interests.
8. There have been no changes in either Garry's or the McColley' circumstances since the Court ordered the original schedule.
9. There have been no new changes regarding Kayla and Sarah's needs since the Court ordered the initial visitation schedule, and neither Kayla nor Sarah have indicated that they want to shorten their visits with their grandparents.
10. Garry has not introduced evidence giving cause for amending Kayla and Sarah's visitation schedule with the McColley's.
11. Wayne and Ruth McColley established an educational fund in Kayla and Sarah's name, after the girl's mother, Tammy, passed away.
12. Pastor Lawrence Nelson swore that trust money was given to the McColleys,'instead to Garry by members of their church, because a number of people and organizations in Dodge County refused to donate if Garry was in any way able to touch the trust fund.
13. Pastor Lawrence Nelson was the first person to suggest that the McColleys start a fund in Kayla and Sarah's name.

14. Garry has accused Wayne McColley of lying about this fund and stealing money donated to the fund.
15. Garry wrote these accusations in a "Communication Tablet," which is used by both parties to communicate before and after visitation drop-offs and pick-ups.
16. This educational fund resides, as of October 12th 2001, at Alliance Bank of Blooming Prairie
17. The fund is listed under the name of Nado Bernard Jr., in trust for Kayla and Sarah.
18. This fund currently contains a substantial amount of money, as is consistent with the McColleys making any and all deposits in their granddaughter's names
19. This court possesses evidence establishing this trust as far back as January 30th 1997.
20. By contacting the Dodge Center Board of Commissioners about concerns regarding his granddaughter's well being, Wayne McColley caused private information regarding Garry to be disseminated in the Dodge County Independent paper. Issue October 18th 2000.
21. The Court met with Garry and Wayne regarding this matter on May 23rd 2001, and firmly stated that both parties must refrain from any same or similar behavior in the future.
22. Wendy has repeatedly requested that the McColley notify her and Garry when the McColleys take Kayla and Sarah out of town during terms of visitation.
23. Garry has requested that the McColleys notify him when the McColleys take Kayla

A FATHER'S QUEST

and Sarah off the McColley farm during terms of visitation.

24. These request are recorded in the aforementioned "Communication Tablet."
25. The McColleys have not introduced evidence giving just cause for failing to comply with Wendy's repeated attempts to request notice from the McColleys when the McColleys take Kayla and Sarah out of town.
26. Wendy and Garry have requested that the McColleys allow the girls to take baths on their own, and that the McColleys not assist in washing when the girls bath at the McColley's home.
27. The above-mentioned requests were recorded in the aforementioned "Communication Tablet.
28. Communication between Wendy and the McColleys, as recorded in the "Communication Tablet," has been fairly and consistently amicable.
29. Communication on Garry behalf, as recorded by the "Communication Tablet" is often confrontational.
30. The McColley's responses to Garry's remarks have been neutral and non-confrontational.
31. Based on the evidence recorded in the "Communication Tablet," and the testimonies of both parties during the motion hearing on this matter, it looks as if the purpose of this motion if to frustrate the McColleys.

Judge Agerter wrote a report on the Conclusions of Law and Order. Part of it contained a lot of legal talk. It was hard to understand. I am going to put the parts of it that the judge didn't put in the MEMORANDUM part.

> 6. The Court orders that the McColleys to notify Garry as to their whereabouts with Kayla and Sarah, including a phone number and place to reach them during visitation, any time the McColleys take Kayla and Sarah more than sixty miles off of the McColley homestead.

Now we knew we wouldn't go more than sixty miles off the farm. I knew if we called him, it would be a problem. What he really wanted was control, and I would have to ask him permission to go somewhere. We had gone to Camp Snoopy at the Mall of America many times. We would have to stop going there.

> 7. The Court orders that the McColleys to stop assisting in bathing Kayla and Sarah when they visit the McColleys, except to the extent that the McColleys may fill the tub, check the temperature of the water, and visually supervise to make sure that both girls are bathing safely.

That was actually what Ruth was doing. We had gone through this ever since we got visitation. First, they were to take a bath, and then he forbade them to take a bath. When the girls were younger, he was hoping they would get burned. Garry's plan was that he could stop visitation with the bath issue.

MEMORANDUM

> After reviewing all the evidence, this Court does not find that circumstances warrant modifying the visitation order. There are no accusations

of endangerment, nor incidences of chronic or unreasonable failure to comply with court-ordered visitation. The court assumes that the parties anticipated Kayla and Sarah's schedules and any possible future changes when they devised and agreed to a specific visitation timetable and the parties have not now offered evidence that those schedules changed. More specifically, a request to modify visitation by two hours, because the girl's parents need more time to get the girls ready for school the next day, does not warrant modification under the statute. This is supported by the fact that evidence in the "Communication" tables indicates Kayla and Sarah have been able to work on their homework and bathe at their grandparents before a Respondent's pick them up, suggesting that there is no real need to cut established visitation short by two hours. As such, the court will not modify visitation and the schedule will remain consistent with the original order.

Garry accused the McColley's of stealing money from his daughters trust, yet had no evidence on which to base this accusation. Garry also wrote confrontational messages to the McColleys in the parties, "Communication" tablet and threatened to drag the McColleys into court if he did not get his way, or if the McColleys failed to supply Garry with information regarding the trust fund. Wayne wrote to Garry and attempted to explain why the trust is under his name, where the money is going, and why McColley would not furnish future information to Garry. The information contained in Wayne McColley's letters to Garry is consistent with testimony from the McColley's Pastor, and consistent with other evidence showing the trust's establishment and account balance. Wayne's letters to Garry were at all times cordial and non-confrontational, and represent a good faith effort on Wayne's part, to put Garry's mind at ease with regard to the trust account and ill will between the two.

Regardless of Wayne's attempts, Garry accused the McColleys of stealing and continued to threaten court. Garry then instituted this proceeding without a shred of evidence showing the girl's interest were harmed, or that his family's circumstances had changed. Future, Garry's daughters indicated that they did not want their visits with their grandparents shortened. The girl's school counselor also wrote that it would be in the girl's best interest to continue visitation as is. Finally, based on entries into the "Communication" tablet, it does not look as if Garry's proposed reason for modifying the order holds muster. Garry claims that the girls need the extra two hours to complete homework, bathe, and get ready for school, yet the tablet indicates that the girls have been doing these things before Wendy and Garry pick them up on Sunday at five. Regardless, even if there is homework to complete and baths to be had before bed, these are goals, which both parties can work out and meet without modifying the existing order.

Based on evidence, history, and testimony, it is clear to this court that this request to modify is nothing more than an attempt on the Respondent's part to punish and frustrate the Petitioners, both emotionally and financially. The Petitioners were essentially forced to pay an attorney in order to defend their right and this frivolous claim, and as such, Respondents must pay for their own endeavor. Therefore, the court awards the Petitioner's attorney, attorney's fee in the amount of $500.00. Hopefully, this award will serve as a lesson to those quick to drag fruitless claims before this court in the future.

L.E. Agerter

We were lucky that Restovich was gone. Garry wasn't too smart when he introduced my letter and the notebook. He introduced evidence against themselves. What was he thinking? But at least he was helping us. Garry didn't think like 90 percent of the people. He would sink himself.

Chapter 20

The Sixth Year after Tammy's Death

Wendy had arranged that Garry and I should go to mediation. I received a letter with a wrong date from ADR Services (Alternative Dispute Resolution Services). We actually met on January 14, 2001. Eventually, the letter was sent after the first meeting.

> Date: January 17, 2002
> Participants: Garry
> Wayne
> Mediators: Gerard Goulet
> Carmen Nomann
> Observer: Liz LaRoque
>
> Mediation has been set for Wednesday, January 30th at 6:30 PM at 1421 3rd Avenue SE, the little brick building at the corner of the 3rd Avenue and 15th Street entrance to the Olmsted County Fairgrounds. For landmarks, there is a sign on the corner Boulevard of 3rd Avenue and 15th Street indicating the above address and a flagpole on the avenue side.
>
> Please be seated in the first floor lobby. ADR Services is looking forward to serving you.
>
> Kate Johansson

On Monday night, January 14, 2002, at 6:30 PM, I met for mediation as requested by Garry's wife, Wendy. During the mediation, Garry said many times about I was so full of anger and needed help and needed to grow up. About an hour or so into the mediation, right after Garry made this statement, the moderator, Gerard Gonlet said, "Let's hold it a minute, I have been sitting here watching and listening to the two of you, and I see no anger in Wayne, it's only coming from you."

Garry said, "So now it's me." And then he just exploded. "You damn right I'm angry, I'm so angry I'd like to beat the hell out of him." Then he jumped to his feet, looked at me, and then said, "Get up and get outside. I'm going to take care of you right now."

I stood up, and he came within inches of me. I thought he was going to punch me right there. The mediators all quickly responded and got him to sit down. I was almost hoping that he would have punched me. I would have stayed down and got them to call an ambulance. Then he would have been arrested for assault and battery. We were in Olmsted County. He would get arrested. If we were in Dodge County, I don't think the sheriff's deputies would have come.

The mediators discussed many things with us. Some we finally agreed on, and some we never agreed on. On the things we agreed, they wrote down, and we had to sign our names to it.

1. Garry and Wayne each agree that they want the best for the two girls, Sarah and Kayla.
2. Garry and Wayne each agree not to bad mouth the other in the presence of the girls.
3. Wayne will not talk to Wendy and Garry agrees not to come to Wayne's place.
4. Wayne and Garry agree to remind the girls to brush their teeth.
5. Wayne and Garry each need to think less about themselves and more about Tammy and the kids.

6. Wayne and Garry agree to not accuse each other and continue to live in the past. The past is gone. They agree to focus on the future for the sake of the girls.
7. Wayne and Garry agree to meet again on Wed. Jan.30, 2002 at 6:30 pm.

They only talked about simple things. Most things were a given, but I had trouble with number 6. I didn't want Tammy gone. Garry never obeyed court orders. Why would Garry honor any of these things? We had the next meeting on January 30, 2001. It was harder to agree to some of these things. On what I agreed to do, I was really going to try to honor these things. Was Garry going to honor anything? These were the things we agreed on January 30.

1. Garry & Wayne agree that it is OK for Wayne & Ruth to call the girls on the phone whenever they'd like.
2. Wayne & Garry agree that a process needs to be developed to handle conditions when the girls have other events they may want to do instead of going to Wayne's. Wayne agrees – so long as there is sufficient advance notice.
3. Wayne & Garry agree that Wayne will encourage the girls to take baths during their visits.
4. Wayne agrees NOT to sign the girls' homework.
5. Wayne & Garry agree to have clothes for the girls at both places. Wayne will supply clothes for the girls at his place
6. Garry & Wayne both agree to follow the court orders in total. One specific item is that Bob will pick up the girls, and "Sometimes "Ruth will do the pickups.

7. Wayne & Garry agree not to go on each other's property. Wayne agrees that Garry can come on his property if the girls are there and are significantly late. Garry will call before coming over.
8. Garry & Wayne agree that it is OK for the girls to call Wendy, "Mom".
9. Wayne and Garry both mutually agree NOT TO bad mouth each other to any others.
10. This Jan. 2001 agreement incorporates all the agreements made in the Jan. 14, 2001 agreement with the exception of paragraph 3. That is, it is OK for Wayne to talk to Wendy.

It really hurt Ruth and me to hear the girls call Wendy *Mom*. Tammy was Kayla and Sarah's MOM. But I knew we would have to live with it. On the bath issue, I didn't agree. When Ruth and I were young, we had a bath every Saturday night whether we needed it or not. When our kids got old enough to take a bath, they decided on their own. Our water was really hot. I think Garry was hoping that one of the girls would get burned. Then he could stop the girls from staying overnight with us. He was still trying to use the bath issue even though the judge had already ruled on this issue.

Two meetings were all we had. Maybe it helped some, or maybe Garry learned a lesson taking me to court. He lost big-time. It really helped us that Restovich wasn't in the picture. We had very little trouble getting the girls afterward. Life was changing, and life was getting better. Brenda and Justin would soon be out of our house. We were planning a big vacation in March.

Our church had its annual meeting in January. Some members went off the council, and we elected some new members onto the council. After the annual meeting was over, the new council met in another room to elect officers. I was elected president. I would have more work to do.

I had to completely remodel the double-wide. I got the complete house in my shop. I made new kitchen cabinets. I hired Lee Loppnow to help me. He changed all the plumbing. We redid every room. People who visited me in the shop couldn't believe that we had a complete house in the shop.

In March, Ruth and I went on a long vacation to Kentucky. My Uncle Cliff lived there now. We stayed at their house for a few days. Then we went to see everything about Ab Lincoln. We stayed at a bread-and-breakfast in an old mansion. We were to come down for breakfast at 8:00 AM. We got up early and waited in our room for eight. When we got down, the man's wife had already left for work. They waited and waited. We had come down at nine. The time zone changed in the middle of Kentucky. We stayed the next three nights at a bread-and-breakfast at a horse farm. We stayed in a double garage that they had made into an apartment. They had a small lake that we walked around. We could walk among the horses. We visited the Kentucky Horse Farm. We were there for hours. We told them about our granddaughters. They said we should bring them here. I said they wouldn't like it because there wasn't a swimming pool. He took me through the house and opened up a door. There was a large swimming pool. He told me that the girls were free to use it anytime. I had planned to go there again, but we didn't.

Jenna, the daughter of Allan and Doreen, was born on April 5, 2002. A week before Jenna's due date, Doreen had a prenatal appointment. The doctors had concerns that the baby could weigh ten pounds at birth. Allan and Doreen went to Plaza Moreno restaurant following the appointment. They had just ordered their meals when Doreen's water broke. Allan told the waitress that Doreen's water broke and they would have to cancel their meals. The staff offered to send towels with them. Doreen was admitted to the hospital. Nurses kept checking on Doreen and the baby throughout the night, but there were little changes. At 10:00 AM, the OB doctors came in and gave them the option to either wait a couple hours to see there was more progress or get the operating room ready for a C-section. Allan and Doreen agreed on a C-Section. Jenna was a day old when the pediatrician diagnosed Jenna with hip dysplasia. Jenna would have to wear a Velcro harness for three months. Jenna had an appointment with Mayo every two to three weeks to adjust the harness. Jenna had no limitations in physical education or activities throughout school. Jenna weighed seven pounds, ten ounces at birth. She was baptized May 12, 2002.

Jenna, Allan and Doreen's daughter

It was the end of May. We were finished with the planting. We had one crew in the yard setting up the home for Brenda and Justin. We had hauled in three feet of fill to build a new machine shed. A crew was working on the machine shed. I was sitting on a pile of dirt where I could watch both crews working. I thought that the next days would be exciting. All of a sudden, a feeling came over me that I should go to Branson. Was an angel trying to work on my mind? Soon, Ruth came out and sat beside me. We talked a little bit about Brenda's home and the machine shed. Then I said, "Maybe we should go to Branson tomorrow." Ruth right away agreed. She immediately went in the house to start packing. Ruth never agreed to go on vacation that fast before. Was an angel working on Ruth too? I couldn't believe that I was doing this. We had two crews working, and I was certain they would have questions for me. What was I thinking? Bob was really angry with me. We were really busy!

We were sitting in the Baldnobbers Theater in Branson. We always went early. I really enjoyed talking to people who sat beside us. We sat in the middle of one row. Ruth was sitting on my left. Right before the show started, a couple come in and sat beside us. The lady sat beside me. Her husband said nothing. I asked her where she was from. She said, "Michigan." She asked me where I was from. I told her, "Minnesota." Then she told me that she had a brain tumor. She had only one month to live. Then the show started. I didn't know what to say. Before Tammy had died, I would have gotten up and left during intermission. As the first half of the show was going on, I started thinking that God had sent me to help her. I realized why we had left so fast with so much to do. I must talk to her. What would I say?

When intermission came, Ruth got up and left without saying anything to me. Her husband left right away too, without saying anything to her. I was really hard of hearing in my right ear. She was sitting to the right of me. All of a sudden, it started feeling like the twilight zone on an old TV program. It was completely quiet in the theater. In my mind, and I'm certain in her mind, we were alone. All I could hear was her. We started talking about our belief in God. I started sharing things with her that I have never shared with anyone, including my wife. I talked about Tammy. I was anxious to see Tammy when the time came for me to die. She said that her husband had been in the military but had retired recently. He was going to take her anywhere that she wanted to go. She wanted to go to Branson. She wasn't afraid to die, but she had two young grandchildren and she was going to miss seeing them grow up. We both talked about dying and going to heaven. Right when the intermission was over, Ruth and her husband came back. I never talked to her again. When we were leaving the theater, I told Ruth about the experience that I just went through.

When we got back home, I forgot about her and the experience that I had at Branson. They were done setting Brenda's house. I

A FATHER'S QUEST

would really have to get busy on the house. But they hadn't done any more work on the machine shed while I was gone. I was kind of disappointed with that. A month later, when I got up in the morning, all I could think about was this lady I had met in Branson.

I told Ruth, "Maybe this was the day she died."

Ruth said, "You should have gotten her number. Then we could call her and see what happened."

I said, "I was not in the habit of getting phone numbers of women."

Ruth told me I should have. I agreed with her. All throughout the day, I couldn't get her out of my mind. Shortly afterward, we had a church council meeting. I was to share a Bible reading. I always wanted to share a reading that was appropriate for the meeting. Instead, I decided to share the experience that I had with this lady in Branson. I based it around how God works in our lives.

Pastor Nelson announced that he was retiring at a church council meeting in the middle of the year. It was a shock to me! Being council president was going to be more challenging for me. I studied the church constitution. I got a lot of advice from the ELCA Senate. We had to elect a nine-member call committee to call a new pastor. After we elected a call committee, the senate wanted us to study the history of our church. I chose not to be on the call committee. As council president, I would be attending all their meetings. I could express my opinion, but I couldn't vote on anything. I thought being on the call committee was the most important thing in your life. Having nine members, someone was always going to have a conflict. You were expected to attend every meeting even if it was your spouse's birthday. One of the questions the senate had for all of us was, "What is a secret ambition you have that no one knows?" After everyone shared their secret ambition, they asked me. I said that my secret ambition was to write a book. The senate gave us a name, Pastor Hagen, whom we hired as an interim pastor.

We took our whole family to the Wisconsin Dells again this year. We stayed in the same condo on a lake that we stayed in last year. We took the girls riding horses every day, sometimes twice.

When school started, Kayla had a school trip to Rice Lake State Park north of Claremont. She wanted Bob to ride on the bus with the kids. Every student could take one person with them. Most were taking their mother or dad. Bob came to me and asked my advice. I said, "If Garry finds out that you rode on the bus with Kayla, he's going to explode. We'll be in real trouble." At first I told him not to go. After thinking more, I told him to not ride the bus. Anyone can go to a public park. Garry cannot say anything about that. Kayla really enjoyed showing off Bob to her friends.

The last months of the year, Wendy started to come to me for advice on how to deal with Garry when she was transferring the girls. By then, I had dealt with Garry for ten years. I kind of knew how. I was trying to help her. When Wendy went home from our place, Garry threatened her and got her to tell what I had told her. Then Garry called me on the phone and told me, "That's not your business to talk to Wendy about me." Then I realized it was best not to even see her. I avoided her as much as I could.

We got through the year not going to court. I didn't have to call my lawyer, Roxanne. I kind of gave up on proving that Garry killed Tammy. How could I do that? Ruth and I were going to take more vacations. I had spent a small fortune fighting with Garry. I couldn't believe that the farm was making so much money. I had a firm belief that God was helping us. Now we were going to spend that money on ourselves, if it was okay with God.

In the fall of that year, I decided on buying a PT Cruiser. I wanted it to be special. I ordered it from the Chrysler dealer in Waseca. We had to wait six weeks for it to come. I had never special ordered a car before. We were excited when they called one of the first days in December. We didn't trade any car in. Bob took Ruth and me to Waseca to pick up the new car. At that time, there weren't a lot of PT Cruisers, but there was some. Whenever we met a PT Cruiser, they turned on their lights. It was an exciting time!

Chapter 21

The End of the Nightmare

We decided to go on a vacation in February of 2003. We left right after we had our monthly visitation with the girls. We drove our new PT Cruiser. We drove through Iowa, Illinois, Indiana, Ohio, and West Virginia into Virginia. We had never been in Virginia before. We spent some time in the Appalachian Mountains and then the Shenandoah Valley. The Shenandoah Valley was simply beautiful. Then we decided to go to the Prestwould Plantation in far south Virginia. We drove hours only to find it closed. I was really disappointed. I studied the map and found several plantations on the James River. We would have to go a long way north and east. I kind of lost my temper. I would have to make up a lot of time. I started driving too fast. Soon a police car pulled me over, and he gave me a ticket. Then I was mad with myself! Before we got home I decided that I wouldn't pay the ticket. I would never go back to Virginia again. When we got home, I had a ticket in the mail. I threw it away. Then I got another one. I started thinking about Virginia. I really thought it was the prettiest state there was. I knew I would like to go there again, so I paid the ticket. Sometime afterward, I got another ticket. So I paid it again. What was I thinking? It would have been cheaper to have paid the first ticket right away.

Then we visited the Shirley Plantation and The Berkeley Planation on the James River. Two of our presidents, William Henry Harrison (1841) and Benjamin Harrison (1889–1893) came from the Berkeley Plantation. There was a lot of history there. After being at these two plantations, it would have been much closer to come right from the Shenandoah Valley. Next we took the ferry across the James River south into North Carolina. That was also a new state for us to visit.

Plantation home called Hope

On the roadmap, there was a plantation called Hope. We went to Windsor, North Carolina. There was a sign pointing us to Hope. Hope Mansion is the restored home of former North Carolina Governor David Stone (1770–1818). Upon his marriage to Hannah Turner in 1793, Stone received the 1051 acres known as Hope Plantation as a wedding present from his father Zedekiah. The mansion was completed in 1803. A precocious youth, David Stone graduated first in his class from Princeton in 1788. His education and various fields of endeavor proved him, like Thomas Jefferson, to be an heir of the eighteenth-century Enlightenment. By 1803, David Stone had built an impressive mansion at Hope to accommodate his wife, Hannah, eleven children-to-be, and his many guests. This served as a fulfillment of his interests in architecture and as a haven to pursue his other many interests. On the second floor of the mansion, there was a large drawing room and a library, which housed Stone's

1,400 volumes. As Ruth and I entered the library, a really strange feeling entered my entire body. I said to Ruth, "I've been in this room before." From the time of my youth, I've always wanted a library. I've bought many more books than I've read throughout my life. I never had a library, but on one wall of my office, which is twelve-foot-wide, there is a built-in bookshelf the entire width.

Next we went to visit my Uncle Lyle and Aunt Kathy in Milton, Florida. We stayed with them for three days. Next we planned to go to Gulfport, Mississippi, to a gambling casino. It was Valentine's Day. We drove to Gulfport casino, and there were no rooms. There also were no rooms in town. At a hotel, they told us to go east to the next exit and there would be a room. We stopped at every exit to Mobile, Alabama, before we found a room. We only got less than eighty miles from Lyle's that day. We wanted to stay in New Orleans. Would we find a room there? I found a brochure in the hotel that showed rooms in New Orleans. Everyone had told us to go to the French Quarters. I thought that we should stay in the French Quarters. I found a hotel listed in the brochure, and I called. They had a room, so we would have somewhere to go. I made a reservation for three days. When we got to the hotel, there was no parking. They told us that we didn't need a car. They told us that they would put the car in an underground parking ramp. They would bring it back when we checked out of the hotel. I felt really uneasy when they took our new car. Would I get it back okay? The hotel was built in the 1700s. The room was really small, but it was clean and kind of nice. The bathroom had really old fixtures.

We could sign up for tours at the hotel. We signed up for a tour visiting plantations one day and another one to go on a riverboat up the Mississippi the next day. We went out for supper the first night in the French Quarters. We went in a restaurant and got a menu. The cheapest meal was a hamburger for $40. We split the hamburger. Walking out of the restaurant, we noticed that there was a menu placed on the outside of every restaurant. The first night, we walked to every restaurant that was somewhat close by. We knew where we would eat the next night.

At seven thirty the next morning, they picked us at the hotel for a bus ride to go on a plantation tour. We went at least fifty miles north. We toured three plantations, and the day was fun. That night we ate at a bar that had a band that played Creole music. We kind of enjoyed it. It was fairly cheap. We both ordered a beer. They never came back and asked us to order another beer. That was okay. They picked us up the next morning and took us a short distance to the river. We spent the day on the riverboat. It was fairly big, and the weather was nice. Late in the day, we went on a carriage ride pulled by mules. The driver told us that mules are more sociable than horses. We went to the same bar for supper the next night.

We were leaving the next morning, but we wanted to walk around the large park that was in the center of the French Quarters first. As we walked around the park, holding on to each other's hands, we noticed several psychics set up in the park. I didn't believe in them. At the last side of the park and not far from the hotel, we saw the carriage and mules. It was the same driver that we had the night before. We stopped and visited with him awhile. Then I told Ruth it was time to check out of the hotel. Hopefully, we would get our car back okay. We walked past the park holding hands. All of a sudden, I dropped Ruth's hand and walked back to the park. I walked up to a psychic. It felt like I didn't have control over my body. Who or what was causing me to do this?

I asked the psychic, "How much do you charge?"

He answered me, "In Louisiana, we are not allowed to charge anyone. Most people give me twenty dollars."

I told him, "I don't know why I walked up to you. I don't believe in psychics."

He then asked me, "What day and what year were you born?"

I told him. He opened up a book, and he read for what seemed like several minutes. He then proceeded in telling me who I was. He described my personality to a tee. I couldn't believe what he had said! How could he have known so much about me?

He then said, "You are a really disturbed person." I agreed with him on that. He then said, "You have marriage difficulties."

I told him, "I don't have any marriage difficulties. I am a happily married man. Everything is going well."

He then said, "You own your own business."

I said, "Yes."

He then said, "You have business difficulties."

I said, "I don't have any problems with my business."

He said, "You don't have problems with your whole business, but only part of it."

I told him, "No!" But I was wrong.

When I got home, I found part of my business was in trouble. We owned a sizable investment in Al-Corn. They were doing an expansion to make more ethanol. The expansion was costing them 100 percent more than they planned. How did he know that?

Finally, I told him, "My daughter was murdered six years ago, and nothing was done about it."

Then he said, "It was your son. No, it was your son-in-law that did it."

I said, "Yes."

He then said, "In six months, your son-in-law will be dead or in prison."

I then said, "If you are right, I'll give you $100. Give me your address, and I'll send you the money when it comes true."

He wouldn't give me his address. Finally, I gave him $10 and left. What was I to think about this? We checked out of the hotel, and they brought our car to us without a scratch. What a relief!

We then drove to Natchez, Mississippi. We crossed the river into Vidalia, Louisiana. We were going to stay there the night. We pulled into a parking lot and started to look at the brochure that we got in New Orleans. We could stay for $55 a night. Which one would I choose? All of a sudden, a lady come up to our car. She wanted me to stay at a new hotel that was recently built next to the Mississippi River. It would cost $125. I told her that we were going to leave early the next morning. I didn't want to pay that much. She called the hotel, and they told her we could stay for $100. I told her, "No." Finally, she told me we could stay for $75. They had a restaurant, and we could get 50 percent off the meal. We finally agreed.

We followed her car to the hotel. We stayed on the fourth floor. The whole end of the room was a window. When we looked out of the window, we couldn't see anything but the river. There was a large riverboat docked across the river. It was staying for the night. There were a lot of lights on it. It was pretty! After supper we went to an exercise room. Again it was all windows to the river. I walked on the treadmill, and Ruth rode on a stationary exercise bike. As we were enjoying the room, I told Ruth, "When we get home, I'm going to build an exercise room in our house with a lot of windows with a view." We stayed at the hotel until the last minute to check out. We really got our money's worth.

New South Room

When we got home, I couldn't get the psychic out of my mind. I told some of my friends and all the people in the support group about the psychic. In the Bible in Isaiah 8:19, it says,

> And when they say to you, seek those who are mediums and wizards, who whisper and mutter. Should not a people seek their God? Should they seek the dead on behalf of the living?

When I looked to the Bible, I couldn't find anything about physics. Did this verse fit to a psychic? Sometimes the Bible is really confusing and hard to understand. I went to Pastor Hagen and told him about my experience with the psychic. Pastor Hagen told me that God sometimes uses strange people to give messages that God wanted someone to know. I had prayed for over six years that God would help me. I had almost given up. Sometimes I really felt praying was helping, but other times it felt like we were taking one step forward only to take two steps backward. Would God help me now? Could I believe what a physic had told me? This whole experience had really left me really confused. What would I do? Maybe I would just have to let it play out and leave it in God's hands. It was going to be a long six months. Would this cause me to lose my faith in God if this didn't happen after what Pastor Hagen had told me?

Several members of our church didn't like Pastor Hagen. They told me that I had the authority to fire Pastor Hagen, being that I was the president of our church council. I didn't know if I had the authority to fire a pastor or not. I told them that if we fire an interim pastor, how would we call a pastor to our church? No pastor in his right mind would want to come to our church after our firing an interim pastor. Pastor Hagen had told a lot of people that soon we were going to build a new church. They disagreed and didn't want to hear this. I thought that Pastor Hagen was doing a good job. Being council president, I worked closely with him. I really got to know him. His job was to get the congregation to get over our former pastor and get them ready for a new one. He was making accepting our next pastor easier. He did the job we had hired him to do.

After we came back from our vacation, the call committee met frequently over the next months. We got a name from the synod of a pastor considering coming to our church. Three of us went to attend church and listen to him preach. We all got a cold feeling from his church. Our whole committee agreed not to call him. Then we got a name from someone right out of the seminary. His name was Justin Boeding. He was preaching at a church, and several members of the call committee went to listen to him preach. I didn't go. Then we decided that the entire call committee would interview him. We wanted it to be at a neutral place. We decided on the Hubbell House. They had a room for us to meet in. Everyone paid for the meal themselves. I paid for Justin. After doing the interview with him, we decided to have another interview. We wanted him to preach a children's sermon with no warning. We also wanted to meet his wife. A pastor's wife could have a big influence on the congregation. We again met at the Hubbell House, and I again paid for the meals for Justin and his wife, Jayne. The call committee met again, and everyone agreed to call him. I didn't vote because I wasn't a voting member. Then several people from the committee wanted my opinion. I agreed to call Justin.

Life went pretty well for the next months. I was waiting for the six months to pass. Maybe I was going to be disappointed. I started to feel this way as time was going by. Then things started to happen in July. We had our normal visitation with the girls. I think on our visitation with the girls, Garry and Wendy broke up, arguing over drugs, and Wendy moved to a trailer in Mantorville. I would find out about this later. Then on July 10, 2003, Officer Brant Richardson conducted a traffic stop on a vehicle in Kasson. The driver was identified as Garry. Dispatch advised that Garry's driver's license was canceled. Garry was unable to provide proof of insurance. Garry was then arrested on an Olmsted County warrant, and the vehicle was towed to the Kasson Police Department, and the plates were impounded. During a search of the vehicle, officers located two white hollowed-out pens located in the center console and the passenger's side door. Both pen tubes had a residue on them that tested positive for the presence of methamphetamine. On July 11, 2003, Garry was formally charged with "Controlled Substance Crime in the Fifth Degree and Driving after Cancellation." Garry then was appointed a public defender, who wrote Garry a letter about the felony he was charged for.

July 15, 2003

Dear Garry

I have been appointed by the Public Defender Office to represent you in the above felony matter.

I will notify you when your next appearance in court is scheduled.

I have written to the Prosecuting Attorney's Office requesting copies of the police reports pertaining to this matter. Once I received them, I will send copies to you for your review.

In the meantime, please call my office to schedule an appointment to discuss this case. I look forward to hearing from you soon.

Sincerely,
Rachael Drenckpohl
Assistant Public Defender

Garry had a hearing with the court soon afterward, and they let him out on bail. His attorney argued that Garry should be released without paying bail. He had always showed up on time for a court hearing in the past. Finally, Judge Agerter released Garry without posting bail.

After Garry got this letter, he called and wanted to know if we could keep the girls until Sunday night. My Uncle Lyle and Aunt Kathy came to visit us. They stayed with us at night but were visiting relatives during the day. Wendy called me and said she had seen a part of Garry that she had never seen before. She was afraid for her life and the lives of the girls. She said, "You have to do something."

I said, "What can I do? We have the girls with us now so they are safe for now. You have to do something. You have to go to the sheriff's office."

I had tried to help Wendy in the past, but I had always got burned. I couldn't trust her. When Uncle Lyle came home, we had a long talk. I wanted his advice. Lyle had always been the person that I had turned to for support. Then we had Kayla call her dad. She got him to say that they could stay another day. We were buying some more time. Hopefully, Wendy would act. I didn't know this at that time, but I would soon learn something. Wendy went to get the mail. There was a letter from an insurance company. She opened the letter. Garry had bought a large accidental life insurance policy on Wendy. She realized that Garry was going to do the same thing to her as he had done to Tammy. Would he get away with this twice?

The next morning, Lyle and Kathy left for home. Late in the morning, Ruth took the girls to the swimming pool in Hayfield. I was working around the yard, and I had to go to town to get something. I went in the house to get my billfold. The phone rang. It was from the sheriff's office. They asked me where the girls were.

I said, "Ruth has taken them to the swimming pool in Hayfield."

The deputy said, "You keep the girls with you until you hear from us."

I completely forgot what I was going to town for. I immediately went to Hayfield and shared the news with Ruth. The physic was right! We didn't know for sure yet, but I was certain that he was right. God had answered our prayers. That night the call committee met at a house on the deck of a call committee member. The call committee and Pastor Justin were there. We were there to call Justin to our church. He accepted. I had really good news to share with everyone about the girls. Now they would be in church almost every Sunday. When I shared the news with the support group, several people said, "How did the psychic know this?"

Wendy had gone to the sheriff's office and turned Garry in. They used an informant to buy drugs from Garry.

A FATHER'S QUEST

STATE OF MINNESOTA DISTRICT
COURT-JUVENILE DIVISON
COUNTY OF DODGE THIRD JUDICAL DISTRICT

In the matter of the Children of:

Garry, DOB: 06/24/59
AFFIDAVIT OF:
Jennifer K. Adamson
CHILDREN:

The following facts constitute grounds to believe the children are in need of protection and services:

A. That on 07/21/03 Dodge County Sheriff's Department executed a search warrant for narcotics at 68073 240th Ave. Kasson, MN 55944. Narcotics were found at the residence and Garry was arrested. At this time possible charges include, but are not limited to, first-degree possession, felon in possession of a firearm and sale of narcotics.

B. That, on 07/21/03 Dodge County Sheriff's Department filed a 72-hour police hold and placed Kayla and Sarah with relatives in Dodge County.

C. That, this social worker recommends it is in the best interests of Kayla and Sarah to remain in an out-of-home placement through Dodge County Department of Human Services due to neglect and safety concerns in the home.

D. That, due to the situation requiring removal of the children, the Court find that reasonable efforts were made by this agency to prevent placement.

E. That, Dodge County Department of Human Services, be granted temporary legal custody of Kayla and Sarah with authority to place in a facility that meets their health and safety needs.

Petitioner, by and through its undersigned agent, hereby verifies that the above allegations are true to the best of the petitioner's information and belief.

STATE OF MINNESOTA
COUNTY OF DODGE

Jennifer Adamson, Social Worker
For the Dodge County Department of
Human Services, Petitioner

The next day Jerry Glenna came to our house. He said he had been assigned to be guardian ad litem for Kayla and Sarah. He said this was going to be an easy job for him. He knew that we wanted the girls and also knew that the girls wanted to live with us. He was a retired officer of the Minnesota Highway Patrol. I wondered what happened to Deb Dibbler. She was second-in-command at Human Services. She had always looked out for Garry. I had fought with Human Services for years. Why were they doing this now? We had a new sheriff now. Maybe it was making a difference.

Human Services told us that we would need a temporary foster care permit to take care of the girls. They came out to our place to do an inspection on our house. The only thing they found wrong was that I had an old gun hanging over the fireplace. The gun was so old that you couldn't buy shells for it. I would have to remove the gun. We were later licensed to do foster care. They would pay us $17.50 per day for each child. I didn't want the money to take care of my own granddaughters. I opened up two accounts, one for each girl, where I put the money to give to the girls someday. We were lucky that we bought the home for Brenda. Now the girls could each have a room to themselves.

I had prayed for years that God would help me. Then a really strange thing happened. The retired sheriff died at a fairly young age of a heart attack. In his obituary, his wife had the same maiden name as Garry's. I don't think they were related, but I don't know for sure. Did this make a difference why he didn't want to investigate Tammy's death? Then the director of Human Services, Brian Hartung, committed suicide. He shot himself in his head in the bathtub. Maybe Brian had a guilty conscience over Tammy's death? He had told my sister Sandy that he wanted to do something but just couldn't. Maybe Deb Dibbler didn't have so much power now? Was Deb or the sheriff responsible for Brian's death? Then George Restovich died of cancer. I would never have to deal with him again. This whole thing felt really strange. Why?

Then Rollie Spriggle advised me that I should get a new lawyer. We hadn't used a lawyer in a year and a half. He said that we had hired Roxanne Heinrich to fight the county. She had gone against a lot of the people at the courthouse, and now the county was now mad at her. Now we needed an attorney to work with the county. He recommended that I hire Kristine Dickie, which I did. I don't know if I did the right thing. It cost me as much in one year as I paid Roxanne in five years. Maybe Roxanne would have done as well. I kind of had a guilty conscience that I didn't stick with her. We had to pay Kristine a retainer of $1,500. We had to agree to replenish the account monthly so that the balance on deposit with the firm was always at least $1,000. We had to pay her $185 an hour. This was going to be different. Roxanne never sent me a bill. She said that God sent her to help us. Maybe I should have paid Roxanne more.

Wendy filed a Harassment Restraining Order against Garry on July 29, 2003. He was already in jail, but maybe the order would keep him in jail. The reasons for Wendy filing this order were the following:

1. He called her residence, work, and her cell phone. She asked him repeatedly not to call.

2. She was not for sure but she was told he was going to walk up to her residence and peek through the windows at night.
3. He was calling family members and my work leaving obscene messages.
4. Said he was going to blow up my trailer in the past.
5. I have seen 1st hand the malicious behavior he has and he has a violent past, known well by others.
6. Bitch of a wife, left on home answering machine.
7. Girls are with their grandparents now but he needs to stay away from them.

On the twenty-third of July, Garry had a hearing to appear in court. He was already in jail. This time, Judge Agerter ordered that Garry had to post $200,000 bail. Everyone that had an interest in this knew that it would be impossible for Garry to post bail this large. Maybe Wendy had a large influence on the judge. Maybe the letters that I wrote to the judge made a difference. Judge Agerter could have asked for much less. Maybe the whole system was waking up to how violent he could be. Why didn't they realize this before? Why did we have to go through this terrible nightmare so long?

On the fourth day of August 2003, we had to go to court. Judge Agerter issued an order:

ORDER

1. The Dodge County Department of Human Services shall continue to have temporary legal custody of the children, Kayla and Sarah, with authority to place the children in such shelter care facility as will reasonable meet their needs.

2. This case is scheduled for pretrial on September 22, 2003 at 1:30 pm and for trial on October 1, 2003 at 1:30 pm.

Ruth and I went to Chatfield early in August to tell Ruth's mother, Edna, the news. We went alone so we could really talk freely about what was happening. We told her about the new room we were building on the house and where I had gotten the idea. Edna had turned ninety in the spring. She was in good health and driving her car. All her children hosted a big party for her. Shortly after this time, her health had started to fail. She was in the hospital for a short time and went to the nursing home. Ruth and I went to see her every other day at the nursing room. I told her that I loved her. She wasn't in the nursing home very long before she died on October 4. She was the best mother-in-law that I could have had. I would really miss her!

Three weeks after Garry had been arrested for selling drugs, Wendy sold drugs to an informant, and she was arrested. Wendy was using drugs so much that she needed the money to buy more. She should have known that she would be arrested. When people have a drug habit, they cannot think clearly. The drugs became more important than anything else in life. I think it was the same informant that bought drugs from Garry. Why did Wendy leave her family to get hooked up with Garry? It never made sense. She made the biggest mistake of her life. It was lucky for her to see the letter in the mail about the large accidental death policy that Garry had bought for her. Otherwise, she could be dead by now.

We had a counselor from Dodge County visit us one day a week for four months to work with all of us. The girls wouldn't talk to her. Garry had forbidden them to ever talk to a counselor. She was a big help to Ruth and me in dealing with the girls and their violent behavior. We had a problem sometimes with the girls fighting. They would kick each other in the stomach. The counselor told Ruth to never leave them at home alone even for a short time. At the end of the four months, the girls never had this problem again. Children behaved like the grown-ups that they were living with. Ruth and I live in a loving situation. We have never hit each other. The girls caught on fast, and the problems they had went away. If we had gotten the girls two years later, maybe we would have had more problems than we could handle. I think God answered our prayers just in time.

> The above-entitled proceeding duly came on for hearing in chambers before the Honorable Lawrence E. Agerter, Judge of District Court, on the 22nd day of August, 2003.
> Based on all the files, records and proceedings herein, the Court now makes the following.

FINDINGS

1. The children in the above-referenced matter are in need of their personal belongings and effects.
2. The child has an independent right of entry into their own residence to retrieve their personal belonging and effects.
3. The Dodge County Department of Human Services has been granted Temporary legal custody of the children with authority to place them in such shelter-care facility as will reasonable meet their needs.
4. Dodge County Human Services has authorized the Guardian Ad Litem to assist the children in retrieving their personal belonging and effects from their home.

ORDER

1. The Guardian Ad Litem is authorized to enter the children's home for the limited purpose of assisting them in retrieving their personal belongings and effects.

BY THE COURT:
Dated: August 22, 2003 Lawrence E. Agerter
Judge of District Court

The girls were going to school in Kasson. We were in the Triton School District. It was never easy for me to change schools. I wondered how this would affect them. They were living with their grandparents. How would this affect them? I thought that most kids were living with a mother and father. How would this affect them? I was worrying about a lot of things, but I would soon learn that I was worrying about nothing. Half of the kids didn't live with a mother and father. Several kids in their grades also transferred from Kasson to Triton. They adjusted well to the new school and never had problems. Why did I have so many problems going to a new school?

We got a letter notifying us that there was a case concerning the girls on October 1, 2003. We always went to any court case concerning Garry even when it didn't concern the girls.

In Re the Children of:
Garry (father) CHILDREN IN NEED
OF PROTECTION OR
SERVICES ORDER

The above-entitled proceeding duly came on review hearing before the Honorable Lawrence E. Agerter, Judge of District Court, on the 1st day of October, 2003. The father of the children, Garry, was present and represented by his attorney, Rachael Drenckpohl. Also appearing were Kim Zvorak of the Dodge County Department of Human Services; Gary ReMine, Assistant Dodge County Attorney via telephone; Jerome Glenna, Guardian Ad Litem for the children; and Kristine Dickie, attorney for Wayne and Ruth McColley, grandparents.

ORDER

1. The Dodge County Department of Human Services shall continue to have temporary legal custody of the children, Kayla and Sarah, with authority to place the children in such shelter care facility as will reasonably meet their needs.
2. The Court finds that placement is necessary because the children are without necessary food, clothing, shelter, education or other required care for the child's physical or mental health or morals because the child's father, Garry, is incarcerated.

BY THE COURT:
Dated: October 3, 2003 Lawrence E. Agerter
Judge of District Court

It seemed like we were going to court for nothing. We were paying our attorney $185 an hour to travel from Rochester to court and the time we were waiting, plus the time we were actually in court. Maybe for the court to remove the children from their home, the court had to jump through many hurdles that the law required. It would take much more time than we expected. It would get really expensive.

Soon the judge said that the girls were to have phone contact with their father. We also had to take them to visit their father in jail. At first Ruth kept a diary of the calls and visits. Garry was to call on Thursdays and Sundays. We were to take the girls to visit him the first and the third Saturdays of the month.

DIARY OF THE CALLS

| Thursday | October 2, 2003 | Didn't call |
| Sunday | October 5, 2003 | Didn't call |

Thursday	October 9, 2003	Didn't call
Sunday	October 12 2003	Called

Sarah didn't want to talk to Garry.

Thursday	October 16, 2003	Called

Wendy called here to let us know that she got him a calling card. He would be calling more.

Sunday	October 19, 2003	Didn't call
Thursday	October 23, 2003	Didn't call
Sunday	October 26, 2003	Called

Garry called but they were on the phone less than two minutes.

Thursday	October 30, 2003	Didn't call
Sunday	November 2, 2003	Didn't call
Thursday	November 6, 2003	Didn't call
Sunday	November 9, 2003	Didn't call

DIARY OF THE VISITS

October 4, 2003	Bob & Wayne took the girls to Red Wing. Bob went in with the girls
October 18, 2003	Bob took the girls to Red Wing.
November 1, 2003	Bob took the girls to Red Wing, but they didn't see Garry. He got moved to Owatonna.
November 15, 2003	Bob took the girls to Owatonna. No visiting on Sat. afternoon.
November 16, 2003	Bob took the girls back to Owatonna. They had a one-hour wait. After thirty-five minutes the girls wanted to leave.
December 6, 2003	Bob took the girls to Owatonna.
December 27, 2003	Bob took the girls to Owatonna.
January 10, 2004	Wayne took the girls to Owatonna.
January 24, 2004	Wayne took the girls to the Waseca jail.

February 14, 2004	Wayne took the girls to Waseca
February 28, 2004	Wayne took the girls to Waseca.
March 13, 2004	Wayne took the girls to Waseca.
March 27, 2004	Wayne took the girls to Waseca.
April 15, 2004	Wayne took the girls to Waseca. Wendy was there.

We had a hearing in court November 12, 2003. The girls' guardian ad litem, Jerome Glenna, wrote a report to the judge. The judge followed his recommendations.

RECOMMENDATION

1. I recommend that the children remain in their present home with grandparents, Wayne and Ruth McColley.
2. I recommend that the children have contact with their father in the following manner. Telephone contact every Thursday and Sunday evening at 7:00 PM with a limit of 30 minutes per child unless there is a special event to be shared. Visits with their father to be held every other Saturday with the children's Uncle Bob doing the transporting to Owatonna. When Bob is not available the grandfather, Wayne, to transport.
3. I recommend that the children be contacted by cell phone so that they will not need to be at home to receive the calls from their father. If the call is to be made at 7:00 PM then It should be made some time between 7:00 & 7:15.

HISTORY & INFORMATION GATHERED:

The children were visiting at the home of their grandparents, Wayne and Ruth McColley when their father Garry was taken into custody and charged with a number of drug-related offenses. The children's mother died in a house fire several years ago. The children's father and stepmother were separated and their stepmother is also in jail awaiting court on drug related charges. Human Services took custody of the children and placed them with the grandparents as caretakers. The children have a very strong bond with not only their grandparents, but also with their maternal aunt and uncle who also reside on the premises of the McColley farm. The children are attending school in West Concord and adapting well to their new residence and school. The children have not been called on a regular basis by their father. They also were not notified when their father was moved from Red Wing to Owatonna. A trip was made and he was moved. They also have been required to go home to await a call from their father which never came… This is why I feel that calling the children should be by cell phone and there should be in a time frame of fifteen minutes in which the call should be made. In this way the children would not have to spend the whole night awaiting a call.

Respectfully submitted,
Jerome O. Glenna
Guardian ad Litem

I knew that we should be getting the Social Security checks for the girls. But I figured that Garry would be more in trouble if I waited awhile. I went to the Social Security Office in Rochester in November 2003. I thought Social Security was meant to be for only people about to retire. The office was full of young people. None of them could speak English. Why did they qualify for Social Security? I had to wait forever to talk to someone. I then called the sheriff's office.

COMPLAINT

Complaint is Investigator Jeff Brumfield of the Dodge County Sheriff's Office, who bases this complaint upon facts obtained from his own investigation and/or that of other law enforcement officers whom he believes to be reliable.

In November 2004, the Dodge County Sheriff's Offices received a report that a number of Social Security Checks for the benefit of two children, were cashed by an unauthorized party and spent. Subsequent to execution of a search warrant at the home of Garry and Wendy in July 2003 and the incarceration of Garry, his two minor children, S. and K. were placed into the care of their maternal grandparents, Mr. and Mrs. Wayne McColley in Dodge Center. The mother of the children was the daughter of the McColley's and because of her death, the children receive Social Security payments of $629.00 each month. The checks had been made out to Garry for each child. Although the children were residing with the McColley's, the Social Security checks continued to be sent to Garry at the address where his wife, Wendy (hereafter referred to as Defendant) was still residing. Defendant then signed Garry's name to the checks without his permission, also signed her name, deposited

A FATHER'S QUEST

the checks into her checking account, and spent the money.

Defendant admits signing her name to the checks, depositing and spending the money on house payments and truck payments, but claims she took the checks to the jails where Garry was housed, and he signed his own name to them. Garry denies that she bought him the checks or that he signed them. The signatures on the checks do not resemble verified signatures of Garry.

The checks made out on the U.S. Treasury were as follows:

Check Number	Dated	For the Benefit of	Amount
3092 89938576	11/03/2003	K.	$629.00
309287912880	10/03/2003	K.	$629.00
309285879175	09/03/2003	K.	$629.00
309283828451	08/03/2003	K.	$629.00
309289939575	11/03/2003	S.	$629.00
309287912879	10/ 03/2003	S.	$629.00
309285879177	09/03/2003	S.	$629.00
309283828450	08/03/2003	S.	$629.00
TOTAL			$5,032.00

COUNT I

    Charge: Check Forgery

    In Violation of: Minn. Stat. 609.631 Subd. 2 (2)

    Maximum Penalty: 10 years in prison and/or $20,000 fine

On or about August through November, 2003, in the County of Dodge, State of Minnesota, the defendant, Wendy with intent to defraud, falsely endorsed or altered checks totaling $5,032.00 so that they purported to have been endorsed by another.

COUNT II

Charge: Offering Forged Checks

In Violation of: Minn. Stat. 609.631 Subd. 3

Maximum Penalty: 10 years in prison and /or $20,000 fine

On or about August through November, 2003, in the County of Dodge, State of Minnesota, the defendant, Wendy with intent to defraud, offered or possessed with intent to offer forged checks totaling $5,032.00, whether or not they were accepted.

Being duly authorized to prosecute the offenses charge, I hereby approve this Complaint

DATE: December 2, 2005 PROSECUTING ATTORNEY'S SIGNATURE

Gary ReMine

To my knowledge nothing was done. Why did the sheriff wait a year to act? Why did Gary ReMine sit on the complaint for over a year before he acted on it? It was over two years now. Our granddaughters never got the money. WHY? Maybe it was the same when Garry's mother forged Tammy's name on the insurance policy. The sheriff didn't investigate that one either. BCA had told the sheriff to investigate, but he didn't. Why? Garry wasn't a suspect in this crime. I should have acted much sooner before Wendy got so much money from the girls. I thought that Garry was the guilty one on this crime and that it would add to his problems.

We were to take the girls to visit Garry's mother and family at Christmas in 2003. When we took them, they didn't know where their grandmother lived. Evidently, Garry hadn't taken the girls very often to visit their grandmother. Kids that old should have known the way. Garry's family and Garry started working on the girls against us. We started having more problems after their visits with Garry. They were not so happy now as they had been. I had to do something. What would I do? When the girls came, they wanted to know if I would buy them horses. I told them we would have to wait until we had custody of them. In February 2004, I told the girls we would start looking at horse stables. We went to look at one southwest of Stewartville. It was a really big barn with a riding arena. The owner said that he gave riding lessons. We decided that if the girls were going to have horses, they should learn to ride first. When I took them twice a week, I started to study the horse stable. How would I build one? I knew we couldn't build one that large. But I wanted to build one like theirs. He used a horse named Mercedes. He told us that she rode as smooth as a Mercedes car. The girls and I fell in love with her. I bought Mercedes for Kayla in March, and we paid $2,500 for her. He said he would find a horse for Sarah. He found Cheyanne. We paid $3,300 for her. I used the money that we had put aside for the girls from foster care and Social Security. That way they would own their own horses. I bought them nice saddles with this money. Now we had to pay him to board the horses, and he charged us the same for the riding lessons. I again used their money for the riding lessons and to have him board the horses. Garry wasn't as successful in turning the girls away from us anymore.

We had started to plant corn in the middle of April. My dad went to the vets' hospital in the cities. My sister and my two brothers went up to see him on the weekend. I knew they would have to go back to work on Monday morning. I would wait until then. Late Sunday, my sister Sandy came to our house to see me. She said that my dad was in rough shape. He wanted to die. He had begged her that she would do something to help him die. Sandy told me that I was to do something and that Dad would die. What was I to do? I went up to the hospital alone Monday morning. Bob was planting corn, and Ruth stayed home in case Bob would need her help. As soon as I got to the hospital, Dad told me that I would have to do something so that he would die. None of the other kids were there. Why did this have to fall on me? Mom and I went into the visiting room. Mom said that Dad had been in terrible pain for a long time. He wanted to die, and she agreed. We had several doctors come to talk to us. They thought that Dad was depressed. Mom didn't agree with the doctors. They couldn't do anything deliberately so that he would die. Finally, we agreed that they wouldn't give him any more pills. He would eventually die. I went back in the room. Dad asked me if I would forgive him for all the rotten things he had done to me. I didn't want to forgive him. It would be hard to do. I had to think for a while. Again, I thought about the Christian law of forgiveness in Matthew 18, verses 21 and 22.

> Then Peter came to him, and said, Lord, how often shall my brother sin against me, and I should forgive him? Till seven times?" Jesus saith unto him, "I say not until three, Until seven times: but, until seventy times seven."

In the Austin group of Compassion Friends, we discussed this Bible reading a lot. If someone asked you to forgive them, you must forgive them. Finally, I said to Dad, "I forgive you for everything." When we looked into each other's eyes, we both knew what we were talking about. It was something that I'm not going to write about in the book. Then Dad went to sleep. Shortly after, he woke and asked me, "Why am I waking up alive?" I told Dad, "You aren't going to die today, but you are going to die soon." He went back to sleep. I never talked to him again. I went home that night, and he never woke up before I left. I told our children, if you want to see your grandpa again, you have to go to the vets' hospital now. They all went up, and Brenda told Dad that she met someone shopping for groceries at John's in Dodge Center. His name was Owen Moe, and he had three girls. The youngest one was five years old. Owen's wife left him and the girls five years ago, and Owen had custody of the girls. He was a dairy farmer. I was planning on going up to the vets' hospital on Thursday. Dad died early Thursday morning on April 30, 2004. In the following months after Dad's death, Mom talked to me about Dad and when they met before the war. He was a completely different person than he was when I knew him. I think World War II robbed me of the dad I should have had. The war changed him. I had become so attached to Grandpa Larson that I didn't like him. Dad became really jealous of my grandpa. He tried to put Grandpa down in front of me. That made me mad! That caused me to not like him even more. I never had a good relationship with my dad. Maybe I inherited this from my ancestors. I am going to take a quote out of the book my brother Dallas wrote.

> FAMILY TIES. The handwriting analysis done by Ruth Gardner suggests that there wasn't a close relationship between Alexander and his sons. There is also some evidence to indicate this may have carried into the next generation too. George, James, and Nathaniel all had farms, but none of their sons carried on the farming operations when those labors became difficult for their fathers. Alexander was my great-great-great grandfather. George was my great-great grandfather.

We decided to build the horse stable in June. By then I was sure that we would get custody of the girls. We built it southeast of the house. It would be a long walk, but we would need a pasture by it. We decided on four box stalls for now, but we would have room for six box stalls. I wanted to have brick pavers in the alleyway. It would require four thousand pavers. I decided to put a drain tile under the floor and through the stalls. We would dig the entire stalls two feet deep. I would cover the tile with pea rock and then fill the stalls with sand. We put in a floor that looked like filler from an egg case. They were made out of plastic three inches thick. They hooked together. When we got them in, we filled them up with pea rook. The stalls would always stay dry. I special-ordered Southern Yellow Pine to build the stalls. It would never rot. I bought the fronts to the stalls from Donnie Allan. He was a neighbor boy of ours when he was growing up. He had a place in West Concord to manufacture them. We also built a fairly good size tack room. I varnished the whole inside. The next year, we built the other two stalls. We had the building built, but we did everything inside ourselves. Bob and I shared the cost of the horse stable. The complete cost came to $50,000.

Bob bought a black horse from a lady outside of New Richland. The horse was a mare about six years old named Brandy. She was a saddlebred paint. I bought an Appaloosa horse from Jeff Steinerngal. He was a friend of my brother Dallas. The horse was also six years old. He was a gelding. I also bought a saddle for $1,000. We took our stock trailer and picked them both up in one day.

On July 8, 2004, we got a report from the guardian ad litem. We were to go to court on July 15, 2004. The purpose of the hearing was for disposition. That meant that we would get custody of the girls. Jerome O. Glenna's report is as follows:

RECOMMENDATION

1. I recommend that the legal and physical custody of the children be turned over to their grandparents, Wayne and Ruth McColley.
2. I recommend that the children continue to have contact with their father thru letters and by telephone.
3. I recommend that the CHIPS petition be closed and the Guardian ad Litem be dismissed.

HISTORY & INFORMATION GATHERED:

The children were visiting at the home of their grandparent's, Wayne and Ruth McColley, when their father was taken into custody and charged with a number of drug-related offenses and possession of a firearm. The children's mother died in a house fire several years ago. The children's father and stepmother were separated and the stepmother was living in Mantorville at the time of the father's arrest. Their stepmother was also arrested on a drug charge but was released on bail. Human Services took custody of the children and placed them with the grandparents as caretakers. The children have a strong bond with not only their grandparents, but also with their maternal uncle who reside on the premises of the McColley farm. The children are attending school in West Concord and are adapting well to their new residence and school. The girls are receiving individual counseling and therapy both at school and outside of school. They are active in extracurricular and church activities. I know that the girls are still dealing with some unanswered questions concerning both their mother and father. None of us are present able to answer these questions but hopefully the counselors and therapists can help them to deal with their feeling. They are at present in a safe and structured environment and I believe they should remain there.

Garry was sentenced to a minimum of seven years in prison so the girls will both be over eighteen by the time he is released.

Respectfully submitted,
Jerome O. Glenna
Guardian ad Litem

When we got his report, we really felt good. The end of the nightmare would soon end. On July 15, 2004, we thought that it would be the last time to go to court. Ruth and I were unreal happy! Then we were shocked! Garry's mother wanted to have custody of the girls. How could this happen? The only time I could remember she saw them was when we took the girls to her house at Christmas. They didn't really know her. Judge Agerter said there would be a trial with witnesses. Our attorney said she would have to talk to witnesses on our behalf and prepare for trial. This whole thing would cost me $7,000. I figured the only reason she wanted the girls was for the Social Security money. Garry had told the girls in the past that when they turned eighteen and he couldn't draw the money, he was going to kick them out. The judge said we would have to allow his mother and family to visit the girls. At least she couldn't keep them overnight. The visits were only to be for two hours. The first time Garry's mother and some of her daughters came, I told the girls to show them the horse stable and the horses. We really wanted them to know the life we were giving the girls. Were the girls willing to give this up? Would the girls be happy with her? At the last minute, Garry's mother changed her mind. She didn't want custody of the girls now. She realized that the girls were not going to be happy with her. I couldn't believe that she never had much contact with the girls. If Ruth and I had been in her situation, we would have seen the girls as often as we could. I had an attorney bill for $7,000 just to prepare for the trial. I was really mad at her for putting us through this.

We had our family summer vacation in August. We went up north fishing at Finn and Feather Resort. We had been there years ago. We stayed in two cabins at the north edge of the resort. It was a high-rate resort with a swimming pool.

We went to court for the hearing September 21, 2004.

Based on the arguments of counsel, and all of the files, proceedings and records herein, the Court makes the following:

FINDINGS OF FACT

1. The minor children, Kayla and Sarah were found to be in need of protection or services on October 3, 2003, as they were without necessary food, clothing, education, or other required care for their physical or mental health or morals because of their father's incarceration.
2. The children were placed in the home of Wayne and Ruth McColley, the children's maternal grandparents, in July, 2003, and they have remained there since that placement.
3. Reasonable measures were taken to prevent the out of home placement.
4. The children's father is now in prison. Their mother is deceased.
5. The Court is in receipt of the recommendations submitted by Kimberly Zoorak.
6. The Court is in receipt of the Guardian Ad Litem report submitted by Jerome Glenna. Renae Streich, successor Guardian Ad Litem, does not advocate for non-custodian visitation.
7. The children and the McColleys had a significant relationship prior to July, 2003 placement and continue to share a close relationship.
8. The children have adjusted well to the placement with the McColleys.

9. The custodians, Wayne and Ruth McColley, are suitable, fit, and willing to assume the role of permanent legal and physical custodians of the children.
10. No other relative or third party requested to be the custodian of the children.
11. All parties, including the father, agree that the children should permanently live with the McColleys.
12. It is in the best interests of the children to permanently live with Wayne and Ruth McColley.

ORDER

1. That the maternal grandparents, Wayne and Ruth McColley, are awarded permanent legal and physical custody of the minor children, Kayla and Sarah. This transfer of legal and physical custody includes responsibility for the protection, education, care, and control of the children, and decision making on behalf of the children.
2. That this child protection case is hereby closed and Juvenile Court jurisdiction is hereby terminated.
3. That the Guardian Ad Litem is hereby discharged.
4. That this Order shall be filed with the Family Court. Any further proceedings shall take place in the Family Court.

Dated:_____ BY THE COURT
Lawrence E. Agerter
Judge of District Court

A FATHER'S QUEST

The judge didn't immediately sign the order. On September 27, 2004, the judge got a letter from Garry's public defender.

> Dear Judge Agerter
>
> I represent Garry in the above-entitled matter which came before you on Tuesday, September 21, 2004, for a Permanency Hearing. Garry agreed to permanent placement of his children with their maternal grandparents with whom they were placed immediately following Garry's arrest for controlled substance crimes in the first degree on July 21, 2003. Although Garry has always opposed that placement, he has had no opportunity to follow the case plan related to this matter and reunify with his children since he was incarcerated immediately upon his arrest and was unable to post bail. He subsequently entered a plea of guilty to resolve his criminal case in hopes that he would receive a downward departure, as he been accepted into the Teen Challenge Program. Unfortunately, Garry was not given that opportunity either but was committed to the Department of Corrections with an anticipated release date of December 29, 2008.
>
> The Court is aware that the maternal grandparents have an uneasy relationship at best, with Garry and his family. At a hearing on July 21, 2004, the Court was made aware that the children had very limited, if any, visitation with their father and paternal relatives. Following that hearing, visitation improved between the girls and their paternal grandmother and Garry's sister, as well as Wendy, the children's stepmother for seven years.
>
> After a discussion with Garry and his relatives it was agreed that placement at maternal

grandparents would not be opposed. However, there was concern that if the issue of visitation was not monitored, once placement became permanent, the paternal visitation would revert back to little or none. Garry was also very concerned that he would not see the girls at all, since he is currently incarcerated in a facility quite some distance from Dodge County. While his relatives are willing to transport the children, his fear is that the maternal grandparents will not allow it and he will not have the opportunity to see his children over the next 4+ years.

The only request Garry made at the permanency hearing was the Court retain jurisdiction over the issue of visitation. Neither Garry nor his family has money to hire private counsel to litigate the visitation issue in family court. Garry, Wendy and the paternal relatives love the children and have a relationship with them. It is clearly not in the children's best interests to force them to break their ties to their paternal biological family. That is not the purpose of the child protection rules, which acknowledge the importance of the family relationship.

It was stated at the Permanency Hearing that the only reason for the Court to retain jurisdiction is to ensure appropriate services are delivered; this is an incomplete statement of law pursuant to the above. In order for the Court to ensure that the best interests of Garry's children are truly protected, an order regarding reasonable visitation by all family members, is necessary. In order to enforce that order, the Court should retain jurisdiction of this matter to ensure that the visitation condition ordered by the Court is met.

> Respectfully submitted,
> Rachael M. Drenckpohl
> Assistant Public Defender

I thought that the nightmare was over. If this was approved, Garry would control us from prison. If Garry would have died and his family would have had our grandchildren, we would have had a relationship with the girls. Or at least we would have tried. His mother or his family never tried. His family and Garry never obeyed court orders. That was why we were in court so many times. We would need a really good lawyer to win on this one.

October 4, 2004

HONORABLE LAWRENCE AG DODGE COUNTY COURT 22 EAST SIXTH STREET EAST MANTORVILLE MN 55955-2220

Dear Judge Agerter:

This letter is written pursuant to the Court Order dated September 24, 2004
   As previously indicated, the visitation rights, if any, of the non-custodians, including the father, are governed by Minn. Stat. Sec. 257C.08. The non-custodians are required to petition the family court for visitation. They would have to prove that they meet the criteria to proceed; that the visitation would not interfere with the custodial relationship; and that it is in the best interests of the children.
   The father and grandmother's potential rights are governed under Minn. Stat. 257C.07

Subd. 2; however, it is unlikely that the either petition would be approved for several reasons, including the limited contact that both have chosen to have with the girls. The grandmother requested to see the girls only twice in the year-long placement. The father had the right to make regular calls to the girls at the McColleys, yet stopped doing so a year ago, while still keeping phone contact with his estranged wife.

Father's sister has no rights under third party visitation statute. The estranged wife can apply under Minn. Stat. Sec. 257C.08 Subd. 4 if the court finds that she actually lived with the father for two years, but the more significant issue of the children's best interests and the potential interference with the custodial relationship clouds her petition.

Ms. Drenckpohl sought visitation for the father, his estranged wife, and his extended family in the child protection case purely for economic reasons ("Neither Garry nor his family has money to hire private counsel to litigate the visitation issue in family court."), yet has created additional expense for my clients due to pretended objections to placement so that visitation might be addressed.

This case is now a family case. Its origination as a child protection case does not negate the statutory requirements that every other third party in Minnesota needs to follow when seeking visitation.

Without requiring these third parties to proceed, the custodians are forced into litigation of visitation requests that have not been properly pleaded or provided through discovery.

The custodians take serious issue with Ms. Drenckpohl's representation that they in any way denied anyone visitation. The girls have visited with father's estranged wife. Father's sister never once requested a visit. Father's mother made no contact with the girls until Christmas, 2003, five months after the placement. The girls visited with the mother and sister at Christmas.

The paternal grandmother's second request to visit the girls was in July, 2004, seven month months after the Christmas visit. She requested the girls for a family reunion that fell on a weekend the McColleys had plans with the girls. The date of the claimed "reunion" kept changing; red flags quickly arose regarding this request made just prior to the permanency hearing.

After that hearing Kim Zvorak arranged two visits for the estranged wife, father's sister, and father's mother. None of those people asked for any further visitation.

Significantly, during the two visits with the estranged wife, the father called and berated Kayla to the point of tears – twice. The father and his estranged wife had to have carefully orchestrated those events, which were obviously detrimental to the children.

The father is a convicted drug felon with a significant criminal history. The estranged wife has drug felony charges pending and a criminal history. They have chosen their paths and exposed the children to an extremely hazardous home environment. They have, by their own actions, significantly compromised the girls' best interests. It certainly is not a "given" that visitation with either of them is in the best children's best interests.

The children have adjusted well to their placement. They do not ask to see any of these people. Forcing 11—and 12 year-old girls to take a regular trip to prison eight plus hours away to see a man that did not even ask to see them any of the times he was brought to Mantorville for court is absurd

My clients' first and foremost concern is the best interests of the girls. They are not going to deny them contact with individuals who support them in their placement. Unfortunately, father and his entourage are all too clear about their dislike of the McColleys.

It is time for finality and an end to the litigation. It is time to let the girls heal. If father, his estranged wife, or his mother insists on litigation, they will consider it important enough to proceed properly. Until that happens, no evidentiary hearing or any further proceeding is appropriate.

Thank you.

RYAN & GRINDE, LTD,
Kristine L. Dicke Attorney at Law

A FATHER'S QUEST

Brenda and Owen's wedding

On August 28, 2004, Brenda married Owen Moe. My late friend, Jim from the Austin group, helped make this happen. He talked me into buying a home for Brenda and Justin. He and we knew that Brenda had a lot of growing up to do. She wasn't going to do this living with her mother. Thank you, Jim. We had the wedding in our church. The church wasn't big enough, so we invited more people to the reception than to the church. I caused some poor feelings with my Uncle Lenard and Aunt Carol McColley. We only invited them to the reception. I wished that they had called me. The church was full, but we could have seated two more. We had the reception on our farm in the shop. I hired a caterer for the meal. Being in the shop, we served a picnic meal. I hired Kent Larson to play early. He was better for the older ones that were not going to stay late. Afterward, they had a person come in to play music. It wasn't a band. Brenda wanted Doreen to be in the wedding. But Doreen was pregnant and was due.

Kayla and Sarah at Brenda's wedding

Doreen had another daughter on the second of September named Valerie Laurie. Laurie was named after Alan's deceased sister. Doreen's second pregnancy was different than with Jenna. Valerie was still in breech position the last couple of months. The doctors would have to schedule a C-section at the Albert Lea Hospital. They would do it on September 2. Doreen and Valerie would be celebrating their birthdays together. While they were getting Doreen ready for surgery, the contraction started. Valerie had respiratory difficulties at birth. Valerie was in an incubator for twenty-four hours and then flown by helicopter to St. Mary's Hospital in Rochester. Doreen was released from the hospital at the same time. Valerie was in the NICU area for nine days. Valerie had her first appointment less than a week later. Valerie's pediatrician wanted her transferred to St. Mary's Hospital. Valerie wasn't gaining weight like the doctors expected of her. Valerie was diagnosed for milk protein intolerance. She was hospitalized for thirteen days. She was put on Pregetmil Formula before leaving the hospital. Valerie had no further issues with food after she got older. Valerie weighed seven pounds, three ounces and was born at 8:59 AM on the second of September. She was baptized November 21, 2004.

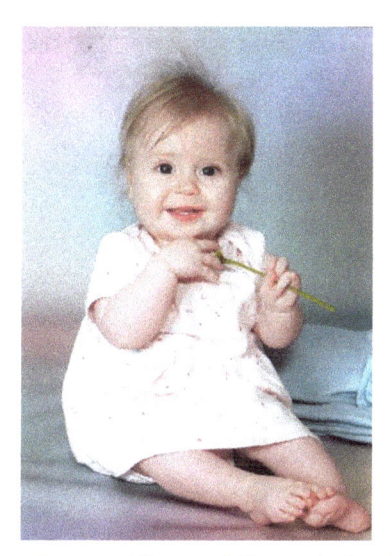

Valerie Laurie, Allan and Doreen's daughter

Finally, Judge Agerter signed an order on December 16, 2004.

ORDER

1. That Juvenile Court jurisdiction is hereby terminated.
2. That any further proceedings shall be brought in the Family Court pursuant to Minn. Stat. 518.18.
3. That the Guardian ad Litem is hereby discharged

4. That all terms of the prior Order in this matter, which are not inconsistent with this Order, remain in full force and effect. Dated this 16 day of December, 2004 By Lawrence E. Agerter

    We had finally won for sure. It was a good Christmas present. Garry and his family could use a public defender if the judge had left the juvenile court open on this matter. It wouldn't cost them anything. They couldn't use a public defender in family court. I think Judge Agerter was getting really sick of Garry and maybe me in dealing with this. I think in his mind, this was the end of it. Garry had made a big mistake in buying the big insurance policy on Wendy. It would sink him. How did the psychic know that this was going to happen? Was Pastor Hagen right when he told me that sometimes God uses really strange people to give us messages? I really thought that I was doing this for Tammy, and we had won. I would give the girls the best life as I could for Tammy. God had finally answered our prayers.

    In the next days, Garry's mother called me on the phone. She wanted to know when she could get visitation. I told her that she had caused a great expense over the years. She was the one that told Ruth and me we wouldn't see the girls again because they liked us more than them. She caused me to get grandparents' rights. "You should get grandparents' rights too." I then said, "I will forget all this and give you visitation if you will tell me why you forged Tammy's name on the insurance policy." She hung up the phone! I have never heard from her again. Rollie had told me that Garry's mother didn't sign the policy. He had a report from the BCA. I asked Rollie for the report, but he wouldn't show it to me. If Garry's mother didn't sign the policy, she would have denied it, but she didn't. BCA had told the sheriff to investigate this. But he didn't! WHY? Garry's mother should have gone to jail for this. How much money did she get from Tammy's death?

    In the beginning of 2005, we went to a convention of Parents of Murdered Children. I drove and Lois Hackbarth and Connie

Sheely went with Ruth and me. The convention was in Kansas City. The first night there, Lois knew several people that we met. It was really fun visiting with them. The next day the men and women separated. I spent the whole day listening to how their children were murdered. It was so sad it was more than I could stand. At the end of the day, I told Ruth to go with Lois. I just stayed in the room. I had no appetite to eat anything. The next day there was a person that talked about cold cases. His name was C. Donald Weinberg. He belonged to a society that investigated cold cases. They had a few wealthy anonymous donors who paid for everything. At the end of the session, I walked up to him. I told him about Tammy's death. He wanted to meet with Ruth and me at eight o'clock in the evening. Ruth and I talked to him almost two hours in the evening. Finally, he said he would take our case. He felt he was convinced that he could find something to prove that Garry murdered our daughter. Finally, something was going to be done. The sheriff had threatened me some years ago to leave Tammy's death alone. He told me that I would lose visitation with our granddaughters if I didn't. Now I had custody. How could they take this away? Ruth and I slept very little that night. We were really glad that we went to the convention. In a month, Donald Weinberg called me. He said he would have to get permission from the sheriff. It would cost Dodge County nothing. The sheriff forbade them to come. Why was this? Maybe they were going to uncover the corruption there was in the sheriff's office and Dodge County. Maybe they didn't want the poor job they had done investigating Tammy's death to come out, or both. We had two new sheriffs by now. Why wouldn't he approve of this? I really thought maybe I should find another avenue. But in the end, Garry was in prison now. We had two girls to raise. We had won the war on the girls, but we would lose the war on Tammy's death. Maybe it would finally be time for the nightmare to end.

Chapter 22

The Horses and the Wagon Trains

My mother always had a love for horses. When I was young, I always had a horse. Both of my grandfathers had a love of horses. When I came home from the Navy, the horses that we had when I was young, Tarzan and Lady, were gone. My mother and my dad had several Appaloosa horses. I was in love with Ruth and never expected to have horses again. When our children were young, Doreen begged me for a horse. A neighbor girl Doreen's age, Lisa, had horses. The first time I remember meeting Lisa, she was standing in the middle of the road. I was going down the road and saw a little kid that couldn't catch her pony. I stopped and caught the pony and helped Lisa get on the pony. We were going through the farm depression, and money was extremely tight. We didn't have a pasture and any buildings to keep a horse in. I told our kids, "We will never have a horse on this farm." But now it was twenty years later. Money was no longer a problem for me. Our oldest daughter, Tammy, was now dead. Tammy had two young daughters. They had now lived with their father for six and a half years after Tammy's death. He was an alcoholic and on drugs. I really felt sorry for Kayla and Sarah. When their dad was arrested for selling drugs, they came to live with us. I really thought that I had failed Tammy. Now I had a chance to make it up to Tammy by giving Kayla and Sarah the best life I could give them. When Kayla and Sarah asked me if I would buy them a horse, I immediately said, "Yes." In a way, the next ten years of my life were some of the best years of my life. I really miss this time and wish I could go back in time.

Kayla on Mercedes and Bob on Brandy

    The horse that I bought for me was an Appaloosa named George. The name reminded me of George Restovich. I decided to name him Dusty. Both girls told me that horses didn't like their names changed. Dusty was not going to like his new name. At first, Bob and I always helped the girls take care of their horses, Mercedes and Cheyenne. Bob's and mine were Dusty and Brandy. After feeding them grain, everyone stood in the stalls and petted their horses while they ate. Dusty didn't like me in the stall with him. He would often try to chase me out. One day while we were all riding the horses down a waterway, Dusty lay down. I had to get off him and then get him to stand up. I then got on Dusty. Soon Dusty lay down again. I had to get off him again. Then I had to get Dusty to stand up. Then I got into the saddle again. We hadn't gone far when Dusty lay down for the third time. That time I didn't get off Dusty. I just stayed sitting in the saddle. I said to Dusty, "It's hard work for an old man to get up onto a horse. I'm going to just sit here until you get up." I don't know if he understood what I told him, but he got up with me still in the saddle, and he never lay down again.

Cheyenne and Dusty

On Father's Day weekend of 2005, Bob, Kayla, and Sarah left on a wagon train. We have a neighbor that went on the wagon trains in the past. Bob went with her one year to help her. She was in her upper seventies, and it was hard for her to go on the wagon train alone. Bob got the idea if he bought a horse camping trailer, it would be fun for the girls to go on the wagon train. Bob paid $55,000 for the horse trailer. When they talked about all the fun they had, I decided to buy a team of horses and a wagon and go on the wagon train with them.

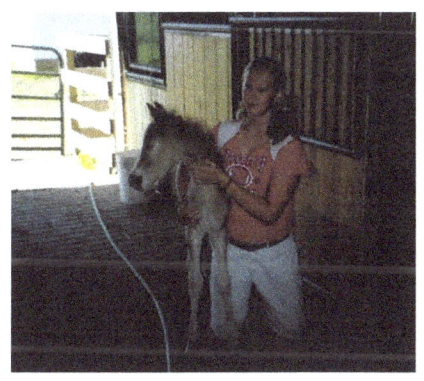

Kayla and Ginger   Sarah and Sapphire

    The year after we built the horse stable, we had to add two more stalls and put in two more windows. I bought two Welsh ponies from Dave Hoenk. Their names were Kit-Kat and Becky. They were both mares and pregnant. I thought it would be easier to drive ponies than horses. Was I wrong! They both had fillies. The girls named them Saphire and Ginger. It was a fun experience for the girls to learn how to lead and to take care of them. Kit-Kat was always wild and hard to catch. They were both sorrels. Kit-Kat had a light-colored mane. When she ran, her mane stood up, and it was fun watching her. I bought a small covered wagon from Jim Plank from Chatfield for $1,000.

Ruth and Wayne

I did a lot of research on where we could take our horses and stay on a dude ranch. Bob just bought a camping horse trailer with four stalls. The camper had a slide out, so there was some room in it. I found a dude ranch about forty-five miles east of the Black Hills. We went in the early part of August. They had a bunkhouse for Ruth and me to sleep in. Bob and the girls slept in the camper. They had a kitchen in the bunkhouse, and Sabrina, the owner, cooked for us. Her husband, Alfred, took us riding every day. I didn't want to leave Ruth alone every day, so I stayed with her some days. Ruth had a sister that lived in the hills, so we visited her one day. One day all of us rode on the 1880s train. Albert took the kids on a cattle roundup and branding. They were chasing cattle one day when they came across a rattlesnake. Albert took his lasso rope and snapped the head off of the rattlesnake. He cut off the rattles and gave them to the kids to keep as a souvenir. Sabrina's dad owned ten thousand acres of this ranch. He had already lost his wife. I spent a lot of time visiting with him. We went riding in the Black Hills one day. Alfred had a big trailer, and he hauled the horses to the Black Hills. Alfred and I were visiting and riding slowly, and the kids got way ahead of us. We couldn't see them anymore, and we didn't know where they went. It was a good experience and fun to track them. When we caught up with them, they were at the trailer. We didn't have to track them. Alfred and Bob always had a couple of beers at night. Sabrina had some goats, and Kayla, Sarah, and Sabrina played with the goats at night. They had two kids at that time. The oldest was a boy named Dirk. I don't remember the girl's name. When it got time to go, no one, but maybe Ruth, was ready to go. We were going to come again next year. When we left, it was 104 degrees temperature with a strong east wind. I drove the PT Cruiser, so I followed them. Bob got two miles to the gallon pulling the big and heavy trailer into the wind.

We were done with harvest in early November. We had a good crop, and we had made money. I went out to do chores early one Saturday morning. I had some feed to grind. I set up the mill and started to grind feed. I didn't have to watch it, so I went down to the horse stable. The plan was to go to town and buy a new van as soon I got done doing chores. The water tank was low on water, so I decided to fill the tank. I got the hose. Dusty came up to the tank. I had trained Dusty to hold the hose. I put the water hose in Dusty's mouth, and he held the hose until the tank was full. There was a shutoff value at the end of the hose. I took the hose from Dusty and shut off the water. Dusty brushed my face with his nose and left. I didn't feel anything. All of a sudden, my mouth started to feel warm. I put my hand up to my mouth. My hand was all blood. I was really bleeding! I took out my handkerchief and put it over my mouth. I got kind of a weak feeling. Bob and Ruth were working in the yard putting away machinery. The sight of blood made me lightheaded, and I began to stagger up to them.

Bob hollered out to me, "What wrong with you?"

As I got closer to Bob, I took away the handkerchief away and said, "I think Dusty bit me."

Bob and Ruth looked at it. I put the handkerchief back to try to stop the bleeding. Ruth started to walk away.

I said, "Do you think I have to go to the doctor?"

Bob said, "Let me look again."

I took away the handkerchief again.

Bob said to Ruth, "Drop everything, and take Dad to the emergency room right away."

When we got to the emergency room, I walked in while Ruth parked the car. I was still holding the handkerchief over my mouth. When a lady asked me what was wrong, I took the handkerchief away and said, "I think a horse bit me." Right away, another lady asked, "Were you kissing the horse?" Then several people came to look. They all started laughing. I didn't think it was funny for me. Right away, they took me to a room and got the bleeding to stop. They would have to call a doctor and team from home to do surgery and fix my lip. It was now about ten o'clock in the morning. Around eleven, the doctor arrived. He looked at my lip and said, "When the team gets here, they would make up a plan to finally fix up your lip." At noon the doctor came in and told me that they finally had a plan. But there was a problem. St. Mary's Hospital had only one operating room where operations were done on Saturdays at that time. One man got stabbed in the stomach. Another man cut his leg deep with a chain saw. These two operations would have to come ahead of me. The emergency room was not busy. I had a nurse that was raised on a farm and had horses, and she was about forty years old. She sat beside me. We talked a lot, and that made the wait seem better. The lip didn't hurt, but my back finally got in severe pain from lying on the bed. I couldn't stand the pain! They gave me morphine for the pain. I got happy being on morphine. Time didn't matter anymore. Around four in the afternoon, I heard maybe they were going to take me to the operating room. Actually, they were going to take the second man into the operating room. I asked my nurse, "Can I go to the bathroom? I want to get up and walk to a bathroom." The nurse helped me to walk to a bathroom. When I was done, I went to the sink to wash my hands. When I looked into the mirror, I couldn't believe what I saw. My lip was all black, and there was a hole big enough to put a quarter in the hole. My teeth showed when my mouth was shut. I thought, for the rest of my life, children were going to be afraid of me. People were going to stare at me. Finally, at ten in the evening, the doctor came to get me. I had spent a lot of time visiting with the doctor. He didn't have much to do on a Saturday night. I told Ruth to go home.

"It's going to be the middle of the night when I get out. Go home."

They put me to sleep to do the operation. Afterward they couldn't wake me when they were done. My doctor came in the room early in the morning. He put up a mirror, and he had me look. I couldn't believe what I saw! There was a lot of swelling, but there was no hole left. Children were not going to be afraid of me. I asked the doctor if they grafted skin from anywhere else. He said that they couldn't.

"There are three different types of skin on your mouth and face. The skin on your lip is one type. The skin above your lip is another type, and the skin in your mouth is another type. So we couldn't graft skin. We cut carefully and straight along the hole and sewed it together."

There is a small scar, but it isn't easy to see. The doctor told me that I could never have morphine again. The morphine made the technicians in the operating room unable to wake me. They were getting very scared that I would not wake up. Sometime later, Sarah, my granddaughter, wrote a story for school: "The Day my Grandpa Got Kissed by a Horse."

We started on the wagon train the Friday night before Father's Day 2006, in Blooming Prairie. My plan was to sleep in the wagon. Dwayne Schmoll went along for a couple of days to teach me how to drive. The team was hard to control, and Dwayne told me, "Do not give them water throughout the day. They will soon cool down. It will be easier for you to drive them." The first night we camped at Hayfield. I went home to sleep with Ruth. The next day, it was cold and rainy. I knew that sleeping in the wagon was a dumb idea. I slept on the floor of the trailer. Rod Friedrich, the leader of the Austin group of Compassion Friends, came on Monday to ride with me one day. We got the lines mixed up at the start. This was the first day for me to harness the horses alone. They left without us, and it took a long time to figure the lines out. When we got started, the team ran the whole way until they caught up with the wagon train. It was a rather hot day, and I didn't give the team any water. Kit-Kat went down just as we were pulling into night camp. Russ and Darlene were in the buggy behind me. Darlene came to help me get Kit-Kat up and to take the harness off. Russ called to Darlene for help. Darlene told Russ, "Do it yourself, I've got more important things to do. Do it yourself." One of the members had a drug that would help. He gave Kit-Kat a shot, and Darlene told me to walk Kit-Kat for a long time. I was to give Kit-Kat water a little at a time. I knew that I had made a big mistake. I would never withhold water from a horse again. Ruth came the next day and stayed the rest of the week. She slept in the bunk with the girls, and I slept on the floor. We went through a gravel pit. We went down a long hill, and there was a creek at the bottom. The creek was completely filled with rocks. Everyone was having troubles to get their horses across it. This would really put a test to my driving abilities. Ruth and I had a lot of doubt, but we finally got across. We had a long hill ahead of us. When we got to the top, I said to Ruth, "This was really something to do this, and we made it!" I felt really good.

The next day, the wagon train got lost. We waited on the road for almost an hour. My team didn't like to stand. I had a super-hard time to control the team. A large truck came by and let the air out of the brakes right beside them. At that exact minute the wagon train turned around and started coming toward my team, Kit-Kat and Becky turned around and started to run. I couldn't control them. Soon the team ran in the ditch. They went through the ditch to the other side and then went in the ditch again. I pulled so hard on the lines that the lines broke. We were back on the road, and we soon would be going down a long hill with a curve at the bottom. I could imagine how bad it was. Now I had no control over the team. Sooner or later, the wagon was going to turn over, and Ruth and I were going to fly out. As we were going down the hill, Bob and Jim Malone each came up, one on each side of the team. Jim grabbed Kit-Kat's bridle and Bob grabbed Becky's bridle at the same exact time. The team stopped! There must have been more than one angel with us to make this happen. I had told Ruth earlier, "If something bad happens, don't scream. It will make it worse." Ruth stayed completely quite. An angel must have been in the seat with Ruth. Some other people had lines that they were able to tie onto what lines we had left. We camped that night next to an Amish tack shop. I bought a new set of lines for $90. The last day there was a long and steep hill. It was hot for the horses. We stopped for a break at the bottom, and I watered the horses. We started and I was behind Paul Vickerman. It took forever to get up the hill. Toward the end of the hill, Paul's horses started to walk super slow. I couldn't hold Kit-Kat and Becky. Soon they went past Paul's team. At that night, when we had our meeting, Paul said, "We should all clap for the small team that passed me." There was man, James Meacham, from Prattville, Alabama. He was completely blind. He rode his horse every day and came many years to the wagon train. We had a ceremony at the end of the wagon train. The wagon master, John Davis, known by JD, gave plaques to some members of the train for helping. JD gave me a plaque for being a newcomer. But everyone told me that it was the booby prize. They were right. In a way, I made a fool of myself. I had a lot to learn about horses and driving a team. We had made lifelong friends. They were family.

In August we went to the dude ranch in South Dakota again. That time Sabrina's sister and her son, Clay, were staying in the bunkhouse too. I think Clay was twenty years old at that time. I really liked him. One of the first nights we were there was a rodeo in New Underwood for children. Sabrina and Alfred's son, Dirk were in the rodeo. It was fun watching him and the other kids. I rode Dusty with Alfred, Clay, Bob, and the girls some but not as much as I rode the year before. One day I hired Clay to give me riding lessons and to work with Dusty. We all went to Devils Tower one day. The temperature was 104 degrees that day. In the night, I woke up in severe pain. I thought I was having kidney stones. I had kidney stones years ago. The pain felt the same. Ruth woke Sabrina's sister to get directions to the hospital. When we got to the hospital, the doctor told me that I didn't have kidney stones. I was just dehydrated. A nurse put in an IV and put a solution in my blood. In a few hours, we were ready to be dismissed from the hospital. I really felt foolish. All I needed to do was to drink more. Bob and the girls were not ready to leave on the last morning. We all said that we would come back again next year. I had mixed emotions. I still felt terrible from my stay in the hospital. Ruth would have to drive home. When we went to load the horses, Dusty wouldn't get in the trailer. Finally, he broke the lead rope and ran back to the corral. There were three horses that stayed in a corral next to where Dusty stayed. Evidently, Dusty wanted to say goodbye to them. His nose touched their noses, and then Dusty came back and got in the trailer. Maybe horses can think and communicate more than we realize. It was getting dark when got to Fairmont. I was finally starting to feel better. We stopped at Perkins to eat.

    We almost tipped over our covered wagon on the wagon train. Ruth had told me that she wouldn't go again with this wagon. One day when I was going to Blooming Prairie, I saw a surrey sitting in a yard. I stopped, and the lady living there said her father had made the surrey. He was from Brainerd, Minnesota. He would make me a surrey. I called him and told him I wanted one with a box on the back to hold water buckets and other things. I needed brakes. We finally agreed on $3,200. I took the stock trailer up to Brainerd to pick up the surrey.

Ruth and Wayne with Molly and Bess pulling the surrey

After the experience we had with Kit-Kat and Becky, I decided we would need a new team. Bob, the girls, and I went to a horse auction in Waverly, Iowa. We soon saw a team of paints. I tried to get them to kick me or bite me. Regardless of what I did to the team, they remained calm. They were mother and daughter. The mother was eleven years old. Her name was Molly. The daughter was eight years old. Her name was Bess. I bought the team for $1,600, and I bought the harness they were wearing for $700 for the pair. I thought that the harnesses were the harnesses that they always wore. I was wrong; the harness didn't fit them. They were junk, and I paid too much for the harness. Bob had to go two hours home to get a trailer to haul the team home. We put up a pen in the machine shed, and we kept them there for three weeks before we put them with our other horses.

I went to St. Charles were several Amish families lived. I found a young couple, and he made harnesses. He would make the set for $1,100. They looked like leather; they felt like leather, but they weren't leather. The material was much lighter than leather. I bought Molly and Bess down to his farm when the harnesses were done. He fit the harnesses to the horses. I really liked the harnesses. Because of their light weight, it was easier to harness the horses.

I soon found out that there was a lot of work to keep paints clean. We took the team on the wagon train the Friday before Father's Day in 2007. Everyone remarked about the good-looking team that I had. My team stood perfect, and they were easy to drive. They stood perfectly still until I told them, "Walk up." When we stopped, I didn't have to tie them up. The team got really excited when we left on the ride. I could tell that they really enjoyed being on the wagon train. My brother-in-law Junior had gone on the wagon train for several years. He had a single horse that pulled a small covered wagon. He made the wagon himself. Eva was with him this year. We met Wallace Turner from Georgia. When Ruth was sitting in the back seat of the surrey, she was sleeping. Wallace was riding his horse, and he had a bottle of water. He threw water on Ruth. It surprised Ruth so much that she almost fell out of the surrey. Wallace was the wagon master of the Georgia wagon train. I met a lot of people that year. Hermann and Sue Von Knobelsdorff were from Goodhue, Minnesota. Bob and Arlene Noser were from Pine Island. Harland and Gini Gekeler were from Waseca. I rode the bus with him when we were in school. George and Barbara Martin were from Mississippi. They had lost a child. Warren Veien went to school with my Uncle David. Elleen and John Campbell were from Georgia. Doug and Penny Brass were from Iowa City, Iowa. Rolland and Brian Weis were from Pine Island. We became friends with more people than I can list. Cheyenne didn't do well with other horses, so I bought a palomino horse for Sarah. Sarah didn't want to ride all the time, so Rod Friedrich rode her horse sometimes. Bob had a hitch put on the semi so he could pull the horse trailer. There were bunk beds in the semi, so we could sleep more people. Rod slept in the lower bunk, and Bob slept in the upper bunk. There were a lot of kids at the wagon train, and the girls really had a good time. Everyone got up at five in the morning and tended to their livestock. At six the trailers were moved ahead to the next campground. Everyone came back in a bus. Herman Transburg was the bus driver. Herman also took the pictures for the book they had made up for everyone at the picnic that they had in September. After the drivers came back, they ate. The wagon train hopefully left at eight. We usually got in around four in the afternoon. After we unharnessed the horses and fed them, we had a meeting to discuss the day. We ate supper at six. The whole time Wallace worked on me to come to Georgia to go on a wagon train with him.

    I called Sabrina to made plans to go to the dude ranch. The dude ranch wasn't doing well. Alfred had taken a job driving truck. He wouldn't be there, but we were welcome to come. I said we had to talk about it. Everyone decided that we wouldn't have fun if Alfred wasn't there to take us riding every day. That was a lot of fun, but we never went to the dude ranch again. I had way too many horses now. I sold Dusty to Curt Miner, my electrician. I traded Dusty for a $1,500 electrical box. Curt bought Dusty for his kids to ride. Curt rode him some. In about three months, I went to Curt's to see Dusty. The other horses didn't like Dusty, and they chased him away from everything. Dusty acted like he didn't know me. I think he knew, me and I could tell that he was mad at me for selling him. Later Curt sold Dusty to a cousin by Preston. He had a big pasture with a lot of trees and hills. I really hope that Dusty had a good life.

If we weren't going to the dude ranch, maybe we could go on the Georgia Wagon Train. Kayla had met a friend, Timera Johnson, who wanted to go along. Sarah said she didn't want to take a horse. She didn't want to ride all the time. We could only take four horses. The team, Mercedes, Kayla's horse, and Timera's horse. We would have to leave by the first of November. We should be done harvesting by that time. But would we be done? The corn was wet, so Lee and Jim Bryselson wanted to wait. They always took their corn right to the elevator in the fall. It would cost them too much to dry the corn. Then they wanted us to pick their corn the first of November. I told them that we were going on the wagon train. "I'll pick your corn as soon we get back." They weren't very happy. I said that I had promised the girls that we were going on the wagon train. I thought maybe they were going to get someone else to pick their corn. We had a very poor plan. We were going to leave Thursday afternoon. Bob was going to pull the horse trailer with his Dodge pickup. Maybe we would need permits to use the semi. I was going to pull the stock trailer loaded with the surrey and hay. We left at four in the afternoon. We weren't going to stop anywhere. I wasn't good at wearing a seat belt, but I put it on. I was pulling a trailer, and maybe a policeman might stop me. The first part of the trip went well. In the middle of Illinois, I became very tired. We stopped in a church parking lot about two in the morning. We were going to sleep a couple of hours. Mercedes made so much noise in the trailer that they took her out and walked her. We weren't sleeping, so we decided to go on. I went ahead of Bob.

Around four in the morning, my shoulder was in pain. I took the seat belt off. I hoped that it was going to be light at five. I was going to have Ruth drive when it was light. I couldn't keep my eyes open anymore. I should have opened the window, but I didn't. Ruth was sleeping so well. I kept dosing off. Ruth would soon be driving. I had the cruise control on. I turned the heater up so that I would really sleep well when Ruth took over. I went to sleep, and Bob could tell by the way I was driving that I was asleep. We went off the road on the left side. The roughness kind of woke me up. I turned the steering wheel too sharp to the right. The trailer started to whip. I overcorrected, and the pickup and the trailer went in the left ditch. The cruise control was still on. Luckily, the left lane of the four-lane highway was some ways apart. I was still kind of sleeping. Maybe I was having a dream. I was going through the weeds in a cardboard box at a fast speed. I heard a crash, and suddenly I was standing beside Ruth on the right side of the pickup. We had a regular cab pickup. The trailer came through the pickup on the driver's side of the cab. My seat was now behind the cab. The driver's door was so crushed that you could see the steering wheel from behind the pickup. I had the center armrest down. The door was so caved in that there wasn't room for me on the seat. Where was I? The pickup was totaled, and the trailer had only a small hole, which I fixed with a small amount of duct tape. Bob and the girls came running, and Bob said, "You are lucky to be alive. Someone most have been looking out for you." If I hadn't taken off the seat belt, I'm certain it would have been entirely different. Ruth and I didn't have a scratch or any sore spots. I think Ruth wasn't fully awake until it was over. God and angels were with us again. Where we went in the ditch was a very, very short distance from a bridge. If this would have happened at the bridge, odds are Ruth and I could have been killed. What would we do now? Bob called 911! We would have to leave for home right now, or we would have to unload the horses. I had some time to think before the police came. My Uncle Cliff lived sixty miles away. They had an acreage, and maybe we could unload the horses there. When the police came and said he would call a wrecker and told us where they were going to take the pickup and the trailer, I called Cliff. He said he would meet us there. Cliff got there about the same time we got there. Cliff told us that he had a next-door neighbor that had horses and that he fenced the acreage on Cliff's land. Cliff said he called the neighbor, and he said that we could unload the horses. Ruth and I rode to Cliff's house with Cliff, and Bob and the girls followed with the horses. Cliff's neighbor volunteered to go and get the trailer and bring it to Cliff's house for us. All of us by now were dead tired. Ruth and I slept in an upstairs bedroom at Cliff's house, and Bob and the girls slept in the horse trailer.

Truck and trailer after accident

My plan was to go home early Saturday morning. After I bought a new pickup, I would have to come back to get the trailer. During breakfast, the girls wanted to stay another day or so. Both Cliff and Linda said we were welcome to stay. Ruth and I were still shaken up from the accident. There were some small fields that were harvested and some woods across the road from their house. Linda told the girls that she was sure that they could ride the horses there. Kayla and Timera rode their horses, and Sarah rode Bess. On Sunday, Linda got on the Internet to look for a pickup for me to buy. I bought my damaged pickup used, but I figured it would be easier and faster to now buy a brand-new pickup. I didn't want to buy a used pickup that I could have any trouble on the long trip. I wanted a one-ton four-by-four pickup with a regular cab and a Chevrolet like the one we had. Linda found a one-ton four-by-four regular cab at Bob Hook Chevrolet in Louisville, Kentucky.

Monday morning, I called them early. I talked to Brooks Phillips, a salesman. I told him I was from Minnesota. I told him about the accident that we had. I told him that I wanted to buy a new pickup over the phone. But I must feel that I got a fair deal. I need a fifth-wheel hitch in the box. He asked me about financing. I told him that I would pay cash. "I'm going to write you a check. I'll give you the name of my bank and the telephone number so you can check if the check is good." He said, "I don't need the name of your bank, I trust you." We agreed on $30,000. Next I called Ag Star in Rochester, the place we borrowed money to farm. I asked to talk to Nan Johnson, a secretary. I told her about the accident. "I am going to buy a new pickup for $30,000. I want you to wire or take the money to the bank in Dodge Center right away." Nan told me that she would to it. By now I had known Nan for twenty-five years.

We hooked up the stock trailer to Bob's pickup. I imagined after I paid for the pickup, they would have to put on the fifth-wheel hitch. It would be late when that was done. Ruth and I would stay in a motel, and we would meet at a rest place along the highway. Cliff came with us, and the girls stayed with Linda. When we got to the dealership, we had to wait a little. Then the salesman came in. I signed the papers and gave him a check. I asked him, "How long will it take to put the hitch on?" He answered, "It's ready to go." I couldn't believe that they installed the hitch on my word. I had no idea what my new pickup looked like. When I saw that it was white and that it was sharp-looking. I was happy with the pickup. Ruth and I followed Bob's pickup and trailer back to Cliff's house.

We all left early Tuesday morning for the wagon train. It was a little bit before six o'clock in the evening by the time we got to Tifton, Georgia. I called Wallace, and he gave me directions to find the wagon train. It would soon be dark when we pulled into camp. After we unloaded the horses, I went for water. The first man I saw was Jim Malone. I said to him, "You are the man that saved my life." We moved ahead in the morning the same as our wagon train. As I pulled in the parking spot, George Marten called out, "You have a nice new pickup. I like it." Wallace had told a lot of people about our accident. But they didn't feed us. There was a food truck that followed us. We could order food and pay for it. On the Minnesota wagon train, JD always lined up the Lions Club or churches to feed us. On the Georgia wagon train, most people cooked for themselves. We had to make sandwiches for ourselves at the noon stop. Sarah rode in the surrey with us. I think soon she wished she had a horse. All the kids had a ball on the wagon train. One day a man rode up to us and asked if Sarah would ride his horse, and he would ride in the surrey with us. My insurance company called me one day on my cell phone. They agreed that they would pay me $15,000 for my old pickup. It was a relief that I didn't have to do anything with the old pickup. As we were pulling into night camp, it was cold and almost dark. Around noon, it was seventy degrees. But it was cold in the morning and at night. There was a man, Slim, who rode a mule and rode with the kids. One night, the kids, including our girls, stole the mule from Slim. He went to every camper and asked where his mule was. He couldn't find the mule. The kids painted the whole mule different colors. We could only ride three days. It was way too short. The train ended at Calvary, Georgia. There was a big celebration that weekend. I felt comfortable when our girls were running around and playing with other kids on the wagon train. But there would be thousands of people here. I was responsible for Timera. They would not like spending all time with Ruth and me. Bob could go with them, but there were three on them. John and Eileen Campbell volunteered to keep the girls and look out for them. I wasn't comfortable. I knew that I would have to have a better plan on going home than I had going down to Georgia. We were going to my Uncle Lyle's in Milton, Florida. It was seventy-five miles always. We were told that it would be almost impossible to leave Saturday morning with the crowd that would be in Calvary. We would have trouble getting the trailers out through the crowds. We decided on leaving the wagon train on Friday night. The girls weren't happy. We were going to leave from Lyle's early Sunday morning and drive to Cliff's. We would stay the night there and come home Monday. When we got into camp, we packed up and left.

It was close to ten at night when we got to Lyle's. Lyle and Kathy's daughter Starlin and her husband, David, had a newer double wide home next to Lyle's house. David had two horses. He had two different pens for the horses. We unloaded our horses in one pen. Ruth and I slept in Lyle's house while Bob and the girls slept in the horse camper. The next morning, Bess had jumped out. She was by the horses, but she was on the outside of the pen looking in. There were several small gravel pits and small woods close by. David rode his horse there. After breakfast, Bob and I harnessed the team. Kayla and Timera saddled up the horses. David saddled his horse and went riding with us. It was fun for everyone, especially David. We had made David's day! We left for Cliff's early Sunday morning. When we got to Cliff's, we had fifteen extra bales of hay. We unloaded the hay in Cliff's neighbor's barn. We stayed with Cliff and Linda's Sunday night and got home Monday night. On the trip down to Georgia, we should have left a day earlier and stayed at Cliff's on the way down.

Tuesday, Bob and I went over to Brygelson's to pick their corn. We couldn't believe how much the corn dried in ten days. Lee thanked me for going on the wagon train instead of picking their corn. They had saved more in drying costs at the elevator then the trip cost us except for the new pickup. The month of November was a warm, clear month. There was more than enough time to finish the fall work.

It was now 2008. Sarah had a new friend from school, Belinda. It was the first of May when I met her. She was with Sarah and Kayla beside the horse stable. She had galloped the horse across the pastures without a saddle or a bridle. I thought that she was a really good rider. But it was her first time. When her adopted mother came over, she told me that I should not be afraid if Belinda got hurt. They had good insurance. I couldn't believe a mother telling me this. As time went on, I started to feel sorry for Belinda. She had lived in several foster homes before she was adopted. I never tried to learn anything about her past. I felt that it was none of my business. In the next years several times, Belinda would call me or Sarah and would ask me if Belinda could come and stay with us for a while. She didn't get along with her adopted family. Belinda even asked me if she could call me Grandpa. She told me, "I wish I could live with you." At one time, I considered trying to get custody of Belinda. She was always well behaved, and we never had any trouble with her. In the end, I didn't try to get custody of her. I knew that Ruth didn't think it was a good idea. I really didn't know how Kayla and Sarah would think about it in the long haul. Belinda came on the wagon train with us for several years. Rod Friedrich also came with me for several years. Rod always came to our farm to ride a horse ahead of time. JD's wife, Monica, always did registration. They met on the wagon train and got married on the wagon train. Their son, Dustin, came on the wagon train before he was born. The girls talked me into letting them clean out the back of the horse camping trailer and putting down bales and letting them sleep in the back of the horse trailer. I knew they would be playing around half of the night with the other kids on the wagon train. There were over 150 people at the wagon train at some time.

It was now 2009 and my fourth year on the wagon train. Paul Vickerman decided that we should do the trip backward. We started at Camp Winnebago. Camp Winnebago was the purpose of the wagon train. It was a camp for disabled children. The wagon train usually raised over $30,000 for the camp. I was a director of Southeast Mutual Insurance Company. I had a sign on my surrey advertising for the company. In turn, they donated $500 for the camp. Ruth went to all our local businesses seeking donations for the camp. Ruth was never a person to do this. All the money that the wagon train gave to the camp was used to pay for the campers to go to the camp. Some years Ruth got over $2,000. We were going to end up at the Austin Fairgrounds. Melba Wood was from Alabama. She was a really good country western singer. She played her guitar and sang almost every night. They had an auction on Tuesday nights to raise money for Camp Winnebago. I always looked everything over and decided what to buy. John Campbell had made a horse and colt standing next to a fence out of wood. It was fairly big. It was painted black. It would look great over the door on the end of our horse stable. I decided to buy it regardless what it cost. That was the most expensive item on the sale. Several people wanted the sign too. Everyone really clapped when the auctioneer said, "Sold." It has now hung on the end of the horse stable for over ten years. It looks like new! I always think of John and Eileen Campbell when I see the sign. Jacque Wennes took care of the porta-potties and the water tank on a truck. She moved to the next campsite after the wagons left in the morning. They sold a song on the auction written by Melba Wood (Al), Wallace Turner (GA), and Eileen Campbell (GA) "Queen of the Port-a-Potty."

John Campbell's sign hanging outside the horse stable

I'm only going to write the last chorus.

The Last Chorus:

She's the queen of the port-a-potty She rules the stinky kingdom A bowl brush is her septor The water truck is her throne
    As she goes from place to place Looking after her toilet seats She's the queen of the port-a-potty Exactly what we need!

The song was auctioned off for $65. It was sung by Karen Whitaker from Minnesota.

We always have a lot of fun on the wagon train. On Thursday, right before we came into camp, the rubber on one wheel started to came off. Ruth always brought the car along. She wanted to know that she could leave any morning or night. She never did. I took the car home and got a drill, cable, and clamps. I fixed the wheel long enough to make the last day. I decided that I would buy a covered wagon next year. JD and Wallace really worked on me to go on the Georgia wagon train. JD wanted my family to go with them. He had a super-long trailer. They were only going to ride horses. He would have room for the surrey and hay. They would exchange drivers, and we were only to take the horse camper trailer, and that way Bob and I could take turns driving. I took the wheel to the Amish to have it fixed.

I called Nan Johnson and told her we were going on the Georgia wagon train. I told her, "Be prepared for me to call you to wire money to the bank to pay for a pickup truck." She answered, "Call someone that is higher than me next time."

Kayla bought a horse from Timera. His name was Thor. He was nineteen hands tall. He walked like he was marching. It was kind of fun watching him. Timera wanted to go again so Sarah would not have a horse. The girls were in contact with Wallace. Wallace told the girls that he would have a horse for Sarah. I told JD that I would furnish all the hay. JD and Dustin came over for the hay the night before we left. Joleen Gundermann was going along. She was from Waseca. Joleen always led JD's wagon train. Bob, the girls, Ruth, and I knew her well. We left early the next morning. Bob and I took turns sleeping in the trailer. We all made it down to Tifton, Georgia, without any trouble. Wallace had a paint horse for Sarah when we arrived. They didn't have a food truck, so we had to cook some. They had a bus that took us to a restaurant most nights. JD, Monica, Dustin, and Joleen cooked most nights, so they didn't ride on the bus. Monica, Dustin, and Joleen rode horses, and JD rode in a wagon or a pickup with someone. The roads down there were all sand. They had kind of a pecking order. We always went last. Bess became lame from walking in the deep sand. Molly never did her share, but now it seemed like Molly knew that Bess was in trouble. She was pulling most of the surrey. I knew we would never make it if we were last. They had mostly mules, and the mules and wagons got the sand so lose. The sand was firm at first. The next morning, I tried to get at the beginning of the line. But they wouldn't let me in. Finally, when one wagon was trying to block me from entering the line, I really gave him hell. I was able to get in the line. Several people complained to Wallace. I overheard Wallace talking to the wagon drivers nearby, "The McColleys are friends of mine from Minnesota. Treat them better from now on." After that day, we never had trouble again. On the wagon train, we saw several fields with peanuts. They had dug them, and peanuts were in win rows. The fields were waiting to be combined. We also saw fields of cotton being picked. Georgia farming was a lot different from Minnesota farming. As soon as we got into Calvery, we all packed up and left. JD didn't want to stay for the celebration. The girls were unhappy that we were not staying for the celebration. They had so much fun on the wagon train.

In 2010, I talked JD into camping one night at our farm. We started out in Austin. Last year Paul Vickerman suggested that we start out at Camp Winnebago and made a large loop over a few years and ended up at Camp Winnebago. We ended at Austin in 2009.

How to Prepare First-timers for a Wagon Train (Written by Barb Bergert)
1. Drink a gallon of water before bed and walk a ½ mile in the morning_ before morning rituals_ so the Pee-Pee dance is perfected. If your walk is like an Alabama gaited mule, you've mastered it!
2. Drive in downtown rush hour traffic—roll your window down and put your arm out and holler WHOA!
3. Enter your truck and trailer in mud bog races.
4. When you're driving and someone flips you off, practice the "Bob Barker Beauties" hand wave.
5. On a 100-degree day, have your first cousin lock you in the outhouse for 20 seconds! (If you don't come out, he couldn't count that high—pick wisely)
6. Eat baked beans twice a day and sleep in your car with the windows rolled up for a week.
7. Take 4 piles of horse manure, put it in 6 inches of grass, run it over with your

4-wheeler a couple of times, then use your plastic road apple picker to pick it up.

If you have passed these few simple tests, you are good to go to hear the words… WAGONS HO!!!

Kayla rode her horse Thor. Sarah rode Cheyenne. Sarah had trouble right away in Austin. She wanted Bob to ride Cheyenne. When Bob got on Cheyenne, she reared up over and over again. People said, "You are really a good rider." Eva took a picture of Cheyenne standing on only one foot while Bob was riding her. When we stopped for a break, Bob unsaddled her. There was a burr under the saddle. How did that happen? Cheyenne was really good the rest of the wagon train. I never thought a horse could stand on one foot, but we have a picture to prove it.

Bob on Cheyenne

It was the first time that Doreen and her daughters, Jenna and Valerie, came on the wagon train. My grandson, Justin, also came.

We camped the first night at Brownsdale. In the morning, we left for Hayfield where we would have lunch. I'm going to copy something from the book that JD made up for us each year.

Sunday, June 20, 2010—Brownsdale to McColley Farm—18 miles

Woke to 61 degrees and partly cloudy skies. Move ahead to Wayne & Ruth McColley's farm went smoothly. Gene & Delores Distad led us out of Browndale—30 wagons, 39 riders. Rain moved in for a wet ride for awhile this morning. By the time we reached the nursing home in Hayfield for lunch, the sun was shining—and the temperature was rising! We were greeted at our lunch stop by many of the residents of the nursing home who were sitting under two canopies. The smiles on their faces were priceless as they watched horses and mules with buggies, covered wagons, and surreys pulling into the parking lot. Surely, it brought back memories to many of them. Lunch was served by the Hayfield Lions was enjoyed by all—residents and wagontrainers, alike. The temperature continued to rise as Wayne McColley's wagon led out of lunch for the afternoon journey to their farm. The cross county route was scenic. We could see the wind turbines getting closer and closer as we traveled toward camp. What is in the distance? A farm lining up equipment for an auction sale? ... Oh guess that is the evening camp! The trucks and trailers lined up in a single row all the way down the hayfield was a site to see! Wayne took us the cross-country route through field and waterway into the back side of the camp. We were all glad to get out of the sun and cool down a bit. Wayne invited anyone who wanted to tour the farm to feel free to do so. Roberta has arrived but hasn't had time to count the donations turned in yet...she'll give a report tomorrow. Evening meal was provided and served by the Dodge Center Lions. Hope no one is planning to lose weight this week—what a meal! Agstar treated us to root beer floats after dinner. Mmmm...they hit the spot! Pat Fuchs & Eva Bernard were the Jouralists. They wrote this part. Eva is Ruth's sister. Roberta Anderson is the Treasurer. She has always been the treasurer. The Distad's lived a few miles east of Hayfield. Agstar Financial Services is the bank that finances my farm. Darrel Ness is my banker and he served the root beer floats.

Wayne and Rod

    Bob had really cleaned up the shop. I bought enough tables so everyone could eat at the same time. For chairs I bought planks and we had cement blocks. My friend, Rod Friedrick, was going to help Darrel serve the root beer floats. Just before starting to serve the floats, Rod got a surprise of his life! His wife, Sandy, his daughter, son-in-law and his grandchildren all came. None of his family ever had an interest in wagon trains. Rod couldn't believe that they were here! Now he had an opportunity to show his family the wagon train and all the horses and mules. His family made the 2010 wagon train special for Rod. Joleen Gunderman and Bob climbed to the top of our grain leg. It's 80ft tall. Joleen took the pictures of the campers in our hayfield. She had five enlargements made and they sold them at the auction to raise money for Camp Winnebago. The pictures sold for $85.00 each. What a way to raise money! We had several other people come; neighbors and people from our church. My mother and my brother, Dallas, and his family came. What fun!! I ordered 12 dozen rolls from the bakery in Byron. I picked them up at five o'clock the next morning. I asked the Wise Guys from our church to serve breakfast. I would pay for the meal. Men that had never gone to Wise Guys before came to help serve the meal.

Camp

Monday, June 21, 2010—McColley farm to West Concord—18 miles

This morning is humid & cloudy, with a little breeze. Rigs pulled ahead on schedule, but road construction made for a delay in the drivers getting back on time, so the train left a little behind schedule. We should be able to make the time up on the road. Breakfast was served by the "Wise

Guys" of Faith Lutheran Church from Dodge Center. Mike Dengler led the day's ride to West Concord—31 wagons, 26 riders. The first mile of the ride we traveled past the field of wind turbines we'd been eyeing yesterday afternoon. We traveled through the edge of Dodge Center then past the Civil War recruitment station in Wasioja and on to the Wasioja Baptist Church for lunch. The meal was served by Kasson-Mantorville Lions—brats, beans, chips. Had our first excitement of the wagon train as lunch break started…a run-away horse and wagon. It ran into a vehicle, where the shaves broke and the wagon stopped, but the horse kept going. The horse was stopped and caught in a short time. No one was hurt, the horse was not injured, and the vehicle had minor damage. The wagon needs fixing, though, so they will pull out the rest of the day. The afternoon was cloudy, with a mid-afternoon shower. The road construction guys let us travel though their construction for the last two blocks in West Concord (sure beat taking a lengthy detour), so we arrived in camp at the old school a little earlier today. The kids took advantage of the swimming pool during the extra time before the evening meal, and showers were available in the pool house for those who just wanted to wash off the day's dirt and grime. The West Concord Community Club served Mexican cuisine for supper—excellent meal. **Total donations: $8,903**

It was my brother-in-law Nado Bernard that had the accident with the horse. Ruth didn't come along that day as she stayed at home to clean up after wagon train camp over at our farm. I called her to come up to Wasioja to help Nado. Eva went home for the day to do something. She always helped Nado with the horse. If Eva had been there, I'm sure there wouldn't have been an accident. Eva and Ruth's niece's son, Abram Pulkrabek, rode with Nado and Eva. He rode with us the rest of the day. We stopped at Herman Tranburg acreage by Northfield. In their yearly enactment of the James Gang Bank Robbery, Herman plays Frank James. On his acreage, he has constructed a western town. He even has a stagecoach. It was really fun to look at the buildings.

Awards Presented for Recognition of Efforts

- Gene & Delores Distad—provided wagons for our special campers to ride
- Mike Mueller—provided wagons for our special campers to ride
- Cindy Stalvey—loaned her horse to traffic personnel and others when needed
- Traffic control—Bob Edwards, Wallace Turner, John Michael Stalvey, Megan Funk, Dustin Davis, Gabrielle Millard, G. L. Stevenson, and Joleen Gurdermann
- Dave & Marlys Delzer—Ran the Peddler Wagon
- Angela Hegland—"Port-a-Potty Princess"
- Herman Transburg—bus driver, photographer, and host for lunch
- Hermann von Knobelsdorff—helped set up wagon train beforehand; provided wagon for special campers to ride; used his sheriff's vehicle to help with traffic control on the last day
- Roberta Anderson—treasurer
- Wayne & Ruth McColley—helped set up wagon train beforehand; host & hostess for overnight stop
- Dave Pagel—for his overwhelming help in setting up our stay in Cannon Falls
- Wagontrainer of the Year—Mike & Pat Fuchs helped set up wagon train beforehand; got us back on the road

after the rainstorm at their house; host & hostess for overnight stop

Jacque Wennes—received a special award "toilet seat" award for being our good-hearted "Port-a-Potty Queen"

Gifts to JD & Monica for all their efforts put forth in making the 2010 Friendship Wagon Train another fun, exciting, and successful year!

Quilt winner—Stephanie Turner (name drawn by her own daughter Josey…Hmmm)

The 2011 wagon train went from Goodhue to Rushford. There were 145 participants. They had a one-day layover in Wabasha. David Kaczmarek was building a building to unload grain into a pit for us. Bob and I went home for the day. Ruth, Doreen, all the girls and the horses stayed. Belinda didn't go with us this year. We never saw her much after this time. The last day, we were going to stop at the North Prairie Lutheran Church for lunch. That was the church where Ruth and I got married forty-three years ago. I really looked forward to that! Right before we got to the church, we had an accident. Russ and Darlene Wright drove a team of horses hitched to a 1912 Studebaker buggy. They both fell asleep right before they came to the church. The team left the rode, and the buggy tipped over. Russ and Darlene flew out. Luckily, they weren't hurt. Traffic personnel and others helped upright the buggy and got it back on the road. The buggy was bent some, but it was still drivable. Later Russ took the buggy down to the Amish to get it fixed.

The 2012 wagon train was different to me. The wagon train started out in Stewartville and went to Camp Winnebago by Caledonia. There were 148 participants. Bob didn't go this year, so we didn't have the semi with the sleeper. I had to pull the trailer with my white pickup. Rod Friedrich never came again. Wallace didn't come up from Georgia this year. Nado and Eva didn't drive a wagon. Nado rode on my wagon with me one afternoon. He even drove the horses a little bit. DeLores Distad and our Doreen Nelson were the journalists. We camped in Chatfield on the edge of town in a nice camp. Nado and Eva Bernard received a plaque for outstanding help in setting up and organizing the FWT's stay in the Chatfield area.

In 2013, there were 129 participants. The wagon train started in Dexter and ended up near Nodine on the Joe Ready Farm. Wallace was there again, but we didn't go this year. By now, Kayla had a job, and Sarah was going to college. Kayla sold Thor. The real reason we went on the wagon trains was for the girls. I would miss it. We all went to visit the wagon train one night. Eva and Nado and Dave and Marlys were the peddlers. Eva and Monica were the journalists. The wagon train started out with nineteen wagons and thirty-five riders.

In 2014, they were starting in Waseca at Farm America. Because of the place they were starting, I wanted to go. When my dad quit farming, he worked for Roy Luken. Roy donated this land to the state to start Farm America. I had worked on this farm when I was a teenager. Neither Kayla nor Sarah went. Kayla was now pregnant. Ruth, Doreen, Jenna, Valerie, and Justin went. We went in the early afternoon. Justin and I talked to an employee for Farm America. He told me that they had the A John Deere that Roy had. I had run this tractor. He invited us to go in a restricted building to look at the A. Just not being on the wagon train one year, I found there were so many people that we didn't know. A lot of the people we met at the first years had gotten too old or some had died. Bob, Kayla, and Sarah weren't there. The fun that we had was gone. There were once again 129 participants. On Saturday morning, there were eighteen wagons and several riders. As the week went on, there were more riders and a couple more wagons. A saddle horse got excited before we left. The rider fell off as he saddle slid under the horse's belly. It took the traffic people some time to stop the horse. The saddle was ruined. We felt that we were going on a real wagon train as we went through a minimum maintenance road. The rains that we had last week left the road still underwater. On the first break, JD fell off his wagon. He fell right on his nose. It looked terrible. We had lunch in Otisco at the church. My Uncle Duane and Aunt Barb came to visit the wagon train while we had lunch. We camped the first night in New Richland. We were going to have lunch in Hartland the next day. About two miles from Hartland, we went by the farms that my great-grandfather and his son, George, owned. My great-grandfather lives in Thor, Iowa. My grandfather, Edward Larson, farmed these farms in 1912 and 1913. It gave me a really good feeling to drive a team of horses and a wagon into the town of Hartland. Maybe my grandpa was driving a team into Hartland at the same time over a hundred years ago. What did Hartland look like then? That was something to dream about. I had known Michael Cunningham from the first. He rode a horse and at first did traffic control. His dad, Pete, drove a wagon with mules. There were in Georgia both times with us. Michael was driving this wagon this year with his dad, Pete, and his mother, Doris, in the back. His parents were in their upper eighties. Ruth and I visited with them a lot. They all wanted Ruth and me to visit them in Tennessee. Wallace was not here this year.

Fellow Wagontrainers,

As we prepare to close out the Friendship Wagon Train of 2014, a smile comes across my face as I think of the problems we had to endure. Not only did I have the opportunity to meet Mother Earth face-to-face if front of the Good Lord and the entire Friendship Wagon Train, I also had a good time.

I feel very fortunate that I have so many friends amongst this group of dedicated wagontrainers. This year was no different than any other year…we all had a good time, and Camp Winnebago received a good amount of donations to help with camperships. All I can say is "thanks again" and "keep up the good work."

Hope to see all of you again next year on the 2015 Friendship Wagon Train.

J.D.

It was not as much fun without Kayla, Sarah, and Bob. I didn't know how much longer Justin would come to help me. Maybe I could get another year out of him. He didn't like horses so much. Jenna and Valarie really enjoyed the wagon train. Maybe as they got older, they could help me. At this time, I didn't know it, but the wagon train was over for us. Ruth got run over by the horses and carriage in August. Just when she was getting over that, Ruth got breast cancer. At that time, I didn't realize the problems that were ahead. As I'm writing the end on this chapter, I can't believe the sadness that has come over me. Some really good friends have died: Jim Malone (the person that saved my life), Dave Hoenk, Paul Vickerman, Rolland Weis, Pete Cunningham, Hermann von Knobelsdorff, Dave Delzer, and others have died. Camp Winnebago is now closed. Bob sold his horse camping trailer in 2017 for $15,000. In the spring of 2019, Bess didn't shed her hair. Sarah tried to cut it off with a clipper. The clipper didn't cut off Bess's hair. I went to Fleet Farm and bought a clipper for $350. It come with a nice box. Finally, Bess's hair was off. On my birthday, December 21, Ruth and I decided to go to Trumblers Restaurant in Albert Lea in the afternoon. We were just pulling into the restaurant at four. My cell phone rang, and it was Bob. He said, "Bess is lying down and kicking her feet." I said, "Maybe you should call the vet." As we finished eating, Bob called back, "She has a twisted stomach. There is nothing that the vet can do." I said, "Tell the vet to put her down." I knew that Bess was in a lot of pain. I didn't want her to suffer. It would soon be dark, and I didn't want Bess to be lying in the cold in pain. It cost me $240 to put down a horse. As we got home, Bob was just finishing burying her with the backhoe. There was eight inches of frost. I felt guilty about the little time I spent with the horses after I had my stroke in 2016. The next morning, I went to the stable and spent a lot of time with the other horses. Bess was the youngest horse at twenty years old. Molly was the oldest horse at twenty-three years old. We still had Mercedes, Cheyenne, and Brandy. As I walked by the harnesses, I realized that we would never use them again. We would never pull the covered wagon, the surrey, or the carriage again. Right now, I think we have much more sadness in life than good times. Why did this have to happen on my birthday? Kayla now has two children—a girl, Jordyn, and a boy, Colten. They live in Kasson. Sarah still lives with Ruth and me on the farm. She takes care of the horses.

On March 18, 2020, Bob came in my office in the afternoon. He said, "Molly is dead." I never expected this. On Sunday, the eighth of March, I went down to the horse stable to see the horses. I greeted all the horses. I spent the most time with Molly. I opened the gate to Molly's stall and let her out. That was the first time since I had my stroke almost four years ago that I had opened the gate. Molly ran out! She appeared to be spry. I asked Bob, "Where did she die?" Bob answered, "She died on the dirt that was left over from burying Bess, next to Bess's grave." No one had any idea that Molly would die. She was now twenty-four years old. It was old but not terribly old. I started thinking, "How much can animals think?" She was Bess's mother. Ruth and I were Tammy's parents. That was a terrible time to go through to lose Tammy. We never got over Tammy's death. Maybe Molly never got over Bess's death. Maybe Molly died of a broken heart. The time when we went to the first Georgia Wagon Train, we ended up going to my Uncle Cliff's. Kayla and Timera went riding on their horses. Sarah rode Bess. Molly almost went crazy being separated from Bess. Whenever we were on a wagon train and Molly and Bess couldn't see each other, they went crazy. The vet put Bess down. But before the vet came, Sarah put the other horses in the stable. Bob buried Bess before the other horses were let out of the stable. Somehow Molly could sense Bess had died and where she was buried. Molly picked Bess's grave to die. This is a terrible time to put an end to some of the best times of my life.

Chapter 23

The Medium

WANAMINGO / PSYCHIC MEDIUM   Sat Oct 2 2010

Heather Allen, the Medium

In the winter of 2009, Ruth and I went to a meeting for Parents of Murdered Children. Lois, the monitor of the meeting, told everyone that she went to a meeting where a medium spoke. She wanted to know if she should invite Heather Allen, the medium, to our next meeting. Everyone at the meeting was curious as to what the medium would say about our deceased children. Everyone there agreed that we wanted to have Heather Allen come to the next meeting. At the next monthly meeting, the medium was there. Lois had a separate

A FATHER'S QUEST

room where she would meet privately with each couple. Ruth and I were the first couple to meet with her. The medium said she was able to communicate with Tammy. She described Tammy as a fairly tall, blond-headed young woman with long hair. Tammy said she was in a relationship that she couldn't get out of. She was really happy now. She was concerned for her brother. He had never dealt with her death. Tammy was happy that we were raising her children and that it was always meant to be. It was a short meeting because so many people were there. She gave us a card with her phone number so we could call her if we wanted to meet with her. At this point, I didn't know what to think. She could have found this information out, but Lois told us that she didn't tell the medium anything about us. But if she didn't have any information ahead of time, how was this even possible?

In the coming days, I thought about the medium most of the time. How could she communicate with the dead? I studied the Bible, particularly the book of Revelation. In a lot of places in the Bible, it is hard to understand, especially Revelation. As I was studying the Bible and the book of Revelation, I came across a verse that made sense to me.

> Now I saw a new heaven and a new earth, for the
> first heaven and the first earth had passed away.
> Also there was no more sea. (Revelation 21:1)

In several places in the Bible, God is going to make a new earth after the old earth passes away. If the heaven was away from the earth, why would God have to make a new heaven? If heaven and earth was at the same place, only in a different dimension, that would explain why a medium had the ability to cross over and to communicate with people from the other side. Mediums have always been on earth since the beginning of time or before the Bible was written. In Isaiah 8:19, it says,

> And when they say to you, seek those who are
> mediums and wizards, who whisper and mutter.

> Should not a people seek their God? Should they
> seek the dead on behalf of the living?

All that had really caused me to be confused.

I went to see Pastor Justin to talk about all these things. I told the pastor that I believed the earth and heaven were together only in a different dimension. I explained to Pastor Justin why I believed it to be true. Pastor Justin said he had just read in a book written by a Lutheran theoretician that said the same thing. We talked about mediums.

Pastor Justin said, "You have to be careful to put all your faith in mediums."

I asked Pastor Justin, "Should I go to see Heather Allen, the medium?"

He said to me, "I think you have enough belief in God that it would not be harmful to you." He wanted to know what Heather told me.

On April 10, 2009, Ruth and I went to visit Heather Allen, the medium. We had a three-thirty appointment in Wanamingo. We had no idea where her address was. We found her place at two thirty. We were way too early, and we decided to drive around a little. We got back to her house at three o'clock and went in. Ruth and I sat on a couch, and she sat on a chair to the right of us. I apologized for being so early. She said it was okay because these other people with us had arrived twenty minutes ago. Ruth and I were surprised that other people were with us. We couldn't see them. She said Tammy was there and that she was in a relationship that she just couldn't get out of. Heather Allen would roll her eyes to the back of her head and be silent for several minutes, and then she would say something. Then she asked us if we knew a Denise. Both Ruth and I said, "No." She asked us several times if we knew a Denise. While I'm writing this, over ten years later, I realize we actually knew Denise. She was a daughter of Ruth's cousin. Denise's sister was killed in an accident when she and her sister were children. I wish that we would have said that we knew Denise. I wonder what Heather would have told us if we would have said yes. Then she said Tammy was concerned about

Robert. She mentioned another name starting with *R*, but then it was Robert for sure. She said he had hard luck in relationships but that he was going to meet a girl with short blond hair. Then she said that Tammy had long blond hair, and we said, "Yes." She said, "Robert is a special person that deserves someone really special, and that is why it's taken so long."

She then asked, "Do you have any questions?"

I then asked, "Do we have any other relatives with Tammy?"

She said, "There is an older lady with auburn red hair. She's wearing wire-rimmed glasses and an apron. She likes to bake cookies." She then asked, "Do you know who she is?"

I looked to Ruth and said, "This is your mother." Ruth shook her head to agree.

She then said, "This lady has heart trouble, and she keeps putting her hand to her heart, she also has a lot of trouble with her feet."

Ruth and I both looked at each other and then said, "Grandma never had trouble with her feet."

Heather said, "She is rubbing her feet now."

I then said, "This part doesn't make any sense."

Heather was right, and Ruth and I were wrong. That evening, we called Ruth's sister Eva. Eva told us that in the last years, Grandma had a lot of trouble with her feet and that was why she had given up the job of being manager of the apartments where she lived.

Heather then said, "There is an older white-haired man with a small slim build with them. He doesn't say anything. It's like they are standing on steps with this man the highest, Tammy next, and then the lady standing below Tammy. Tammy and the lady are holding hands with a boy with brown hair and a small build. His name is… It starts with a *J*."

She then said, "John."

I said, "No."

She then said that it was a really short name.

I finally said, "Jim."

She then said that Jim wanted to tell us that he always wanted long hair, but no one else wanted him to have long hair. He wanted everyone to know that he now has real long hair. She then said there was another short man there with a mustache. Neither Ruth nor I could figure who that was. She then said all these people wanted us to know they were really happy. When Ruth told her sister Eva about Jim and his long hair, she told Ruth that Jim always wanted long hair, but they wouldn't let him have long hair. How did the medium know this? The order they were standing on the steps was the order that they died.

I then asked if Tammy was with us most of the time and was able to follow her daughters' lives? She said that Tammy was almost always with us and that she tucked the girls into bed every night. After they are asleep, she pulls the covers up a little bit. Soon afterward, we talked to the girls about this. Kayla told us that when it's dark in the room, she can see a shadow standing at the foot of the bed. I then asked Kayla, "Does this scare you?" Kayla then said, "No, it doesn't scare me. It gives me a comfortable feeling." Heather then said that Tammy was seeing things in both girls that they were taking after her. But right now Tammy was concerned about the youngest one because she was having trouble in school. Sarah was having trouble getting along with certain kids. Tammy also had this problem. Tammy said she played little tricks on us. Something about always tipping over something in the living room. Neither Ruth nor I could relate to this. Then Heather said Tammy was always doing something to the freezer door, always opening something. Ruth right away knew what she was talking about. On our refrigerator freezer, there was a door on the ice maker. Sometimes it was open. Ruth closed the door. A short time later, when Ruth went in the freezer, the door was open again. On a holiday dinner some time later, Ruth had a candle holder with Tammy's picture on it. Ruth lit the candle and put it on the center of the table. During the meal, Ruth opened up the freezer several times to get something out. The door was always opened. Ruth closed the door. The next time Ruth went into the freezer, the door was opened again. Was Tammy with us? Heather said that Tammy never did these things to the girls because she didn't want to scare the girls. I said to Heather, "I wished Tammy would do these things more often." Heather Allen got a mischievous look in her eye and said Tammy was excited that we would enjoy these things. She would surprise us.

I then asked if Tammy could tell us anything about her death. She said the days before and right after her death was like she had amnesia. She had no memory. Maybe God didn't want Tammy to remember her death. She said she didn't know how to get away from him. She thought she was sleeping at the exact time of her death. She didn't feel any pain. She was glad that he took the girls out of the house. Garry was out of control. She was trying to stand up for herself but wasn't able to. He was always so jealous; if she would talk to anyone, he would think she was having an affair. She didn't realize how dangerous he was. He would often try to strangle her. She was glad that the girls were not in contact with him now. She wanted us to tell the girls what happened to her. She didn't want her daughters to get into a relationship like she was in. She just couldn't get away. He had too much control over her. She always tried to see the best in people. She was way too trusting. I then asked, "Was Tammy at her funeral?" She said she was there with her faith guide. Everything was fuzzy. She had gone to sleep in one life and had just awakened in another life. Everything was so confusing. She saw all the people who were there, but that was about it.

I then said to Heather that I had read several books about psychics and I understood what faith guides were. I had never read a book about psychics until after we were in New Orleans and I had met the psychic there. He had gotten my interest up after he said that Garry would be dead or in jail in six months. "Is there a faith guide with Ruth and me in this room now?"

She said, "There is one with you, and there are two with Ruth."

I then asked, "Did Tammy choose to have such a short life?"

She said, "Tamm's life choice was to learn forgiveness and that she had accomplished everything she had set out to do. A lot of people on earth did mean things to her while she was on earth, and she had learned to forgive them and that she was really happy now."

That was the only time that Heather used the name Tamm. I never called Tammy "Tamm" to her or anyone else. Ruth called Tammy "Tamm" all the time. But Ruth never said Tamm to Heather. Why did Heather say Tamm now? She then said that Tammy was really happy that we were raising her daughters.

I then said, "I really feel guilty sometimes. I really like the life that I have with Kayla and Sarah and if Tammy hadn't died, I wouldn't have this life now."

She said, "You shouldn't feel guilty. It was always meant to be that you would raise Tammy's daughters."

I then said to Heather, "I feel that my life's purpose was to learn responsibility."

Her face got a big smile and said, "Your faith guide is shaking his head yes." Heather then said, "You have a big responsibility raising two families."

I then said, "You also told me that you are also a psychic, and I have a couple questions along that line. I have run for county commissioner three times, and I have lost. Do I have any political future, or should I just give up on this? I have a feeling that there's more that I'm meant to do."

Heather then rolled her eyes and acted if Tammy was talking to her. "Tammy is saying something about getting a job without an election. You are on the town board."

I said I was on the town board, but I had just gotten off.

She said, "Tammy was saying that you are good on boards, people listen to you and respect you." Then she said, I think you are meant for a much bigger and more important job."

I think my most important job was taking care of Ruth when she had cancer in 2015. Maybe I was to write a book also.

"Will I ever have a daughter-in-law and more grandchildren? I have only one son, Robert."

She said that Robert was going to meet a girl with short blond hair. "You are going to have five grandchildren."

I said, "We have ten grandchildren already."

She then backtracked a little and said the girl that Robert was going to marry and that she would bring one child into the marriage and that they would have two more and Tammy's girls were the other two, making five. She was wrong, but maybe not. Bob married a blond, but she had long hair. She had two grown-up daughters. Her oldest daughter had a boy in 2018. Bob takes his grandson everywhere with him, including the tractor and semi.

Heather then said, "You have a big house. Do you do your laundry in the basement?"

Both Ruth and I said that we had a big house but we did not do the laundry in the basement.

She said, "Someone is doing their laundry in the basement, and Tammy is making the lights flicker when that someone is doing their laundry." Well, she was right. Our daughter Doreen had a big house, and she did the laundry in the basement. The lights were always flickering. Doreen called an electrician. The electrician could not find anything wrong. After checking the lights twice, he replaced all the bulbs in the basement.

Heather then asked, "Did you go on a train on a family vacation?"

I answered, "We took Tammy and our other children when they were young."

She then said, "It had a black engine, but part of the train was red. You took the girls on the same train some years later."

We were really surprised that she knew that. Tammy was telling her. Both Ruth and I said that the train was in the Black Hills. It was an 1880 train.

It's now five o'clock, a half hour past our ending time. I asked her if I owe her any extra money for staying late. She said, "No." So I wrote her a check with some extra money for coming early and staying late and then left. What were we to think about what she said? I was taking notes throughout the visit we had. As soon as we got home, I wrote down everything we had talked about so I would not forget anything as time went by. We saw her several times in the future. Both Ruth and I had more questions. I took notes every time we went, but the notes became less and less. I wish now that I would have written everything down.

The next time we went to see Heather, she talked about the medicine cabinet doors in our bedroom bathroom. There are three doors. There is a touch latch on the doors. You touch the door, and it opens just a little. I had been noticing lately that the doors were opened just a little. I asked Ruth if she was opening the door.

Ruth said, "No."

No one else ever goes in our bathroom. Who's opening the doors? Heather told us that Tammy was doing it. If the right one was open, she was telling me that she agreed with me. If the left one was open, she was telling me that she disagreed with me. Tammy hardly ever opened the middle door. Heather then told me that I had trouble with the radio in the field yesterday. I told Heather that the radio was all static. It didn't work. She said that Tammy was doing it. "In your car, all of a sudden, the radio changed stations by itself."

I agreed with Heather that it happened often. She told me that Tammy was doing it.

She said, "Tomorrow you better pay attention. Tammy is going to do something."

I had a self-propelled sprayer. I filled it with water and chemicals and left the yard for the field. I had the radio tuned to music. It was a song by Tom T. Hall called "Old Dogs and Children and Watermelon Wine." It started out, "I just turned sixty-five some months ago." I was sixty-five years old. Then the radio changed to static. When the song came to the part "I just turned sixty-five some months ago," the radio was clear, and then it changed to just static. That went on through the whole tune. The next song was "El Paso" by Marty Robbins. It was my favorite song. The whole song was clear. When the song was over, the station changed to all static. In a while, I turned the radio off. Sometime later, I was riding with Bob in his pickup. The radio changed stations by itself.

I asked Bob, "How often does this happen?"

Bob said, "That hasn't ever happened before."

When Kayla turned eighteen, she wanted to go to a casino and stay overnight with her ex-stepmother, Wendy. I forbade Kayla to stay overnight. We got into a serious argument. Wendy, at one time, had an addiction to gambling. I didn't want Kayla to get addicted to gambling. The next morning, when I got up, the medicine cabinet's right and the middle doors were wide open. Tammy agreed with me. How long would it take for Kayla to forgive me? In a couple of days, Kayla came to me and said she went to the casino with Bob on her birthday. They stayed for two hours. She thanked me for making the right decision.

We were having the annual picnic for the Austin Companion Friends in August 2010. At the previous meeting, I asked everyone, "Do you want me to invite the medium to our picnic?" They all agreed. By now we had quit going to the Rochester group. I called the leader of the Rochester group and invited everyone to come. We had just finished off our garage. We decided to meet in the garage instead at the shop where we usually had the picnic. That way, Heather Allen could meet with the people in our south sunroom. Ruth and I couldn't believe how many people that were here. A lot of people we didn't know. We never saw them again. Heather brought here son along with her. Justin was here, so he played with her son all day. Heather started to meet with people before noon. She met with the last couple at six o'clock in the evening. At first, the people couldn't believe all the things that Heather told them about their deceased children. Toward the end, it was not so accurate. Heather had to be getting really tired trying to communicate with so many spirits.

One time when we went, Heather said that Tammy wanted to thank us for letting Sarah get a small brown dog. We were making a lot of points with Tammy. How did Heather know about the dog? We told her that we were soon going on vacation. She said that Tammy was going with us. We would know that she was with us. On the morning that we left, we stopped at the car wash in Dodge Center. When we were going through the car wash, all of a sudden the back window went down. Water came into the car. I'm positive that neither Ruth nor I did it. Neither Ruth's hands nor my hands were even close to the doors. The only way we could think that Tammy must have opened the window.

On September 19, 2014, we went to see Heather. She said that there were three relatives with us. Tammy and my mother and another gentleman. He was about five feet, ten inches. He was thin and had black hair. He sometimes had a mustache. At one time he was a smoker. He was 4F and didn't go in the war. I said he was my Uncle Stanley. He was my mother's brother. Mom wanted to thank us for taking care of her during the last part of her life. She said when she was with us, she couldn't turn on the TV. Now she can do it. Ruth had been giving me hell for not shutting off the TV when I went to bed. Heather said my mother was making the small scooter cars play a tune. Sometime ago, in 2012, on a Sunday afternoon, we were in the south room where mom slept while she was with us. The scooter cars were there. Our younger grandchildren rode them while they were with us. At two in the afternoon, Ruth got off her chair and was leaving the room when she got in the exact spot the scooter car played a tune. It happened often when Ruth got in the exact spot. We couldn't figure out why the scooter car played a tune when Ruth was in the same spot. The scooter car was left in difference places in the room from time to time. When my sister Sandy was sick in the hospital, the tunes stopped. When Sandy got home, the tunes from the scooter car started again. But Ruth had to be in the exact place. When Sandy died, the scooter car never played a tune again. Tammy told me she changed the station on the radio. She didn't like my station.

    I took Ruth to see Heather in the summer of 2015. Ruth was in a wheelchair. Heather said Tammy was there alone. When it got time for Ruth to die, Tammy was going to come for her. Ruth would see Tammy right before she died. It was an upsetting visit with Heather. Was this terrible news, or was it good news? In a way, it would be comforting knowing that Tammy was coming for Ruth. Heather didn't tell Ruth when Tammy was coming. By 2016, Ruth was walking again. Sometimes my radio still changes stations but not so often. Once in a while, the medicine doors are open but not so often now. We have never been back to the medium again. Almost everybody has strange things happen sometimes. Why is it? I still go to church and worship God almost every Sunday. I don't worship a medium. But the medium has made me believe in God more. I definitely know where I am going when I die. I have no fear of death. It would really be fun to open the windows of cars while they were going through the carwash. I still have some things to do. When things get much harder for me, I look forward to death. I also hope it is years and years away. On this part of the book, I would put my hand on the Bible and swear to God that everything is true to the best of my ability.

Chapter 24

Life after We Got Custody of the Girls

In 2005, I took everyone in my family up north fishing. We went to Finn and Feather. We rented the newer four-bedroom cabin that we had in other years. Doreen and Allan and Jenna and Valerie had one bedroom. I think Jenna slept with Kayla and Sarah in one bedroom. Valerie was a baby. Brenda and Owen had one bedroom. Owen's girls—Samantha, Morgan, and Haley—had one bedroom. We rented a second two-bedroom cabin where Bob, Justin, Ruth, and I slept. I rented a nice boat with a windshield. We took turns fishing from the boat. The boat was also big enough to pull tubes in the water. They also had a nice swimming pool by the lodge. I hope everyone looks back on the trip and thinks it was fun. I paid for everything.

I wanted to have the girls to have an experience with a horse camp. I knew that the girls had gone to camp before. I had to find a way better camp than the one they attended in the past. I found a camp on the Internet. It was called West Wind Stables and was run by Martin and Shari Thomas. It was for girls between the ages of eleven and thirteen. Kayla and Sarah went in 2004. They stayed together in a bunkhouse with other girls. They were assigned a horse that they would have for the week. They had to take care of the horse, and they got riding lessons. Bob, Ruth, and I took the girls to the camp and picked them up after the end of the week. They had a big ceremony at the end of the week. It was fun, and they wanted to go back next year. So in 2005, they went again. Kayla was too old to go in 2006. Sarah didn't want to go alone. They offered Kayla a job as being counselor for the younger girls. It was an excellent opportunity for Kayla. The only catch was, she would have to stay the whole summer. Kayla didn't want to lose out on the other things we were doing. I would have to plan something that was better.

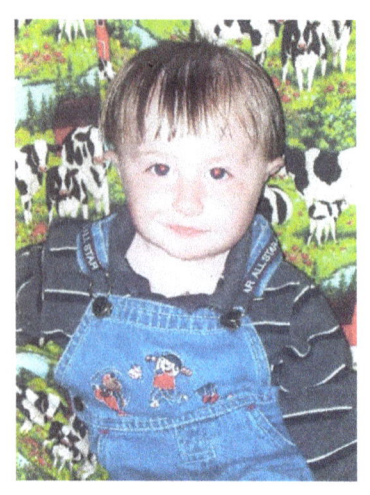

Braeden Harold, Brenda and Owen's son

Owen took Brenda to the hospital at 6:30 AM on Tuesday, July 5, 2005. The due date was on the Fourth of July. Brenda was induced to go into labor. Nothing happened, and they decided to break her water at 6:00 PM. Braeden was born at 10:45 PM.

In 2006, we decided to make a big change to our house. Because of all the work, I decided not to buy pigs back right away after we sold the pigs in the spring. The carpenter that had helped me for several years, Lee Loppnow, had suggested that we put the kitchen in the dining room. We would take out the wall between the kitchen and the dining room, making it all one big room. The way it was now, everyone came into the house through the kitchen. Ruth didn't like people standing in the kitchen. After we were done, everyone would enter the house through the dining room. I made a new set of kitchen cabinets with fancy doors in the shop during the winter. I also hired a neighbor boy, Ricky Flint, to help us. Ricky helped me for several years. He always slept in our house when we went on vacations. I didn't feel comfortable leaving the farm alone. The plan was to take off the roof over the kitchen. We would have a fourteen-foot ceiling. One morning when we were starting on the dormer, Ricky said, "Today, I think I'm going to be the boss." I thought it was funny, but Lee didn't think so. Lee didn't want to work with Ricky anymore. When Bob or I had other things we had to do on the farm, I thought Ricky could help Lee. We finished the roof and got part of it shingled. We got the new cabinets installed. We got the counter tops installed, and Lee put in the sink and did the plumbing. Ruth could use her new kitchen. We got the old cabinets out by July 3.

On July 4, while Lee was walking across his yard, he passed out. An ambulance was called, and Lee went to the hospital. The doctors determined that Lee would have to get a pacemaker. He couldn't do anything for at least six months. I was really glad I didn't have pigs now. We were going to go to the dude ranch in August. How would I get everything done now?

Kayla and Sarah had two girls that were in their grades in school. They lived in the country and had two horses. Their dad shingled houses and barns. These girls were at our place often playing with Kayla and Sarah. They wanted Sapphire and Ginger. Kayla and Sarah both said I should sell the colts to them. I got a price from their dad to finish shingling the house. He said his bid was $800. I traded the colts for shingling the house.

Aerial picture of the house

South view of the house

I dreaded taking down the ceiling on our old kitchen. There was 120 years of dirt that was going to come down when we started to pull the ceiling down. Would it take all day? We got the trailer next to the porch to put everything in. I started to pull something down when Ricky said, "I'll go in the attic and kick everything down." I thought a while and then said, "Be careful that you don't get hurt."

Ricky went up and started kicking. I started carrying everything out with a shovel. In an hour, we were completely finished. We never got any dirt down our necks. Why did I worry for days about how bad a job it was taking down the ceiling? Then we had to frame everything in and insulate the room. I decided to hire someone to do the Sheetrocking. Curt Miner suggested a man. I hired him and got him to promise that they would be done when we came home from the dude ranch. When we got home, they were not done. There was white dirt everywhere. We got home late, and Ruth spent half of the night cleaning up the dirt. He did a very poor job. When I questioned him about the job, he had me go in the south room that I had built. He pointed out two places where it wasn't perfect. I told him, "I'm an amateur, and you are a professional, and my job is better than yours." I had him work for days, but it was a terrible job. Then I made a mistake having the rooms wallpapered. Dennis Vang did the wallpapering. He picked the paper on the kitchen side, and I picked the paper on the dining room side. The paper on the kitchen side was very expensive. I figured I could save some money on the dining room side. The dining room took twice as much paper as the kitchen side. Now fourteen years later, the kitchen side is perfect. The dining room side needs to be papered again. I should have listened to Dennis. Next, I installed a solid oak prefinished floor with Ricky's help. We put on siding when we built the bedroom addition in 1998 and the south room in 2003, but we didn't paint it. Lee had put steel soffits on the eaves. What we had done to the house really looked good, but the outside of the house didn't look good. I was sixty-two years old now. My knees were shot from working with the pigs. If I didn't buy pigs back, I would have enough money to completely reside the whole house with vinyl siding. We wouldn't have to paint again. The more I thought about this, I thought maybe it was finally time to quit raising pigs. I hired Darrel Roe, a member from our church, to reside the house. It turned out good, and the house appeared to be new. By now, we spent $37,831 on the house this year. I didn't borrow any money to do it. Ruth was really happy with her new kitchen.

Ruth's new kitchen

    Not having pigs, we didn't need the barn nor the granary. I didn't want to leave the opportunity to ever starting to raise pigs again. Curt Miner was the fire chief at the fire department in Hayfield. I talked him into burning the barn down. It would be a training exercise. I wanted him to burn down the granary too, but he wouldn't. I finally talked him into having a cat pushing the granary next to the barn. The day that the fire department burned down the barn, we had several people come to watch. The first water truck went past our farm and went in the ditch trying to turn around. Bob had to take a tractor and pull the truck out. At first, several people and I stood between the old shop and machine shed to watch. All of a sudden, it got so hot that we moved to the porch. Then the fire got so hot that the firemen started to put water on the old shop and machine shed. All of a sudden, they were concerned that the whole farmstead was going to burn. After a scary twenty minutes, they finally had the fire under control. Curt Miner told me that they would never burn a barn again. They had set a large pool up in the yard. The water trucks dumped water into the pool. The fire trucks that had hoses sucked water out of the pool. After the fire was out, all the firemen threw the man that ran into the ditch into the pool. Ruth and I had lunch for everyone when they finished.

Burning of the barn

After we buried the barn foundation and pit, Bob decided to build a new shed where the barn was. He hired Dave Kaczmarek to build the shed. It was sixty by eighty feet with eaves and two cupolas on the roof. It was seventeen feet tall and had a twenty-four-by-fifteen-foot roll-up door at the front. It also had a smaller roll-up door at the side of the shed. It also had three large windows. At first, we were going to use the shed as a riding arena. Bob and I knew that after the girls were grown up, it would be a machine shed.

Bob bought an eighty-acre farm from Harlan Bryngelson with Lee and Jim Bryngelson's help. Harlan lived in Springfield, Missouri. We agreed with Harlan that we would go to Branson and he would meet us there. We stayed at the Quality Inn. Ruth, the girls, and I went with Bob. Quality Inn offered us a room where we could close the deal on the farm. They also offered a secretary to make copies of everything.

Early in 2007, a lady from Wells Fargo bank called me. She told me to take the funds for Kayla and Sarah and move it to another bank. She said that Wells Fargo had really raised their fees. The fees that they were now charging was way more than the funds were making from investments. I hired a lawyer, Daniel Ziebell from Kasson. He said it would be impossible to do anything with the funds without Garry's permission. Garry was in a prison at Moose Lake. It was close to Duluth. Ruth and I figured it would be a waste of time to go and see Garry and ask his permission to invest the funds somewhere else. But we felt we had to try. We always enjoyed Duluth. We would spend two days in Duluth and go to the prison on the way home. We went right after we finished planting. As we approached the prison, we could see a tall fence with wounded up barbed wire at the top. The prison looked really secure. I didn't want to be there. It was a gloomy place. A guard escorted us into a big room. There were several tables, and there were people visiting prisoners. Garry was sitting at one table. When I asked him about the money, He said, "You trying to steal the money away from me and the girls." That was what he did to the girls' money. He always spent the money that the girls got from Social Security. He thought that everyone was going to do as he had done. I took it as an insult.

"I never stole anything from you or the girls."

We got up and left. I never took any money from the girls. The little money that I spent was directly for the girls. I didn't take no money for raising them. I got a lot of satisfaction seeing Garry in prison. Both girls got $35,000 each. By 2007, it was worth considerably more. When they got the money in 2013 and in 2014, they only got $35,000. Wells Fargo had this money for seventeen years, and they made no return. The money that was donated to the girls at Tammy's funeral had doubled by this time. Garry was worried about my stealing the money when Wells Fargo was actually stealing the money. The girls really suffered from Garry's decision. They should have had $70,000 each.

When Sunday school was starting in the fall of 2007, some of the people that were in charge of Sunday school wanted me to bring my team of horses and the white carriage into the church lot and give the children rides. Pastor Justin was going to hold the services in the east parking lot. I parked the team and the carriage right outside of the parking lot, right behind of where Pastor J. was preaching. About halfway through the sermon, the horses became tough to control. I decided to drive them around the block. After the services were over, I told Pastor J., "The horses got bored and wanted to leave." We both had a laugh. When I gave the kids rides, I had only one rule: "An adult must ride with the kids for safety reasons." After the first ride, one girl asked me, "Do I have to get out? I want another ride."

In 2007, the Dragsten Farm was for sale. Palmer Dragsten had died by now. Palmer's widow and his children wanted to sell the farm by now. I had always rented the farm from Hoysler Real Estate. Farryl

A FATHER'S QUEST

Kluest was the person I always dealt with on renting the farm. Farryl gave me a price on the farm: $575,000. I thought the price was fair. Bob and I were going to buy the farm together. I told Bob we would pay the full price. But when Bob and I went to sign the papers, the family wanted $645,000. Why did Farryl give me the price on the farm before having Palmer's family put it in writing? I didn't feel this was fair. Finally, I offered $600,000. Palmer's family felt guilty about what had happened. They finally agreed to accept our offer.

Ruth, Bob, and I were working on taking corn out of a bin. The sump was plugged up. The bin was over half full. Bob went up and opened the top of the bin. I took up a twenty-foot rod. I was poking the rod down, trying to unplug the sump. The unload auger was running, and there was a tractor running. The PTO from the tractor was running an auger, taking the corn into a wagon. But there was no corn running. Ruth was by the tractor. Bob was in the bin with me. We were poking the rod with no luck. Bob decided to go out of the bin. All of a sudden, the corn started to run. I wasn't concerned at first. All of a sudden, I started to go down with the corn. I tried to get out, but the more I tried, the faster I went down. I hollered to Bob and Ruth, "Help, help, help!" There was so much noise; no one could hear me. The corn was now up to my chest; in seconds it would be over my head. I never had time to be scared. It was the end of my life. I think an angel was at work. Ruth shut off the auger just in time. My hands were above the corn. As Bob entered the bin, I had managed to dig myself out of the corn. It took several days for my legs to quit hurting from the pressure of the corn. The first two bins that we built had tunnel ventilation. They hardly put any rerod in the floor. The floor was badly cracked. This allowed corn to seep out of the bin and rats to get in. This situation caused the sumps to pug. The new bins that we had built had loads of rerod in the floor. A foot above the floor, we had another full floor for ventilation built out of steel. We never had any problem with the sumps plugging. I came close to losing my life over this problem. I had done this many times before with no problem. But maybe it was going to be Bob next time. In the early spring of 2008, we had the bins moved alongside of Bob's new machine shed. We hired someone to remove the old cement, put in fill, and pour new cement. We then moved the bins unto the new cement. We put in the augers and power sweeps and new ventilation floors. We never had this problem again. Why didn't we do this years ago?

Corn bins

We decided to build a hay shed in 2008. For four years, we stacked the bales in a machine shed. It was a lot of work throwing the bales up. I figured that if we built a shed and put a door at the top of the shed, we could use a bale elevator to unload the bales. That way it would be easier to just move the bales of hay away. We wouldn't have to throw the bales up. There wasn't room to build it close to the stable. We built it right south of the machine shed or horse arena. We always used the John Deere Gators to haul the hay to the stable. So it didn't matter where the hay shed was.

On May 28, 2008, Brenda and Owen were at our farm. Brenda's water broke, and Owen took her to the hospital. It was way too early for the baby to be born. Brenda would have to stay in the hospital for six weeks. On June 9, Owen asked Ruth to come over to watch the kids as he was going to the hospital alone to visit Brenda. Ruth went to their farm at six in the morning. I went outside at the same time to start my day. The weather was really calm. Way off the sky to the southwest was really black. My first thought was, "It's really going to storm." First, I went to put the horses in the stable. I knew that Bob was going to do something to the 4430. I opened the shop door and drove the tractor in. Normally, I would have left the door opened for the day. But as I looked to the sky, it was getting blacker and blacker. Rain wouldn't matter. But now the wind was coming up. I decided to close the door. There was nothing I could do outside in the rain, so I decided to go up and sit on the porch and watch it rain. It was still early and Bob hadn't got up. Soon the wind was really blowing, and the sky got completely black. Sitting on the porch, I couldn't even see the porch railings. It seemed like the wind was eighty miles an hour. I could really hear the wind roaring like a freight train. Then it started to get light, and wind became calm. As I looked across the yard toward the hog house, I could see an auger blown over. We had left it in the lowest position. How did the auger blow over? Bob was now up, and we decided to go out and look. As we got down to the bin site, we could see a thirty-thousand-bushel bin lying on the ground. There were about five hundred bushels of corn on the ground. We had five augers, and they had all blown over. We had two tractors sitting on each side of the bin that had blown over. The bin was sitting within four inches of each tractor. One was on each side of the blown over bin. There was no damage to the tractors. Bob had a taller bin setting east of the bin that had blown over. At the top on this bin was a big dent next to the eave. The wind had thrown the bin up into Bob's bin. Bob and I next walked around the house. A large limb off a tree had landed on the roof. We found out from a neighbor to the southwest that an object in their yard was on the west side of their garage, and now it was on the east side of the garage. A straight line wind couldn't do this. A straight line wind couldn't throw a big bin up into another bin. The weather service didn't say there was a tornado, but I'm certain that we had a tornado. I called Ruth and told her about the damage that we got in the storm.

At this same time, Owen was visiting Brenda in the hospital. A nurse came in to find a heartbeat of the baby. She couldn't find one. At the same time, Brenda told the nurse that she had to go to the bathroom. The nurse told Brenda, "Go to the bathroom, I'm going to check on another patient, and then I'll be right back." Brenda went in and sat on the toilet. She could feel something. She put her hand down there and could feel the baby's head. As she got up from the toilet and started to leave the bathroom, she was holding the baby's head. She told Owen, "The baby is coming." Owen hollowed at the top of his lungs, "We need help now." When he got to Brenda, the baby fell out, and Owen caught the baby. All of a sudden, fifteen people were in the room. They really needed help! The reason the nurse couldn't find a heartbeat was because the baby was already in the birth cannel. The baby was a boy, and he weighed two pounds and seven ounces. They put the baby in an intensive care unit for babies. He probably would be in the hospital until his due date. The baby got out of the hospital on September 6, 2008. The baby now weighed seven pounds. They named the baby Emery. Owen wanted to see Dallas's book. He would find a name from the book. Emery was my Great-grandfather McColley's name.

Emery Lincoln, Brenda and Owen's son

Dick Swanson came out from North Star to adjust the claim. I knew Dick. I didn't have enough insurance on the bin to pay for a new bin. I had the bin insured for $30,000. The new bin costs me, $40,000. It was a lot of work to take a bin apart on the ground. Bob owned the taller bin. Bob got about $2,500 to replace the two sheets that were damaged. Bob decided against repairing the bin. He got the money, and the dent would serve as a reminder of the storm. Dick went up on the roof of our house. He gave me an estimate. I hired Lee Loppnow to repair the house. He did the repair for about 30 percent of the estimate. They paid me for the five augers.

Harvesttime would come faster than we wanted it to come. Bob and I had a lot of decisions to make. What would we do? After a lot of thinking, we decided to build a grain leg. We wouldn't have to use augers anymore. Hyland Grain Systems built two bins for us in 2000. One of these bins was destroyed by the tornado. We got a bid for the leg. It was eighty feet tall, and it was capable to move five thousand bushels an hour. Eighty thousand dollars was their bid. I thought it was too high, but if we were going to use it in the fall, I didn't have time to shop. They had the leg on hand. I really wanted a 7,500-bushel-per-hour leg, but I would have to settle for this leg. We had Hyland build the new bin and grain leg. They used a section of the auger that we had going to the wet bin to take the grain to the leg. This was temporary. Bob paid for half of the leg. Between the two of us, we paid cash for the project.

Owen called Ruth one morning at the end of June. "The baby is dying, come over and watch the kids. I'm going to the hospital." Ruth told me, and I decided to go along with Ruth. When we got to Owen's farm, we could tell that Owen had finished milking and had just chased the cows across the road to the pasture. Owen was sitting on a pail beside the road. He had his head in his hands. I told Owen, "I will take you to the hospital. The shape you are in, it's not safe for you to drive." That was a really scary day for everyone, especially Brenda and Owen. But in the end, prayer was answered. A guardian angel was with Emery. The next day, the danger was gone.

Our church had a benefit for Emery. I took the team of horses with the white carriage to the church to give everyone rides. It again took an hour and fifteen minutes to drive the team into town. It took forty-five minutes to go home.

In 2009, the church built on a big addition. Gary Norstad approached me and asked me to pay for a stained glass window over the altar. I agreed that Bob and I would pay for it. Gary was on the church counsel, and they selected a committee to work on the window. After the window was installed, I got up in front of the church and made a speech. I wrote a speech on my computer and saved it. I learned the speech by memory and never looked at it when I was giving the speech. My mother and several of my family came to hear me give this speech. I am going to copy the speech.

Our family is donating this stained glass window in memory of our mother, sister, and our daughter Tammy.

Stained glass window at church

A FATHER'S QUEST

We have a selfish reason for doing this. After Tammy's death, Ruth and I joined a couple of support groups for parents who have lost their children. An overwhelming common theme was that everyone was afraid their child would be forgotten. Our church has changed greatly since Tammy died. Some of you remember her, but many of you do not. It is our hope that when you come to church and look up at the window that you will remember her.

Tammy was born on May 5, 1969. She was baptized at Gloria Dei Lutheran Church in Rochester. She was confirmed in this church by Pastor Nelson. She died a mysterious and questionable death in a house fire on January 5, 1997 at the age of 27. Her funeral was at this church.

Tammy at Confirmation

We don't want to portray her as a saint. She had her faults, just as I do, and most of you do as well. The thing I remember most about her and admire the most was her compassion for people. As a child she had a dream of being a nurse. School was hard for her, especially science. After high school she went to Vocational School and became a nursing assistant. She worked at Fairview Nursing Home. Sometimes I would want to talk to her alone and would go to the nursing home at the end of her shift. The rest of the employees would all come out at the end of the shift. Sometimes Tammy would come out a half hour later. She was busy taking care of a patient or just visiting with a patient. They were more important to her than getting off from work. On her days off she would take her young daughters to the nursing home to visit with the patients. Kayla and Sarah were three and four years old when she died. I'll never understand why she had to die so young.

I want to especially thank Gary Norstad for helping me research where to get the window and the design and going with us to the building committee to get their approval for the window. Someone on the committee had decided to have the cross put in the window and we wanted to highlight it. We especially didn't want to take anything away from it.

When Mike and Stephanie came to the church to measure the window they said they could put something in the window which would have a special meaning to Tammy. We said that Tammy's daughters, Kayla and Sarah, were the most important things to her. She was a really devoted mother and it really showed when she was with her two girls. Stephanie said they would put Kayla and Sarah's names in the window. No one would see them but we would where they were. She then asked if we would like Tammy's name in the window. We said that it would be really nice. She said that we would need one more name to make it work. I picked the name Jesus. They are in the circle of the small yellow round circles around the cross. Tammy, Jesus, Kayla and Sarah. Mike told us that it's common for stain glass windows in real old churches to have messages written in the windows.

I would like to thank Charlene Louks, Carol Johnson, Gary and Mary Norstad, my wife Ruth, and my son Bob for going to the

Rochester Stained Glass shop to help pick out the design and colors. And a special thanks to Bob for helping me pay for it.

And a special thanks to you the congregation for allowing us to do this. Thank You!

Kayla graduated from high school in 2010. I decided to finish off the garage where we would have Kayla graduation party. I had Lee Loppnow help me. We put up Sheetrock, taped it, and painted everything white. I put on a paneling that looked like tile on the bottom three feet. We set up tables in the garage for people to sit at. Ruth had the food in the kitchen. In the fall of 2010, Kayla went to Minnesota School of Business in Rochester. She was going to take up veterinarian technician. After two quarters, she dropped out. I was not happy, but she was now an adult. I couldn't make her do something that she didn't want to.

Kayla's senior picture

I traded corn dryers that summer. We bought a new tower dryer. It was fifty-five feet tall. It held 1,100 bushels of corn. It would be a lot more efficient. We could dry a lot more corn in a day. We could dry between five hundred and one thousand bushels an hour depending how wet the corn was. It was capable that Bob could run the dryer anywhere with his smartphone. It cost $100,000. I paid $50,000 down and financed the rest with FSA, a government office. Without the leg, we never would have been able to buy the dryer. Thinking back on the storm now, it was the best thing that could happen. Maybe God had a plan for us.

In the fall of 2010, I got a call from Jan. Jan is the daughter of Marion, one of Ruth's sisters. She said she was homeschooling her kids. Matthew was a senior, and she figured for him to have a rounded-out education, he needed to spend a week on a farm. Could he spend a week with me? I immediately said, "Yes." Matthew came down on a weekend with his dad, Merritt. Matthew didn't know us, and I think it made it easier for Merritt to go along. Merritt just stayed the weekend. I knew who Merritt was, but I didn't really know him. Matthew rode in the combine some, but he rode in the tractor mostly hauling the corn from the field to the corn dryer. He was a big help. We talked about everything. Why couldn't I talk about these things with my own kids? The week went way too fast for me. Matthew never came again, but Merritt came again the next year for three days. After that, Merritt came every year, but only longer. He wanted to learn everything about farming.

My mother's birthday was November 9, 1920. She would be ninety years old. She was living alone and still driving her car. For the last couple of years, she had trouble with bladder infection, but otherwise she was in good health. At least I think she was in good health. She never shared her problems with her children. When my brothers, sister, and I told Mom we wanted to have a big party for her on her birthday, she said, "No." On her birthday, Ruth and I took her out to eat at noon at the Pheasant's Café in Waseca. My brother Rick also joined us there. We all went to Mom's house afterward. Rick and I went for a walk to look at the old cemetery stone in the pasture. We walked across the field that we knew as the flat when we were growing up. It had crops then. It was now all trees. All of a sudden, a pickup came up to us. The driver hollowed, "What are you doing here?" I told him that the farm was our grandfather's at one time. We just wanted to walk across it again. He gave us permission. We had the party against Mom's wishes on November 14. We had the party at the Senior Citizens Center in Waseca. It was a huge success. Mom really enjoyed the party, and she thanked all her kids for throwing the party.

On December 9, Marsha, Dallas's wife, took Mom to the doctor for bladder infection. The doctor put Mom in the Waseca hospital. The bladder infection was getting worse, and the infection had gone into her blood, and they took Mom by ambulance to the Mankato Hospital about a week later. Finally, they got the infection under control. They called all of Mom's children to the hospital on December 21. That was my birthday. The Austin's Compassion Friends had a Christmas meeting that night. Ruth wanted to go to that. We didn't know how long it would take, so I went alone. Mom was supposed to be walking some, but she didn't want to. We could tell that Mom had given up. We talked about putting Mom in a nursing home. They had to dismiss Mom from the hospital now. I knew if they were putting her in the nursing home, they were sending Mom to die. We all went out to eat in the evening, and then I went home.

I had an insurance meeting the next day, Wednesday, December 22. I had an hour's drive. As I was driving, I was praying to God. Maybe I was just talking to God out loud the whole way. "What should I do? I'm not ready for Mom to die. You have to tell me what to do." When I got to the meeting, I was just as confused as when I left home. On the way home, I felt that God was telling me what to do. "Bring her home to your house, and take care of her." What would Ruth think about this? We had never talked about having Mom live with us. How would I surprise Ruth with this? When I got home, I said, "I'm going to ask you something, and I don't want your answer until tomorrow morning. I want to take Mom out of the hospital and bring her home to live with us." Ruth answered, "I don't have to have a day to think about this. Bring your mother home." Maybe God didn't give me an answer on the way to the meeting because God or an angel was working on Ruth. God didn't want to tell me until he knew what the answer would be. I then called all my siblings and asked them to give me permission to take Mom to our house. They all agreed. Ruth and my mother always got along well, but they were not as close as they were at the end of her life.

Ruth and I went to the Mankato Hospital early the next morning, Thursday, December 23. I informed the staff that I was going to take Mom home. I was surprised that they agreed. They told Mom that I was taking her home to live with us. Her mood immediately changed. Now she had something to look forward to. On Wednesday, Mom refused to try walking. Now today, she was eager to try walking. Mom had an IV, and they were giving her medicine twice a day through the IV. I would have to this. Suddenly, I thought that we were getting into something way over our heads. How would I do this? When I was in school as a teenager, a counselor told me, from the adaptive tests that I had taken, I was most qualified to be a male nurse. I was scared to hook up an IV. Would I change my mind now about taking Mom home? We could tell that Mom now had something to live for. Soon a social worker came in to talk to us. They would send a nurse to our house to hook up the medicine to the IV. They would train me to do it over the next few days. A nurse would visit Mom every week. They would send a therapist to our house twice a week to work with Mom. They would also send a lady to our house twice a week to help Mom take a bath. Medicare would pay for everything, and it would cost us nothing. The social worker had taken a big weight off my shoulders. I never thought in my wildest dreams this was possible. Thank God, he wouldn't tell me to do something without helping me. Thank you, God. We were going to have Mom sleep in the south sunroom. I would need a bed. My parents had a folding bed. I talked to Mom about the bed. Mom told me that for years, she slept in the lift chair that my dad had. She wanted me to go and get the chair. I called Bob, and he went to get the chair. Dallas's son, Alex, helped Bob to load the chair in his pickup. The day really went fast, and late in the afternoon, they said they would need more time to get everything arranged. We would have to come back the next day. Mom would be home with us on Christmas.

We always celebrated Christmas on Christmas Eve on odd years, so we didn't have to get ready for Christmas Eve this year. Ruth and I went to Mankato to pick Mom up on December 24. When we got home, Mom was really tired from the trip. Everyone went to bed early that night. On Christmas Day, all of Mom's children came to our house to celebrate Christmas with her. Ruth didn't cook a meal. Everyone brought snack foods. On Sunday, December 26, Dallas's son, Dana, and his wife, Kathy, and their three boys came to visit grandma. We celebrated Christmas the evening of the twenty-sixth. Ruth always had Swedish meatballs with all the trimmings. Afterward we opened up the presents.

We had bought a baby monitor. We had one unit in the room where Mom slept. We had the other unit in our bedroom. Then we could hear if Mom had problems. One of the first nights, I heard Mom calling me. I ran into her room. Mom was sitting on the floor. She got up to go to the bathroom. When she was going back to her lift chair, she sat too close to the foot of the chair. The chair tipped, and Mom fell to the floor. I couldn't get Mom up by myself, and I had to get Ruth. The next night, the same thing happened again. When I came into the room and saw Mom sitting on the floor, I couldn't control myself. I started laughing. Soon Mom started laughing too. She learned how to get back into the chair, and it never happened again.

Outside of taking care of the horses every morning, I didn't not have much work to do. Mostly, I visited with Mom all day. We talked about her childhood and when she met my dad. We talked about all the horses that she had. She talked about racing the race horses that Dr. McIntire kept at my grandfather's farm. She talked a lot about her Uncle Steve. She then told me, "Of all of my kids, I never expected that you would take care of me." Kayla and Sarah rode their horses up to the house almost every day. Mom enjoyed seeing the horses and the girls riding them. We were kept quite busy with company between the nurse, therapists, and the bath lady. Someone was there almost every day. Dallas, Marsha, and Alex came over every second Sunday. My sister Sandy and her husband, Gary Pittman, came over often mostly on Saturdays. My brother Rick and his wife, Carol, came some. Rick worked a lot of hours, some weekends. Carol worked some weekends too. Once in a while, Rick came alone. My Uncle Duane and Aunt Barb came often. After my mom died, they continued to visit us often. My Uncle Roger and Aunt Lorna came a couple of times. It was hard to get Mom to eat. Shilo stayed right beside her. She snuck her food to Shilo. Mom spent hours trying to get Shilo to talk. Shilo made whining noises to my mother. January and most of February went well. We offered to take Mom home to visit her house several times. She never wanted to go home. But then we had to take Mom to the doctors more and more often. Her bladder had started to fail. She would have to wear a catheter all the time. If she wore the catheter all the time, she was always going to have bladder infection. It seemed now that we couldn't win.

Archway entering the farm

In early January, we bought a bus trip to Washington, DC. I paid extra for the trip, so if we had to cancel, I would get all my money back. Sandy was going to stay at our house when we took the trip, and she and Bob were going to take care of Mom. We had several changes to the farm. We traded combines. We got a 9560 JD Combine. Bob drove it home from the dealership. Mom watched Bob drive it into the yard. I made a drawing of the fence that we going to build. It was an overhead structure with McColley 1971 on the top. 1971 was the year we bought the farm. Mom said, "I can't wait to see it." I built the fence in 2012. Bob and I went to central Illinois and bought a John Deere 4700 self-propelled sprayer. We had Troy Voth from Lodermeirs out several times. We were going to put a pit in the ground to unload grain. We were going to build a building over the pit. I got a big surprise phone call one night during supper. It was from Jon Sutherland. He had bought fifty acres from his folks two years ago. He paid $4,000 per acre. I felt really bad when he bought the farm. I wanted to buy it at the time. Jon said he now wanted to sell me the land. I offered him $6,000 per acre, and he accepted my offer right away. I was on the phone less than one minute. When I came back to the table, I told Mom, "I just bought a farm." I bought the Newman farm with Bob. We each owned thirty-seven acres. The Neuman farm was right next to the fifty acres that I just bought from Jon. I told Bob, "I will sell you the thirty-seven acres for $5,800 per acre." I took out a fifteen-year loan to pay the difference. I could have bought all the land myself, but I figured Bob should own as much land as possible. It would be easier for him when I retired and when I was gone.

The morning before we went on the trip, I could sense that Mom wasn't so well. Ruth and I took Mom to the doctor in Kasson. The doctor checked Mom over and admitted Mom to the St. Mary's Hospital in Rochester. I told Mom that we would cancel our trip. "I'll get all the money back." Mom told us to go. She planned to die. She said, "Tell your brother Dallas to take care of my funeral and wait to have it until you get home." Neither Ruth nor I wanted to go on the trip now. Mom insisted that we go. I had a talk with Bob. He assured us that he would take care of Mom. We should go.

The same night, we drove to Mason City and stayed at a hotel. We could leave the car there. We got on the bus the next morning to go to Washington, DC. Mom had talked to us about being in Washington, DC. She had been only in the train station. We had a tour of the train station. The same clock that was on the wall when Mom was there was on the wall now over more than sixty-five years later. We didn't go in the White House, but we stood on the outside of the fence. A man that was with us had his cap blow off and over the fence. I was a young sixty-seven years old then. It was easy for me to jump over the fence and get his cap. As I picked up his cap, I could see several police cars coming toward me. Would I be in trouble now? I quickly jumped over the fence again. The police cars turned around. What a relief! Some of the people on the tour told me that I would be arrested. When we went to look at the memorials and I saw the Vietnam War Memorial and saw all the names of the veterans that got killed, I almost got sick to my stomach. The wall went on forever. I never want to see the wall again. Looking back at the war now, it didn't make sense. All these men died for nothing. We went to the Ford Theater where President Lincoln was assassinated. We watched a play that took place the day after Lincoln died. We went to Gettysburg and President Eisenhower's Farm. The trip was fun, and it was good to see Washington, DC, once. Everyone should see it once. But once is enough.

When we got home, Mom was in the Lakeshore Nursing Home in Waseca. My sister Sandy really praised Bob for arranging everything. We went every day to visit her. The first few days we could talk to Mom and tell her about our trip. As time went on, Mom slept more and more. Bob went every night and took Shilo, our dog. Bob never put a leash on Shilo. She got out of the pickup and walked into the nursing home. She visited Mom and then went down the halls and visited the rest of the patients. The nurses told Bob, "Shilo can get up on the bed and sleep with your grandmother." Eventually, some days, Mom was never awake. But we stayed four to five hours a day anyway. On April 25, Brenda and her family visited Mom. We couldn't believe what we saw when we arrived. Mom was alert, and she was playing with Emery. Doreen and her girls came later. When we left, Mom told me, "Goodbye, you were a really good son to me. Thank you for taking care of me so good." When we arrived the next day, she was unconscious. The nurses said she was awake early in the morning. She was really mad that she woke up. She had planned to die before morning. Medicare paid for twenty-one days in the nursing home after being dismissed from a hospital. Twenty-one days were up today. A lady from hospice came in to talk to me. Mom had made me promise her that we wouldn't do anything to keep her alive. She wanted to know if I wanted Mom to be on hospice. After some thinking, I said, "Yes." How come I had to make this decision for both of my parents? Mom was on oxygen. The lady asked if she should take the oxygen away. She said, "If your mother feels any discomfort, I'll put the oxygen back on." I didn't think the oxygen was a machine, but Mom had made me promise that I would never keep her alive on a machine. I told her to take the oxygen off. A half hour later, she told me, "She is going to die soon. Call your family." Dallas and Marsha, Sandy, and Carol soon came. Doreen was there too. I sat on a chair beside Mom's bed. I held on to Mom's right hand for about one hour. Her hand was still warm, but I could feel that she died. I told everyone that Mom was dead. I got up and left the room and went to the nurses' station. I brought a nurse back, and she confirmed that Mom was dead. It was April 26, Dad's birthday. Rick's daughter, Melissa, came right after Mom died. All the nurses said that they would really miss Shilo. I think that Mom now realized it was spring. She knew that now we would be busy. She didn't want to impose on us anymore. I thought she had three more months of her life now than if she would have gone to the nursing home at Christmastime. Maybe I needed time to say goodbye. At Mom's funeral, I put my hand on Mom's shoulder as to say goodbye. I would really miss it to call her on the phone and tell her what was going on. I should have visited her more.

The rest of the year was really busy. Sarah graduated from high school. We had the same party for her as we had for Kayla the year before.

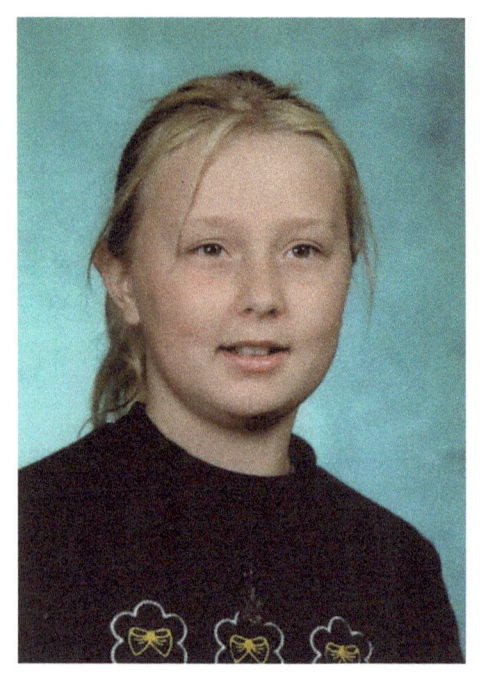

Sarah

    We ran a new tile line from the field. We had to cross three other lines to get the tile deep enough to get it under the pit that we were putting in. We had to dig a hole twelve feet into the ground. The crew put the pit down into the ground. Then the crew put an eighteen-inch auger from the pit to the leg. It was a five-hundred-bushel pit. I paid extra money to put on a bigger grate on the top. Then we had Dave Kaczmarek build a building, thirty-six by forty-five feet, over it. We never finished the inside walls, but Dave put white steel on the ceiling. Justin and I built a room on the inside of the building, eight feet by eighteen feet. Justin was now fourteen years old. I showed Justin how to do it, and I watched him. We poured the floor ourselves with Bob's help. I had always told Bob, "After I retire, you have to build a building so I can unload corn inside." Well, I did it myself. We had to take two six-thousand-bushel bins down. They were now in the wrong spot. There was not enough room to drive in the new building with them there. We would lose storage. Under Obama's tax law, we could write off the full cost of the building in one year. Year 2011 was the only year that we could do this. I had Curt Miner, our electrician, move the control box for the corn dryer into the dryer building office. We could run the dryer from inside. I also had Curt put lights in the grain bins. We had two boxes in the office with a series of lights so we would know how full the bins were. When a bin got full, the dryer shut off. I've made the mistake of running a bin over. Now it won't happen again.

I had my fiftieth high school graduation party in 2011 in late August at Miller Armstrong Center in Waseca. When I was walking across the room, I bumped into Jerry Cauley. Jerry showed me around the school when I first went to school in Waseca. He asked me, "What have you been up to?" I said, "I have been living the American dream." He then said, "What do mean by that?" I answered, "I wasn't raised on a farm. I had no chance of being a farmer. I started farming with no outside financial help from families, and now I'm a successful farmer. That is the American dream." He said he was raised on a farm, but his dad sold the farm to send him to college. He had never been on a farm since that time. He said, "I haven't been on a farm for fifty years." We talked farming for some time. Then he said, "Can I visit you some time?" I took his number and told him, "I will call you when we are doing harvest." Jerry came down during harvest and spent all day. First, I gave him a tour of the whole farm, including my farm office, and I explained crop marketing. We had a screen where the market was there all the time. We went in the shop, to the horse stable, and into the machine sheds. I showed him all our machinery. He rode in the combine with Bob. Ruth brought him lunch at noon. He rode with me in the afternoon in the tractor hauling corn. I was really proud to show him the new corn dryer and the new building and the office where we were unloading corn. When he got home, he sent me a note.

> Wayne,
>
> Just a quick note to tell you how much I enjoyed our visit yesterday. It was truly one of the most interesting and informative days I have spent in

a long time. Please thank Ruth & Bob for me also. All of you were so hospitable and patient in answering all of my questions. You really helped me move forward fifty years in my understanding of the business of farming.

As I was driving home last I experienced one big regret. That is, why didn't we spend more time together and become closer friends in high school?

Let's take the opportunity to stay in touch from now on. So, if you come to the Cities & have time give me a call. Same for times you go to Florida in the winter. Also I would be glad to help you put together a spreadsheet.

Thanks again

Jerry

Jerry spent much of his life working with computers. After harvest, Ruth and I went to the Mystic Lake Casino in the cities. I gave Jerry a call, and he came to the casino, and he ate with us. Jerry and I met at Perkins in Owatonna several times to talk farming.

Fall went well, and I made a lot of money, and I still needed more tax deductions. We bought a forty-thousand-grain bin from Lodermeirs. We had enough fill from digging the pit. It took seven loads of concrete to pour the floor. Four trucks unloaded at the same time. We could reach the bin from the leg, but we couldn't reach the top. The next spring, we put in a grain pump to fill the bin from the leg. The bin cost $74,000, and the grain pump cost $20,000. The year was so good that I paid cash for the building and the bin.

In 2012, I was sixty-eight years old. I hadn't taken Social Security yet. Many of my retired friends told me that I was leaving money on the table. I could have taken the full amount at age sixty-six. Between sixty-six and seventy, the amount increased 8 percent per year. That was a good increase on investment. Many friends had told me, "Maybe you won't live long enough to get your money back." I answered, "If I die earlier, Social Security won't make a difference to me." All my life, I never wanted to bet one way. The age sixty-eight was halfway between sixty-six and seventy. I wanted to buy a new Chevrolet Equinox. We had been looking at them for two years. If I signed up now for Social Security, I would have enough money to pay for the car this year. I signed up for Social Security at sixty-eight years and four months. A lot of people, especially farmers, never wanted to pay any taxes. After 1994, I always made good money. That was a time that I started to think about retirement and Social Security. As a farmer, I could have avoided taxes. But if I was going to draw considerable money from Social Security, I had to pay a good amount of taxes.

We put a retaining wall around the bins that we moved. The ground was higher for these two bins than the other bins. In 2012, we built another bin. It was only a fifteen-thousand-bushel bin. I built it only because the bin setup would look better because of this bin. There was too much of a space between two bins. Then we poured concrete between all the bins. Weeds wouldn't grow anymore. It would be easier to clean, and it would look better. Now I had a bin setup that I could be proud of. We had two hundred thousand bushels of storage.

In July 2012, Ruth and I decided to take a vacation with our new car. We visited Ruth's sister Marion in the Black Hills first. Then we went to Cody, Wyoming, to visit Marion's son, Perry Rockvan. Then we went to Yellowstone National Park. It was raining when we come up to Old Faithful. The many parking lots were all full. We drove around all of them, but we couldn't find a parking place. We wanted to see Old Faithful, but in the end, we didn't stop. Ruth and I talked about coming again in September of another year. It wouldn't be so busy then. We should have gone in 2013, but we didn't. Our health was soon going to change. We went through the corner of Utah and on into Colorado. We stopped at the top of a mountain to read a sign. I started to visit with a young man from Utah. When I told him I was from Minnesota, he said his girlfriend went to school at the university in St. Paul. He said they were going to go to visit some friends in Minnesota in September. I invited them to visit our farm. They came for a day. They said they had never seen corn nor soybeans close up. I took them out to the field to look at corn and soybeans. I took them to the Hubble House. It was fun!

Karen, her husband, and Wayne

In March of 2013, Ruth and I drove to Phoenix, Arizona. We spent a month on the trip. We visited my cousin Lynn and his wife, Debbi. Lynn was my Uncle Marlin's son. I hadn't seen Lynn since when we were kids. We also visited my pen pal, Karen, from the Navy. We were only home for a few days when Ruth's brother-in-law died. He was Donna's, husband, John. He died on April 17. He was only seventy years old. I asked Ruth if she wanted to go to Florida to go to the funeral. Ruth told me that we just got back from vacation; she didn't want to go. Shortly afterward, Ruth's sister Phyllis called me. "I think it a disgrace that none of Donna's brothers or sisters are going to John's funeral." She said that Allan and she were going to fly down. She asked Ruth and me to go along with them. I told Ruth that we had to go. We flew out of Minneapolis to Orlando, Florida. Al rented a car, and we drove to Vero Beach. We stayed at a Holiday Inn. When we were leaving the hotel, Al didn't know where to go. He was studying the map on this smartphone. They had been there before, so I thought he would know the way. Phyllis said, "Just go." Then she said, "Just go." Then she said it again. Al put the car in

A FATHER'S QUEST

reverse. Al backed into the car behind us. Ruth and Phyllis and her sisters are all back seat drivers. They got that from their mother. It really irritates me when Ruth does it to me. Phyllis was the blame for this accident. The first day, Donna showed Phyllis, Al, Ruth, and me around. The next day, we went to John's funeral. We met a lot of John's family. I really liked the pastor at their church. I wanted to see him again. Ruth and I really enjoyed ourselves. John was a Christian, and he wasn't afraid of death.

I met a man at the Austin Companions Friends in the winter of 2013. He said he was looking for a building for him to tear down and move it. I told him about the hog house that we built in 1978. He came out and looked at the building. He wanted $5,000 to take it. I agreed to pay him. When I told Justin, he told me that he would to it for $5,000. "Why are you going to pay someone else?" The man that I first made arrangements to take down the hog house never showed up. I told Justin that he could take the hog house down and that I would pay him the $5,000. Justin and I took the steel out of the inside of the building, and I sold the steel to McNeilus Steel in Dodge Center. Steel at that time was at a high price. Owen, Bob, and I helped Justin tear down the hog house. Then I hired Mark Dikes to bury the pit. That cost me $5,000. It cost me $70,000 to build the hog house in 1978. Now, thirty-five years later, it cost $10,000 to get rid of it.

In 2013, my brother-in-law Nado Bernard Jr. had a large sale because of health reasons. I always called him Junior. He collected various things, but Farmall tractors were the main things. He also restored many tractors and the Model T Ford pickup. The auction company had two rings selling all day. They started early, and it was late in the afternoon when they finished. I first saw the Model T in the 1970s. It was just junk. I couldn't even tell that it was a Model T. But I had told Junior back then that when he finished it that it would be fun to have it. Junior had to search for a lot of things to restore the pickup. He just got done with the pickup right before the sale. When I went to the sale, I knew that I would buy the pickup. I was willing to pay $10,000 or maybe more. I wanted the sale to go well for Junior. I was bidding against two people. This was the only sale when I bid on something that I wanted someone to bid against me. One of the bidders dropped out at $6,000. The other bidder bid was $7,000. I bid $7,100. I bought the 1920 Model T Ford Pickup.

1920 Model T Ford Pickup

My sister Sandy had a lot of problems with her back even when Mom died. She was going to a chiropractor, but it wasn't helping. Finally, she went to the Mayo Clinic. She had cancer in her back. The cancer had eaten out three vertebrates. They gave her chemo, but it didn't help. Then her doctor told Sandy that they would do a bone marrow transplant. I told Sandy that they could take my marrow. But the doctors were going to take her marrow out and put a chemo in it and put the marrow back in her back. Sandy and Gary stayed in the Ronald McDonald House for six weeks during the transplant. Toward the end of their stay, I told Sandy I wanted to take them out to eat. Sandy agreed. I called Michaels Restaurant to make a reservation. I told them about Sandy going through a bone marrow transplant. They had a separate room for us. We had a waitress to take care of us. She wouldn't wait on any other customers while we were there. It seemed like the transplant was a success. On the fourth Sunday in

August, we had a family reunion for my sister and brothers and their families. Sandy seemed good at first, but she later got cold. Ruth went up to the house to get a blanket. All of Sandy's grandkids were there. Sandy wanted to watch them ride a horse. Bob got a horse and gave all the kids a ride. Sandy really enjoyed watching them. Around four, Sandy and Gary left for home. They had a good evening at home. When morning came, Gary couldn't wake Sandy. Gary called the ambulance and they took Sandy to Mankato. She never regained consciousness. I couldn't believe what had happened.

We took a short trip, and when we got home, Bob told us there was a farm that would be sold at an auction. He wanted to buy it. We talked to Darrel Ness and arranged a loan. The sale was held at the Community Center in Dodge Center. I told Bob we would go early and sit in the front row. We would never turn around, and we didn't want to know whom we were bidding against. Bob did the bidding. If I had been bidding, I think I would have stopped. When the auctioneer said, "Sold." Bob had bid $10,600 an acre. That was the highest price of any farm in Dodge County.

Bob brought a new sixteen-row John Deere corn planter for $175,000. The boom on my sprayer didn't match. I had a sixty-foot boom that matched a twelve-row planter. I would need an eighty-foot boom to match a sixteen-row planter. It was December 2013. Ag Power in Owatonna had a 2011 4630 John Deere self-propelled sprayer. They wanted $145,000. I was willing to buy the sprayer. The salesman said that they had listed it on the auction that they would have in December. I would have to buy it at the auction. It was extremely cold that day. Ron Gelhing was the auctioneer. I knew Ron; I had bought an auger from him in 1982. Bob and I sat in the car most of the sale. About a half hour before they sold the sprayer, I told Bob we would have to go and watch to see how the bidding was going. Ron wasn't the auctioneer. Ron was working the crowd. I stood right beside Ron and talked to him from time to time. Bidding was going slowly. When they got to the 4630, they tried to start it at $150,000. They couldn't get a bid. They dropped it to $145,000. Then they dropped it to $140,000. Then Ron looked to me and said, "Help us out." I said, "$100,000." Ron said, "Sold." I couldn't believe what had just happened.

Chapter 25

The Calm before the Storm

It was 2014, and I was seventy years old. Everything was going well. Little did we know that at the end of the year, Ruth would be in serious trouble. Sarah turned twenty-one on January 15. We had raised Tammy's two daughters and had now felt we were done with that part of our lives. Luckily, we had taken many vacations. I told Ruth many times, "When we are ninety years old and we are sitting in a nursing home, we will wish we hadn't spent so much money on vacations." That was a joke. We were planning a big trip. The last few years the farm was making a lot of money. We decided we would stay at more expensive hotels. Once in a while, we would stay in a cheaper place.

In February, we were sitting in a church pew early one Sunday morning. We had just got a new pastor. Her name is Pastor Barb. All of a sudden, she was sitting in the pew directly behind us. She said she wanted to have church on the farm. She wanted Ruth and me to host church on the farm. The church had never done this before. Ruth and I agreed to do this. We had a beautiful farm with a big shop to hold the services in. We had hosted many parties before. It would be fun.

On March 5, we left for a month-long trip. We stayed the first night at a casino in Wisconsin Dells. In the morning, when we got up, the fire alarm went off. Over the loudspeaker, a voice said, "Leave the hotel right away." I wanted to get on the road early. I looked out into the hall. There was no smoke. I told Ruth, "We are not going to leave without our suitcases." We quickly packed and left. When we got to the lobby, there were a lot of people standing around. We saw a fire truck, but we didn't ask anyone anything. We went to our car and left.

Our first stop was Nashville. We were going to visit Michael Cunningham. We had met him on the wagon train and became good friends. We stayed at a Hampton Inn in Nashville two nights. We visited two old plantations while we were there. Michael's whole family was at his folks' place where we visited. They all showed us a good time. Michael was about ten years younger than we were. His mother and dad were in their upper eighties. They wanted us to spend the night with them. We had met them before at a wagon train. But we had a hotel rented, and we wanted to leave early Sunday morning. Sunday morning, we stopped at President Andrew Jackson's plantation, The Hermitages. We had a really good tour guide driving a wagon. I was really impressed with the plantation. Jackson treated his slaves really well. He never split up families. His slaves were allowed to have guns and to go hunting. He wanted his slaves to be happy, and then the plantation would prosper. When he died and his son took over the plantation, it started to fail. I wish I could go back there again.

We stopped at a museum in Mississippi. They didn't have tour guides, but we were visiting with an older lady working there. She ended up showing us the whole museum. She really made it fun for us.

We then visited my Uncle Lyle and Aunt Kathy in Milton, Florida. We stayed with them for three days. Two of the mornings, we went out for breakfast. They were used to going out for breakfast, and they knew everyone there. It was a lot of fun. Lyle's son, Lyle Dean, was in the hospital with lung cancer. We visited him. He would shortly die. I asked them to pick an expensive place to eat. I was going to buy. They wanted to go to The Red Lobster. I did not like any seafood on the menu. I ordered a steak, and it was the best steak I have had in my life. We met most of my cousins and had a really good time.

Next, we went to visit Ruth's sister Donna in Vero Beach, Florida. We stayed close by in Quality Inn Hotel. It was not the best place. It was cheap. The other hotels were a lot farther away. We stayed there four days. We went to a Baptist church with Donna on Sunday. I met her pastor at John's funeral eleven months ago. I really liked him. After church services, we left for St. Augustine, Florida.

St. Augustine is a really old town. There is a lot of history there. We stayed there two nights. The first night, we went on a horse and carriage tour. It was warm, and it was just getting dark. The lights were pretty reflecting off the water. It gave us a feeling of being young and in love. We had planned to take the ride in the daytime the next day. Maybe an angel was looking out for us. The next day was cold and raining. There were no horse and carriage rides that day. Looking back on the ride, it was more fun taking a ride in the carriage at night.

The next day we went to Savanah, Georgia. We stayed at a hotel along the interstate. We rested up awhile and then drove into Savanah. We didn't know where to go. Savanah was better than we imagined. We got a Hampton Inn Hotel room for the next two nights in the tourist district. It was expensive, but it was worth it. It was really nice. I hope I can go back there again and stay there. Savanah is laid out where there is a park in the middle of every block. If my memory is right, there were thirteen parks in thirteen blocks. In colonial days, they could bring their livestock in for protection. We took a tour of the area and walked around a lot. That night we walked to a seashore district where they had fixed up some old warehouses into a tourist area. We ate at a really old-looking and expensive restaurant. It was fun. The next morning, we walked to a place where we went on a horse and carriage ride. A lady was driving the carriage, and she was really interesting. She made the ride fun for us. After the ride, we left for Charleston, South Carolina.

We stayed at a Merritt Hotel along the seashore and half of a mile from the tourist area. It was expensive but really nice. They had a really good restaurant that we could order breakfast off the menu, and it was free if we were staying in the hotel. We had a view of the harbor and the sailboats from our room. It was beautiful. We went on a tour of the Boone Hall Plantation. It was warm, and we spent a lot of time there. The movie *The North and South* was filmed there. We had a tour of the fields that were now being farmed on the plantation. Several of the slave cabins were there, and they had set up displays on the life on the plantation before the Civil War. The plantation was interesting, and we enjoyed ourselves. It was a really good day that we wouldn't forget. We ate our evening meal at a brewery that brewed beer. There were vats of beer sitting in the middle of the restaurant. We had pizza and beer. It was really good, and we had fun. The next day we went by boat to Fort Sumter. Part of the fort was still standing after the Civil War. We met another family there. We spent a lot of time visiting with them. We had pictures of our farm, and they really liked looking at them. I can't remember where they were from.

The next day, we left for Gary, North Carolina. It was part of Raleigh. We went to visit Norma and Kenny Muhlbauers. We stayed with them for two nights. Kenny had beginning stages of lung cancer. Norma had bladder cancer, and the doctors had recently removed her bladder. I felt guilty for staying with them. They both said that we were doing them a favor. It gave them something different to think about than their troubles. A good friend of Norma brought a roast beef dinner with all the trimmings for supper one night. It was simply delicious.

The next day we went to Windsor, North Carolina, where The Hope Plantation was. We had visited it several times before. I belong to the Hope Foundation and send them money every year. We got a personal tour for free.

We were planning on going to Mt. Vernon next. We had been there before when we visited Washington, DC, in 2011. We wanted to see Mt. Vernon again, but snow was in the forecast, and snow would ruin it. We decided to go to Montpelier, the home of President James Madison, instead. When we got within thirty miles, it was snowing so bad we couldn't see the road anymore. All of a sudden, we saw a small hotel sitting next to a Burger King. There wasn't anything close by that we could see beyond the windshield. It was early, but we stopped. It wasn't a nice place, but it was cheap. We didn't like fast-food places anymore, but we could walk to the Burger King, so that was where we went. In the morning, the snow had stopped, and it was melting. We drove to Montpelier. I think it was the prettiest place we had ever seen. The scenery was unreal from the plantation house. They were doing a lot of work everywhere. We had planned to go back again. The same day we visited Ash Lawn Highland, President James Monroe's home. It was kind of disappointing. There was a simple small farmhouse.

Next, we drove to Ashburn, Virginia. It was on the edge of Washington, DC. My mother had three cousins that lived there. I was told they worked in the White House all my life. Mom had talked about them often her whole life. I had met two of them at a family reunion once before. I was looking forward to getting to know them. We stayed at a hotel nearby. The next day, we visited Jim and Joyce Kelly's place. They lived in a big retirement home. Joyce wasn't home as she was visiting her brother in Minnesota. Jim's two brothers—Jack along with his wife, Jean, and Joe—came shortly. We had lunch at the cafeteria at the retirement home. We all had a nice visit. After Jim's two brothers left, Jim and I visited the rest of the afternoon. It was really fun for me. It's things like that that make a vacation really fun.

Next, we went to visit my really good Navy buddy, Bob Cunningham, in Pittsburg. We stayed with them four nights. When we stopped at Bob's, I had a goal in mind. I wanted to talk Bob, Pat, and Colleen into visiting us that summer. Ruth and I had a lot of fun with Colleen over the years. She was a pretty girl. Would I be successful?

Next, we went to Detroit, Michigan, to visit the Ford Museum. We were told that Detroit was a dangerous city. We stayed about fifty miles away. We went early in the morning to the museum and then left in the middle of the afternoon. I thought that the museum was better than the Smithsonian Museum in Washington, DC. It took hours to see it. By the time we left, we were so tired we couldn't walk anymore.

Our last stop was at Jim and Kay Borgen's home in Belvidere, Illinois. We stayed one night with them. Over the years, we had visited Ruth's uncle and aunt, Ray and Alice Borgen, many times. They always took us to visit their son Jim. When they went to the nursing home, Jim and Kay invited us to stay at their home. We went there many times and had lots of fun.

The vacation was now over. The weather forecast for home was cold and snow. I said to Ruth, "Why not go to Branson instead of going home?" But Ruth was homesick and wanted to go home. We had a really fun vacation. Bob, Pat, and Colleen would be visiting us in August. Little did we know, this would be the last vacation while we had our health.

Chapter 26

Leading up to the Power of Prayer

On July 13, 2014, Kayla's daughter Jordyn was born. My Grandpa Larson was born on that date 128 years earlier. Kayla's mother, Tammy, was baptized on July 13, forty-five years before Jordyn was born. I really wish Tammy was alive to meet her granddaughter Jordyn.

On August 16, we hosted the Borgen family reunion. There was a big crowd, and everyone had a good time. Bob and Justin gave horse and carriage rides. Everything went well. There were a lot of cousins, and all of Ruth's brothers and sisters were there. I had told everyone before the reunion, "You never know what the future will be. Everyone should get together now."

Bob and Justin giving carriage rides

A FATHER'S QUEST

On August 17, we hosted a Compassion Friends' picnic. We had a good crowd. My good buddy from the Navy Bob and his wife, Pat Cunningham, and their daughter, Colleen, were also coming that day to visit us. Ruth and I were really looking forward to it. The last time they were here was 1982. I think Colleen was three years old at that time. We were going to give horse and carriage rides. Justin was going to drive them. We hooked the horses to the carriage by the west door of the shop. Ruth and Justin were standing in front of the horses and holding them. I turned and went into the shop, asking who wanted to ride first. The horses ran! They knocked Ruth down. Ruth quickly turned over so she was lying on her stomach. One of the horses stepped on Ruth's legs. The carriage ran over Ruth's legs. Ruth was really lucky that the horses didn't step on her head or back. She could have been seriously hurt or killed. Within fifty feet, Justin stopped the horses. His whole chest was bruised. Ruth got up right away. I didn't realize that Ruth got run over. Justin didn't want to drive the horses now. I realized that if you unhooked the horses now and put them away, you would always be in danger of them running away again. Justin got up on the carriage reluctantly. Some people got in the carriage, and the ride went smoothly. People who had the first ride didn't realize that Ruth got run over. When Justin and the horses left for the ride, I was told Ruth got run over. One of our guests, Julie Learn, was a nurse. She took Ruth into the bathroom and examined her. Ruth had a lot of bruises and a little swelling on her legs. Julie said we should take Ruth to the emergency room. That was the only thing a nurse could say. Ruth would need x-rays to be sure she wasn't really hurt. Ruth didn't want to go. She wanted to be home when Bob and Pat got to our place. Many of our guests stayed wondering how badly Ruth got hurt. Eventually, Bob, Pat, and Colleen arrived around four thirty. Ruth visited with them for about a half hour. Doreen took Ruth to the emergency room at Saint Mary's. I should have gone, but we had a lot of guests. Some of the guests from Compassion Friends stayed, hoping Ruth would come home soon. They left at eight o'clock. Bob and I along with Bob, Pat, and Colleen left the shop and went to the house. They took their suitcases in. Bob made everyone pizza for supper. Bob was a perfect host. It was midnight when Ruth and Doreen got home. There were no serious injuries. But Ruth was in pain. We all went to bed at twelve thirty.

The next morning, Ruth was in pain, and her legs were all black and blue. She got up before six in the morning. She started breakfast. Ruth wore long pants so no one could see the bruises. She never let on that she was in pain. We planned to visit Mayo Clinic and Mayowood. We had a tour at the Mayo Clinic. We visited the offices of Dr. Charley and Will Mayo. It was the same as it was in 1940. The next day, we went to the Mayowood Mansion. Little did we know at the time that the Mayo Clinic would become the main social life that we would have for years. We went for our noon meal to Michaels Restaurant. It was in the downtown area close to Mayo. It was a high-end restaurant that is now closed. The next day, we had our noon meal at the Hubbell House in Manorville. It was a famous restaurant. I took Bob C. and Bob took Colleen out to our fields on our gators to look at our crops. Later Bob and Colleen drove the horses, and Bob, Pat, Ruth, and I rode in the back of the carriage and had a tour of the farm and fields. Bob went horseback riding with Colleen. But she wasn't comfortable riding. Soon the two Bobs went riding together. I gave everyone a long ride in my Model T pickup. We hated to see them go on Thursday. Ruth went everywhere with us. We had all learned something. Ruth was one tough lady. Maybe God and the angels were with Ruth. There was something much worse soon to come. Ruth would have to get really tough to survive what was ahead.

My Uncle Lyle died on August 31. I wanted to go to his funeral. But Ruth was still in pain. I didn't think she could make the trip. I asked Uncle Duane if they were going. He said he didn't think Barb could make the trip. They wouldn't go. Finally, I decided not to go. I really wanted to go, but it would be impossible. Lyle was born on the first day of summer, June 21, 1932. He was eighty-two years and two months when he died. I would miss him.

We had church on the farm September 14. There were about 180 people here. My old country school friend Charles Priebe and his wife and Charles's mother, Agnes, were here. When I was a boy,

I stayed at their house many times. My country schoolteacher, Ruth Mittlestadt, was also here. This was a special day for me. We had a polka service with a band. While the people were sitting and the service was going on, our dog, a boxer named Shilo greeted everyone. I think it was too big of a day for her. On the way to the house at night, I think she had a heart attack. She fell on the lawn and stayed there quite a while, and then she appeared to recover. Bob and Justin gave horse and carriage rides to everyone. The kids really enjoyed the rides.

Jordyn was baptized during the church service. When she is grown up, I hope she will think it was a special day for her being baptized at her great-grandfather's farm. I wished that Tammy could have been there.

Chapter 27

The Power of Prayer

Harvest had started; soybeans were done. We had started corn. It was early October. Merrett was down visiting us. It was a Saturday. I was out early in the morning unloading the corn from last night. When I was done and had a set of wagons out in the field, I had some free time. I came in the house. Ruth told me that there was something wrong and that she would have to go to the doctor. I asked, "What's wrong?" She told me to feel her left breast. I could feel a lump. I couldn't believe it! Soon it was time to start hauling the corn. That was all I could think about. Why hadn't I noticed a lump earlier? For the last two months, when I had tried to touch her breasts, she pushed my hand away. I thought she was sore from the horses knocking her down or maybe she wasn't in the mood. I think Ruth had known it for a while, but Ruth said she didn't. It was almost noon. I was unloading corn. I should call the doctor. I didn't know the number. All of a sudden, an angel was helping me. I dialed the number. A lady answered instantly. That never happens when you call the Kasson Mayo Clinic. She said, "I will get you in first thing Monday morning." I couldn't believe it. Merrett told me that he would take over for me as long as it took.

We went to the doctor at Kasson Mayo Clinic first thing Monday morning. A young lady doctor examined Ruth. She said she wouldn't tell anyone that they had cancer without additional tests. But she was positive Ruth had breast cancer. Ruth would have to go to the Mayo Clinic in Rochester immediately. The doctor went with Ruth and me to the appointment desk. She stayed there until the appointment was made. I have never seen a doctor do this before. We had an appointment for one o'clock that day. It would be too early to go, so we went home to wait. Ruth called Brenda, and I called Pastor Barb. They both came to our house promptly. Pastor Barb said we should join hands and she would pray for Ruth. Pastor Barb held Ruth's hand. Ruth held my hand. I held Brenda's hand, and Brenda held Barb's hand. When Pastor Barb started to pray, our dog Shilo laid her head on Ruth's and Pastor Barb's hands. Shilo always begged Ruth for things for years. Ruth always asked, "Why does Shilo always come to me?" From that day, Shilo never begged to Ruth again. She was able to sense that Ruth was really sick.

They did a mammogram of Ruth's breasts at one o'clock. They confirmed that Ruth had breast cancer. We would have many more appointments that week. They did a needle biopsy, and it confirmed cancer. When they were done with the tests, we met with the cancer doctor. On Ruth's right breast, they said there was a really small tumor. It was a really slow-growing tumor. They said they thought she had it for ten years. On her left breast there were several tumors. It had spread into her lymph nodes under her arm. It was fast growing, and they didn't think Ruth had it for long. The one tumor in her breast was so close to her chest cavity they didn't think they could remove it. They would have to come up with a plan how to beat the cancer.

I thought that if it was fast-growing, they would start treatment soon. We didn't hear anything. In two weeks I called Mayo. They said they didn't have a plan yet. It was in December before they had a plan. They would give Ruth a chemo called Texel. They would give Ruth twelve treatments, once a week. Then they would give Ruth a different kind of chemo four times. Then they would remove Ruth's breasts. Then they would give Ruth radiation five days a week for six weeks. The tumor that was so close to her chest cavity and close to her heart that radiation could injure her heart. I didn't think that sounded good. But if we didn't do it, she would die. She would have to be really tough to get through it. Maybe God had prepared Ruth for this.

We had a Blue Cross supplemental plan for our Medicare. We had a chance to change the plan in December. We knew Ruth had cancer. It would get expensive. We picked a plan where Blue Cross would pay everything. We would be paying a premium that would be two and a half times higher. We figured it would be worth it.

They started the Texel treatment right before Christmas. We went to a room where there were six patients sitting in chairs. The chairs reminded me of a chair in a barbershop. Everyone was getting chemo. The chemo took two to three hours. Sometimes there was someone to visit with. Other times everyone was so busy with their smartphones there was no one to visit with. Ruth always slept. On those times I would go walking in the subway or visit with someone sitting in the piano area. We met good friends there. The couple was Joan and Jim Hoffman from Owatonna. Joan had breast cancer like Ruth. They lived on a farm northwest of Owatonna. They were friends of Pastor Barb. The treatments at first were going well. It was like they were giving Ruth a high. She looked forward to it.

Mayo told Ruth that she would lose her hair. She didn't want anyone to see her bald. Mayo sold wigs in the subway. Medicare would pay for it. Neither Ruth nor I liked the wigs that Medicare would pay for. We started to look at other wigs. We found one that cost $300. It was an auburn color. When Ruth put the wig on, she looked exactly like her mother. I couldn't believe it! I always got along with Ruth's mother really well. I thought it would be neat if Ruth looked like her mother. At chemo they gave Ruth many nice-looking caps for her to wear. When her hair started to fall out, Ruth asked our son-in-law Owen to cut off all her hair.

In February, everything was going well. The tumors were getting smaller. The doctors said they would skip a week on the chemo. We decided we would go on a vacation. We would fly to Las Vegas. We would rent a car and go to Laughlin. We would stay at the Colorado Belle Casino. It was a building, but it looked like a riverboat. We had stayed there many times before. When we got to the casino, our room wasn't ready. Ruth played on a video poker game close by. She got a royal flush, and she won a lot of money. Ruth would need to have a lot of bad luck to lose money on the vacation. She was always ahead. The first night Ruth had pain in her legs. We didn't know it at the time, but Ruth was getting neuropathy in her legs. The next night they hurt so badly that Ruth couldn't stand it. It helped to walk, so we walked in the casino in the middle of the night. They were worse at night. In the daytime, Ruth didn't have as much pain. Ruth's feet swelled up, so we had to buy bigger shoes. We took a jet boat to Lake Havasu, Arizona, one day. Curt and Beth Vaith, who wintered there, picked us up from the boat dock and took us out to eat. That day was really fun. The last night of the trip we, stayed at the Golden Nugget in downtown Las Vegas. They had built a dome over the town years ago. We wanted to see that. We had a real early fight home the next day. It was still dark when we went to the airport. Ruth was in a lot of pain. The airport was really big. It was a lot bigger than when we had gone to Las Vegas several times in the late 1980s and early 1990s. I told Ruth that we would get a wheelchair for her. I could get someone to push it. Ruth wouldn't stand for it; she told me that she didn't need a wheelchair.

Colorado Belle Casino

We had our annual meeting for the Southeast Mutual Insurance Company on March 4. After the meeting, the members of the board met to elect officers. I was elected president of the insurance company. It was an honor.

I was now doing all the grocery-shopping. I had never done this before. Ruth still made a list, but I couldn't find anything. The other ladies shopping could see my difficulties. Many of them helped me. I was grateful for that.

All our married life, Ruth was not good at being a nurse. I had always expected if I got sick, Ruth was not going to take care of me. When I had surgery for a hernia a few years ago, it took too long. Ruth became scared. She thought that I might die. I think she made a deal with God, if I lived, she would really take care of me. After I wrote this, I asked Ruth, "Am I right on this?" She said "Yes." I couldn't believe the care she gave me! Maybe it was in God's plan for Ruth and later for me. I knew I had to take care of Ruth really well.

When we went back to Mayo, the doctors said Ruth wouldn't tolerate any more Texel chemo. They would have to quit it early. They prescribed Gabapentin for the neuropathy in her legs. It was a drug for nerve pain. We had to start with a little and steadily give more. We couldn't quit it. We would have to wean Ruth off the drug. When we got up to sixteen pills a day, Ruth's arms and hands shook so badly that she couldn't eat. Bob held her hand still so she could eat. Bob was now doing all the cooking for us. It took several days to cut back the Gabapentin to the right amount. Ruth was still in terrible pain. Ruth wanted me to hold her in my arms at night. When she went to sleep, I was afraid to move. I might wake her up. Ruth woke up often in terrible pain. Mayo put her on a narcotic, OxyContin. I could give her two pills every four hours, twelve a day. Ruth was begging to give her more pills in less than two hours. I didn't know what to do. I couldn't stand to see Ruth suffer. Mayo finally said I could give the pills to her sooner. I had to write down in a tablet the time I gave Ruth the pills and to bring it in every time so they could look at it. No way could I give her more than twelve narcotic pills a day. I was lucky that Ruth was sleeping enough that I never had to give her more than twelve a day. I was getting so tired that Bob and my girls had to watch Ruth some nights. On those nights I slept in another bedroom. Mayo did some more tests. The cancer was growing again. They would give Ruth a different chemo. They said it would not make the neuropathy worse. They would give Ruth four treatments two weeks apart. They gave the first one Thursday, March 19.

On Saturday night, Ruth was really bad. She was in a lot of pain. She couldn't move anymore. The medicine wasn't working. I called Bob to come over late in the night. I realized we would need more help. We knew that we needed to take Ruth to the hospital. I told Bob that I wanted to go to church and talk to Pastor Barb. People from church had volunteered to help us. I didn't think they would be that much help. I would have to train each one of them. Ruth would need a lot of care. I asked Pastor Barb if she could help me hire a woman two days a week to help Ruth and us. I could afford to pay her.

Right after church, we took Ruth to St. Mary's Hospital. I stayed in the hospital with Ruth that night. Monday morning, a group of doctors came into the room. They asked Ruth to raise her legs. As much as Ruth tried, she could barely lift her legs one inch. They didn't know what to do. Soon some good friends, Greg and Kathy Holtz, came to the hospital to visit us. Pastor Barb also came up. Pastor Barb said we should get around the bed and join hands. She would pray for Ruth. It was a long prayer that God would help Ruth recover. Soon they all left. A couple of hours later, the doctors came into the room again. There were some new ones this time. They asked Ruth to raise her legs. She raised them eighteen inches high! The doctors couldn't believe what they saw! Now they could come up with a plan. They said they would have a therapist come right away to get Ruth moving. I called Pastor Barb and gave her the good news. "I think you have an inside track with God."

A therapist came into the room shortly. He tried to get Ruth walking. He said Ruth couldn't lift her feet high enough to walk. He said he would get a person from prosthetic laboratories to come to the hospital and make braces for Ruth's legs. A man come shortly to make them. I had to buy a new pair of shoes that were big enough that the braces would fit in the shoes. The shoes were the only clothing item I ever bought for Ruth that she liked. A pain doctor worked on Ruth's pain and thought he had it under control. Pastor Barb called me with a name and phone number of a woman who would work for us, Jackie Short. Jackie was a member of our church. Wednesday, they were ready to dismiss Ruth from the hospital. It was late in the day, and they had to have a nursing service lined up to come to our home. They didn't have one yet. We would have to stay another night. The doctor said Ruth wouldn't be taking anymore narcotic pills. I argued with the doctor. "What am I going to do if Ruth has terrible pain at home? I want a prescription for a narcotic." He said Ruth wouldn't have pain. We argued more, and finally, he gave me a prescription. I had been staying with Ruth at the hospital. I thought it would be safe to go home tonight and take a shower. I should have stayed.

I came back to the hospital early in the morning. Ruth's door was shut; it was normally open. I opened the door, and I could see Ruth was in terrible pain, and she was crying. I went to the desk and asked the nurses why Ruth was in terrible pain. "Why is Ruth crying?" The nurses said they had orders from the doctor not to give Ruth any narcotics. The doctor would not be in until ten. I went back into the room to see Ruth. She said she had pushed the call button for the nurse around midnight. The nurse said they couldn't give Ruth anything for pain. Finally, they closed the door so they wouldn't have to listen to Ruth crying. The nurses never checked on Ruth the rest of the night. I called the St. Mary's administration office. I told them what had just happened. They said they were going to investigate it. The doctor was there before someone from administration office came. The doctor blamed the doctors who were working that night in the hospital. The doctor was at fault. He never changed his order when I had the argument with him the day before. He gave Ruth the pills, and the pain got better. When people from St. Mary's finally came to investigate it, they apologized. But an apology didn't mean much to us after Ruth was in severe pain for ten hours. There was plenty of blame to go around. They finally had a nurse service lined up to come to our house, and Ruth was dismissed from the hospital.

Ruth didn't wear the wig much after this time. It was hard for Ruth to get the wig on or off to care for it. She thought having no hair was the least of her problems. Bob and I took Ruth to church in a wheelchair. She didn't wear the wig or caps. She had too many other problems to worry about. Hair wasn't a big deal at that time.

    Jackie and I agreed that she would work eight hours a day on Tuesdays and Thursdays. That would give me time to do other things. Jackie was an excellent cook. She made things we could warm up in the microwave. It would be easier for Bob. I encouraged Jackie to spend some time just visiting with Ruth. She did all the housekeeping, laundry, cooking, and helped Ruth with everything. She was a really fast worker. All of us really liked her. All of Ruth's visitors really liked Jackie too. Ruth was getting a lot of visitors at this time. My Uncle Duane and Aunt Barb came every week or two. They were really concerned about Ruth. I think company was really helping keep Ruth in a better mood.

    The nurse came out to our home. She said that Ruth would need therapy at home. Ruth was already in the wheelchair we got when my mother was here. The wheelchair was one my dad had. The wheelchair would not go through the bathroom's doors. The nurse said it would be easier for Ruth to have a smaller wheelchair so she could get into the bathrooms. She could get around more easily. Medicare would pay for it. The therapist gave Ruth exercises to do. Jackie helped Ruth the days when she was here. Ruth refused to do them for me. Our kids could get Ruth to do them.

    We had an appointment with the cancer doctors. Ruth's sister Linda wanted to go along with us. They would give Ruth another chemo treatment April 9. We had a long wait until the next appointment. The three of us went to Victoria's restaurant and had a leisurely meal.

    The next appointment was with a doctor that would look at Ruth's legs and feet. It was a three-thirty appointment. The doctor never came. Ruth was in severe pain. We finally got Ruth out of the wheelchair to a couch. Linda got Ruth pillows and sat with Ruth and comforted her. The doctor didn't come until after five. The doctor did a long examination. He never came up with a solution to help Ruth. He suggested that maybe we should try acupuncture. They didn't know if it would work. Medicare would not pay for it. It would cost $200 a time. Ruth could hardly walk. Oftentimes I had to lift

Ruth into bed and into the wheelchair. We had to try something. It was after six when we got out.

Ruth got chemo on April 9. Her birthday was April 10. On the night of the tenth, Ruth was really sick and in pain. Bob, Sarah, and I took Ruth to St. Mary's Hospital at six in the evening. At eleven o'clock, they decided to take Ruth to the Methodist Hospital. That was where they treated cancer patients. They told me Ruth would be there for some time. They would take Ruth by ambulance. That was free when they transferred patients between hospitals. I could ride in the ambulance. I told Bob and Sarah they should go home. It was after one when we got in the room. They brought a cot for me to sleep on. Most of the first night, there was someone asking me questions. I hardly got any sleep. Ruth never got out of bed Saturday. She was too weak.

On Sunday morning, a therapist came into the room. He asked Ruth to dance. He got her up, and he tried to dance with her. Ruth was in a good mood. She looked a lot better than yesterday. Stan and Linda came up to see her. They were having a nice visit when two nurses came into the room. They had Ruth sit on a large chair with rollers. They took Ruth into another room to give her a shower. I visited with Stan and Linda while Ruth was gone. When Ruth came back into the room, Stan and Linda said goodbye. They got Ruth up to weigh her. She passed out. She fell back into the chair. One nurse run out of the room. The other nurse was sitting on the floor shaking Ruth's hand. The nurse was crying and saying over and over, "Ruth, please don't leave me, please don't leave me." I got up and came closer to Ruth. I couldn't believe what was happening. I thought Ruth was dying! How could this be happening? A code was said over the intercom. All of a sudden, a dozen people ran into the room! They pushed me out of the way. Nurses were putting an oxygen mask and monitors on Ruth. At the same time, they were lifting Ruth off the chair and unto the bed. They lowered the head on the bed and raised the foot of the bed. Ruth came to. They put her belongings on the bed. They ran out of the room pushing the bed. I could hardly keep up. They took her to another floor and to a room where they could monitor her heart. She was in an intensive care unit.

When they got Ruth to the room, they started to hook her to the monitors. A crash crew nurse said she was going to take care of Ruth. Ruth was going to be her only patient the rest of the day. She said Ruth couldn't have much company. When they got everything hooked up, Ruth didn't look good. The nurse stayed with Ruth most of the time the first two hours. I called all our kids and told them what had happened. She was in another room under intensive care. She couldn't have much company. Next, I called Eva, and I asked her to call her brothers and sisters. Palmer came up right away. Throughout the rest of the day, Ruth's whole family come up to see her. When church was out, I called Pastor Barb. She said she would come up soon. In two hours, the nurse said Ruth now looked better. She could have as much company as she wanted. They took Ruth out of intensive care at eight o'clock in the evening and moved her to another room. That was a scary day for everyone, especially me.

One day in the hospital cafeteria while I ate, I saw Jim and Joan Hoffman. Joan's twin sister had cancer and was in the hospital. They were visiting her. They come up to Ruth's room with me to see Ruth. We had gone out to eat with Jim and Joan and her twin sister and her husband before.

In the next days they did many more tests. The cancer was growing again. Ruth couldn't tolerate any more chemo. They would do surgery May 24. Then after she healed up from the surgery, they were going to give radiation, five days a week for six weeks. I decided to go home one night to shower. I was hungry for pancakes. I stopped at Perkins. There weren't many people there. After I ordered I decided to call Ruth's two brothers and fill them in about Ruth. I didn't think I was talking loud enough for anyone to hear me. When I went to pay the bill, the waitress told me that someone had paid the bill for me. It touched me so much that I started crying. Ruth got out of the hospital on April 17.

Soon we had an appointment for acupuncture. We went into a small room. There was a small bed and a very uncomfortable couch. I took Ruth into the room in a wheelchair. When Ruth lay on the bed, I sat in the wheelchair. A lady came in and stuck twenty-one needles into Ruth. Some went in her head, ears, right shoulder, legs, and feet, some between her toes. Ruth was getting pain in her right shoulder, and it was from the accident she had with the horses. Then she put on a relaxing film on TV. Then the lady turned the lights down low and left us alone for an hour. Ruth and I fell asleep. Ruth didn't experience any pain from this. I think she wanted Ruth to relax so much that she would sleep. The lady came back into the room in an hour. She counted the needles as she took them out. Sometimes she had to really look to find the last one. We were to come twice a week for two months and then come once a week.

We had an appointment at Mayo shortly before May 24, when she was due for surgery. The doctors said Ruth was too weak to do the surgery now. They would move the surgery date to June 24.

Ruth's brothers and sisters got together at a point in Lake City where some of her sisters had mobile homes in the beginning of June. She sat with her sisters for a long time together at a table. Ruth was in a wheelchair. Then some of her sisters came to me and said, "You can't allow the doctors to give radiation to Ruth." Without the radiation, it was possible she could die. How could I allow this to happen? Ruth was a little stronger, and two sisters took both of Ruth's hands and helped her walk. They spent some time at this. When we got home, I asked Ruth about this. Ruth said she had been through too much. She couldn't face radiation. She said they could do the surgery but wasn't going to have any more treatments.

Ruth's sister, Donna, came with us to some of the appointments we had at Mayo. She wanted to hear what the doctors said. She also wanted to see how acupuncture worked. When Donna was with us, we ate at a restaurant in the Kahler Hotel next to Mayo.

We then went to visit Heather Allen, the medium. I took Ruth into the house in a wheelchair. She said she could communicate with Tammy. She said that Tammy was going to come to get Ruth. She said Ruth would see Tammy when she came. She didn't tell us when Tammy would come. She didn't tell us whether it would be soon or years to come. We didn't want to know. But I started to think, maybe I should prepare myself for the worst. I was scared!

It was June 24. We had to go to the hospital shortly after five in the morning for the surgery. I really dreaded it. They would remove

Ruth's breasts. But I wanted Ruth to live, so this was necessary. There was a lot for the nurses to do before the surgery. They wanted my cell phone number; they would call me after the surgery. They would have to send everything to the lab and check for cancer. They put a dye into Ruth's veins where the dye would go to her sentinel lymph nodes. They would take them out and check for cancer. Maybe they would have to take all her lymph nodes out. They took Ruth to surgery at eight. I was to sit in a big waiting room with a lot of people. I was alone. I had a long time to wait. I kept praying that the doctors would get all the cancer. Time went really slow. I kept praying. Finally, the phone rang. The doctor told me to leave the waiting room and go into the hall. I became really scared! When I was in the hall, the surgeon told me that they couldn't find cancer in Ruth's left breast and lymph nodes. There were some remains of the tumors, but the cancer was gone. In Ruth's right breast, there was a really small cancer, and they were positive that they got it all. I got so emotional I started crying. I couldn't believe it! It was a miracle! Everyone was praying for Ruth for a long time. God had answered our prayers! It took Ruth awhile to get out of recovery. They had thin tubes in her chest, and they had to train me to empty the tubes. They would leave them there one week. Ruth didn't have any pain from the surgery. We went home later in the day.

After a week, over the phone, a Mayo doctor told me I could pull the tubes out. I was surprised! The tubes were nearly six feet long. Ruth started to get better. She started by setting the table. She was able to stand and put the dishes on the counter. Then she sat in the wheelchair and put the dishes and silverware on her lap. She could put them on the table from the wheelchair. Everyone put the dirty dishes on the counter above the dishwasher. Ruth was able to put the dishes in the dishwasher and take them out while sitting in the wheelchair. Soon Ruth started cooking from the wheelchair. She could stand at the stove a minute at a time. The acupuncture was starting to work. The pain was going away. Ruth was getting stronger.

We had to go to Mayo to meet with the radiation doctor. The doctor told us that if they didn't do radiation, the cancer would come back. Ruth said she was now finally feeling better. She was not going to have radiation. She said she couldn't face going through any more treatments again. She didn't want to be sick again. She had been through too much. I told the doctor, "If you said you didn't get it all, maybe we should do radiation, but there is no cancer left. We don't need radiation." I now felt comfortable not doing radiation. When you look back on what Ruth went through, you see God had cured the cancer. I really believe in God and prayers.

Ruth's hair was finally growing back. It came in black and curly. Ruth had never had black hair before. The curls looked good on Ruth. Finally, the hair got so long that Ruth wanted it cut. The curls were gone; they didn't come back. The black hair was gone too. Her natural color came back.

Ivar and his family

Ivar Scrumpstad and his family would be visiting us from Norway. Ivar was a MAST student in 1984. We were really excited, but it would be hard for us to have them stay with us. What was I to do? I finally asked Bob, "Could they stay in your house and you sleep in our house?" They would have a house for themselves. I asked Jackie, "Would you clean Bob's house?" I also asked Jackie

A FATHER'S QUEST

if she would work every day while they were here and cook for us. I think it was fun for Jackie to visit with someone from Norway. It would not be easy to go anywhere. We would have to entertain them at the farm. I think they enjoyed looking at the farm, and we enjoyed showing it to them. Ivar's two sons enjoyed shooting the rifle at targets and shooting traps with a shotgun. Ivar's daughter enjoyed horseback riding. We all had a horse and carriage ride. I think it was fun for all of us.

Mayo said we could now go every other week for acupuncture. Jackie started coming one day every other week. This allowed Ruth and me to do more things.

Ruth had now gotten where I could help her walk a little. We could go to a restaurant without the wheelchair. We decided to try going on a short vacation. Most of the time, Ruth was in the wheelchair. We first went to Jackpot Junction, a casino by Morton Minnesota. We then went to Walnut Grove. Laura Ingalls Wilder Museum was there. We really enjoyed it. We spent the next night in Spirit Lake, Iowa. Ruth was able to walk with my help into a restaurant in Spirit Lake. The next day we ran into a casino in northern Iowa. I took Ruth into the casino in a wheelchair. We didn't stay their long. We both won $20 really fast. We decided to leave while we were ahead. We then went to the Humboldt County Historical Museum. We had been by it before but had never stopped. It was really good. I pushed Ruth in the wheelchair where I could. She sat in the car while I saw the rest. There was an old church that they moved in from Hardy, Iowa. It had the most beautiful colored windows I have ever seen. We stayed overnight in Humboldt. The next day we went to Thor, Iowa. We went to the farm my grandfather lived on when he was born. We had been there many times before. We always stopped to visit the lady who was living there. She wasn't home. Next, we found the farm that Gary Norstad's great-grandfather Lars Norstad lived at. Lars's wife was an aunt to my great-grandmother. We spent the last night at Diamond Joe's, a casino north of Clear Lake, Iowa. I have never won any money at that casino before, so we lost.

Ruth started to go grocery-shopping with me. We walked together a short distance into the store, and then Ruth rode on a scooter. Grocery-shopping was a lot easier for me. It was finally fun to be able to go places with Ruth and not to go alone.

Soon we decided to visit Ruth's sister Marion in the Black Hills. Marion had breast cancer years ago too. We stopped at Walnut Grove again. Then we went to De Smet, South Dakota. Laura Ingalls and her family lived there after Walnut Grove. Her parents were buried there. We went to the graves. There were 160 acres to look at. Ruth couldn't do it. When I went into the store where they sold tickets, I told the lady working there we wouldn't be able to see it. I told her that Ruth had breast cancer and neuropathy and couldn't walk. She told me that she had breast cancer and neuropathy too. She got over it and was okay now. It really gave us hope! She said, "There is a golf cart here for you to use." We spent a lot of time there. We looked at the farm buildings and the house. We went to a church and to a schoolhouse on the golf cart. It was fun! We stayed in a hotel in Deadwood while we visited Marion. We went gambling with Marion and Sid, her husband, once. We went to Hills City and rode on an 1800 train. We had done this several times before with our kids and grandkids. We ate across the road from the train at Ruby's restaurant. It looked like a restaurant from the 1800s. I had spaghetti and meatballs. The restaurant was fifty miles from Deadwood, but the meal was so good that we drove back there the next day to eat.

In the middle of September, Shilo died. She was going to come in the house late in the afternoon. She collapsed on the porch. I was working in the office, and Ruth called me. Ruth sat on the porch in the wheelchair, and I knelt down beside her, petting her. I think she had a heart attack. She heard Bob coming in with a tractor. She tried to get up but couldn't. Bob picked her up and brought her into the south room where she had a bed. We all ate supper, and then we all sat by Shilo. Ruth never liked dogs. But after Pastor Barb prayed for Ruth the day Shilo put her head on Ruth's hand, Ruth become attached to Shilo after this time. When she was young, she barked so much she drove us crazy. She lost her voice in later years from barking too much. Shilo was Justin's dog. When Brenda got married and she and Justin moved away, they took Shilo. She was always chasing things and barking. Owen milked cows, and Shilo wasn't going to work there. Shilo started to live with Bob in the house I had built for Brenda on our farm. Ruth and I went to bed at night, and Bob sat up all night with Shilo. Six thirty the next morning, Bob came into our bedroom and said that Shilo just died. I took her out on the porch with her bed. In the afternoon, Brenda and her boys came over, and we buried her west of the horse stable. Justin's Little Shilo was born on August 30, 2001. If she had lived a few more days, she would have been fourteen years old. She had a long good life. Soon afterward, I wrote the story "The Dogs throughout the Years."

I didn't have to stay with Ruth all the time. Ruth was able to do more on her own. I was able to help with harvest. Merritt came more, and he took my place while I took Ruth to acupuncture treatments. It still took some time to take care of Ruth. Harvest was really good. Soybean crop was the highest yield we had ever had.

We had ninety thousand miles on our 2012 Chevy Equinox. I had never bought new tires. I was hoping Ruth and I could do a lot of traveling. The vacation that we had in September went well. I would have to buy new tires or buy a new car. We went to Lakeville, and we bought a new 2016 Chevy Equinox. I didn't want everyone to know we bought a new car. We bought a white one exactly like the old one.

Ruth and I took Doreen's girls, Jenna and Valarie, Christmas shopping in December. We went to Walmart in Albert Lea. I helped Ruth walk into the store. There was a scooter for Ruth to ride on. Ruth started to run into things. The girls and I found it to be embarrassing to be with Ruth. We pretended we didn't know her. Maybe we were mean to Ruth.

Acupuncture treatments started to hurt when the lady put in the needles. Ruth had never experienced this before. Ruth soon didn't want the treatments anymore. I thought that it was now really working. Neuropathy was now soon going to be over. Mayo decided that we should only have the treatments once a month. Ruth agreed to this. Only three times I got a bill from Mayo for the acupuncture treatments. I paid them right away. I figured the bill would be ten thousand by now. I never received another bill. I never asked them.

In a way, I blamed Mayo for causing the neuropathy and all the pain Ruth went though.

We had Christmas at our house. Doreen and Brenda brought the meal to our house on Christmas Eve. We still took the grandkids with us to pick out their Christmas presents. We gave money to everyone else. Going shopping was now getting harder. Little did we know, it would soon get even harder.

After the February acupuncture treatment, Ruth didn't want them again. They hurt too much, so Ruth quit them. We also decided we didn't need Jackie to help us anymore. It was a mutual decision; Jackie had too much to do. We would miss her.

We had the annual meeting for the Southeast Mutual Insurance Company on March 2, 2016. I was now the president of the company. I had to conduct the meeting. I was happy that Ruth could go along.

We had just got a new car. We had cold weather and snow at home. I thought Ruth would get better sooner if we went south. Little did I know that in two months, I couldn't take care of Ruth anymore. Ruth would have to get better. Our first stop was St. Louis. An old Navy buddy, Steve, and his wife, Judy Hubbert, lived there. We stayed two nights in a hotel close to their home. I think if I remember right, the four of us ate supper at The Cracker Barrel. The next day, they picked us up at the hotel. I think Steve drove my car, as we had to take the wheelchair for Ruth. We went to a neat house where there was a restaurant. It was a neat unusual place. Then we went to a museum. I had to push Ruth in the wheelchair both places. Spending time with them was fun.

Next we went to Murray, Kentucky to visit my Uncle Cliff. We had always stayed at their place several times before. We always slept in an upstairs bedroom with a bathroom. It was nice. This time we stayed in a hotel. It would be easier for me to take care of Ruth. We never went to their house. We went out to supper with Cliff and my Aunt Linda.

We then went to Milton, Florida, to see my Aunt Kathy. We had always stayed at their home many times before Lyle had died, and it would now be different. We stayed at the Red Roof Inn three nights.

It was close by. We were invited to their house for dinner Sunday. We had a good visit with my Aunt Kathy and my cousins. I really missed Lyle. I was really glad that I saw him five months before he died. I asked Kathy if she would take us to Lyle's grave. Lyle was buried in a tiny family cemetery close by. Lyle had taken me to this cemetery several times before. He always took care of it. I couldn't remember where it was. My cousin Starlin showed me how to use Facebook and got me started on it. She said, "Maybe we could share our vacation with them." We didn't like the breakfast that they served us in the hotel. There was a Waffle House next to it. We always ate there. I needed to get Ruth walking better. We walked together. We spent the next day at Moline, Alabama. We visited an old fort there. Ruth was in the wheelchair. We left on Tuesday morning. We decided to find Lyle's grave again by ourselves so we could find it again.

We got to Ruth's sister's home early in the afternoon in Vero Beach, Florida. It was sunny, and the temperature was in the eighties. Donna lived on the second story of her building. Donna wanted us to stay with her. There was no elevator, so we would have to climb the outside stairs. Ruth had never done this after she had neuropathy. I think it was helping her get stronger. Donna and I helped Ruth climb the steps. Ruth, Donna, and I visited the Hallstead Farm that day. It was a 120-acre citrus farm started in the early 1900s. Only one family had lived there. Next, we visited a train museum. We spent the first part of the afternoon on a two-hour boat trip on the Indian River. We saw many dolphins. That was fun! We also saw many beautiful mansions from the boat. We went to church and Sunday school with Donna Sunday morning. I really enjoyed meeting her pastor again. In Sunday school, Donna introduced Ruth to the Sunday school class. She told them that God had answered their prayers. In the last few days, Ruth was getting stronger. Ruth got a pep talk from "Mother Donna." We both agreed with what she said: "It is going to take a lot of work from both of you to get Ruth back to normal." God had answered prayers from a lot people who were praying for Ruth.

We then went to St. Augustine, Florida I pushed Ruth around in the wheelchair this morning. We ran into places that were not wheelchair assessable. The traffic got terrible as the day went on. We wanted to take a tour of the city. The red train tour looked the easiest for Ruth to get on. There was no place to park. Finally, I pulled into a trolley tour place. The trolleys were built higher up than what we had planned. How could I get Ruth on the trolley? There was no parking place. We would have to park the car a long way away. It would be impossible. Suddenly, there was an angel helping us! A girl from the ticket place came up to us and said, "Just leave the car here." She would give me a permission slip to put on my windshield so they wouldn't tow my car. She would help me to get Ruth on the train and off. I think God and angels are with us all the time.

We stayed the next night on Jekyll Island in Georgia. We stayed in a beautiful Hampton Inn. We had a large room with a sitting area and an outside balcony overlooking the pool. We had supper that night in a really nice restaurant on the wharf. We met a couple there that was from Blaine, Minnesota. Afterward we went on a horse and carriage ride through the historic area. We had a beautiful day the next day. We were thinking about everyone in Minnesota enjoying the snow. Jekyll's Inland was a place for the extreme rich to spend the winters there. They built cottages that were more like mansions. The rich that lived there controlled most of the money in the world at the time. In World War II, German U-boats were spotted off the shore. Everyone left and never came back. Today it is a park, and everything is kept perfect. It is simply beautiful. In the morning, I pushed Ruth around in the wheelchair. The streets and sidewalks were made out of tabby, a cement made out of seashells. It was a large park of mansion after mansion. Next we sat on the beach. There was no one in the water as it was too cold. But the air was warm, and there were many people just sitting on the beach. Next, we took a red train tour for two hours. I got off the train and looked at many mansions. The weather was so nice that Ruth enjoyed just sitting on the train and looking at everything. We felt bad that we had to leave the next day, but we were extremely tired tonight.

The next day, we went to Hofwyl-Broadfield planation. It was a perfect day, and it was a beautiful place. There was no mansion. At the beginning, the family lived in Savanna. The plantation had a regular farm house. The family eventually lost the mansion but saved the plantation by changing it to a dairy farm. The last member of the family died in 1973, leaving the plantation to the state. We had supper at a seafood restaurant on the water with all glass windows with a beautiful view. We stayed the night at a Hampton Inn in Georgetown, South Carolina.

The next day, we spent all day on the road. The first part of the trip the traffic was terrible, and we never thought we would get past Myrtle Beach. The second half the traffic wasn't so bad. After sitting in the car too long, I could hardly move. When people saw Ruth and me walking, they must have wondered who was helping whom walk. We spent the night in Edenton, North Carolina. It is a historic town. We had supper at a fancy seafood restaurant. When we looked at the menu, everything was $20 to $30, and we had no idea what most things were. We ordered a hamburger, and the total bill was $15. We had an excellent table right next to the window facing the historic street with a view of the waterfront. All of a sudden, a police car come by with flashing lights. Then came fifty people carrying crosses followed by another police car. It was Good Friday. When we left, Ruth had trouble getting down the steps. Then a young man jumped up and took Ruth's arm and helped her to the street. Angels are sometimes people. We were going to stay there three nights. It was going to be Easter. We thought we would have trouble traveling. We had to spend Easter somewhere.

Wow, what a day! I was lucky to have an understanding wife, because Ruth sat in the car while I toured two plantations. First, we went to the Hope Plantation. We had been there several times before. I have been a patron member of the Hope Foundation for many years. In 2015, they printed a book on the Hope Plantation. My name is in it, and I am labeled as a patron member. I bought the book at a reduced price. I got a special tour, and they told me that I could take pictures of the mansion. After the tour, we visited a while in the office, and the lady who gave me the tour told Ruth she wasn't getting away without a hug. Next, we went to Somerset, a plantation about forty miles away. It was the biggest plantation in North Carolina. It started out as one hundred thousand acres and over eight hundred slaves. There was a mansion and a lot of buildings. There was a lot there, and the tour took two hours with an excellent tour guide. We had spaghetti at an Italian restaurant in the historic district. Another excellent day with the weather.

It was Easter the next day. Ruth and I attended a United Methodist Church. Service started at eleven o'clock. Before the service, the pastor came down the aisle and shook everyone's hands but didn't ask who we were. It was a good message on who had the last word. It was raining when we got out of church, so we went out the back door to our car. Our plan was to go to Kitty Hawk. We had a late dinner at Mel's Diner. Many people reading this are probably too young to remember the TV show *Mel's Diner*. We had an excellent meal. Next, we went to the Wright Bros. National Park. It was lightly raining, and Ruth sat in the car while I went in the museum. We drove completely around the Albemarle Sound. We crossed several bridges miles and miles long. One of them I checked, and it was three and a half miles long. It was a pretty trip even if it was raining.

Next, we went to Kenny and Norma's house in Cary, North Carolina. We stayed there one night. Norma seemed well, but Kenny was sick with lung cancer. We took Norma out to eat while Kenny went for treatments. When we left, I sure hoped that we would see Kenny again, but it was not to be. Kenny lived two more years.

Another wonderful day. We spent several hours at Appomattox National Park. The Civil War ended there. They have restored everything as it was in 1865. Everything was simply beautiful. There were a lot of buildings. At first, I pushed Ruth in the wheelchair. We looked at everything from the outside. Then Ruth told me to leave her sitting on the wheelchair and go in as many building as I wanted to. They had real like lifelike statues of General Grant and Lee signing the peace treaty. It made me think I was in 1865. I hope we can go back there again. The weather was warm, and Ruth enjoyed just sitting and watching.

Pat Cunningham called us and asked us to come one day earlier than we had planned. We skipped some things that we going to do. We got there on Thursday night. Thursday night, we went to visit Pat's brother David. Bob had to work. David has an elaborate

Christmas and train display. It takes up most of his house. He had left it up from Christmas so we could see it. It is simply unbelievable! Friday, we visited a history museum. There was more there than we could possibly see. It was good, and we took many pictures. Ruth was in the wheelchair. Their house was in the mountains. We came into the garage, and there were steps going to the main floor. The bedrooms were upstairs, and there was another flight of steps. I wondered if Ruth would make it. I helped Ruth with the steps. Ruth got stronger every day. I think visiting Bob and Pat really helped Ruth get better. The visit went well.

We spent our forty-eighth wedding anniversary on April 6 at a casino hotel in Waterloo, Iowa. It was now time to go home the next day. We really had fun, and Ruth was now getting to be like the wife I had married forty-eight years ago. God had really answered our prayers.

Shortly after we got home, we went to Mayo, and the doctors said Ruth was cancer-free. We had really enjoyed the vacation and were planning many more. That was not to be! In less than a month, I would be fighting for my life.

Chapter 28

Dogs throughout the Years

The End of an Era

The morning of August 11, at 6:30 AM, Justin's little Shilo died. She was a very special boxer dog. Probably only pet lovers can relate to the deep sorrow we feel. On August 30, she would have been fourteen years old. She had a long life, and she had been failing for the past eleven months. The evening of August 10 at 7:00 PM, she wanted to go outside. Ruth watched for her to return to the porch. When she got to the door, she collapsed. Ruth called for me, and we both sat on the porch with her. She was unable to get up. After about forty-five minutes Bob, our son, came home with the lawn tractor from mowing grass at his hog house. When she heard the tractor, she tried to get up. I helped her, and she made it into the house, but she couldn't control her direction, and she went down again. I carried her into our sunroom and tried to put her on her doggy bed. She wanted to stay up and struggled some but finally lay down. Bob came in the house and petted her. We all sat and watched her for about an hour. We have two houses on our farm. Bob lives in one alone with Shilo; she has her own bedroom. Bob called her, and she tried to get up to go home but couldn't. Bob tried a couple more times but it became obvious that even though she wanted to she couldn't. Eventually, Ruth and I went to bed, and Bob spent the night sitting in a chair beside her. At four in the morning, I checked on her and remarked to Bob that she didn't look good. At six thirty, she tried to stir and move; she put her head on Bob's foot and passed away. Bob came in our bedroom and said, "Dad, Shilo just died."

The Beginning

I was born during World War II. As my dad was serving in the Army, I spent the first two years of my life living with my maternal grandparents. The first dog I remember was You No. My mother told the story many times about how they were afraid to have me around dogs when they were visiting. It wasn't that they were afraid that I would be bit but that I would grab the dog by the head and bite its ears; the dogs would then run away howling. When I was two, the war was over. My parents moved to a rented farm next to my paternal grandparents, and we had several dogs. The two that stand out are a rat terrier named Patsy and a yellow collie named Lucky. We were dairy farmers, and Lucky was an excellent cattle dog. We had lived there ten years when my parents had a sale and quit farming. We lived on several farm sites and always took the dogs with us. Then my parents moved a house onto my mother's parents' farm where they lived the rest of their lives.

When I was fourteen, I knew for sure that I would someday become a farmer. That could be another story.

In 1968, I married a wonderful girl and had a job as a cabinetmaker in Rochester. We lived in an apartment the first year and then built a new house. Our first daughter, Tammy, was born at that time. I couldn't wait to get her a dog. My wife, Ruth, didn't like dogs, but I finally persuaded her. We got a small toy Chihuahua named Taffy. Our second daughter, Doreen, was born in 1970. In the spring of 1971, I sold the house and bought a 160-acre farm. It had been abandoned some years before. The windows were broken out of the house. Ruth was not happy but finally moved in June 1971.

The First Era

Our son, Bob, was born April 6, 1972, on our fourth wedding anniversary. I had bought some sows and was going to farrow pigs.

I had also bought a border collie that we named Sheba. I was on the top of the world. I had a sweet loving wife, two beautiful daughters, a son to take over the farm, and a really good dog. Life couldn't be any better than this. Sheba was a black-and-white, medium-sized border collie. She was a natural livestock dog.

We had sows and pigs in pastures, and sometimes they would get out. I continued to work as a cabinetmaker. Ruth would call me at work mad saying the pigs were out. I would try to explain that I couldn't leave work and she would have to deal with it. By the time I got home at night, the pigs were all in. Sheba had rounded them all up and put them back in. She had to actually see us making attempts at fixing the fence, or she wouldn't put them back the next time.

In 1974, I quit my job and started farming full-time. In 1975, I bought another farm, and in 1976, we rented another farm, so the farm grew fast. We also raised more and more pigs. Sheba was always with me when I did chores. When we were farrowing, I always went to check the sows at ten in the evening. Sheba always went from crate to crate with me. By eleven, when everyone else was in bed sleeping, she would always bid me good night. She wouldn't go in the house, and if I locked her in the barn or another building, she would chew up the doors to get out. It didn't matter how cold or how much snow she had to be outside. We had a small space under the step to the house, and that was where she slept. One winter morning, I could hear her crying. I opened the door and could see her through the storm door. She couldn't move. I went out another door and found that her fur had frozen to the step. I got some warm water and got her free, but she wouldn't come into the house.

We still had Taffy, and she and Sheba got in a disagreement one day, and one of Taffy's eyes popped out. We took her to the vet, and they removed the eye. We could never tell if it affected her.

In the fall of 1976, our youngest daughter, Brenda, was born. When it came time to potty train Brenda, Taffy did it by always sitting in the bathroom next to her. Around this time, I bought a wired-hair terrier named Corky. He was a fighter, always taking on a wild animal and always winning.

A FATHER'S QUEST

I don't remember when Taffy died. I think it was around 1980. It was in the summertime, and she died in front of the house. Corky was standing watch over her. As the sun changed throughout the day, he moved her all the way around the house always, keeping her in the shade. We couldn't get him to leave her. I was afraid to bury her fearing that he would dig her up. When night came, we got him in the house, and I buried her in the dark. That fall, Corky was run over by a neighbor pulling two wagons of corn by our place.

After Corky died, we bought a miniature schnauzer. He was for the kids and was a house dog. Snokey right away became my dog. I taught him to sit up and beg, roll over, and to march like a soldier making square turns. He was a fast learner, and I only worked with him for a few minutes at a time during breakfast with bacon. He loved to show off and never once let me down when I wanted to show him off. I used to eat breakfast barefooted, and we had a Swedish student named Jan that year. Snokey had made a mess on the floor of my office, and I went to get something during breakfast. I stepped in the mess. Jan had the laugh of his life as I tried to hop on one foot to the bathroom. Snokey became extremely fat from all the treats I gave him, and he only lived to nine.

From 1977 through 1979, we put up many buildings on our farm: a large hog house, a machine shed, and a grain drying set up with two bins. On almost all the pictures, Sheba is close by watching.

In 1980, we rented more land and started having foreign students though the University of Minnesota. They spent a year living with us, studying American agriculture. We had twenty students over the next sixteen years. Sheba always welcomed them.

The farm crisis started in the 1980s, and times got tough. In 1983, I decided I had to make changes on the farm. I decided to quit farrowing pigs. I don't remember when exactly, but around this time, Sheba died of old age. She had really slowed down. She had lived to be a livestock working dog; I thought it was fit to bury her behind the barn where there was a row of trees. The trees are now long gone, and the barn is gone. New buildings have been built. I don't know anymore exactly where I put her. Sheba was gone, the sows were gone, no more late nights in the barn. I had a young family, and it was tough times. I don't really remember mourning her. The farm had made a huge change, and it was the end of an era.

The Second Era

In the spring of 1984, I just had to have another border collie. Money was extremely tight; I could get a male a little cheaper than a female, so I got a male puppy and named him Jack. We were then buying feeder pigs. With no pigs in outside lots, we had less fence to keep up. As Jack grew up, he became very hyper. He might have done better on a cattle farm with a lot of work. If I let him run loose, I was getting a call from a neighbor. Jack was chasing their chickens or cows or something. I had to keep him tied, but he ran steady from one end of the chain to the other. One day when he was loose, he was hit by a car. I think he had a head injury as he was unconscious for several days. He just lay in the barn. He finally came to and was kind of okay for a month. He was no companion. He soon started running again. He was soon hit by another car. This time he died. I was sad for almost one minute.

Things got really hard financially in 1985. The kids wanted another dog. I wasn't sure we wouldn't lose the farm. If we had to move, another dog could be a problem. One day I saw an ad for a free puppy that was part blue heeler. She was mostly white with very, very little brown and black spots, short-haired, and medium-sized. We named her Ginger. Ruth didn't want her in the house, so she was to be an outside dog. She was okay with sleeping in the barn and did fairly well outside in the cold during the day.

She was really good with the pigs. When we loaded pigs to sell, she would stay right beside Ruth, and the moment she knew which one needed loading, she had it on the truck. The barn had a low ceiling, so I could go up in the hay barn with just a step ladder outside the barn. We bedded the pigs I kept in the old sow building with straw. Several times a week, I would go up in the hay mow for straw, and she would climb the ladder and go along. She came down the ladder headfirst. She was a real companion! She went every place with me.

One day I could hear her barking in the machine shed. I went to see what was wrong. I had left an extension ladder fully extended next to a deck where we stored something. There must have been a cat on this deck because Ginger had climbed completely to the top of the ladder; she was right to the roof. She couldn't get back down, so I had to climb up and carry her down.

Once in a great while, I would give her a ride in the pickup. She really liked this. If I would say, "Ginger, do you want to go along?" she would go right to the pickup and get in as soon as the door opened. If I didn't ask her, she never went near the pickup. She never begged for a ride.

The farm economy started to get better. Looking back, I think it was getting better before we thought it was at its worst. We were able to rent more land, and the farm started to prosper again.

In 1988, I had a Danish student who wanted to help me build a mudroom and farm entryway on the house. That winter after the entryway was finished Ginger got real sick one day. We suspected she had drunk antifreeze. I took her to the vet. He said he would try something but held very little hope. He said to leave her and that I could come and pick her body up in the morning. The kids felt terrible. We got up in the morning, had a very quiet breakfast, and normally, I was out working before the school bus came. I stayed in until they left for school. It was a long ride into town; I felt terrible. How would I bury her with all the ground frozen? Was I surprised when I entered the vet's office. She greeted me at the door. We were all so happy. I called the school to tell the kids. Ruth said she could sleep in the new mudroom. She eventually became a house dog.

During the fall harvest, I always got up in the night to check the corn dryer. Because Ginger was in the house, she would go along. She would chase the light from the flashlight. She would come in the dryer shack with me, and I would check some samples of corn and sit and pet her awhile and back to the house with her chasing the light. This went on for seven harvests.

As she became more and more a house dog, she became less and less a pig dog. She became a real member of our family. She became really social and enjoyed all our children's graduation parties.

She never bit anyone or bothered any people visiting the farm. She wasn't much of a watch dog. But let a stray dog or cat or any wild animal enter the farmyard, and she stood her ground and chased them away. In the summer of 1996, she was eleven years old, and life was getting harder. One day I looked out, and there was stray dog entering the yard. She also saw it and attacked it. It was running down the road. I was surprised she could still do this.

That summer for the first time ever, we had $5 corn. I had the bills paid up and enough corn to build a new farm shop. It would be fifty-four by eighty feet with three thousand feet of hot-water pipe in the floor for heat. I thought this will be nice for Ginger as she could spend her days with us while we were working; she wouldn't have to experience so much cold. This was not to be.

In September, she got sick. I took her to the vet. She had some female problems, and with her age, there wasn't much to do. By the end of the month, she could hardly move. One night she couldn't get up the steps from the garage to the house, so we made a bed in the garage for her. The next morning she was dead. I buried her in the lawn southwest of the house.

I didn't realize one could get so sad. I didn't care to live anymore. Harvest was terrible, she wasn't with me to check the dryer, and I missed her so.

The kids were all grown. We had the last foreign student in 1995. Bob was now farming with me. He had bought two farms, and I had bought more land. Farming would be much different with the warm shop. It was again the end of an era; life had made a great change.

By the end of the year, I was still mourning Ginger. I missed her so much I was sick. I didn't realize that in a week I would have a real loss that would forever change my life. This loss was one that I would never get over.

The Era of the Boxers

When Ginger died, I said to Bob, "I will never live on the farm long enough for another dog, so you get the next dog." I had planned that Bob would get married and that Ruth and I would leave the farm. After harvest, he bought a female boxer puppy named Daisy. I always called her Muggsy because of the shape of her nose.

On January 5, 1997, our oldest daughter, Tammy, died in a house fire. This forever changed everything in all our lives. It was a Sunday morning, a blizzardy day. We decided, because of the weather, we wouldn't go to church. At eight thirty, we saw Tammy's car go by, toward her house. She lived four miles east of us on the same road. She must have worked the night before. Early afternoon, we got a call that Tammy's house was on fire. We left to go, but our car got stuck in the snow. Bob had his pickup on the road. Ruth told me to go with Bob. As we got close to her place, we could see the flames. I said to Bob, "I hope everyone got out." As we turned past her place, I saw her sitting in the front seat looking back toward the house. I saw our granddaughters in the back seat. I was so relieved. We walked past the car toward the house without stopping at the car. When we got close to the house, someone said that Tammy was still inside. I looked back to the car, and she was gone. She was twenty-seven years old and had two daughters. Kayla was four years old, and Sarah was three years.

Whenever I asked her husband anything about the fire, he would tell me it was none of my business. He did not want us to see our granddaughters because we might talk to them about the fire. We were never emotionally able to ever talk with them about that day. There was a huge amount of life insurance. On two of the policies, someone else had signed Tammy's name. We eventually had our grandparents' rights established in court to have visitation with Kayla and Sarah. This is a long story in itself for another day.

Also at this time, our youngest daughter, Brenda, was pregnant. We weren't happy about this at the time. On March 9, 1997, she had a baby boy whom she named Justin. You could have not asked for a better baby. He was always happy, never fussed. They lived with us in our house. Ruth and I were so sad about Tammy. It was hard to get out of bed in the morning. Justin gave us a bright light in the day. It was like he was a gift from God to get us through this.

In the summer of 1997, we added a grain bin, giving us 40 percent more storage. We also added an air system to blow the corn to the bins. This saved us from moving augers from bin to bin, making harvest easier. We still had to check the dryer at night though.

In the following spring, Ruth and I took a short vacation, and when we came home, we learned that Daisy had been run over by the school bus at the end of our driveway. She wasn't on the road. The school bus didn't stop at our farm. I've never figured this out. Bob buried her beside the driveway.

Boxer puppies were quite the experience, so Bob and I decided we would try raising them. I bought a female in western Minnesota and named her Lady. Bob bought a male north of the Twin Cities that he named Tramp. They both were born March 3, 1998. Now we had Lady and the Tramp.

In August 1998, we added two and one half bedrooms and a bath on our house. Our bedroom was really small. We would add on to our bedroom. Now Brenda and Justin would have a bedroom downstairs, and our granddaughters would have a bedroom when they visited. I hired a friend of mine to help with this. Justin, who was a year and a half, and these two puppies were often out with us. It was so much fun to watch them play together. Bob also built a two-thousand-head hog house on his farm that summer.

We had no puppies until spring of 2001. I had given up on this ever happening. Lady had seven puppies. Justin and I would lie under a tree and play with these puppies. I was a small child again. What fun! When we sold the puppies, it was a sad time, but we got enough money to put central air in our house.

Brenda wanted me to keep a puppy for Justin, but we wanted to raise more puppies, so I bought him a female puppy. They named her Shilo. She was the nicest puppy you could ask for. She was easy to housebreak, never chewed anything or caused any problem. She was a real sweetheart.

It was the first day of harvest. Ruth was filling the car with gas at our fuel barrel. She got in the car and drove ahead; Shilo was killed. Justin wanted her buried under his bedroom window. He was four years old. I bought him another puppy again, almost right away. We got her from a lady in Walnut Grove. This puppy was a half sister to the first one. Because the first puppy's registered name was Shilo and they still wanted that name, this puppy's name was Justin's Little Shilo. She was born August 30, 2001.

She wasn't anything like the first Shilo. She would quickly jump on the couch and pee. What a disaster! How could this have happened? If anyone has seen the movie *Marley and Me*, she was Marley. She was always getting into something, always chasing everything, barking until she would drive you nuts.

In the summer of 2002, Shilo had a litter of ten puppies. Lady had also had puppies again before this. I had told Brenda she could have all the puppy money if she took care of them and sold them. Brenda did a really good job of this. She wrote to the people who got puppies, getting some word-of-mouth business. It was easy to sell the puppies.

In the spring of 2003, Shilo had another litter of puppies, ten again. We had sold all of them in June. On July 21, 2003, Kayla and Sarah came to live with us permanently. The second week in August, our whole family went to a resort in Northern Minnesota. I had hired a sixteen-year-old neighbor boy to stay at and watch the farm. One of the first days up North, I got a phone call from him. Shilo was run over by a motorcycle. He took her to the vet in Dodge Center, and she would need surgery. It would cost $700. I said, "Okay." A short time later, he called back. "It's a bigger surgery than they want to do, and they want her to go to Rochester. It will cost $1,500." Justin, who was six years old, was right beside me. He said, "Don't let my dog die, Grandpa," so I gave the okay. A short time later, I got another phone call. The vet in Rochester was going on vacation; he didn't have the time for the surgery. Again, Justin said, "Don't let my dog die, Grandpa." Shilo should go to the University of Minnesota, but our sixteen-year-old neighbor didn't feel comfortable taking her to the Twin Cities. We had sold one of the first puppies to a really nice lady named Gloria. The vet's office knew her well and said maybe she could do it. I called her, and she agreed. Her mother was having surgery in the cities on that day, and she would take Shilo home with her after the surgery. A couple of hours later, I got a call from Gloria.

"Wayne, this is going to cost you $3,500, but I know you can afford it." Justin was still beside me, saying, "Please don't let my dog die, Grandpa." By now, all this had gone too far to back down, so I said okay. In the end, it cost me over $4,000.

As soon as we got home from our trip, we went to Gloria's house to pick up Shilo. I have never seen a dog so happy to see us as she was. After that time, she never liked to be left alone. After this, she slept in Brenda's house in Justin's room.

I am going to backtrack here. In the late fall of 2001, I bought a double-wide mobile home. It was in really bad shape. I put it all in my shop and completely rebuilt it during the winter. In the spring, I had it set up on our farm just east of the shop. Brenda and Justin had moved into it about a year before Kayla and Sarah had come to live with us. This made everything easier when Kayla and Sarah had come to live with us. Bob still lived with us and really took on the father role for them. In many ways, he had taken on this role shortly after Tammy had died.

Also in 2001, we took down the trees where Sheba was buried. We also hauled in a lot of fill and built a new machine shed.

I bought another boxer female from the same people in Walnut Grove and named her Molly. The boxers always lived and slept in the shop. We sold two litters of puppies from Molly.

As soon as Kayla and Sarah came to live with us, they asked, "Grandpa, will you buy us a horse?"

In the winter, we started having the girls take riding lessons. In the spring, I bought the horses they were taking their lessons on. Kayla got the horse named Mercedes, and we bought Cheyenne from the same person for Sarah.

Bob and I also each bought a horse. Later I bought a team of driving horses. We stayed on a ranch out west twice with the horses and went on many wagon trains. We went twice to the state of Georgia.

In July, we started to level the site for the new stable. There were a lot of tall weeds there. Bob backed up with the backhoe, and there lay Lady dead. We didn't even realize she was there. She was only six years old. We buried her right east of where the building was to be built, right where she was run over.

On August 28, 2004, Brenda married Owen, a dairy farmer who lived twelve miles north of us. They tried to take Shilo with, but she caused too much trouble, always chasing something. They had too much traffic in their yard and were afraid she would be run over. They tried a couple of times, but it just didn't work. Shilo went back to sleeping in the shop, and Bob moved into Brenda's house.

In the spring of 2006, we had a wet cold night, and all the boxers got in a fight. This happened very rarely, when one of the females was in heat. Molly was injured. It was very late at night, and we put straw down in the shop and left Shilo and Tramp outside. We had other buildings they could get into. In the morning, Molly was dead. We buried her on the east side of the horse stable with Lady. For a long time, I didn't have anything to do with Shilo or Tramp. We quit raising pigs in 2006.

By the summer of 2007, Tramp was slowing down. He liked to lie on a bench on our porch. He did not like it if we wanted him to move. Ruth was a little afraid of him. Shilo hadn't changed. She chased and barked steady at the lawn mower. We had two John Deere Gators that Kayla and Sarah drove often. She always chased them. She was often tied or locked up. Tramp disappeared one day. Bob looked everywhere for him. He was always Bob's dog and often rode in the semi when Bob was hauling grain to the market. A neighbor called. They found him dead in a fence line. Bob and Owen went to get him and buried him alongside Lady and Molly.

We took down the barn and granary in 2007. Bob built in their place a sixty-by-eighty foot machine shed. The first couple of years, it was used as a riding arena for Kayla and Sarah. At times we had so many horses that some stayed in there.

After Tramp was gone, Shilo had one more litter of puppies. They were a Lab cross, I think. There were only three. Thank heavens! I paid the vet bill and gave them away. I was just glad to find them good homes. We also had Shilo spayed so there would be no more puppies.

With all the other boxers gone and feeling sorry for Shilo not having her puppies, Bob started to let Shilo sleep in his house. She had Justin's old room where she slept years ago. Kayla and Sarah started letting her come in our house, and Ruth slowly became okay with this. Shilo also lost her voice. I think she barked so much she couldn't do it anymore. Not being able to bark, she quit chasing things. She slowly started to become a companion and a better dog.

Shilo and Bob started to become extremely close. She started to ride in the semi often. She would sit in the passenger seat like a person. I started calling her trucker. She would also ride in the tractors once in a while. In the following years, the farm really changed. We were in a very profitable time. Our land base never grew. We sold some farms and bought some farms. We bought some farms that we were renting and lost some rented land, buying other land. All the machinery was updated to the newest technology. We built a state-of-the-art grain-drying and storage setup. Bob now checked the dryer from his smartphone from anywhere. We only go out at night if something is wrong.

On November 8, 2010, we celebrated my mother's ninetieth birthday. She had always had a great love for horses and dogs. She was in fairly good health, but six weeks later, she was in the hospital. It looked like we were going to have to put her in a nursing home. I'm on an insurance company board of directors. In the car on the way to the December meeting, I prayed out loud almost all the way to God to tell me how to handle this. On the way home, it was as though God was telling me to have her live at our house. I said to Ruth, "I have something to ask of you. I don't want an answer now. I want you to sleep overnight on it and answer me tomorrow." She asked what it was. I said, "I want my mother to live with us." She said she didn't have to sleep on it. "It's okay." I brought my mother home on the twenty-fourth of December.

Shilo immediately liked my mother. When no one was watching, Mom would slip her food to Shilo. Shilo always stayed right beside her. My mother would spend hours trying to get Shilo to talk to her. They would sit looking at each other, and Shilo would be moving her mouth and make a whining sound. She could no longer bark.

My mother lived with us three months. She lived in the sunroom. We had many doctor visits and different therapists visiting our home. Shilo got a doggy bed or mat so she could stay beside my mother. She still slept at night at Bob's house. Ruth and my mother always got along but were never close. This changed, and Ruth and my mother became extremely close, and Ruth got closer and closer to Shilo. Every few days, our granddaughters would ride their horses close to the windows so my mother could see them. Bob and my mother had always been close, but they became closer. My mother's mind was perfect, and it was fun talking about her childhood.

Ruth and I had a bus trip to Washington, DC, planned in April, and my sister Sandy was going to stay with Mom. The day before we left, she didn't look well. I took her to the doctor. He put her in the hospital. She insisted we still make the trip. When we got back, she was in the nursing home. My sister shared with me how impressed she was with Bob because he had taken care of everything. Mom was in the nursing home twenty-one days before she passed away. Bob visited her every night with Shilo, unleashed; she got out of the pickup and went to my mother's room. Then she went up and down the hall visiting all the patients and staff, then went and lay by mom's bed. After Mom passed away, several of the staff told us they were going to miss Shilo.

After that time, Shilo would always go to Ruth and sit looking at her, moving her mouth and whining. She always wanted something. She never did this with anyone else. Ruth sometimes said, "Why always me?"

In September 2014, we had church service on the farm. Kayla and Brandon's daughter Jordyn, our great-granddaughter, were baptized in our shop that day. There were 185 people there. While the pastor was preaching, Shilo went up and down each row of chairs greeting everyone. Someone was always petting her. The church put on a meal, but she never begged for food. Late that afternoon, after everyone left, she had a spell on the lawn. We think she had a heart attack. She was thirteen years old, and I think the day was too much for her. After a while, she got up and came in our house. That evening when Bob came to take her home, she went okay; she seemed fine again.

In October, Ruth noticed a lump in her breast. We went to the doctor in Kasson right away on Monday morning. The doctor made an appointment for Ruth that afternoon in Rochester. We knew it was cancer. We came back home. Ruth called Brenda, and I called Pastor Barb. They both came right over. Pastor Barb said we should all join hands and pray. Shilo got up and put her head on Pastor Barb's and Ruth's hand.

Ruth started chemo in early December. Everything went well until late February, when Ruth got neuropathy in her legs so bad that early April, she couldn't even walk. We had many doctor visits during this time. Shilo didn't like being left alone and was always happy to see us come home. She had made it through the winter really good. She had a big scar from being hit with the motorcycle. I always thought this would bother her in old age, but we could never tell it. The grandkids would come often, and she was really happy to see them. Her short tail would go like crazy. It didn't matter how rough the grandkids would treat her; she would never bite or snap at them. In December, when we got company and were sitting in the kitchen, she would come to Ruth, whining with her mouth going. We finally figured she wanted a doggy bed in the kitchen because she had to be with us. Sarah bought her another one.

After February, she never came whining to Ruth again. She knew Ruth couldn't help her. When Ruth was at her worst, Shilo wanted to be in the same room. She really wanted to be in bed with Ruth. Ruth never liked to pet animals, but I would catch Ruth petting Shilo.

When planting time came, Ruth needed 24-7 care. Bob had to do everything alone. I had always done the spraying, and Ruth had always helped fill the planter with seed. She always had the seed exactly where he would need it. Shilo suddenly started waking Bob at 4:00 AM. She wanted to go outside but would never go back in their house. She came over to our house, and Bob had to let her in. Now

A FATHER'S QUEST

he was up and might as well get to work. When the planting and spraying was done, she quit doing that.

She had always liked to ride in the semi like Tramp, but now that was also hard. She had a couple more spells like last September.

Ruth had started to recover and could walk a little. She had surgery, and even though she could never finish the chemo treatments, the cancer was gone. Our prayers had been answered.

Bob had just come in our bedroom. Shilo just died. Ruth and I got up. Jacki, a dear lady that had been helping in the house, arrived. Ruth and Bob and I sat with Shilo. Brenda, Owen, Justin, Braeden, and Emery arrived. Brenda and the small boys sat on the floor beside her. We were pouring cement that morning. I dragged her doggy bed outside on the porch. It had short soft sides; I then covered her with a towel.

After we were done with the cement, Bob had to load pigs. Brenda, Owen, and the small boys went home. Justin stayed. About three thirty, Bob took the backhoe and dug a hole off the west side of the stable, south of the stable porch. We buried her in her doggy bed. Bob and Justin put her in the hole. Justin pet her for the last time and neatly folded the towel over and around her. Justin and I then shoveled dirt until she was covered. Then Justin finished with the skid loader. In the sunroom where her doggy bed was and where she died sits a Precious Moments angel about sixteen inches tall with her hands folded. We miss her so.

Shilo always knew she was Justin's dog. She always got excited to hear his voice or to see him. When he petted her, you could see it meant the world to her.

The end of another era. Ruth would never help again in the fields. I would soon be retired too.

What's the next era? I hope and pray Bob would have his own family on this farm and that there would be many happy times with more great dogs.

—Wayne McColley

Chapter 29

The Stroke

We had a nice vacation, and now Ruth was on the mend. I know I would have to take care of her for some time or maybe forever. When we were at Uncle Lyle's, my cousin Starlin taught me how to use Facebook. I wrote almost every day on the trip. When I got home, I decided to write about farming and the new technology involved. I am going to start this chapter on May 1, 2016.

Sunday, May 1, 2016

Today was a different day. We were invited to a Polka service in Waseca by my country school teacher Ruth Mittlestadt. She was my teacher from 3rd through 7th grade. She deserves the credit for my success in life. An excellent teacher! Our daughter Doreen and her family were there. Also, my brother and sister-in law, Rick and Carol, were there. The pastor had an excellent message that leaves many questions.

Monday, May 2, 2016

Nice to see the sun today. Bob hauled soybeans today. For some years we have hauled them to a processing plant in Fairmont, Minnesota, 100 miles away. That was always where we could get the highest price. This year for some reason that changed and we are taking the soybeans to the river market in Winona, Minnesota, 70 miles away. They are going to the export market. Bob also sprayed seven acres of corn again. We had alfalfa planted there and alfalfa doesn't die easily. Afterwards, Bob washed up the sprayer. I checked on the waterway work that was taking place. Then I mowed some lawn. Ruth always did that job and I never appreciated her enough. I like to have the farm look really good and with the amount of grass that we mow we never really finish. At the end of the day I saw Bob filling the planter with soybean seed so hopefully we can go back to planting tomorrow.

Tuesday, May 3, 2016

My social life almost got in the way of farming today. I was getting ready to go to Wise Guys at church when Bob called me on the phone saying he needed seed. I said, "I'm leaving just now for church to go to Wise Guys." He asked me, "Are you going to make me come home with the planter for seed?" GUILT TRIP!!! Luckily I had my coffee and my mind was working. I quickly took the seed to the field and had Ruth follow in the car. Then I took her home and went to Wise Guys. We had biscuits and gravy and an interesting discussion. While I was at church the guy building the waterway called saying it was done. I then made a quick trip home to talk to him. He drove his Cat to the next farm to continue with the waterway. When he is done with the waterway he's coming back to our farm to take a lot of trees out along a creek for me so he will be there for days. There is a huge amount of dirt left over from building the waterway. I want to move it ¾ of a mile to the other side of the farm to fix a problem there. I have never seen anyone do this before. Planting soybeans is a little different than corn. I will write a little about that tomorrow. It was Senior Day at the grocery store today so we had to go shopping. It will be nice if Ruth can go alone someday. It will be a long time. Tonight is pizza with a group of friends so it has been a very hard day.

I didn't know it at that time, but it would be some time before I wrote on Facebook again.

We went for pizza at the Pizza Cellar in Blooming Prairie. One other couple that came was Greg and Kathy Holzt. We ordered pizza and I ordered a beer. We were having an interesting conservation. I had finished half of my beer. All of a sudden, I got a terrible pain on the left side of my head. It was more than I could stand, but luckily, it lasted less than a minute. I looked to Ruth and said, "I just had a stroke." I never even thought of having a stroke before. I didn't know any symptoms of a stroke. Why did I tell Ruth that I just had a stroke? Maybe my guardian angel had put these words in my month. Greg and Kathy got up and told our waitress that I had a stroke. They called 911. A policeman came in almost immediately. I figured that I could finish my beer. I wasn't able to pick up the bottle. An ambulance was soon there. They bought in a gurney to put me on it to carry me out. I told them I could walk out. But they didn't let me try. I told them that I wanted to go to St. Mary's in Rochester. But they told me they could only take me to Austin or Owatonna. I was never afraid. Why wasn't I afraid? Maybe my guardian angel would stay with me the whole time.

I talked all the way to Owatonna with the attendant that was with me in the ambulance. Greg and Kathy took Ruth to the hospital in their car. Kathy called Bob. He was almost done with a field. He told her, "When you know something, call back." Bob called Brenda, and Brenda called Doreen. At the hospital, they administered a medicine that was supposed to bust up the clot that I had on my brain. It didn't work! Then they told me that they were going to take me to Abbot Hospital in St. Paul. I didn't what to go there. It would be very hard on Ruth and my family to be so far from home. "Why are you taking me to Abbot? I want to go to St. Mary's in Rochester." I had to argue a lot, but finally, they told me that they were going to take me to St. Mary's. They loaded me again on an ambulance and gave my clothes to Ruth. Kathy called Bob again and told him that they taking me to Rochester. They were following with Ruth in their car. Bob was now done planting that field and was now home. He told Kathy that he would meet them in Dodge Center. He was going to take Ruth to the hospital. As they were going, Ruth looked at my clothes. She said, "The shoes are missing." Kathy called George Sierakowski, from the support group in Austin, and he said he would go to the hospital right away to get the shoes. He lived fairly close in the hospital in Owatonna. When they got to Dodge Center, Bob, Brenda, and Justin were there waiting. Greg told Ruth they would go back to Blooming Prairie and pick up my car and take it to their place. I talked all the way to Rochester with the attendant. I could tell where we were going without looking.

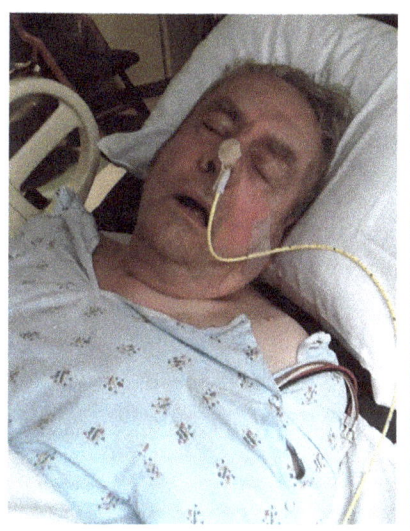

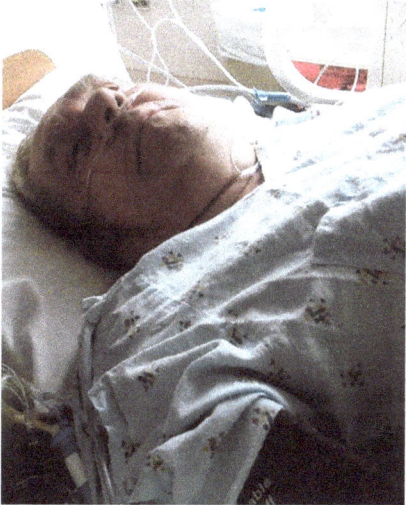

Wayne in the hospital after surgery

As soon as I got to the hospital, they took me into the operating room and operated on my brain. They partially removed part of the clot. When I come to from the operation, I couldn't talk or swallow. I was completely paralyzed on the right side or my body. I couldn't believe that the doctors went into a vein though my groin and operated on my brain. They made no cuts! The only thing I remembered the first night was Pastor Barb and Jackie Short had visited me. I experienced a strange thing. I lay unable to move, unable to move my head, and unable to talk. I had a tube down my throat. I couldn't swallow. I could still think. I was never afraid. Was my guardian angel right beside me at that time? I could tell what was happening around me when it happened, but I had almost no memory. Much of what happened the first few days, I had trouble remembering. All of my family and Ruth's family came to visit me. I couldn't remember, but when they told me they were there, I remembered. Ruth stayed with me the first night.

My sister-in-law Carol wrote on Facebook, Wednesday, May 4, 2016:

> In need of The Power of Prayer for Wayne McColley, Rick's oldest brother. Got word last night that Wayne had a stroke. He is at St. Mary's Hospital in Rochester. Visited today and found out that speech, strength, and his right side is affected. Wayne totally believes in God's love and God's prayers are needed to uplift this whole family. Feeling very thankful for our blessings. They are two short days of being done planting. May they be uplifted and carried through this trying time. One day at a time and be thankful for each wonderful day! We shared Sunday polka Church service with both of them. Love and hugs to all of you!!!

Carol wrote on Facebook again, Thursday, May 5, 2016:

> Update on Wayne McColley. Brain scan showed that the blood is a small area. On the left side and in a bad area. Wayne is nodding his head yes or no to respond. Bob said that Wayne raised his hand and motioned for him to leave and shook his head yes. When Bob asked him if he wanted him to stay. That alone is good news that he is aware of his surroundings. Keep the prayers flowing. We thank you and so much for your concern and love and understanding. That is why God put us on earth together to do! Another beautiful day! Thanks!

Sarah wrote on Facebook, Friday, May 6, 2016:

> Update on my Grandpa Wayne McColley. They did a MRI today and confirmed that he had a stroke that affected the lingual area of the brain. They said that it looks like he has also had a smaller stroke previously by the looks of the MRI. MRI and echocardiogram show some cholesterol build up in the heart and carotid arteries and could possibly cause it. The right side of his body is still paralyzed but unlike before he can feel when you rub his arm or leg or am holding his hand. He is trying harder to be able to talk. It is still hard for him to communicate and he starts to get frustrated but it is an improvement. Thank you everyone who has been praying for him.

Carol wrote on Facebook, Saturday, May 7, 2016:

> Update on Wayne McColley. Heard today that Wayne was sitting up in a chair. Had the feed-

ing tube removed and has ate some meatloaf and potatoes. Very frustrating for him that he can't talk. Will be here at least for another week. This is good news! Couldn't believe it myself. Feeling blessed! Thanks for all the prayers!

Carol wrote on Facebook, Tuesday, May 10, 2016:

Update on Wayne McColley. He is being transferred this afternoon to the Dodge Center nursing home. Praying for his speech to return and strength and motion to his right side! May God bless him in abundance with healing at this time of recovery. The first three months of therapy are usually the most successful according to the doctor. Prayers for the family as well to give them strength to get them through this trying time as well. God bless you all!

Dallas wrote on Facebook, Tuesday, May 10, 2016:

Yesterday was Marsha's day off so we went to Rochester to see Wayne, but I wasn't sure what to post! Update on Wayne McColley. It was a hard day emotionally, as I'm sure every day is for Wayne, Ruth, and the kids, and grandkids. I found some encouraging signs, but also see that it is going to be a long hard road too. One of the aspects with speech seems really good. He easily counted to ten with most words quite audible. It also seemed quite good when Bob asked him to repeat words. But, I also saw where Wayne wants to say something and the first couple of words come out (though not always audible) and then things just stop and he can't say more. That is probably normal for this stage, as it is far more complicated process. And it also makes things very frustrating for him.

I think it is also a very good sign that he wants his leg and foot rubbed; it feels good to him. That should be a good sign of the nerves coming back. Doreen tickled the bottom of his foot, and he definitely felt that. He didn't move his leg/ foot or arm/hand when we were there, but others have said he has moved his foot. He moved his shoulder, but I don't know if he could always do that.

He is also aware of everything going around him. So please pray for him and the family for a steady path of healing!

In case anyone didn't see Carols posting today, Wayne should have been transferred to Dodge Center Nursing Home this afternoon. Thanks.

Sarah wrote on Facebook on May 10, 2016:

Update of Wayne McColley. He is able to communicate with us. Before it was hard for him to talk and now he is able to get the words out better and talk! While before he couldn't move his right leg at all but now part of his physical therapy is lifting his knee and bending it and he has to push his leg out straight. He can do this now! Such improvement in just a matter of days! He still hasn't been able to do anything with his right arm but I have faith in him and know his strength and determination will persevere

He is now at the Dodge Center nursing home as of this afternoon. He is up to visitors at any time. He says he will be home in a month.

I know some of you have been worried about grandma. She is doing really well. She has been going up to visit him daily, spending the night with him a couple of times. She comes home to get a good night's rest and will get a ride through a family member or friend to go back up to spend time with him again. She will pack some food and water with her or go to the cafeteria for something. Bob has been going with her the past two days (since he has gotten all of our beans and corn planted and sprayed) and he has been making sure she is taking well care of herself.

Thank you Richard Carol McColley and Dallas McColley for all of the updates and providing information for everyone keeping grandpa in our thought and prayers. So much improvements in just a matter of days and if I know how determined and stubborn grandpa can be much more will be occurring. Thank you again to everyone for all the well wishes and prayer sent this

The nurses figured that Ruth required too much care. They ordered Ruth to go home at night. On Thursday morning, Gary and Mary Norstad brought Ruth to the hospital. I remembered that they were here. It was getting easier to remember, but it would take a couple of more days to get all my memory back. Our neighbor, Lloyd Henslin, brought Bob dinner every day until he got done planting. Friday, Bob was done planting, and he brought Ruth to the hospital. By Friday, they got me out of bed and got me sitting on a chair. They took the tube out of my throat. The tube in my throat was put in through my nose. Now I could swallow. I could move my head. They had a therapist come to try getting me to talk. After a few days, I could say yes and no and count to ten. Saturday, they used an overhead hoist to take me into the bathroom to give me a shower. Justin came often to see me. He would push my right leg up. I was able to push my leg against him. He did it every time for many times. Justin and I could tell my leg was getting stronger. Bob told me about a nursing home in Rochester. The wife of this person worked there. It seemed like I would get better care. Phyllis and Al visited me often. Al said if I stayed in Rochester, they would visit me often. I liked the way the nurses and other people cared for me in the hospital. Why couldn't I just stay in the hospital? Monday, they gave me bad news. I would be going to the nursing home in Dodge Center on Tuesday. I dreaded the news that I would be in the nursing home. I let Bob know that I didn't want to be in the nursing home in Dodge Center. But I couldn't talk. All I could say was, "No." I thought that Medicare would pay for twenty-one days like they did with my mom, then I would have to pay the bill. As they took me to Dodge Center, I had in my mind that I would be back to normal in a month. I would walk out of the nursing home and go home. Then I would take care of Ruth again. How would Ruth make it now? That was something that really worried me.

When I got to the nursing home, all I did was sleep the first day. The first day, Bob tried to get me transferred to a nursing home in Rochester. The social worker, Jodi Liebenow, who accepted me into the nursing home, didn't want me either. She thought it would cost them too much to take care of me. Medicare would never pay enough for the condition I was in. The McColleys would cause her too much trouble. Tammy worked at this nursing home when she died. Management remembered her. Management told Jodi, "You have to do something to keep Bob and the McColleys happy." Thursday they took me to therapy. They tried to get me to stand between two bars. It took two girls to get me up. As soon as I was standing, I started to throw up. They took me back to the room. I was unconscious most of the day. For a brief moment, I came to, and my cousins Judy and Shirley were there.

Carol wrote on Facebook on May 13, 2016:

> Update on Wayne McColley. Heard physical therapy didn't go well today. Wayne collapsed.

Heart rate down and throwing up. Not sure why or how come. Praying that things are more stable tomorrow. And they aren't any added concerns! May God continue healing and hold him tight! Love and hugs to the family!

Carol wrote on Facebook on May 14, 2016:

Update on Wayne McColley. Went to visit Wayne yesterday. This guy is a real trooper! Bob and Ruth were there also. We stayed for a few hours. Wayne ate supper with Bobs help. His food is puree yet. Wayne was able to share and speak to us. His voice is still weak. He has physical therapy 3 hours. Along with other types. He is not able to read yet. His right foot was moving while we were there. Wayne said he wasn't moving it. Wayne and Bob went for a walk outside with Wayne in the wheelchair. Asked Wayne if he still plans on his stay only on being a month and he smiled and said, yes. It is definitely easier for the family having him closer. May God continue to bless Wayne with healing and strength and Gods love! Love and hugs to all of you!

A nurse checked me in the middle of the night. My heart was in A-fib. She had me breathe in a paper sack. Then she called the ambulance to take me to St. Mary's. I was there for two days before they took me back to Dodge Center.

Carol wrote on Facebook on May 15, 2016:

Update on Wayne McColley. Just in case any of you were thinking of visiting him today. Wayne was sent back to the hospital to monitor a rapid heartbeat and possible dehydration. Not sure at

> this point if just today or how long. Prayers sent up for him and his family!

Carol wrote on Facebook on May 17, 2016:

> Update on Wayne McColley. Heard he went back to the Rest home on Monday. Praying for continued healing!

When I came back the second time, I decided that I would make the best of it. I wasn't happy, but I would act happy. Medicare would pay for one hundred days if I made progress the whole time. That gave me a lot of incentive. Michelle was the therapist that got me walking. Holly was the therapist that worked on my arms. My right arm was paralyzed. They couldn't do anything with that arm. But Holly wanted to get my left arm stronger. I was right-handed. My right arm was the stronger arm. Now my left arm would have to do the work of both arms. I had to lift weights with my left hand. When she told me to lift it ten times, I did it twenty times. When she told me twenty times, I lifted it fifty times. Then she gave me a heavier weight. Maybe it took me a few days to get up to fifty times, but I always made it. At first, Michelle just got me to stand between the two bars. Then she got me walking. She put her knee on my right knee as I walked between the bars. Then they called in a person to make me a brace for my foot and ankle. I thought Michelle was the best therapist that I had. When I was in the hospital, unable to move, I never thought I would walk again. Michelle was the one that got me walking again. I could never thank her enough. One day when I was walking between the bars, my pants fell down. That was the first time since my stroke that I laughed. I couldn't stop laughing. They gave me a pair of suspenders to wear. At least my pants wouldn't fall down again. Oftentimes stroke patients couldn't control their emotions. When bad things happen, they start laughing. That was what happened to me. When good things happen, many patients start crying.

The first week, Bob took Ruth to the nursing home every morning at eight. He pushed her in the wheelchair. She stayed all day every day. Bob visited me every night and took Ruth home. Then a surprising thing happened the second week! Ruth drove the car and walked into the nursing home. I thought this would be impossible. God knew I would never be able to take care of Ruth again. It was time for Ruth to get well. She would now have to take care of me. God never leaves us completely alone! Ruth came every morning at eight, and she stayed till eight at night. I didn't like their coffee, so Ruth always brought me coffee. I tried to be done with breakfast before Ruth came. I couldn't get up by myself. I couldn't dress myself. I got really impatient waiting for someone to get me up. Would I be done with breakfast before Ruth came?

Bob called Bob Cunningham, my Navy buddy, and gave the bad news to Bob.

Bob C. posted on Facebook on May 23, 2016:

> Hi Wayne, I talked to Bob yesterday and he said you're reading Facebook. He also told me that you are improving every day. I know you must be frustrated with all that's happened. But, with therapy and time and prayer you'll get back to your old self. Until I talk to you again, say Hi to Bob and Ruth. Keep the faith buddy, we all love you!!

Bob posted on Facebook on May 30, 2016:

> Dad had therapy Friday and Saturday when they had him walk between the poles he was able to walk without them blocking his knee today. He was able to step his right leg forward. He did really good. They started the shock therapy on his arm to stimulate it. Hopefully they get it to start moving. They plan to do it every day. Yesterday I pushed him to church in the wheelchair and back. Last night I pushed him in the wheelchair

down the street south of the nursing home. It gave us something different to look at. Tonight we were going down a couple of different streets we had not been on before. We were invited to their patio to have strawberry short cake. Ruth walked with us.

They had a therapist to work on my talking. She always came to my room. She wanted me to say men's names. I couldn't think of any, including Bob. On the second day, I thought of my dad's brothers. They were an important part of my life. "Dale, Marlin, Lyle, Lenard, Duane, David, and Clifford." The therapist was really helping me. That was an amazing day! Those was the first words that I spoke except for yes and no and counting to ten. The next day she had me work on men's names. "Roger, Stanley, Bob, Allan, Owen, Justin, Dallas, Richard, Howard, Palmer, Junior, Al, John, Stan, Braedon, and Emery." She worked with me about forty-five minutes at a time. My brain was really tired. I couldn't think about anything after this short time. I couldn't realize how tiring this was. The next day she wanted me to say ladies' names. At first, I couldn't say any names. Until now, I had never said, "Ruth." That was the first lady's name that I said. How did I first think of men's names? Ruth had five sisters. "Marion, Eva, Phyllis, Donna, and Linda." The forty-five minutes was now up. I couldn't make my mind think anymore. The next day I came up with, "Doreen, Brenda, Kayla, Sarah, Jenna, and Valerie." The third day, "Deloris, Sandy, Carol, Marsha, Barb, and Audrey." The next day, she had me work on animals. Next, she worked on sentences. I could say words, but I couldn't really talk. She started with short and simple sentences. When a stroke takes your speech, it takes a long time to get it back. Now almost four years later, I still have problems coming up with words.

I really wanted to go to Justin's graduation at high school and to the party at their farm. The high school was close. We went by the high school when Bob pushed me to church. Maybe Bob could take me to graduation in the wheelchair. But how was I going to get to their farm?

Bob posted on Facebook on June 4, 2016:

A couple nights ago Justin came to see Dad. He was taking his graduation tassel and rubbing it on Dads arm. It was driving him nuts and he was trying to kick Justin but couldn't. He tried to grab him but couldn't. When Justin got ready to leave Justin gave dad a hug. Dad reached around Justin and grabbed under his arm and tickled him. Next thing Justin was on the floor and there were both laughing really hard. I think it was a good thing for both of them.

Thursday when they did the shock therapy there was a couple times the shock was a little than it should have been. Fridays shock therapy started out good then all of a sudden the shock was a lot more and the girl didn't realize it right away. Then she shut it off. Then she said that they would have to send it in to be fixed. Hopefully they would have it back next week.

Today Justin and I came in to have lunch with mom and dad. After we were done eating we went outside with mom and dad. Justin and I went home to do a few things. Later on I went back and Dad said they almost had a disaster when they came back into the room. Dad was going to get back into bed. Mom said she had to go to the bathroom. So dad waited and waited. Mom didn't come back so Dad decided he would go back to bed by himself. He got up and fell into bed but couldn't get turned around the right way. He thought about pushing the call button but he knew he be in trouble for trying without help. So he just laid there until Mom came to help him.

A FATHER'S QUEST

At this time, they gave me a twelve-inch-wide board, three feet long. I could put the board between the wheelchair and the bed. I could slide along this board to move from the wheelchair to bed or to get from the bed to the wheelchair. I was never to try this alone.

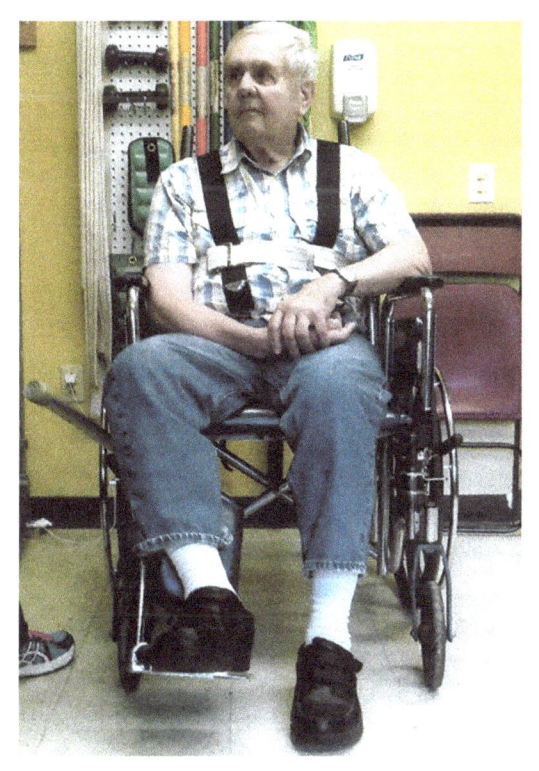

Wayne at physical therapy

When I could talk some, I had Bob call several people. I started having a lot of company. This really helped me get over the stroke. It helped me get my speech back. Jerry Cawley visited me one day. On the sixth day of May, he took his son to the Mayo Clinic. I was to visit them at the Mayo Clinic. I never showed up. Jerry was wondering why I didn't show up. I didn't remember this at all. Things like this were helping me to remember again. Don and Heather Myers visited me several times. All my cousins from my Uncle Dale's family visited me once. My brothers and Ruth's brothers and sister visited me several times. Uncle Roger and one of his daughters visited me. Uncle Duane and Aunt Barb visited me often. Glen and Barb Borgan visited me. Gary and Mary Norstad visited me many times. Dave and Jeremy Wahlstrom also came a couple of times. I got many calls from my Navy buddy, Bob Cunningham.

It seemed like when I first came to the nursing home, everybody was in a bad mood. When I saw anyone, I always said, "Smile." After a few days, when they saw me, they automatically smiled. I thought that the mood of everyone had really improved. I didn't have to say, "Smile," again to a person I knew. When I was in therapy and another patient came in, many of them didn't want to do anything. It was almost impossible for the therapist to get them to do anything. But many of them had been in the nursing home for a long time. They didn't have anything to look forward to. I always liked therapy. I wanted to spend all day at therapy. It was better than spending all the time in my room. I knew the date when I was going home. I had something to look forward to.

Oftentimes when I was in the therapy room, Jodi would come in and visit with me. I liked her, and it was fun when she was there. When Bob was visiting me, often Jodi and Bob sat in the gathering area and talked. Maybe the reason that she spent so much time with us was what management had told her: "You have to do something to keep Bob and the McColleys happy." One day when she came into the therapy room, she was carrying a can of Mountain Dew. I told her that Mountain Dew was bad for her. I told her that I forbade Ruth from buying any Mountain Dew. I didn't want my kids to get the habit of drinking Mountain Dew. "It's habit-forming." She said, "I'm going to sit with your son and get him hooked on Mountain Dew." I answered, "You are a wicked woman." From that time on, whenever I saw her, I always said, "You are a wicked woman."

My roommate also had a stroke. He and I had trouble talking. I couldn't understand him, and he couldn't understand me. It would have been fun if we could talk to each other. He had a television, and he controlled it. I never liked his programs. When he wasn't in the room, I sometimes had Ruth change the channel. When he came back, he called the nurse aide in to change the channel and to tell me to never change the channel again. Bob brought me a seven-inch CD player. The noise from the player interfered with his TV. He told me that I couldn't use the player. How would I handle this problem? I had Bob buy me a set of earphones. The problem went away.

They had the bed where my right arm fell out and just hung there. I couldn't really feel that it happened. It didn't wake me up. When I sat on the toilet, my right arm just hung. Often they would let me sit there thirty minutes before an aide came in to get me up. A nurse noticed a separation in my shoulder. It was because of my arm just hanging. She showed Bob and Justin. There was room for a finger between the separation on my shoulder. Soon I started to have a lot of pain. They had me wear a sling during the day. It hurt so bad that I started to wake up at night screaming. They had a solution called Icy Hot that they rubbed on my shoulder. If they really massaged my shoulder when they put Icy Hot on, it helped. If they just wiped it on and then left, it didn't help much. Deb Roe worked at night, and I was happy when she was there. She really massaged my shoulder. One night a nurse aide came in and told me that she was not here to give me a massage. I told management that I wanted another room. My right arm should be next to the wall. Then my arm couldn't fall out. My roommate had an oversized bed and a stuffed chair. Ruth never had a stuffed chair to sit on because of the oversized bed. They wanted to turn my bed the opposite way. If they did this, he couldn't have an oversized bed. When they got him a regular bed, his wife said, "Why are you complaining all the time?" I told her that I never complained before about anything. I needed a bed where my right arm was against the wall. I would have preferred to have a different room. Ruth always had to sit on a hard chair. Neither one of us ever complained. After they changed the bed, they got a stuffed chair for Ruth to sit on.

It was finally June 5. Justin was graduating from high school. I got up early and had breakfast. This was something I was really looked forward to. Ruth came in at eight. She gave me coffee. All of a sudden, I didn't feel good. I told Ruth to take me back to my room and help me get into bed. When we got back to the room, I felt terrible. I said, "Go get a nurse."

Bob posted on Facebook on June 5, 2016:

> This morning Dad got up and had breakfast and was looking at the newspaper when he felt a little dizzy and he said to mom that he wanted to go to his room. Shortly after he laid down he told mom to have a nurse check his blood pressure. They did it and he was 220 over 120. A nurse called me on the phone. I came in right away and she asked me what I wanted to do. I thought we should take him back to Rochester. At that moment they were talking to a doctor. He said they changed his heart medicine the last time he was there. The nurses gave him a pill that was supposed to slow his heart down. They kept checking it every half hour and it came down a little. All other vital signs are good. He has been really tired all day and he was looking forward to going to Justin's graduation. We all came here to see him after the graduation. Hopefully tonight goes good and he is better tomorrow.

The minute after Justin walked across the stage and received his diploma, he left the school and immediately came to the nursing home to see me. He didn't wait for the end of the ceremony. Justin's family came to the nursing home to congratulate Justin.

Michelle told she would help me go to Justin's graduation party at their farm. She would practice with me getting in the car. It went much better than I imagined. I think Michelle and I were amazed at how well it went. She told Ruth, "Maybe we could go for a ride."

Carol posted on Facebook on Wednesday, June 8, 2016:

> Just got a phone from Bob McColley. He said he was in the field putting on anhydrous. He said he had two visitors. You will never guess who! It

> was Wayne McColley and Ruth. Heard Ruth has been doing driving for physical therapy. Wayne was learning to get in a vehicle. They went for a spin out to the farm. This is BIG NEWS FOLKS AND A BLESSING!

The therapist knew that I was on Facebook before I had the stroke. She was teaching me how to talk and said, "If you write on Facebook, you'll learn how to talk better." The first day, it took me an hour to type just eleven words with her help.

I posted on Facebook, Thursday, June 9, 2016:

> My first getting in the Car and going for a ride.

I posted on Facebook, Friday, June 10, 2016:

> I have been practicing getting in the car. I have travel to the farm and looked at each of the fields. We travels to Justin's and looked at the start of the dry cows building. We are going to Justin party Sunday afternoon to celebrate his graduation. Bob and I are going to the insurance monthly meeting Wednesday Morning. I had a great amount of coaching help from my therapist.

I thought I made a huge improvement in one day. I went from eleven words to seventy words. I made a few mistakes but overall I thought that was something! I'm right handed. To type with my left hand was something!

Gary Norstad posted on Facebook on June 11, 2016:

> Big surprise this afternoon when Bob McColley drove out to our house and with him were Wayne McColley and Ruth. Way to go Wayne!!! Good

to see tremendous progress. Shows what determination can do. My hats off to you.

On the twelfth day of June, we went to Justin's party at their farm. Bob had been practicing on getting me in and out of the car. Michelle wanted to know if it would be safe to take me without their help. Bob was successful in taking me to Justin's party. On June 15, he took me to St. Charles to go to the insurance meeting. I had only missed one meeting from the time that I had the stroke. I was president of the company. Bob got me out of the car and into the wheelchair. I had to sit in the wheelchair during the meeting. Bob sat beside me. Don Sexton, the vice president, led the meeting. I said very little. I still had trouble coming up with words. But the meeting went well for me. The next day, when I met with the speech therapist, I told her that I wanted to lead the next meeting. She assured me that she would make it happen.

On June 18, an aide was getting me up. She had me sit on the bed. All of a sudden, I stood up with no effort. It felt so good to stand by myself! I didn't want to sit down. She said, "Sit down right away." I think she was afraid that I might fall. She really gave me hell, and then finally, I sat down. That was something! That felt so good.

On June 21, 2016, Bob posted on Facebook:

> Last Sunday we took dad to church, He was able to stand for a little while during service. After church I brought him home and Kayla and I were able to roll him up the stairs to the porch. We got him in the house and into his chair. We stayed there until five. Justin and Owen helped me get him down the stairs. Monday morning the staff chewed him out for doing this stuff on his own. They said it could be unsafe for him to do these things on his own. He told them that he wasn't going to just lay around and do nothing because he was afraid of what could happen. They finally agreed with him at the end. Monday morning at

physical therapy they had him walk between the parallel bars. They had him walk to the end and then turn around and then walk back. They then said he could set down for a little. He said, "No." He wanted to walk again. So he did and when he got back the next time he sat down. He sat for a bit and then walked it again. Tuesday they had him walk with a one hand walker He walked 20 feet across the room and turned and walked back. They said he should walk down the hallway on the carpet. It was harder. He walked for 60 feet on his own. They had him set down He said he could have walked future. There was a staff person on both sides of him in case he fell. He did really good with no help. After that they brought him to the room and practiced getting up from the wheelchair and setting on the bed and getting up and setting back in the wheelchair. They had a sliding board that he could slide between the bed and the chair. He did so good that he was able to get rid of the sliding board. During dad's physical therapy she gave him a 4 lbs. dump bell and told him to do different movements. She said that it was so easy for him so she gave him a 5 lbs. dump bell. She asked him to do 20 each of different exercises but he always did 50 each the different exercises. After the therapy he slept for an hour. When he woke up he was really sore. He guesses that he is was getting new muscles. It was an awesome day and a lot of improvements.

I posted on Facebook on June 22, 2016:

I walked 120 feet today and walked up stairsteps once. I am going to get braces for my right foot

Thursday or Friday. It should help. Another awesome day!

Then a good thing and a bad thing happened in a short time. The good was that I went home every Saturday and Sunday. On these days, I didn't get therapy. It was really boring to just lie around my room. I left every Saturday right after breakfast and stayed at home until eight at night. On Sundays, Bob took Ruth and me to church at first. Then we stayed at home until eight at night. Some Saturdays, we drove around. I didn't mind being at the nursing home too much anymore. Now for the bad news. Two therapists told me that I would never move my arm again. "You will have to get used to it." That really made me mad. "How do you know I will never move my arm?" I would prove them wrong. I thought of my Uncle Lenard. He lay in a body cast for months unable to move. He was told he would be unable to walk. Lenard was a really stubborn person. He walked like a regular person. I would be even more stubborn than Lenard. When someone got the news they gave me, half of the people would accept the news, and maybe it would be easier on them. The other half would be like me. I would prove them wrong. Maybe it would be harder mentally. How did they know ahead of time which way I would accept this news?

Bob posted on Facebook on June 24, 2016:

> Tonight I came to see Dad. He said one of the therapy girls told him she was treating his arm for six weeks and she didn't think his arm would never move again. I was messing around with his hand and he was working real hard. He got 4 fingers to move. I felt his fingers as he moved them. To see if it was nerves or if was doing it and you could see the muscles in his hand and arm moving. I would slide his arm away from his side and he would slide it towards his leg. I thought some of it was coming from his shoulder but his

shoulder did not move. He even picked it up off the bed.

Bob posted on Facebook on July 8, 2016:

> Update on Dad. Yesterday in therapy they had him raise an aluminum pole 3 feet long above his head 3 times with both hands. He is able to push the therapist hand with his right hand. He stood for 13 minutes holding on to the walker. They had him stand without the walker and pull 64 pegs out of a board and put them back in without using the walker testing his balance. This morning he walked 180 feet and this afternoon he walked 200 feet. Tuesday he got the brace for his foot. He is learning to walk with it. He has to walk lifting his leg with his hip. Today the therapist told dad that 2 weeks ago when she told him his arm wasn't going to get better. She said she told him that to get him so mad he would push himself a little harder.

Doreen posted on Facebook on July 9, 2016:

> Dad showed us how well he could walk with the half walker. He did an awesome job. We love you Dad and thanks for showing us what you can do. We are proud of you Wayne McColley!

I posted on Facebook on July 13, 2016:

> A happy birthday to Jordyn, a real sweetheart. I walked 180 feet Monday. 270 feet on Tuesday and 310 feet today. All was done without resting between. I also got undressed and dressed by myself including the snaps on my shirts and the

button on my pants. I was able to raise my hand up a little at the wrists. I was also able to turn my hand side to side at the wrists.

I posted on Facebook on July 15, 2016:

> I had a goal of 400 feet this morning. On Monday it was 180 feet. On Tuesday it was 230 feet. On Wednesday it was 310 feet. On Thursday it was 360 feet and today it was 400 feet. There was no resting in between. I will have to aim higher next week.

We had the insurance meeting on July 20. Bob took me and took me in the building in the wheelchair. I asked Bob to leave and come back at eleven thirty. I led the meeting as president. I'm sure the rest of the board had a lot of patience with me. I felt a lot of satisfaction to do this so soon after having a serious stroke. I wasn't going to allow a stroke beat me.

Carol posted on Facebook on July 27, 2016:

> Went to see Wayne McColley on Mon. He has made the decision to go home in the middle of August. Medicare runs out. He now had dislocated shoulder. Ruth is thinking he should stay. Praying they have some good help lined up for care. His therapy at the rest home is still possibility for after he gets home. Still not of progress happening to his right arm. Wayne and Ruth, we love you dearly. We would love to help out in any way that we can. Prayers, love and hugs to both of you and family!! Praying for more healing to take place. Had a wonderful talk about farming and politics! Have you ever known a McColley to not have an opinion about that? Lo!

Ruth had a great fear of taking me home. How would she take care of me? How would she help me go to bed or get me up in the morning? For me to go home, someone from the nursing home would have to go to our house and do an inspection. They wanted our home safe for me. The social worker Jodi and the head therapist Holly came out. Ruth and I also came. Everything that we would use was on one floor. I had no need to go upstairs. I would have to have a chair to sit up to the table with arms. A lift chair would be helpful. I told Bob to give them a tour of our farm. I knew that Bob always wanted to marry a thin blond woman. Jodi wasn't married. She was a thin blond-headed woman. I had been eyeing her for some time as a daughter-in-law. How was I going to make this happen? Would I be successful?

I posted on Facebook, Thursday, August 4, 2016:

> Last Thursday I walked 1220 feet which was my goal with a cane and with no rest. On Friday I walked 850 feet outside on the sidewalk and on grass and gravel. It was a little harder walking. They said I wasn't able to set any more goals. Time was running out. I had to more things to do than just walking. On August 19 I was to go home. At home I will be using the cane and will not be using the wheelchair. Last Tuesday I bought a lift chair and a chair with arms to set up to the table at Trademart Furniture in Rochester.

On the nineteenth of August, I went home. Bob came over in the morning and helped Ruth to get me up. He also came at night to help Ruth to get me to bed. In the next days, Bob asked my opinion on something.

"Should I take Jodi on a date?"

I said, "What are you waiting for?"

We still went back to the nursing home for therapy twice a week. I could move my arm more. Bob had a date with Jodi on the twenty-ninth of August. Merritt was down helping Bob to get ready for harvest. Merritt went with Bob on his first date with Jodi. Merritt came and helped Bob with harvest in the fall. When Bob started harvest, he quit helping me to get to bed or up in the morning. Ruth started this chore. By then, she was comfortable with doing this.

Bob helped me get in a tractor and chop stalks. Every day I always needed help to get in the tractor, but I could get out with no help. One day when I was getting out of the tractor, I dropped my cane flat on the ground. I couldn't walk without the cane. Now what would I do? No one was around. I managed to bend over and pick up the cane. That was something! I didn't think I could bend over that much anymore. I really expected to fall to the ground. One day Merritt and Bob helped me to climb up and get in the combine. They took a picture of me waving at the top of the ladder. I was so proud to show the therapist the picture. But that was a big mistake. They told me that if I could do this, I didn't have to have therapy anymore. Jodi came from work almost every day to ride with Bob in the combine. When they were done with harvest, Jodi moved in with Bob.

In early November, I got off my chair to go to bed. I didn't go three feet when I fell over backward. My head hit on the chair. I had no warning. I didn't feel that I lost my balance. How did this happen? Maybe I passed out momentarily. But I didn't feel that I had passed out. Ruth called Bob. Bob came over right away and got me up. I wasn't hurt!

I posted on Facebook on November 17, 2016:

> I'm in the hospital. I had a bad fall Tuesday, November 15 in the morning. I had just got dressed and was going to the bathroom to wash my hands and comb my hair. I don't know what happened. What I know now is I may have passed out for a second. I hurt my hip and my arm. I thought my arm was broken. At the emergency room they took my shirt off for the X-ray. I complained about the pain I was having in my hip. The doctor said I should try to walk. I made

two steps with a lot of pain in my hip. The doctor wanted an X-ray of my hip, too. I got back into bed and I became really dizzy. I passed out. They gave me a shot and put something on my chest to bring me back to life. Just as they were to do it I woke up. The doctor was afraid that my brain was without oxygen for too long. They rushed me to have an MRI done on my brain. Luckily I was okay. It seemed forever to take the X-rays. They also took several of my chest and my heart. Nothing was broken; thank heavens. By night they told me that I would need a pacemaker. I had a very painful operation on Wednesday. The doctors told me that the operation wouldn't be painful, but it was. I felt them cutting and stitching it up. I asked them to give me more pain medicine. They said they didn't have any more. They were almost done before they had more. I can go home today if I can walk. My hip is so painful I can't step on it. They want me to have therapy again. I am looking forward to that.

I posted again on Facebook on November 17, 2016:

The therapist was just here. They stood me up. I couldn't move my right foot at all. Finally, I moved it 1 inch, then two inches, then six inches. I could believe what was happening! Next I walked 200 feet. They are going to let me go home. I had expected that I was going to the care center. I was worrying about nothing!

I posted on Facebook on November 21, 2016:

The true story of my hospital stay is finally coming out. At the hospital Bob told me I hadn't completely passed out. I couldn't figure out why Doreen, Brenda, Kayla, and Sarah came to the emergency room. Ruth tried not to look worried. I was completely out. They had a whole team to bring me back. When I passed out they turned the whole bed with my head lower than my feet. If I had low blood pressure, I should have come to. My heart beat was so low my brain was not getting oxygen. I think it was more than two minutes which Bob told me. The doctor asked Bob if they should try to revive me or to just let me go. Bob said that I wouldn't want to be kept alive on a machine. The doctor told Bob he didn't have to think, he had to decide immediately. He said, "Try to bring him back." They gave me a shot and the doctor said, "Open your eyes!" over and over. Ruth finally told me this. Then they put a gel on my chest and were ready to shock me when I opened my eyes. It would have been scarier for Ruth and Bob to see them use the paddles on my chest. I don't think I would have felt it. The doctor told me that I was without oxygen to my brain too long. They rushed me to have an MRI. I think prayers were answered. It was okay! I don't remember what was next. They X-rayed both of my hips, my arm, my shoulder, my chest, my heart and my lungs. Nothing was broken and my shoulder had healed itself from the separated shoulder at the care center. They put in a pacemaker the next day. I was lucky to be at the emergency room. If I had been at home, I would have died. I feel that God was watching over me. I can't understand why this had to happen.

After being in the hospital, I had to meet with my regular doctor at the Kasson Clinic. The doctor said I should have therapy at the

Kasson Clinic. When I went to therapy, the therapist told me that he couldn't help me.

He said, "When you have a stroke, you have to have therapy on your brain. That is what they do at St. Mary's in Rochester."

In December, Bob asked me if I wanted to go to Branson. Jodi and Ruth went too. Bob had bought a female boxer puppy south of Des Moines, Iowa. We would pick the puppy up on the way back. Part of the time, I was in the wheelchair. But I walked in the Bald Knobbers Theater and walked to the front of the theater to sit. On the way back, we stopped at Sedalia, Missouri, to visit my old friends Chuck and Mary Matz. They introduced Ruth and me when we first met. Mary had cancer at that time. Sadly, it was our last time to see her. We stopped to pick up the puppy, Zoe, on the way back.

We celebrated Christmas on the night of the twenty-sixth of December. Around nine at night, I had to go to the bathroom. I had Ruth take me. When I sat on the toilet, I quit breathing. Ruth hollered for help. Bob came right away. My whole body had a gray look. I was not breathing. I appeared to be dead. Bob left the room to call 911. Doreen, Brenda, and Jodi also came in the bathroom. Jodi knew how to give CPR. She was planning on getting me on the floor. But she had to get me off the toilet to the floor, and there wasn't much room. Brenda shook my hand and hollered at me. Suddenly, I opened my eyes and started breathing. All of a sudden, a policeman walked in the bathroom. I was sitting on the toilet with my pants down. Why were there so many people in the bathroom with me? Why was there a policeman here? All of a sudden, there was an ambulance crew in the house. Why was this happening? They got me off the toilet and into the south room next to the bathroom. They had me sit on the lift chair. They checked me over and decided to take me to the emergency room. At the emergency room, they found nothing wrong. They said, "When you are on the toilet and straining, this sometimes happens." I had just gone to the bathroom to pee. I wasn't straining. I questioned if my pacemaker caused this. They said there wasn't anything wrong with the pacemaker. But I couldn't remember what happened. We went home.

In January, I started therapy at St. Mary's Hospital. That was to last a long time. It was well over a year. Ruth took me two days a week. There was a man that worked there. He worked at the door and helped me get out of the car. His name was Kevin, and we became good friends. They really worked on my arm. But I realized that it would take a long time. Now, four years later, I can move my fingers and thumb a little. I can move my hand and arm more. But I can't do anything with them. They got me really walking more, but I always had to use the quad cane.

I was planning on going to the insurance convention on March 5–March 7, 2017. We always went to church early. I walked all over around the church. Bob was going to take Ruth and me up to the hotel in the Twin Cities Sunday afternoon, and he was going to pick us up when it was over. Ruth, Bob, and I went to church early. I wanted to walk a lot. I had to build up my confidence that I was able to do this. Bob was walking with me. All of a sudden, I fell over backward. Bob stood me up, but my toes on my right foot were curled. They stayed curled forever, and they only got worse. I was unable to move my toes since I had the stroke. Why did all my toes move for the first time on my right foot? But I was unable to move them again. They just stayed curled. I could hardly walk. I called one of the guys going to the convention and told him that I wouldn't be able to come. I called the hotel and got them to reimburse the insurance company for my room. That was a terrible disappointment. I have never been able to walk well since.

I wrote on Facebook on Tuesday, December 5, 2017:

> We are in Pigeon Forge, Tennessee. Bob and Jodi took us. It's like Branson, only bigger. Ruth took me to breakfast in the hotel in the wheelchair. I couldn't believe the number of people who went out of their way to help us. They told Ruth, it's too hard for you, let us push. There are a lot of good people. Last night I walked into the theater. We had seats at the front. It was a long way and it was steep down. It was scary! I thought it would

be easier coming back up. It was not as scary but it was harder work. The first night we saw a show with horses. Really good!! Yesterday we drove in the Smokey Mountains. We went to County Tonight last night. Today we are going to go to Dollywood. We are having fun!! It feels good to go on vacation again.

I wrote on Facebook on Wednesday, December 6, 2017:

I wanted to share the picture at the Grand Old Opera but I'm not smart enough to do it. I bet not one of you reading this has done this before. I sang on the Grand Old Opera stage. If you have seen the picture you will see the microphone in my hand. Being that it was Christmas I chose Dashing Through the Snow. Maybe I will be famous! We are having a good vacation! We stopped at the Keenland race track. I said, "This is where I got the idea of all of the white fence." Jodi said, "We will build a white fence along the whole pasture." I said, "Who is going to paint it?" She said, "I will." I have got the best daughter-in-law there is.

I kept telling Jodi, "I made the most money selling puppies. It took less investment than all the other enterprises." Jodi and Bob decided to buy a male boxer. They named him Jax.

I went to the Mayo Clinic to a foot specialist. The doctor said that they would have to break my toes and I would have to be in a cast for three months and unable to walk. I decided to wait. Maybe they would get better on their own. I was going to therapy. If I had the operation, I would have to quit therapy for three months. I didn't want to quit therapy.

First, I went for one hour for my legs and walking, and then I went for one hour for my arm and hand at St. Mary's. I went twice a week. In about three months, the therapist that worked with my legs said that I had therapy enough. The last thing we did was trying to get up without help from the floor. I was afraid to get on the floor at first, and it was hard to do. But I would have to get used to it. After getting on the floor four times, it became easy. I was able to get off the floor with a chair, and I could stand up. For my arm, they had several machines to use. They had one machine where they could suspend my arm in cables. Then I didn't have the weight of my arm working against me. For my arms, I went almost a year after they quit working on my legs. They tried many things. They had me pick up things with my hand and release them. After a while, I was able to pick things up, but I was never able to release the objects.

I wrote on Facebook on Monday, November 20, 2017:

> I went to therapy at St. Marys Hospital today. For the last three weeks the therapist has been giving me electric stimulation to my right arm. I sit on a machine where I paddle with both hands. They are putting electrical stimulation to my right arm making it move in a way that I wasn't able to move it. I have not been able to move my arm in that way since I had the stroke. Today she tried something different. She put electrical stimulation to different muscles to make me pick up a spoon and put something in my mouth. It hurts! But, I believe you have no gain without pain. She turned it up high enough where I could hardly stand it. I held a small bowl in my left hand with ice chips. She turned on the power. I was able to grab the spoon with my right hand and get ice in the spoon and get it in my mouth and eat the ice. I did it over and over. The therapist said, "See if you can do it without power?" I did it twice without electric power. I cannot control my emotions since I had my stroke. I started crying. That was a big thing!! The therapists told me, a year

ago, I would never move my arm. I hope that I can do it again. I spent an hour and forty-five minutes working on this. The therapist was really surprised at what just happened.

I wrote on Facebook on Friday, December 1, 2017:

> I was sad at therapy yesterday. My therapist told me she was leaving Mayo. I will really miss her. She gave me a big hug. I told Ruth, if I were young again I would ask her out, but I am not young. I don't think I made any points with Ruth. The therapist told me many times to say something if I had pain. I said, "You will never know if I am in pain." There was twice it hurt so bad I couldn't hide it. I have been getting happier from the electrical treatment. I have been getting in a better mood. I sometimes think there is such a relief for her to turn off the electric and maybe that is why I am in a better mood. I am moving my arm more and maybe that is why I am in a better mood.

After my favorite therapist left Mayo, the other therapists didn't like using electrical stimulation. By the end of February 2018, they told me that Medicare would only pay so much every year. They told me in case something happened and I had to go to therapy, I had better save some time. I argued, but it didn't do any good. They dismissed me. What would I do now? I couldn't just sit every day. I couldn't watch TV all the time. I was bored very little in my life. Would I be bored now? I had to have something to do. That was when I decided to write a book. Heather Allen, the medium, told me that I was going to write a book. I decided to name it *A Father's Quest*. When Diana Vang, a retired schoolteacher, heard that I was writing a book, she volunteered to correct my writings. She made me a better writer. Our kids were in her class at school.

In the fall of 2018, my toes started to curl more. I couldn't move my toes at all. Why was this happening now? I went back to the foot doctor. He told me that if he didn't fix my toes soon, it would be impossible to fix them. I would be laid up for three months. I couldn't put any weight on my foot. I would be in the wheelchair all the time. I decided to have it done right after the holidays. He scheduled the surgery for early January. I would have it done at the clinic. I would go home the same day. I really planned that my walking would be as good as it was before I fell at church and my toes curled.

When I went for surgery, they put a screw in my big toe. They would permanently leave the screw in my toe. For the other four toes, they were going to permanently remove the knuckles in my toes. Then they were going to put long pins through my toes into my foot. They were going to leave them there for one month. Then they were going to take the pins out. After the operation, there were over forty sutures in my foot. They had my foot wrapped in so many gauzes or bandages that it appeared my foot was in a cast.

We had bought a portable ramp to put on the steps to the porch. We also bought a turntable where I could step on with my left foot and turn to sit down on the bed. It was just a small piece of plastic. At the most, maybe it cost $25 to be made. It cost us $150. I wasn't to put any weight on my right foot, but it was almost impossible. I tried extra hard not to abuse my foot. I went back in two weeks when they took the bandages off. They x-rayed my foot and the doctor told me that it turned out well. Then they put a cast on my foot. Mayo did all this on the fifteenth floor. The rooms had a lot of windows, and there was a good view of the city. All the people that worked there made it fun for me.

A FATHER'S QUEST

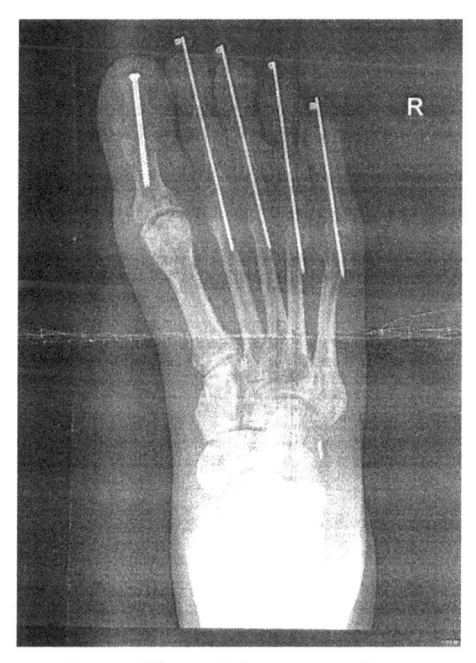

X-ray of foot with screw and pins

In a month I went back. They took off the cast and x-rayed my foot. The doctor was happy. Then the doctor said he was going to take the pins out. I figured that it would really hurt. I said, "You are going to put me under so I won't feel anything?" The doctor said, "No, you won't have much pain." I didn't know what he meant about not having much pain. I wasn't looking forward to it. As he got everything ready to do it, almost everyone that worked in the area came to watch. I told everyone, "I should charge you admission if you are going to watch." The doctor had a pliers like we used on the farm. He just pulled out the pins rapidly. It was a surprise for me! I hardly felt anything. Then they had to put another cast on for a month. There were two workers that put the cast on. They told me, "You will do better with a John Deere cast." I had always talked to all the workers a lot. All of them knew I was a farmer with John Deere tractors. They put on a green cast with yellow stripes. Then they put on a John Deere emblem. I was proud of the cast! I really enjoyed showing the cast off.

It sure felt good when they took the cast off. I could walk again. The doctor wrote a subscription for me to get therapy. We decided to have therapy at the care center in Dodge Center. I started in April and went two times a week until November. Michelle was again my therapist. But she wasn't the main therapist. Most times I worked with someone else. I was disappointed. I figured she was the best therapist that there was. I went for one hour at a time for my leg and another hour for my arm. I started out with Morgen Larson for my arm. She was from Waseca. I really liked her! But she never was there on Fridays. I went on Mondays and Fridays. As time went on, Morgen Larson was never there. Finally, Holly told me that she was going to take care of me. I could pick up things with my right hand and release them. Finally, after years of therapy, I could to it. Things really came slowly. They had an exercise where they had a rope with handles through a pulley suspended from the ceiling. I was to use both hands to pull it up and down. I did this exercise when I was at the nursing home. But back then, the therapist had to tie my right hand to the handle. At that time, I had to do all the work with my left hand. My right hand was just going along for the ride. Now I could hold onto the handle without being tied to it. I was able to do the work with both hands. I was to do it for fifteen minutes. I told Holly one day, "I bet you twenty dollars that I can do it for the whole hour." I knew I would lose. She wouldn't bet with me. Holly then put weights on my wrists, making it harder. In about twelve minutes, my right hand just dropped off the handle.

My goal for walking was to walk a quarter of a mile. They were going to discharge me from therapy in November. Michelle told me on the last day that I would have to meet my goal. She had her dog at therapy that day. She put her dog on a lease, and they walked with me. Toward the end, I got so tired that I wanted to give up. I could hardly lift my legs. Michelle told me that I didn't have far to go. Would I make my goal? I would have to get more stubborn. Finally, I made it. Ruth had a wheelchair waiting for me to sit down when I finished. Michelle pushed me out to the car and helped me get into the car. When we got home, I made it up the steps, but Ruth had a wheelchair waiting for me when I got into the house. Ruth took me to bed that night in a wheelchair. I had overdone it! Holly had me come to therapy a couple more times for my arm. I think she would have done it longer if they wouldn't have discharged me for my leg.

Chapter 30

The Journey through Cancer

In early July of 2017, I was sitting on my lift chair in the south room. Zoe, the boxer, jumped up on the lift chair. She put her paws on my stomach. I felt it! Sometime later I had to go to the bathroom. My urine was all blood. I thought right away that it was cancer. I went to the doctor in Kasson. He thought it might be bladder infection. But he said, "Just to be safe, you should go to the Mayo Clinic in Rochester to have it checked out." I lay on a table where the doctor put a camera through my penis and looked into my bladder. I could see everything on a computer screen. I saw cancer before the doctor told me that I had cancer. Maybe Zoe had just saved my life. The cancer was in the beginning stages. Maybe if she hadn't stepped on my stomach, the cancer would not have been discovered for months and months. It could have been too late. The doctor said that they would operate soon.

Mayo doctors operated on August 9, 2017. We reported to the clinic early in the morning. A nurse called me into a room where I sat on a chair. The chair was adjusted so it became a bed. Ruth got me undressed and got me into a grown. There was a locker in the room for my clothes. The nurse and several other nurses came into the room. There were several things for them to do, including putting in an IV. It all took about two hours, but the time went fast. Then a person that worked in the operating room came to get me. They put an oxygen mask on over my nose and mouth. Then they injected a medicine into the IV. They said, "Breathe deep." I was out right away. The next thing I knew, they were trying to wake me. When I completely came to, a person wheeled me back to the original room. Ruth helped me get dressed, and we went home. I had a catheter that I would have for one week. The doctors told me that they had to put a stint between my kidney and bladder. The cancer was at a place where it damaged the tube between my kidney and bladder. The doctor assured me that there would be no permanent damage.

In the first days, I was really sick. The day when I was the sickest, I just lay in bed. Jax, Bob's boxer, came into the bedroom. He put his paws on the bed. He put his head right next to my head. He stayed there for almost one hour. He was trying to comfort me. He could feel that I was really sick. Animals can think much more than we think. Jax is the most caring dog we have ever had.

I posted on Facebook August 17, 2017:

> I finally feel like a man today. The 9th of August I had surgery to take the tumors off my bladder. It was cancer! It was cancer and it didn't spread. They put in a catheter and we left in six hours. The first day I had severe bladder spasms and then I got sicker every day. I got constipated. Monday I was sitting on the toilet. Bob came in and then I passed out. Bob called the ambulance. Justin was here and he and Bob carried me to the south room. I was confused when the ambulance arrived. I spent Monday night at the hospital. It was late Tuesday afternoon when I got home. This morning at 8:00 in the morning they took the catheter out. I ate a roll and drank two cups of coffee. When I went to the bathroom everything worked. Ruth, Doreen, Bob and I met with the doctor and now we have a plan. We went out for dinner. I feel so much better. In the last week I felt it would have been better to die. I have a month to heal and then the chemo treatments begin in six weeks. They have to operate again

to take the stint out. It will not be fun. Say a PRAYER for me.

I think the only reason I thought I felt like a man was because they had taken the catheter out. The same day when we met with the doctor, I went back to emergency room. The doctor didn't think there was anything wrong with me. I insisted that they put me back in the hospital. Finally, they took me to a room. The next morning a person from the admission office came to see me. He said, "You are here for observation, Medicare won't pay. You will have to pay the bill." I still felt terrible, and I argued with him. The doctors didn't find anything wrong with me. But I knew there was something really wrong with me. But in the end, I didn't want to pay for another night. So I went home Thursday afternoon.

I woke up at five in the morning on Friday, August 18. I felt terrible! Just before six, I called Bob to come over. I didn't know it, but Bob was almost at Lyle with a load of corn. Bob called Jodi and asked her to check on me. I started throwing up blood in bed. It was all over the sheets. It was black, and it looked like tar. When Jodi came into the room, she called 911 immediately. Soon the ambulance was here. They took me out of the bedroom and put me in the ambulance. The attendant was checking my vitals all the way. When we went through Kasson on the way to Rochester, the attendant hollered to the driver, "Turn on the siren and don't stop for anything." I felt the end was here. When we got to the emergency room, they immediately admitted me to the hospital. Why did they let me go home yesterday? I felt terrible when I went home. They could have saved Medicare a huge cost, and they could have saved me a huge amount of pain. Why did it have to get so bad for them to act?

About midnight that night, a nurse come into the room to check on me. I was burning up. She called the doctor, and they both worked on me for over two hours. My temperature was 105 degrees. They packed me in ice. Finally, after two hours, my temperature started to come down. A group of doctors came in the next morning, and they felt that the infection had gone into my blood. They took me for a test where they would put a camera down my throat and they could look at my heart. They told me that they couldn't put me under but I wouldn't remember it. I didn't remember when they put the camera down my throat, but I woke up clear when they were doing the test. It didn't hurt, and I felt no discomfort. I lay so quietly that they didn't know the medicine that they gave me, to take my memory away, had run out. When I was back to my room, a doctor came in to tell me the results of the test.

"Your heart really looks good, but there is an infection on the leads to the pacemaker. If we don't take it out, you will be dead in less than one week. We will monitor your heart until we can put the pacemaker back in."

When the doctor left, I started to think about all this. I could easily spend a month in the hospital. Bob and Jodi were going to be married on Tuesday, August 29. It was the first anniversary of their first date. If this was the case, I would be unable to go to their wedding. On Monday, August 21, they did an operation and took the pacemaker out. It was a painful operation just like when they put the pacemaker in. They put a catheter in. That was something I didn't like. They never stitched up the wound from taking the pacemaker out. So on Tuesday they did another operation to close everything

My urine started to have blood in it. The blood started to clot. The clots plugged up the catheter. When this happened, I started to have severe pain. It was so bad that I screamed. I didn't have to call the nurse. She could hear me screaming. She had to call urology to have a man come to irrigate the catheter. Sometimes it took a while for them to come. The pain never left me until they irrigated the catheter. Soon I had another nurse work on the tube from the catheter to the storage bag. She got it running somewhat again. But I still needed someone from urology to come. After that I always talked a nurse into doing this while we waited for urology to come. The pain was not as bad, but I was still was in pain. I had this problem every two to three hours around the clock. Dying would have been better.

Then finally I got some good news. They had me on a machine that monitored my heart. After six days the doctors told me, "There is nothing wrong with your heart. When we put the pacemaker in, your brain was not sending the right messages to your heart. Your brain has repaired itself. Now it is sending the right messages to your heart." That was good news! The doctor told me that it wouldn't be so painful the next time. But I didn't believe him after all the pain I had last time. Now I wouldn't have to have another operation to put the pacemaker back in. What a relief! How could my brain repair itself so soon? Maybe I would get out early enough for Bob's wedding.

I figured that the catheter was causing me all the problems. The catheter was causing the clots. If they would take the catheter out, I could walk to the bathroom. I would get more exercise. I finally talked the nurses into taking the catheter out. At first it felt so good! But when I went to the bathroom, I was bleeding. I left a blood path on the floor all the way to the bathroom and back. I had to go every forty-five minutes. Soon I had clots that I couldn't pass. It hurt so bad that I begged the nurses into putting the catheter back in. At least now I would have severe pain every two or three hours instead of every forty-five minutes. Those were the most miserable twelve days I had in my life. I was almost to the point of praying that I would die. If it was not for Bob's wedding, I'm sure they would have kept me longer. I asked the doctors if I could leave the hospital for two hours and then come back. They said, "If you leave, you will have to be discharged. You can't come right back." The doctor reluctantly released me on Monday, August 28.

On the twenty-ninth, I still felt terrible. It was Bob and Jodi's wedding day. I had no business coming home from the hospital. I still had the catheter. I was not comfortable with that. Part of the time I was dizzy when I stood up. I told Ruth to go alone. Ruth didn't feel comfortable to leave me alone. I didn't want Ruth to miss the wedding. Finally, two hours before the wedding, I agreed to go. The wedding was four o'clock in the afternoon. There would be only fifty people there.

Ruth and I got to the church an hour before the wedding. The first people we saw were Jan and Merritt. They could tell that I didn't look good. The first thing they asked me was, "How much have you been drinking?" It wasn't alcohol. I admitted that I was not drinking enough. I felt it was embarrassing wearing the catheter. On purpose,

I didn't want to drink anything. How would anyone know I was wearing a catheter? But the bag could show on my ankle. I didn't want the bag to get full. Jan wanted to get me something to drink. I finally told her to get me a bottle of orange soda. She went to Kwik Trip. After I drank the soda, I started to feel better.

Jodi's daughters, Janessa, Ashley, and a friend from Florida, Lisa, stood up with her. Merritt was Bob's best man. Justin and Doreen's husband, Allan, also stood up with Bob. All of Ruth's brothers and sisters and their mates except Marion were there. My two brothers and their wives were there. My Uncle Duane and Aunt Barb were there. In the last years, they had become close to Bob. Of course, Doreen, Brenda, Kayla, and Sarah and their families were there. There weren't many people from Jodi's family there. She didn't have a big family.

Bob and Jodi's wedding day

The wedding was like something I never saw before. Most of the time, Bob and Jodi sat on chairs on the altar. The attendants sat in the first row of the pews. That was different! But I'm sure it was easier sitting rather than standing the whole time. Pastor Barb did a great job. The wedding was nice! After the wedding at church, everyone came out to the farm for lunch. Everyone had decorated the shop. We had sloppy joes, chips, salad, and cake. Jodi made the meal. Have you ever heard of a bride cooking the meal for the guests? I think I just got a great daughter-in-law. They would have never met if I didn't have a stroke and went to the nursing home in Dodge Center. At first she said that the McColleys would cause her too much trouble. Was it true? Now she was a McColley. I had been praying for years that Bob would get married. God answered my prayers! But in the end, I had paid a big price for this to happen.

In the next few days, I started to feel better. Bob and Jodi were going to have a big party on Saturday night on our farm to celebrate their wedding. I asked Jodi one day, "When did you first feel romantically toward Bob?" She answered, "It was the first time when I saw your farm." I was planning on having her as my daughter-in-law when I first told Bob to show the farm to them. Maybe she fell in love with the farm first and then fell in love with Bob. At that time, I didn't know that Jodi wanted to be a farmer. Maybe when they got married she didn't want to be a farmer. Maybe that would come later. She told me that the total wedding was going to cost less than $2,000. They had a wedding dance on Saturday night. One of Jim Bryngelson's daughters, Laura, played in the band. The band cost them $700. Jodi bought dresses for the girls who stood up with her. She bought her wedding dress. She bought red shirts for the men that stood up with Bob. They wore black jeans. They had a meal including pulled pork. Jodi again made the meal with help from a husband of a great friend, Lisa from Florida. They came up for the wedding. Jodi's daughters served the meal. I couldn't believe that she did all that for less than $2,000. They had two hundred people for the dance. There are so many people that get divorced today. I think the more they pay for the wedding, the more apt they are to get divorced. I knew that she would make Bob a great farm wife.

They got some chairs from church for the wedding and the party. We were going to have church on the farm again in September. We would need the chairs for that day. Janessa was going to take the pictures. It was a super nice day, and Ruth and I went down to the shop in the middle of the afternoon. Jodi wanted to have a picture of them and us standing next to the Model T Ford Pickup. We didn't know Janessa, but she spent some time with me, especially when I was walking. I immediately liked her, and I knew she was a caring person. We had met Ashley before. Ruth and I always enjoyed when she came over to our house. During the party, Ruth and I sat with George and Jean Sierakowski and Gary and Mary Norstad. Ruth walked around and visited with a lot of people. I was in the wheelchair, and it was hard to get around with so many people there. I got a chance to visit with Gary Pittman, my brother-in-law. He was married to my sister Sandy. His daughter, Michelle, and her husband, Mark, brought him to the party. My sister Sandy always wanted to go to Bob's wedding. It's was not to be. I thought of Sandy many times during Bob's wedding. Gary had kidney cancer, and I never saw him again. He died on December 16, 2017. Some people started to leave at ten at night. Ruth and I were really tired, and we went home. Ruth brought our car to the shop, and Janessa helped me get into the car.

On Tuesday, September 5, 2017, the doctor looked into my bladder. He decided he could take the stint out. Bob was in the room with me, and he watched. The stint was over six inches long. I can't believe how they did this. They put the stint in though my penis and got it between my bladder and the kidney. The doctor also left the catheter out. He wanted me to stay in the clinic until I could pee. I wanted to go home! I agreed that if I hadn't peed in three hours, I would come back. On the way home, I got severe pain in my kidneys, and I threw up over and over. We were lucky that Ruth had an empty box in the car. When we got home, I was sick again, so we went back to the clinic. A male nurse, Andrew, took me to the restroom. I was able to pee. There was a lot of blood in the urine. I felt that I had very low blood pressure. The doctor debated putting me in the hospital. I had an appointment with a doctor in Kasson the next day. So he let me go home. When I went to the doctor in Kasson on Wednesday, my blood pressure was a little bit better. I was sick again Tuesday night. The doctor decided that they would put a medicine in my veins every day for two weeks. Jodi was a nurse before she became a social worker. Jodi administered the medicine.

I had therapy at home. I had a therapist who was raised on a farm by Lanesboro, Minnesota. The first thing she did was to have me walk holding on to her hand without the cane. She wanted to know how much pressure my hand was putting on the cane. She walked with me a lot outside. I really liked her. But I made a big mistake by talking too much. I told her that Ruth and I went out to eat. She told me that she could only work with me if I was homebound. I really regretted that I told her that. Why couldn't I keep my big mouth shut? I had lost considerable weight in the hospital, and I lost a lot of muscle. I really needed therapy, but now I wouldn't get it.

On September 17, 2017, we had church on the farm like we had it in 2014. Jordyn was baptized as a baby in 2014 at our farm. Colten was going to be baptized this time at our farm. But now Colten was not a baby like Jordyn was. He was twenty-four months old. Pastor Barb was going to have Jordyn help her baptize Colten. It was a big disappointment for Pastor Barb. Colten didn't want to be baptized. He was afraid! He started crying, and it wasn't easy for Pastor Barb. We had about two hundred people there. Bob and Jodi gave horse and carriage rides to all the kids. It was a fun day! Bob and Jodi said they wanted to do it again.

I started treatment on my bladder September 26, 2017. It was on a Thursday. I picked Thursday because the third Wednesday was my insurance meeting. I was still president of the company. I figured that I had six days to get over the treatment. The nurse put a killed tuberculosis in my bladder. It didn't make sense, but that was what they called it. Shortly after we arrived at the clinic, a nurse come out and asked how I was feeling. Then she ordered the drug. It usually took an hour. Then a nurse came to get me and took me into a room. I had to pull my pants down and lie on a small bed. The nurse had to put on a protective gown and a mask. She then put a catheter in me. By then I was used to it, and I didn't have pain. The medicine came in a small container, and she poured the medicine into the catheter. I wasn't supposed to go to the bathroom for two hours, and then I was to pee and get rid of it. I did this every Thursday for six weeks.

I felt good when I got home from the clinic. I even worked in the fields that afternoon some days. I felt good on Fridays. On Saturdays morning, I started having bladder spasms. I had spasms every hour for twenty-four hours. And then there were gone. What a relief! Ruth and I missed church for six weeks.

I wrote on Facebook on Thursday, November 2, 2017:

> Last Thursday was the last of my cancer treatments. I hope now that it gets better. I have a January 19th appointment to look in my bladder to see if everything is okay. I hope I don't have to go through it again. Today I had electrical treatments on my arm. The therapist used electrical stimulation on five different muscles at the same time. The therapist put my hands on a machine where I paddled with both hands. She had to tie my right hand to the paddles. When she turned it on I was really in pain, but I got used to it. It had a thing showing how much each arm was doing. When I paddled backwards I was able to keep both arms at 50%. When I paddled forward I was able to get my right arm doing 70% of the work. The electrical stimulation in my right arm was making my muscles really work. I got in two and a half miles. It took an hour. I am supposed to have this treatment twice a week. Four hours later my right hand still feels like it is still moving. I really look forward to doing this!

I wrote on Facebook on Tuesday December 5, 2017:

> We are in Pigeon Forge, Tennessee. Bob and Jodi took us. It's like Branson, only bigger. Ruth took me to breakfast in the hotel in the wheelchair. I couldn't believe the number of people who went

out of their way to help us. They told Ruth, it's too hard for you, let us push. There are a lot of good people. Last night I walked into the theater. We had seats at the front. It was a long way and it was steep down. It was scary! I thought it would be easier coming back up. It was not as scary but it was harder work. The first night we saw a show with horses. Really good! Yesterday we drove in the Smokey Mountains. We went to County Tonight last night. Today we are going to go to Dollywood. We are having fun! It feels good to go on vacation again.

I wrote on Facebook on Wednesday December 6, 2017:

I wanted to share the picture at the Grand ole Opera but I'm not smart enough to do it. I bet not one of you reading this has done this before. I sang on the Grand ole Opera stage. If you have seen the picture you will see the microphone in my hand. Being that it was Christmas I chose Dashing Through the Snow. Maybe I will be famous! We are having a good vacation! We stopped at the Kleenland race track. I said, "This is where I got the idea of all of the white fence." Jodi said, "We will build a white fence along the whole pasture." I said, "Who is going to paint it?" She said, "I will." I have the best daughter-in-law there is.

On the way back home, we stopped at Uncle Cliff's in Kentucky. We went out to Cliff's place, but we didn't go in the house. I just wanted to show Jodi where they lived. We stayed at the Best Western Motel. There was a restaurant close to the motel. We took Cliff and Linda there for supper. They seated us at a round table away from everyone. With the shape I was in, maybe I would embarrass the other costumers. But the food was good, and it was easier for us to visit with no one else around. We had a really good evening.

From Cliff's we went to St. Louis to visit my Navy buddy, Steve and Judy Hibbert. I thought it would be fun for Bob and Jodi to go up in the Arch. It's six hundred feet high. Bob and Jodi had never seen it before. Ruth and I were in it three times during the years. They dropped us off at Steve's house. Steve and Judy took us out to eat at the Cracker Barrel. Afterward we came back to Steve's house. We had an interesting conversation. If was really fun to see them again. In the middle of the afternoon, Bob and Jodi came back, and we had to say goodbye. We left, and they figured we could make it home that night. It would take about eleven hours. Bob was really speeding, and a Missouri highway patrol car put on his red lights, and we had to stop. He came to our car, and he asked Bob for his license. Bob was going twenty miles an hour over the speed limit. A short time later, the highway patrolman came back to our car. He said, "You have an expired driver's license. It has been expired for over eight months. You better take care of it." He then left. I couldn't believe Bob didn't get a ticket. Bob has been picked up for speeding many times. He has never gotten a ticket.

Bob and Jodi took Ruth and me to Gary Pittman's funeral on December 19, 2017. Afterward we stopped at Uncle Roger and Aunt Lorna's house. Lorna was almost blind. I sat about six feet from her. She could see someone was there, but she couldn't recognize me. We had a good visit. She was praying to die. When we left, she told me goodbye. I knew that I would never see her again. Lorna died at eighty-seven years old on April 9, 2018. That September, Roger was in the hospital in Waseca. Ruth and I went to visit him. We talked about many things when we were younger. It was a fun day. When we left, I told Roger, "We'll see you soon." I never saw him again. Roger died at eighty-nine years old on October 2, 2018. When we went to Roger's funeral, Roger's four girls told me, "My dad always looked to you as a younger brother."

On January 18, 2018, the doctors looked at my bladder again. He said I got cancer back, or maybe it never went away. The doctor told me, "This time we are going to give you nine treatments of the same medicine, tuberculosis." I really dreaded this now. Nine weeks was a long time. I started asking God, "Why are you doing this to me?" I knew I was a sinner, but I didn't think I was that bad. On the INTRODUCTION of my book, I wrote, "We planned our lives with God's help before we were born." A lot of my life was really good. I lived the American dream. I have escaped death many times. God was always with me. But then there was very a painful part of my life. We lost our daughter Tammy to murder. "Why did this happen?" I thought it was bad enough to have a stroke. "Why cancer too? Why did I plan on learning a lesson from all this?" Maybe when I go to heaven, I will understand all this. If I was to escape death again, I would really need God to be with me. The doctor told me that electrical stimulation can cause cancer. I quit therapy at St. Mary's at this time. When I quit therapy at St. Mary's, several therapists said that I had more determination than anyone that they worked with. I had been going there for over a year. I would really miss it.

I had bladder infection, and they would have to take care of this before I could start the treatments. I again wanted the treatments to be on Thursday. But this time I started to have bladder spasms on Friday. On Friday nights I got really cold. Ruth couldn't give my enough blankets. The spasms were much the same as the other time. They lasted for twenty-four hours, every hour. But by Saturday night, I always slept well, and we were able to go to church on Sundays.

I wrote on Facebook June 7, 2018:

> I think your prayers for me were answered today. Monday I had a scan of my stomach and it show something wrong with both of my kidneys. The right one has a small lump. It hasn't changed in a year. The left kidney didn't look good. They said if I didn't have much bleeding from removing the bladder cancer they would go in the left kidney and look at it. They would have to put in a stint between my bladder and the kidney. I had this done on the last surgery. They left the stint in

for two months and it bothered me. I don't look forward to this again. When they did the surgery they found that the tumor was really small. There was almost no bleeding so they looked into the kidney and found nothing wrong. They didn't have to put in a stint. That was really good news! The last time they had a catheter in for six weeks and I hated it. Now they say that they will take it out in five days, next Monday morning. They will have to wait for the lab work but there is a chance that I won't need an additional treatment. I had nine treatments last time with terrible pain. This was really good news for me! I ended up in the hospital twelve days last time.

Bob and Jodi decided to build a new house. They would buy a prefab home. They wanted it on the same place as I had the double wide mobile home for them. We sold the mobile home for $5,000 to the same company they bought the new home from. Bob's two boxers, Zoe and Jax, always slept in the mobile home. The day they moved the mobile home away, Jax couldn't figure out was happening. Jax just sat on the empty spot and cried. Bob and Jodi were going to live in the shop until their new home was done. Jax cried all night every night. After three nights, they wanted Jax to sleep at our house. Jax stayed on the floor on my side of the bed and cried all night. We didn't get any sleep. Jax was so tired that he slept all day. Sometimes he got up on the bed. Ruth always pushed him off the bed. One night when Ruth got up to go to bathroom, Jax got up on the bed. He got completely under the covers next to me. Would Jax get away with this? Ruth didn't see him. I didn't say anything. At least he was not crying now. Ruth never liked dogs. She warmed up to Shilo somewhat. But Ruth grew to love Jax. She was always watching for Jax so she could let him in the house. Jax got ice cream every day.

In November, the doctor decided I should have that same treatment again to my bladder. I had a few treatments, and I still had problems with bladder spasms. But it wasn't as bad as the other times. I went for a treatment to my bladder on Thursday, December 6, 2018. It went fairly well. On Friday, December 7, I had an appointment at the Mayo Clinic at eight thirty to have my eyes checked. Ruth was driving the car to Rochester in the morning. About halfway between Byron and Rochester, a thought came into my head: "I'm going to die today." I wasn't afraid or worried about it. When we went into the clinic, this thought was still there. We were there a half hour early. We had been sitting there about forty-five minutes. My hip and my back were in pain. I could hardly stand it. All of a sudden I got really dizzy. I said to Ruth, "I don't feel good at all." At the same time a man came to get me. When he got me into the treatment room, a doctor came in and started asking me questions. I heard the questions, but I was unable to respond to them. I think the doctor thought I was having a stroke. My condition matched with the symptoms of a stroke. He called a crash team. By the time the crash team came into the room, I was unconscious. Ruth actually thought I was dying. Ruth never thought I was dying before when I had close calls. Now Ruth knew I was dying when they took her to another room. She called Bob, but Bob was loading hogs and he didn't answer the phone.

The crew dragged me out of the wheelchair to the floor. They checked my blood pressure, and it was 40/20. They cut off my favorite shirt. They put a defibrillator on my chest. I came to a little. I could feel that I was on the floor. There was a thump, thump, thump feeling on my chest. I thought a man was doing this. I tried to take my left hand and push him away. There was no one there. Then I was unconscious again. I came to for less than a minute when they loaded me in the ambulance. I felt the cold. They had a man that took Ruth to the hospital in a van. Finally, Bob called back. Ruth gave her phone to the man that was driving the van. He told Bob what was happening. Bob called Jodi. She was almost to Byron to check on a patient she was taking care of. Jodi went to St. Mary's right away, and she got there about the same time as Ruth got there.

I came to briefly when they were running down the hallway of the hospital pushing me on a gurney. I remember when they started the MRI, but I don't remember when they finished. Bob called Brenda, and Brenda called Doreen at work. After they were done with the MRI, they took me to a room in the emergency department. Ruth and Jodi were there. A nurse stayed with me the whole time. When Doreen and Brenda got there, the nurse told them, "Your dad is in terrible shape." I think they had the defibrillator hooked to the blood pressure. I felt the thump, thump, and then it went away. All of a sudden I could feel the thump, thump again. I finally came to. It was one o'clock. I had been unconscious for four hours. Evidently, a lot of people were praying for me. I was prepared to die, but God has more things for me to do. I'm not done writing the book yet. Maybe there are other things for me to do. If I were home instead at the Mayo Clinic, I'm positive I would have died.

The doctor came in the room and said, "There is something wrong with your heart. I think we will have to put the pacemaker back in." They put me in a room where they could monitor my heart. After monitoring my heart for twenty-four hours, a group of doctors came in my room. The head doctor told me that there wasn't anything wrong with my heart. The cause for all this to happen to me was the tuberculosis that they put in my bladder. They would never do this again. When they gave a treatment of tuberculosis, I always got cancer back. It was not worth the risk.

Ruth had an appointment to be checked for breast cancer. The doctor's assistant, Dee, did the examination. She was the doctor that Ruth always met with. She found a small lump just below Ruth's left shoulder. Soon they did an operation and took the lump out. It was cancer. Dee was certain that they got all the cancer. Dee wanted Ruth to have radiation in January. Ruth had refused to have radiation in 2015. She had been through too much. But now it was three and a half years later. Ruth agreed to do it. Ruth started it in January. She was to have it forty times, five days a week. Bob took her sometimes, and sometimes Ruth went alone. Bob and Jodi went to Mexico on vacation the end of January. Bob had made arrangements with Jim and Pat Bryngelson to take Ruth if the weather was bad. They took Ruth three days. Ruth wanted to pay them, but they refused. One day they stopped for groceries. Ruth put $100 bill in the grocery bag.

Pat sent a nice card with $100 bill back to Ruth. Pat said that it was an honor for them to do this for Ruth. It was the middle of February when they were done. Ruth had made many friends during this time. She said that she would miss the people, but she wouldn't miss the radiation. She was sunburned quite bad.

I had the operation on my foot in January of the year 2019. In February, I was due to have the test for bladder cancer. My foot was in a cast, and I was unable to walk. They had an overhead hoist to lift me out of the wheelchair and put me on the table. I watched the computer screen when the doctor looked in my bladder. I could see that I had cancer again. That was bad news! When I met with the cancer doctor, we discussed my options. The doctor said, "The best thing that we can do is to take your bladder out. Then you will never get bladder cancer again." I know two people personally that have had it done. They are doing well. Then the doctor said, "Because of your stroke, you'll have to take blood thinner the rest of your life. If we take your bladder out, you will have to be off the blood thinner too long. There is a good chance you will have another stroke. You are not a good candidate to have this done." He then told me that another option was not to do anything. I asked, "How long will I live if I don't do anything?" He said, "Maybe two years." I then said, "I'm seventy-five years old, do you think I will live to be eighty years old if I do everything possible?" He then said, "I don't think so." He then explained to me the problems with surgery. "Every time you have surgery, you will have more scar tissue on your bladder. If you get too much scar tissue on your bladder, your bladder will no longer work." I didn't want to live if my bladder didn't work. I didn't think I had too much scar tissue yet, and I would ask the doctor every time they looked into my bladder. With God's help, I would prove him wrong. I decided to have the operation. I asked him if would be safe to wait until April when my foot was out of the cast. He said, "It will be safe to wait until April." This would be my third surgery for cancer in twenty-three months.

It was so peaceful to be put to sleep for the operation. I enjoyed it! When they were trying to wake me up, the first thought that come into my mind was, "God, why are you waking me up to this?" Again

I had to have a catheter, but it was for only five days. I didn't suffer too badly from the surgery. When would I have to have surgery again? The doctors had told me that they couldn't do anything to keep the cancer from coming back. Then I got an appointment with a doctor. He said there was another medicine to try. It is only 25 percent chance for it to work. He assured me that I would have no problems with this medicine. After the first treatment, I had some problems. When I met with the nurse, she said I was going to have more problems with this treatment than the other treatment. Why did the doctor tell me that I wouldn't have problems? After I got the second treatment out of six, I had severe bladder spasms right away. At the longest they were three hours apart. But mostly they were one hour apart. I thought that they were going to last one day like before. When they lasted for six days, Ruth told me, "I can't stand another night of this. You have to go to the hospital." I was scheduled for another treatment the next day. How could I do this again on Thursday? On Wednesday afternoon, Bob took me to the doctor at Kasson. They were going to put a catheter in me and then send me home. I knew that I could have bladder spasms with a catheter in. Ruth wanted me to go to the hospital. I refused the catheter. The doctor told me that they had to put a catheter in me. Finally I agreed. A nurse came to put the catheter in. She tried and tried, but she couldn't get the catheter in. I think my guardian angel was preventing this. The nurse said, "I've done these hundreds of times. This is the first time I couldn't get it." The doctor then told Bob, "Take your dad to the emergency room at St. Mary's Hospital. I'll call ahead so they will be waiting for you." I think by this time, I was too stubborn and the doctor didn't want to deal with me.

When we got to the hospital, they were waiting for me. They took me into the examination room. The doctor that came in wanted to put a catheter in me and then sent me home. I again refused! I told the doctor, "Admit me in the hospital." Ruth was with me, and I knew this was what she wanted. The doctor said, "We can admit you for observation, but Medicare won't pay." At this time, I didn't care what it would cost. Ruth didn't want to spend the night with me. I argued with the doctor, "I'm not here for observation. There really is something wrong with me." If I went home, who would spend the night with me? I reminded the doctor about the last time I was admitted for observation. I didn't want to pay, so I went home. The next day an ambulance brought me back almost dead. He admitted me for observation. A man from urology finally came and put a temporary catheter in and drained my bladder. He had no problem. Why couldn't the nurse in Kasson get the catheter in? It was already ten at night. I told Bob and Ruth to go home. I got a room at eleven at night.

A young doctor, Nathan Nielsen, came in to admit me. We talked for almost an hour. I really like him. He said, "It isn't good for you to have a permanent catheter left in. It's better to put in a temporary catheter when you need it." This doctor didn't admit me for just observation. I got bladder spasms later in the night, and the nurses heard me screaming. A man from urology came up and put a temporary catheter in and drained my bladder. The next day the doctors suggested I could use a catheter at home. I knew that Jodi had done it as a nurse. But she didn't want to do it to her father-in-law. Ruth refused to do it. I didn't have use of my right hand because of the stroke. It would be impossible for me to do it. A doctor told Ruth they would train her to do it. Finally Ruth agreed. A man from urology came up twice that afternoon to train Ruth. Ruth still wasn't comfortable, so I stayed another night. I had fun with the nurses. We laughed a lot. I liked St. Mary's Hospital. I told the nurses, "I plan to die at St. Mary's Hospital. I'll keep you laughing until the end!" They kept a urinal on a tray next to the bed. At home for three years, when I had to go the bathroom, I always woke Ruth up to bring me the urinal. I was awake in the night, and I saw the urinal sitting on the tray. I could get it off from the tray and use it and set it back on the tray. I tried it, and it worked. We could place a small table next to the bed at home where I could reach it. Ruth would get much more sleep. Why didn't we think about it before? Ruth came up to the hospital the next morning. Someone from urology came up twice to train Ruth. She did a good job, and we finally went home.

At first we used the catheter every morning and night and about two in the afternoon. The reason I was having the problems was my bladder was not emptying itself completely. Soon we quit doing it at two in the afternoon. I always went to the bathroom right before Ruth put the catheter in. We were catching less. I first told Ruth, "We will try not doing it at night." I slept well! In three weeks after we started doing it, we stopped. I haven't had a bladder spasm since.

I soon had another appointment with the cancer doctor. I told the doctor that I was not completely getting rid of the medicine in two hours like I was supposed to. I was retaining too much urine. The doctor agreed. He said he wanted me to complete the program. He wanted me to have the remainder four treatments. The doctor told me that they would do it different this time. A nurse would put the catheter in and administer the medicine. Then she would put a plug in the catheter and leave it in. I was to stay in the room for two hours lying on the examination table. Then a nurse would come in and pull the plug out of the catheter and completely drain me. The nurse pressed on my stomach several times to be sure all the urine was gone. That really worked, and I had no discomfort afterward. In September, the doctor again looked in my bladder to check for cancer. I didn't have cancer this time. The doctor said I would only have 25 percent chance that it would work. But 25 percent chance was enough. The doctor wanted me to have four more treatments. On December 29, 2019, they looked in my bladder again. They found no cancer! The medicine was working! Then I was to have one treatment per month for a year. They were going to look in my bladder again April 29, 2020.

We always took our combine to the dealership at the end of harvest. They checked it over and fixed everything that they found wrong. This year it would cost us $23,000. Bob only had $11,000 of the work done. I figured we would have problems next year. But Bob was now in charge of everything. I figured it was not my place to question Bob's judgment. I rented eighty acres to Bob for next year. I still had 42 percent of the farm. But I planned on renting more land to Bob every year. It was not easy to get out of farming without giving it all to the taxman. Darrel Ness, my banker, had told me several years ago, "Remember how hard it was to start farming. It's going to be a harder time to quit farming." I paid Bob to custom-farm my land. I owned the combine, and Bob owned the heads. We had a 9560 John Deere combine. It was a 2007 model that we bought in 2011 when my mother was living with us. It was the fifth combine that I had owned. We had had it long enough that it was time to trade. Then a John Deere salesman from Owatonna came out. I told him and Bob that I didn't want to buy another combine. It was a 2014 S660 JD combine. It had 1,500 engine hours and 1,100 separate hours. It had more hours than I would have liked. I checked with SEMA, a John Deere dealership. A salesman came out. He had two S660 combines, and he gave us prices. Finally I told Bob I would pay for half of it. SEMA had told us that we could get it for zero interest for three years. That would save us several thousand dollars. We got the salesman from Owatonna to agree. We finally bought a different combine. That would save me some money on taxes.

In January 2020, Jodi had inherited some money. She wanted to buy a new JD Gator with a cab. Bob had a Gator that he put tracks on in the winter. They used it every day. It would be warmer with a cab and a heater. Bob come over one day and said, "You should buy a Gator too. We can get a better deal if we buy two." I always said that when I got the loans paid off on the land, I was going to buy a Gator with a cab. Bob said, "What are you waiting for? You will enjoy it now. You never know what the future will be." Bob and Jodi were going to buy a cheaper model. But Bob wanted me to buy the most expensive model. Finally I agreed. The list price for an 835R was $27,000. They bought an 835M model. By buying two, the price was $24,500 on mine. I had a 2012 825 model to trade in. After the trade, I paid $18,000. At least I could deduct it on my taxes. Last fall I wanted to take the Gator out to the fields and watch them harvest. It was always too cold. Now I would have a heater and air-conditioner. I like to have the boxer dog, Jax, ride with me. But I was always afraid he would jump out when we were away from home. How would I get him back in? Now I wouldn't be afraid because he couldn't get out of the cab.

On April 15, 2020, I had an appointment for the doctors to look in my bladder for cancer again. I was again cancer-free. I then got another treatment in my bladder for cancer again. I got another appointment on May 13, 2020, to have another treatment for cancer to my bladder. I am going to have one treatment per month. They are going to look in my bladder again in July for cancer. The more times they look and don't find anything, the better. Maybe the cancer is gone for good with God's help.

Ruth and Wayne

"Damn the torpedoes, full speed ahead!"

The End

WAYNE McCOLLEY

The McColley Farm

About the Author

Wayne McColley served in the US Navy Reserve aboard the USS *Enterprise*, the largest warship in the world at that time, during the Vietnam War, and received an honorable discharge. After the Navy, Wayne got married to a woman that he met while he was home on leave. Then he became a cabinet maker. An angel told the author when he was a kid that he would be a successful farmer. Wayne couldn't get this thought out of his mind. In 1974, the author quit his job and started farming full-time with his wife, Ruth, without any family financial help. Wayne's Grandpa McColley had a saying that his father had told him: "You can do anything that anyone else can do, but only better." Wayne would become too stubborn for his own good.

CPSIA information can be obtained
at www.ICGtesting.com
Printed in the USA
LVHW071535081121
701271LV00009BB/1